Conservation in the United States

Conservation

in the United States

A. F. Gustafson, *Late Professor of Soil Technology*

C. H. Guise, *Professor of Forestry, Emeritus*

W. J. Hamilton, Jr., *Professor of Zoology*

H. Ries, *Late Professor of Geology*

Cornell University

Third Edition

Comstock Publishing Associates

A DIVISION OF CORNELL UNIVERSITY PRESS

Ithaca, New York

Copyright 1949 by

Comstock Publishing Company, Inc.

First Edition, 1939

Second Edition, 1944

Third Edition, 1949

Second printing, July 1949

Third printing, September 1950

Fourth printing, February 1953

Fifth printing, August 1954

Sixth printing, August 1957

Printed in the United States of America by the Vail-Ballou Press, Inc., Binghamton, New York

Preface to the Third Edition

The third edition of *Conservation in the United States* is presented at a time when the problems of natural resource conservation are more critical than ever before. The exhausting demands during the years of World War II accelerated a drain that has always been steady and severe. The shortages of food, lumber, and metals during the war years still exist. Yet the need for every product that the soils and mines can provide is greater than it has ever been in previous times of peace.

Natural resources are essential to a normal national economy; they are imperative for national defense. Aid to the war-torn countries is primarily a matter of natural resources in one form or another.

With much of the country's natural wealth reduced to alarmingly low levels, and a demand greater than ever before, the public must take stock of its resources and plan on a broad scale for the near and distant future.

A. F. GUSTAFSON
C. H. GUISE
W. J. HAMILTON, JR.
H. RIES

Ithaca, New York
October, 1948

Contents

"The Conservation of natural resources is the key to the future. It is the key to the safety and prosperity of the American people, and all the people of the world, for all time to come. The very existence of our Nation, and of all the rest, depends on conserving the resources which are the foundations of its life. That is why Conservation is the greatest material question of all." —Gifford Pinchot, *Breaking New Ground,* 1947

Introduction

CONSERVATION of the waters, soils, forests, grasslands, wildlife, and minerals of the United States is the subject of this book. As applied to natural resources the term *conservation* implies efficient and continuing use of existing supplies for the benefit of both present and future generations, the avoidance of destruction and waste in their extraction and use, the restoration and sustained development of renewable resources, and the establishment of constructive long-range policies that will make these resources serve the people as a whole, perpetually, to the fullest advantage.

The natural resources. The natural resources of the country are of two broad classes: those that are renewable and those that are exhaustible. The renewable natural resources include the forests, grasslands, other natural vegetation, and animal life. Though severely exploited, and in some regions almost exhausted, plant and animal resources can, to a large extent, be restored. The nonrenewable resources include primarily the soils and the mineral wealth of the country. The soils must be placed in the class of exhaustible resources because though their fertility may be restored, soil formation requires ages. If soil is washed or blown away, it is gone forever. Mineral wealth includes the metallic ores; the mineral fuels, including coal, oil, and gas; and the nonmetallic minerals, examples of which are phosphate, potash, salt, gypsum, and sulfur. When these resources are gone they cannot be replaced.

The natural resources contained within the present boundaries of the United States were originally of many kinds, vast in amount and great in value. Thought to be inexhaustible, these resources have been developed, used, and wasted without consideration of the future. Within a span of little more than three centuries of time, much of the original natural wealth of the country has vanished.

The problems of conservation. The problems attendant upon the conservation of natural resources are extremely complex. The resources are of many kinds, widely distributed geographically and held by various classes of owners. Much of the country's natural wealth is under private ownership. To establish suddenly the long-range plans that would theoretically be most satisfactory would undoubtedly restrict many of the activities of the individual owners and adversely affect the present economic life of communities, cities, and entire regions. Some resources are widely distributed throughout the entire country; others are found only in local regions where the prosperity of the inhabitants depends upon a continuing supply of raw materials. Industries that have already been developed pay taxes, employ great numbers of wage earners, and purchase large quantities of material. Drastic changes in the method of operation of these industries might quickly bring serious economic dislocation to many people.

Furthermore, close and complex interrelations exist between waters, soils, vegetation, and animal life. The wise management of one invariably benefits others. Conversely, the abuse of one adversely affects those that are closely associated with it. If forests or grasslands on hills and mountain slopes are destroyed by severe exploitation, or by fire, the protection afforded the soil by the vegetative cover is lost. The removal of this cover immediately destroys in large part the shelter and food supply of the animal life living there, with the result that the wildlife must either migrate to other sections or perish. The removal of the protective cover diminishes greatly the watershed values of the slopes: excessive runoff of water takes place; surface soil is washed away; flood damage is increased; streams and reservoirs are filled with silt; and recreational and wildlife values are lost.

Extensive and ill-advised swamp drainage projects have been undertaken from time to time with the aim of making the swamp lands available for agriculture. Great areas in the Midwest and in the Everglades region of southern Florida have been drained, with entirely unexpected results. The soils have dried out unnaturally, fires have destroyed much of the organic content of the soil, wildlife has perished or been forced to migrate, and in some sections important tourist and recreational features have been destroyed.

In parts of the Southwest the protective cover of grass has been destroyed through unwise agricultural practices, with the result that damaging wind erosion has taken place. Many western farms have suffered severe soil losses.

Nature has its own set of checks and balances; and where human activity disturbs the fundamental relationships of natural control, widespread destruction of many kinds takes place. Plans of conservation must be integrated; they must take into account the manner in which various resources are related and the ways in which they influence one another. Though vaguely aware of the scarcity of many materials formerly available in abundant quantities, the public generally is poorly informed on the status of the country's natural resources. Political considerations on both federal and state levels often make difficult the effective solution of existing problems.

Depletion of natural resources. In the exploitation of the country's natural resources, enormous quantities of materials were utilized in ways that were necessary to the nation's development. Forests had to yield to agriculture. Timber and minerals provided in countless ways the structure, equipment, and fuel that enabled the country to develop with a constantly improving standard of living. Grasslands supported the livestock from which a large proportion of the meat, leather, and wool supply of the country has always been obtained. In many regions wildlife provided food, fur, and recreational pleasures. These resources were used in almost unlimited quantities and have contributed in large measure to the country's progress, prosperity, and protection.

But in addition to utilization there has been waste and destruction. Forests and forest lands over wide areas have been ruined by destructive logging and fire. The larger part of the agricultural soils of the country are faced with serious problems of erosion and loss of fertility. The western grazing lands have been declining in forage value for years; much of the great western range is in a state of severe depletion. Floods, stream pollution, and river and reservoir silting are matters of local and national concern. Swamp drainage, stream pollution, unrestricted hunting and fishing, and the transfer of forest and grassland to agriculture, to the raising of livestock, and to urban use have reduced the wildlife population to a small fraction of what it once was.

Of minerals, only iron, magnesium, salt, bituminous coal, anthracite, phosphate, potash, and molybdenum are available in ample amounts of usable grade to last one hundred years or more. Further, twenty-two essential minerals have dwindled to a thirty-five year supply or less; the supplies of manganese, vanadium, and tungsten are practically gone. Other essential minerals of which the known supply will last less than thirty-five years are petroleum, copper, lead, tin, zinc, and nickel.[1]

Public and private ownership. During the period between the close of the Revolutionary War and 1853, the federal government acquired its public domain, which in all aggregated a billion and a half acres, an area that was three-quarters of the land surface of continental United States. To encourage settlement in all parts of the country and the development of resources, early steps were taken to transfer most of these public lands to private ownership. As a result lands in vast amounts were sold or given to individuals, to business corporations, and to various states. By 1934 when the Taylor Act virtually put an end to the disposal of public lands, all but some 455,000,000 acres had been either transferred to private ownership or reserved by the federal government for national forests, mineral lands, and reservations of various types.

The issues involved in public and private ownership are many. Natural resources in public ownership need not be exploited for immediate economic gain; instead these resources can be developed and used for the maximum long-time welfare of the public generally. A tremendous role has, however, been played by private ownership in the creation of national wealth. The private operation of agricultural lands, as well as of much of the country's mineral, forest, and grazing resources, is fundamental to the American way of life. It is desirable that private and public ownership operate side by side, the one emphasizing industrial activity, the other seeking to aid industry and at the same time to use national wealth for the maximum benefit of both present and future generations.

Unquestionably the time has come when private owners must operate their properties with a minimum of waste and destruction, looking to the future as well as the present. If this course of action is not followed, the growing scarcities will inevitably bring about public laws that will force a conservative use of privately owned natural wealth. At present, in order to conserve the natural resources for the benefit of the country as a whole, the federal and state governments have enacted legislation to control the use of great areas of land in private ownership. Certain forms of regulation now exist in connection with the protection of forests, with the preservation of wildlife, with the handling of certain minerals, and with the conservation of

---

[1] *Annual Report, Secretary of the Interior,* 1945 (Washington, 1946).

agricultural lands. The steps taken thus far are probably but a slight indication of the restrictions that are likely to be established in the future to control the exploitation of the natural resources now in private ownership.

Natural resources and national welfare. An ample and varied supply of natural wealth is indispensable to the prosperity and security of a nation. The United States has always been in a favored position in respect to the abundance of its natural resources. After the early years of struggle in which rich soils, forests, and wildlife did much to enable them to survive, the early settlers began to establish their own industries and to develop an export trade in timber and other forest products, and in various agricultural commodities. As the population increased and pushed the frontiers farther to the west, new supplies of forest and mineral wealth and vast areas of fertile agricultural soils were waiting for use. Agricultural, industrial, and commercial development proceeded at a rapid pace.

Because of the abundance of resources, the ease of acquisition, and the ability to utilize and make the products available, the country has developed in a material and economic way until it has provided standards of living for its citizens that have been the envy of the entire world. The exploitation of the country's resources has been accompanied by much that is tragic in waste and destruction, but the fact remains that the natural wealth has been largely responsible for the building of this nation.

If a nation is to survive and live in a state of freedom and security, it must be able to defend itself against attack and aggression, it must be able to protect its international trade and commerce, and it must have the power to hold the respect of other countries that may plan to interfere with its mode of existence. The maintenance of national security, essential to national well-being, demands that the country be provided with adequate and effective military, naval, and air forces. To provide the equipment needed for the country's armed forces, the first requirement is an abundant supply of natural resources.

Thus natural resources supply the essential materials for foods, housing, clothing, and protection, and in many other ways provide the necessities and comforts of everyday life. So abundant have these resources been that the individual has come to take them for granted, and to give little heed to their exhaustion. The result is that some resources are practically gone and many others are known to be distinctly limited in amount. Certain changes in the use of natural wealth must take place if security and prosperous conditions of living, manufacturing, and commerce are to continue. Otherwise a continually decreasing level in living standards is inevitable.

Natural resources and national defense. Twice within a span of twenty-five years the United States has been forced into wars of unprecedented magnitude. Wars create abnormally heavy demands on human and physical resources. The war that this country entered in 1917 was exacting in its call for men and materials. Severe as these demands were, they were insignificant in comparison with the drains that were made by the struggle that started on December 7, 1941, at Pearl Harbor.

Success in both World Wars came only through the efforts of a large and thoroughly trained army, navy, and air force, backed by a united citizenry and completely equipped with the implements of war. War requires ships, tanks, airplanes, guns, munitions, lumber, fuel, clothing, food, and countless items of special equipment. To meet these requirements great quantities of iron and steel, copper, aluminum, nickel, and other metals, gasoline, oil, coal, and almost every other conceivable material that the country's soils, mines, and forests can produce must be provided as long as war lasts. The war machine also calls for many materials like tin, manganese, tungsten, chromium, mica, antimony, graphite, and asbestos, which must be imported partly or wholly from other countries. It was only because skilled workers had available vast reservoirs of minerals, forests, and other natural resources that this country could speed its war production as it did during World War II. It is not without irony that a war may have been the most effective of all agencies to bring the public to an understanding of the importance of its natural resources and the need for their perpetual conservation.

This country is destined to play a leading role in world affairs. The army, navy, air force, and merchant marine, essential to this role, will be far in excess of anything that the nation has had in previous peace times. The maintenance of these branches of service will always be a heavy drain on the country's natural resources.

The scope of conservation in the United States. It is the aim of this book to present the basic principles of conservation so that the reader may gain an understanding of both today's and tomorrow's problems and be in a position to assist in dealing effectively with them. The presentation is made in four general sections, preceded by an introductory chapter dealing with the conservation movement. The first section deals with the soil and water resources of the United States; the second, with the forests, the western grazing lands, and the national and state parks; the third, with wildlife; and the fourth, with minerals. With each of the major resources is presented a discussion of their value and importance, their regional occurrence, the extent to which they have been used, the causes of depletion, inventory estimates, and the steps essential to their conservation.

CHAPTER I

The Development
of Conservation

CONSERVATION deals with all natural resources in all forms of public and private ownership.

Up to the present, progress in conservation has, for the most part, resulted from public endeavor. The administrative needs of great areas of publicly owned lands, the centralization of authority to deal with these areas, the wisdom of the people in preferring long-range benefits to all rather than immediate economic returns for a few, and the presence in public service of farsighted and forceful men who believed in the principles of conservation have been important factors in the leadership of the federal and state governments. The federal government has established policies that have profoundly influenced the individual states. Over the years these policies have also had an impact on the individual and corporate owners of natural wealth.

To a major extent the country's agricultural soils, grazing lands, forests, and minerals are privately owned, and to these resources the basic principles of conservation must ultimately be applied. Such a course is imperative for the security and prosperity of the citizens of this country. If conservation is not followed voluntarily, the public will, without a doubt, demand a different kind of stewardship of many of the natural resources now privately owned.

The conservation movement has been supported vigorously by conservation associations, by organizations of scientists, and by a number of farsighted citizens who were aware of the need for better management of the nation's resources. With a slow start and in the face of many discouraging setbacks, the movement has steadily forged ahead. Many factors have contributed to the awakening to the need for conservation, but basically it resulted from the wasteful use, destruction, and rapid depletion of the country's natural wealth.

A history of the major steps in the development of conservation starts with the manner by which the present pattern of land ownership in this country has evolved, taking into account the lands in the original colonies as well as the lands that originally made up the great public domain. The story continues with the legislative enactments that provided for the withdrawal and reservation of public lands from private entry; for the establishment of departments in federal and state governments to administer the public lands; and for public regulatory activities, where necessary, to control the operation and use of privately held properties. Other parts of the history of conservation are the progress made as a result of established policies and laws and the present status of conservation with respect to lands under both public and private ownership.

PUBLIC LAND POLICIES

Lands in the colonies. Vast areas of heavily forested land, situated both within and beyond colonial boundaries, were conveyed to the original colonies by patents and charters from the crown of England. Many of these lands were retained by the colonies when they became free and independent states. In some cases grants were made directly to individuals for the purpose of furthering colonization in the new country. Timber and various agricultural crops were of primary importance in both the domestic economy and trade with Europe. Consequently as time passed, extensive tracts, publicly or privately owned, were subdivided and sold, or otherwise conveyed, to various parties, who acquired them primarily for the exploitation of their timber and other resources. Many properties changed hands by subsequent retransfer. In some cases, large properties were split into smaller areas, but in other instances large holdings were created by the assembling of smaller units.

The acquisition of the public domain. Beyond the boundaries of the original thirteen colonies, private ownership of land is associated closely with the building up and disposal of the public domain. By the *public domain* is meant the lands owned by the United States as a whole and subject to sale or other disposition by the federal government. When the colonies declared their independence in 1776, there was no public domain. Seven of the new states claimed practically all of the territory of the United States east of the Mississippi, with the exception of what is now Florida. These seven were New York, Virginia, Massachusetts, Connecticut, North Carolina, South Carolina, and Georgia.

Shortly after the Revolutionary War Congress persuaded each of the states to cede to the federal government all the lands beyond their boundaries to which they claimed title. These lands thus passed into the possession of the central government, and the public domain, established for the benefit of all the people, came into being. By 1802 the domain totaled 266,000,000 acres. Large as this area was, it was insignificant in size compared to the vast territories added to it during the next fifty years. The territories acquired by the Louisiana Purchase, by conquest from Mexico, by the treaty with England involving the Oregon Territory, and by subsequent additions from Spain, Texas, and Mexico increased the public domain by 1853 to 1,442,000,-000 acres, and rounded out the area of the continental United States as it is now known. The United States at that time owned an empire of tremendous size, including the magnificent timberlands and other forms of natural wealth, most of which were later to be transferred by one method or another into private ownership.

The expansion of the public domain is presented graphically in Figure 1. This map shows the location of the land areas acquired and the sources and dates of acquisition.

The disposal of the public domain. The public domain was of value only as it could serve the people as a whole. It was natural, therefore, that steps leading to its use and disposal should be taken. Early policies controlling its disposal were formulated with three objects in view: to encourage settlement in the West, to obtain as much as possible in financial return to support the activities of the central government, and to stimulate education and the construction of roads, canals, railroads, and other internal improvements essential to the country's development.

Soon after the first steps in assembling the public domain were taken, federal laws began to be enacted that provided for the transfer of the public lands by sale to settlers and by gift to war veterans. Later came other laws that provided for land disposal in a variety of ways. Great areas of public land were granted to individual states for the support of education and for internal improvements, and to railroad corporations for the purpose of promoting the construction of trans-

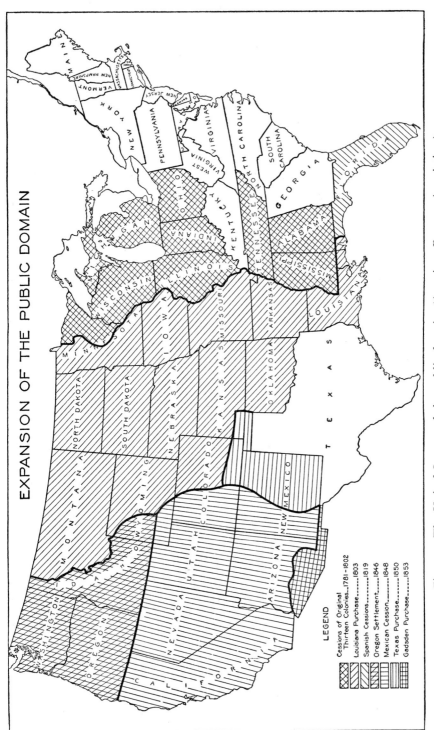

Figure 1. The United States and the public domain. (American Forestry Association.)

portation lines. Tremendous sections of the finest forests were granted outright to a small number of the western railroads. Space is not available to describe in detail the laws and methods by which public lands were transferred to private ownership. Special mention should be made, however, of the Homestead laws, the first of which was enacted in 1862. This law of 1862 was more responsible than any other for stimulating the agricultural settlement of the West. Also of great importance was the Timber and Stone Act of 1878, which permitted the acquisition by industry of many of the great holdings of timberland in Washington, Oregon, California, Idaho, and Minnesota. Other laws which helped transfer public lands to private ownership were the Pre-emption laws, the desert land laws, and the Timber Culture Act.

Every law enacted for the disposal of the public lands resulted, directly or indirectly, in the private ownership of vast areas of timberlands and of other natural resources in every section of the United States. Practically all the valuable agricultural lands, all the areas containing the metallic minerals, and the greater part of those bearing forests, forage, and the nonmetallic minerals were alienated from public ownership. Lands conveyed in small amounts were, in many cases, later consolidated into large holdings. Many of the areas granted to states and railroads were subsequently subdivided and sold or otherwise transferred to lumber operators or to industrial corporations. Much of the legislation was badly framed, and, as a result, land speculation, monopoly, and fraud were inevitable.

Of the vast area of federal land, which included almost all of the United States beyond the borders of the original colonies and Texas, 72 per cent, or 1,031,500,000 acres, have been disposed of to individuals, to corporations, and to the states. Some of the lands originally transferred have been reacquired through exchange. The records of early disposals do not permit exact statistics, but the approximate areas of public land disposals are shown in Table 1.

Four hundred and thirteen million acres, or 28 per cent of the public domain, have not been transferred. Of this area, approximately 233,000,000 acres, 16 per cent, have been withdrawn and reserved by the federal government for conservation and defense. Prior to 1910 the government reserved the lands now making up the larger part of the national forests because of a realization of the reckless speed with which the forests of the nation were being cut and wasted. Also included in the major withdrawals by the government are lands reserved

Table 1. Approximate Area of Public Lands Disposed of Under the Public Land Laws * as of June 30, 1943

	Acres
Total area disposed of	1,031,500,000
Disposed of by methods not elsewhere classified	300,000,000
Granted or sold to homesteaders	285,000,000
Granted to states	225,400,000
For support of common schools	77,500,000
For reclamation of swamp land	64,900,000
For construction of railroads	37,100,000
For support of miscellaneous institutions	20,600,000
For purposes not elsewhere classified	16,000,000
For construction of canals	4,600,000
For construction of wagon roads	3,300,000
For improvement of rivers	1,400,000
Granted to railroad corporations	91,300,000
Granted to veterans as military bounties	61,000,000
Confirmed as private land claims	34,000,000
Sold under timber and stone laws	13,900,000
Granted or sold under timber culture laws	10,900,000
Sold under desert land laws	10,000,000

for reclamation and power projects, for national parks and monuments, for wildlife and game refuges, for Indian reservations, and for military needs.

By 1934 all but 180,000,000 acres, 12 per cent, of the public domain had been disposed of, or withdrawn into federal reservations. Settlers and industries are not interested in these lands since they are for the most part deserts, semideserts, and unproductive uplands. The largest areas remain in Nevada, Arizona, Utah, New Mexico, Wyoming, Oregon, California, and Idaho. Because of the forage resources on this tremendous area, these unreserved federal lands have been used freely by stockmen for pasturing their grazing animals. A gradual but steady deterioration of the greater part of these lands, as a result of overgrazing, has taken place. To provide for their better management the Taylor Grazing Act of 1934 was passed, creating grazing districts to be administered by the Department of the Interior; most of these vacant

* From an unpublished report prepared by the Office of Land Utilization of the Department of the Interior, 1946.

lands are now included within the districts established under the provisions of this act.

The federal government at present owns 455,000,000 acres, 24 per cent of the area of the continental United States. Of these 455,000,000 acres, 413,000,000 are lands that were a part of the original public domain. The other 42,000,000 acres were acquired by purchase or by the acceptance of donations. Of all federally owned land, the Department of the Interior has jurisdiction over 268,000,000 acres and the Department of Agriculture over 166,000,000 acres. The greater part of the remaining areas are administered by the Army and Navy departments.[1]

The areas and percentages of the lands in federal ownership, classified by the departments and divisions thereof administering them, are presented in summary form in Table 2.

TABLE 2. AREA IN ACRES OF LANDS IN THE CONTINENTAL UNITED STATES IN FEDERAL OWNERSHIP, 1944

	Thousand acres	Per cent
Department of Interior		
Bureau of Land Management	181,546	9.6
Office of Indian Affairs	55,280	2.9
National Park Service	13,585	.7
Bureau of Reclamation	14,475	.8
Fish and Wildlife Service	2,760	.1
Others	66	
Total (Interior)	267,712	14.1
Department of Agriculture		
Forest Service	157,618	8.3
Soil Conservation Service	7,481	.4
Others	881	
Total (Agriculture)	165,980	8.7
War, Navy, and other departments	21,954	1.2
Grand totals	455,646	24.0
Land area, United States	1,905,362	100.0

[1] *Study of Problems in Connection with Public Lands of the United States* (House of Representatives, Report 1884, 78th Congress, 2d Session; Washington, 1944).

FEDERAL LEADERSHIP

Conservation in colonial times. Conservation was initiated and its early stages of development were influenced primarily by the rapid depletion of the forests. As long as forest supplies were abundant and the forests appeared to be unlimited in extent, action in the field of conservation could scarcely be expected. Yet it was apparent to a few farsighted citizens that in some regions the forests were being depleted of certain types of the more valuable trees, and that a long-continued trend in overcutting and general waste would lead to serious consequences.

As a result evidences of forest conservation began to appear in colonial days. As early as 1681, William Penn established an ordinance to the effect that for every five acres of land cleared, one acre was to be left in forest. In 1691 came the well-known proclamation known as the Broad Arrow. This edict from the English government ruled that white pine trees, 24 inches and larger in diameter, were to be marked with a broad arrow, and that trees so marked were to be reserved for the Royal Navy. The edict of 1691 applied to the woods of Massachusetts, but in 1710 it was extended to cover all of New England, New York, and New Jersey. During this period a number of minor laws aiming at the better handling of local forest resources were enacted.

Somewhat later than the colonial era, but long before serious attempts were made in forest conservation, was the Santa Rosa project. In 1828 during the administration of President John Quincy Adams, a federal law was enacted authorizing the purchase and reservation of lands on the Santa Rosa Peninsula of Florida for the growing of live oak and red cedar, highly valuable woods for shipbuilding. At that time it was thought that the future supply of ships for mercantile and naval purposes would be dependent on a constant supply of timbers of various kinds. Some 30,000 acres were acquired, and part of this area was planted to live oak. Little technical knowledge was available on how to grow the trees, the experiment failed, and the project was abandoned within a few years after its inception.

These projects are of historical interest, since they give evidence of early interest and concern for the perpetuation of forests. They accomplished little, however, and it was not until the latter part of the nineteenth century that forest conservation actually began to develop.

Conservation 1872 to 1891. Some seventy-five years ago, in 1873 to be exact, the national government began to give serious attention to the forestry problems of the country. Matters of this kind move slowly, but the early efforts started a progressive movement that has never stopped, and that has been characterized by a succession of forward-looking steps. Out of them have developed directly the national forests and national forestry on other federal lands. In addition, the examples set by the federal laws and the impacts created by them have had a far-reaching effect on state and other publicly owned forests, as well as on the forest policies controlling the handling of many privately owned lands.

Specific mention should be made of the establishment of Yellowstone National Park in 1872. The lands constituting this park were withdrawn in order that the phenomena therein might be reserved in perpetuity for the benefit and enjoyment of the people of the nation. Though Yellowstone was a specialized type of conservation, withdrawal from commercial exploitation of all the resources of the area committed the government to the principle of reserving certain federal areas and maintaining them for all time for the benefit of all the people rather than for a few.

In 1873 Franklin B. Hough presented a paper before the American Association for the Advancement of Science at Portland, Maine. In this he emphasized the evils of forest destruction, spoke of the relation of forests to the regulation of stream flow, and made a plea for the retention of large areas of public forests. Two years later the American Forestry Association was organized, an association that has had great influence in furthering forest conservation as a national policy. It is now a powerful nation-wide organization.

As a result of the efforts of these two associations, Congress enacted legislation whereby in 1876 a forestry agent was authorized in the Department of Agriculture. To this position Mr. Hough was appointed. Though he had few resources with which to work, this step was of great significance to the conservation movement. It was the start from which ultimately developed the Forest Service, which at present administers almost 158,000,000 acres of national forests.

Another important step was the study made by Major J. W. Powell of the United States Geological Survey of the western arid lands. His findings were published in 1879 in his *Report on the Lands of the*

Arid Region of the United States, which emphasized the problems of irrigation and flood control.

Because of the growing pressure on Congress as a result of the influence of the American Association for the Advancement of Science, the American Forestry Association, and other organizations, Congress in 1891 enacted one of the most important laws ever passed dealing with forests and the public lands. In some respects this law may be said to be the start of real conservation in the United States. It authorized the President of the United States to withdraw lands from the then existing public domain and to create forest reserves (which later became the national forests). These reserves were placed under the United States Department of the Interior, though the promotive and investigative work was in the United States Department of Agriculture. This was not a satisfactory arrangement, and changes were later made to put all aspects of the management of the lands under one department.

President Harrison withdrew 15,000,000 acres, and President Cleveland, who followed him, reserved 21,000,000 acres more. All of this land was in the West. Quite understandably there was much opposition from many of the citizens of the states in which the reserved lands were located.

This law was of vital importance because it stopped for the first time the policy of giving away the public lands and started a trend whereby the public lands were to be retained by the federal government for the benefit of the people as a whole. The impact on the conservation movement was tremendous. While the law dealt with the creation of forest reserves, its influence extended to the country's other major natural resources on public lands.

Theodore Roosevelt and Gifford Pinchot. Although the forest reserves were created under the Act of 1891, no provision had been made for their administration. This unsatisfactory situation was remedied by another federal law enacted in 1897, which was the organic act under which the national forest reserves were to be administered. In 1898 Gifford Pinchot, whose influence on the conservation movement in general was probably greater than that of any other man, became the Head of the Division of Forestry in the United States Department of Agriculture. In 1901 Theodore Roosevelt became the President of the United States. Being vitally interested in the conservation of all natural resources he formed a team with Gifford Pinchot to bring about the most spectacular era of conservation in this country. As a result of the team play between Roosevelt and Pinchot, tremendous interest was engendered in the entire conservation movement, and in this forestry played a leading part.

The Reclamation Act of 1902. During this period the arid lands of the West were also receiving serious attention. In 1902 Congress enacted the Reclamation Act, which authorized the Secretary of the Interior to withdraw lands from the public domain both for the construction of reclamation works and for the establishment of farms later to be irrigated. It was the aim of this law to reclaim arid public lands for agricultural use, with water from federally constructed irrigation projects. The user was to pay a fee to the government for the water supplied him. As a result of this act, almost 20,000,000 acres of arid and semiarid lands were withdrawn from the public domain. Some 10 per cent of all irrigated land in the West obtains its water from federal irrigation projects, the balance being supplied by works established with private capital. Many people have been benefited by federal reclamation, and the act is definitely one of importance in land conservation.

The Forest Service and the national forests. In 1905 the national forest reserves were transferred from the Department of the Interior to the Department of Agriculture. In the same year the Bureau of Forestry in the Department of Agriculture became the Forest Service. In 1907 the forest reserves became the national forests. Since that date the Forest Service administering the national forests has been in the United States Department of Agriculture, although at times attempts have been made to transfer the national forests to the Department of the Interior.

President Theodore Roosevelt, under the law of 1891, withdrew 148,000,000 acres from the public domain to add to the already existing forest reserves, and, from the standpoint of area, the national forest system in the West is at present approximately as it was created by him. Also there were set aside 1,500,000 acres of land valuable for water-power sites, 30,000 acres of coal lands, and 5,000,000 acres of phosphate lands. In addition there have been reserved 5,000,000 acres of oil lands, 4,000,000 acres of oil-shale lands, 9,000,000 acres of potash deposits, together with additional millions of acres of power and reservoir sites. During President Roosevelt's administration more than

200,000,000 acres were reserved to be the permanent property of all the people.

The Antiquities Act of 1906. An important federal law that enabled the President to withdraw lands for the establishment of national monuments was the Act for the Preservation of American Antiquities, of 1906. This law authorized the President, by proclamation, to set aside as national monuments lands owned or controlled by the United States containing historic landmarks, historic or prehistoric structures, and other objects of historic or scientific interest. This was an important law since it made possible the reservation of many areas that have since been incorporated in the national park system. It has resulted in the establishment of eighty-five national monuments, aggregating more than 9,000,000 acres. Whereas national parks must await authorization by Congress for their creation, speedy action on the reserving of a national monument is possible through presidential proclamation. Many of the most famous areas in the United States have been withdrawn under this act. In some cases bitter controversies have ensued as a result of the reserving of areas that contained large amounts of exploitable resources.

The White House Conference of Governors, 1908. As a result of a suggestion by the members of the Inland Waterways Commission, which had been requested in 1907 to make a study of waterway transportation, President Theodore Roosevelt called a conference of governors of all states to consider the problems of conservation. The members of the Waterways Commission requested this study because, they said, all problems of conservation were interrelated and a single commission dealing with only one small phase of the problem could accomplish little. The White House Conference of Governors was held May 13, 1908. This meeting was attended by the governors of the various states, the Vice President, the Justices of the Supreme Court, members of the Cabinet, the Senate, and the House of Representatives, and many other interested persons. At this conference the soils, water resources, forests, and minerals were discussed.

This conference was a landmark in the conservation movement. Resulting from it was the National Conservation Commission of forty-nine members with Gifford Pinchot as chairman. This commission prepared an inventory in three volumes of the nation's natural resources; it was the first time in the nation's history that such a study had been made. Another result of the conference was the establishment of state conservation commissions by the governors of forty-one states.

On December 8, 1908, a second White House Conference of Governors was held at which the findings of the National Conservation Commission were endorsed and on January 11, 1909, presented to the President; from this resulted the North American Conservation Conference of February 18, 1909, a conference which included representatives from the United States, Canada, Newfoundland, and Mexico. These conferences were important since they focused the interest of the government and the people on the public lands and on many phases of their constructive management. Congress was reactionary in its attitude and, by refusing appropriations for the expenses of the commission, caused it to go out of existence. An aroused public then formed a National Conservation Association with Charles W. Eliot, then President of Harvard, as honorary president and Gifford Pinchot as the active president. The influence of these developments was far-reaching, and for the first time in the nation's history conservation became a significant part of the American way of thinking.

Charles R. Van Hise. At the Conference of Governors was Dr. Charles Richard Van Hise, then President of the University of Wisconsin, who had always been deeply interested in conservation. In 1910 Dr. Van Hise published *The Conservation of the Natural Resources of the United States,* the first book of its kind dealing with this subject. For twenty years this text, containing much information from the reports of the National Conservation Commission, was the only book on the conservation of natural resources. A revision and enlargement of this book was published in 1930. Numerous other texts have followed treating the subject in various ways.

The Ballinger-Pinchot controversy. As a result of the interest engendered in the conservation movement, the public has been quick to sense any irregularities in the handling of the public lands. In 1910 occurred the Ballinger-Pinchot controversy over the manner in which Alaskan coal lands were being handled by the Department of the Interior. The controversy was important in national affairs and once more brought to the attention of the public the need for safeguarding the disposal of the public resources.

The Weeks Law of 1911. Prior to 1911 the national forests had all been created by withdrawals from the public domain. In 1911, however, the Weeks Law was enacted, primarily as a result of the efforts of Henry S. Graves, who succeeded Gifford Pinchot in 1910 as the Chief Forester. The Weeks Law was important in that it made possible the purchase of lands at the headwaters of navigable streams for inclusion in the national forest system. Before the enactment of this law all the national forests were located in the West. By means of the Weeks Law it became possible to purchase lands in the East and to create those national forests that now exist in the eastern states. This law has been subsequently amended so that lands can be purchased in other parts of the country.

Figure 2. The forest—a natural resource. Great forests like these supply wood for many industries, provide cover and food for wildlife, regulate stream flow, prevent soil erosion, and contain many areas for recreational use. The forests shown are in the southern Appalachian Mountains. (U.S. Forest Service.)

The Mineral Leasing Act of 1920. Up to 1920 the public mineral lands were disposed of by laws of 1866 and 1872. Even today the metallic mineral lands are still acquired by individuals under these laws. However, in 1920 the Mineral Leasing Act became law, and under its provisions public lands containing oil, gas, oil shale, coal, potash, phosphate, sulfur, and sodium may be leased to individuals upon a basis of royalty payments, and under conditions that call for maximum recovery and minimum waste. Though public lands contain not inconsiderable amounts of nonmetallic minerals, these amounts are relatively small in relation to those that have passed into private ownership. By far the greatest part of the lands containing metallic minerals are in private hands, vast areas having been acquired as agricultural lands. Metallic minerals on public lands, to which this act does not apply, are still extracted on the basis of free exploitation; conservative mining practices are matters for each operator to undertake.

That the public was aware of the great value of the federally owned minerals is evidenced by its reaction to such events as the Teapot Dome and Elk Hill oil scandals in the early twenties. At present if attempts are made to obtain by irregular procedures publicly owned mineral wealth, an immediate and searching investigation by Congress and other federal authorities takes place.

The federal Water Power Act of 1920. Also in 1920 was passed the federal Water Power Act, a progressive piece of legislation. This law made possible and encouraged the private development of water power, under provisions that safeguarded the rights of the people using this power, as well as the interests of those investing their capital. By its terms royalties are paid to the government; the leases expire at the end of fifty years, when the government may take over the plants with an equitable reimbursement. Much power development by private capital has resulted from this act, with immense benefit to the people able to make use of such services.

The Clark-McNary Act of 1924. An event of great importance in forestry was the co-operative Clark-McNary Act. By the provisions of this law, the federal government grants annually to the individual states sums of money that must be matched by state appropriations; the total sum can then be used for protecting forests from fire and for certain other designated forestry activities. This act has been primarily responsible for the great progress made in protecting state and privately owned forests from fire. It has stimulated reforestation tremendously in all parts of the United States, has brought about the greater part of the development of extension work in farm forestry, and has extended the provisions of the Weeks Law in connection with the purchase of lands for national forests.

Conservation of wildlife. Inasmuch as most of the fish and game have been held to be publicly owned, it has been the responsibility of public agencies to protect and to provide adequately for the perpetuation of this valuable resource. The establishment of game refuges, the restrictive laws dealing with hunting and fishing, the restocking of streams and lakes with game fish, and the steps essential to creating and maintaining suitable habitats for all important types of game have been given much attention both by federal and state governments. Numerous constructive laws have been enacted to perpetuate and develop wildlife species.

Figure 3. Moose are still common in a few western states and Alaska. A picture of this sort requires much effort and is treasured far more than a mounted head of the same animal. (U.S. Forest Service.)

Federal game refuges are set aside by executive order, by special acts of Congress, by the Migratory Bird Conservation Act of 1927, and by other legislation. Because much of the bird life is migratory, treaties have been made by the United States both with Canada in 1918 and with Mexico in 1936.

The federal Wildlife Restoration Act of 1937 gives federal aid to the states for acquiring and developing lands under state jurisdiction for purposes of wildlife conservation. Federal money for these grants is obtained from excise taxes on sporting arms and ammunition.

The federal government has set aside a number of refuges, both for big game and general wildlife. There is, however, still need for additional refuges to provide adequately for the survival and increase of most forms of mammal and bird life.

The Soil Conservation Act of 1935. The serious problems of soil loss through water and wind erosion and of exhaustion of soil fertility through improper agricultural practices have long been recognized by soil scientists. But it was not until the great dust storms of the Southwest occurred in 1934 that the general public sensed the vital need of

Figure 4. Former South Carolina cotton field (1936). Only a few years ago this badly gullied field was productive cotton land. Many years of soil building through the growth of legumes and forest trees may restore such land to productivity once more. Further washing, however, should be checked at the earliest possible moment. (A. F. Gustafson.)

immediate constructive action. In 1933 the Soil Erosion Service was organized in the Department of the Interior. In 1935 a federal law, the Soil Conservation Act, was passed in order to attack the menace of soil erosion and other forms of soil deterioration. To administer the provisions of this act, the Soil Conservation Service was established in the Department of Agriculture. As a result of later legislation in 1940, the functions of the Soil Conservation Service in dealing with lands under the jurisdiction of the Department of the Interior were transferred to that department. The Soil Conservation Act was of great importance in the conservation movement. It has resulted in an active program aimed to halt the depletion of the soils of the nation.

Franklin D. Roosevelt and conservation. During the administration of President Franklin D. Roosevelt many noteworthy activities were initiated and carried out. Among the outstanding events were the establishment of the Civilian Conservation Corps in 1933, the start of the Tennessee Valley Authority in 1933, the formation of the Soil Erosion Service in 1933, which became the Soil Conservation Service in 1935, the enactment of the Taylor Grazing Act in 1934, the creation of the National Resources Board in 1934, and the passage of the federal Wildlife Restoration Act of 1937.

The activities under the provisions of the Soil Conservation Act, the Taylor Grazing Act, and the Wildlife Restoration Act are treated in other parts of this book. The Civilian Conservation Corps was one of President Roosevelt's first conservation projects. To provide work for a large number of unemployed young men, 1,500 camps, each with a capacity of 200 men, were established in various parts of the country. After a period of successful operation, the number of camps was increased and in September, 1935, 2,652 were in operation. Soon after this date the number of camps started to decline. Because of the demand for men in war industries, in agriculture, and in military service, the need for the camps diminished and in June, 1942, the Civilian Conservation Corps was discontinued. These camps were well distributed over the country. Many of them were located in the state and national forests, others in the parks, and still others were placed wherever useful work was found.

The Tennessee Valley Authority. The Tennessee Valley Authority, a project whereby the entire drainage area of the Tennessee River, with all its resources, was to be developed for the maximum social and economic betterment of the citizens, was approved by Congress in May, 1933. The river and its tributaries, farms, forests, and minerals were to be brought to a high stage of development through integrated and unified control. Power development, flood control, navigation, soil conservation, mineral development, forestry, and social progress were all included in the plans. The Tennessee is one of the country's larger rivers, and the success or failure of the T.V.A. will undoubtedly influence the extent to which other regional river-basin developments will be authorized. It has been in essence a pilot plant. The administration of the T.V.A. is of a new type in that the control and development of all resources are integrated in one basic plan and administered by a group of three virtually independent directors.

The National Resources Board report. In June, 1934, President Roosevelt established the National Resources Board with Harold L. Ickes, then Secretary of the Interior, as chairman. Aided by a group of distinguished men, the Secretary transmitted the *Report of the National Resources Board* in December, 1934. This report is a voluminous document, containing inventories of all the natural resources of the nation, with recommendations for future action. The 1934 report is the first complete report to appear since the report of the National Conservation Commission of 1908.

Federal agencies and their present activities. The conservation activities of the federal government are, to a major extent, concentrated in the Department of the Interior and the Department of Agriculture. Reference to Table 2 (p. 14) will show the various bureaus that are included in each of these two departments and the approximate areas of land that each administers.

In the Department of the Interior the Bureau of Land Management, the Office of Indian Affairs, the National Park Service, the Bureau of Reclamation, and the Fish and Wildlife Service are the principal divisions dealing with conservation matters. In the Department of Agriculture the Forest Service and the Soil Conservation Service are the two principal agencies in conservation.

In addition to the various bureaus and services found in the Departments of the Interior and Agriculture, other departments of the federal government, as well as a number of independent authorities and agencies are also concerned in one way or another with our natural resources. Divisions of the National Military Establishment control large areas of land. Some of these lands contain mineral resources of great value. Independent agencies and authorities, of which the Tennessee Valley Authority is an example, also deal constantly with problems of conservation.

The various agencies, services, and authorities have developed over the years and operate within a legislative framework that has been set up to meet the needs of natural resource administration. Many new problems are certain to arise, and as they do it will be necessary to provide additional legislation to deal with them. Probably every bureau in the federal government could do more if it had additional funds and additional personnel. As it is they are doing excellent work in handling the many problems of a routine nature as well as meeting successfully the new issues that are constantly arising.

One of the problems that constantly confront the administrators of the federal agencies is that of holding the gains that have already been made. Constant efforts to alienate resources from national forests, national parks, and grazing districts not only create controversy and dissension between the federal government and private interests, but often cause disputes between major departments of the government relative to the jurisdiction of lands. These situations are unfortunate but unavoidable. The gains that have been made in the past fifty years in conservation are extraordinary. It is to be hoped that the various agencies can hold the ground that has been won and continue to expand constructively in undertaking essential assignments as they develop in the future.

The work of the federal agencies will never be static. On the contrary each agency must be constantly alive to every opportunity to expand its work in the interest of the people and to safeguard, to the maximum extent possible, the resources that each now administers.

CONSERVATION IN THE STATES

Development of state conservation. The efforts to adopt policies of natural resource conservation in most of the states were, until the turn of the last century, of relatively minor importance. As the territories were settled and as the states were formed, the agricultural lands, the forests, and the other resources, each to the extent of their value, were forms of basic wealth on which the economic development of the states was to take place. As a result forests were cleared for agriculture and cut to provide lumber and other products. Where mineral wealth and grassland resources existed, they also were used, frequently well in advance of general settlement. An abundance of fish and game was taken for granted.

The use and exploitation of the resources caused little concern to the public in general, though a small number of thoughtful leaders realized that the natural wealth of their states would not last indefinitely. But with most of the people it was the old story of apparent inexhaustibility. And even if the resources were depleted, all that seemed necessary was to move into new regions and tap new supplies.

As with federal conservation, the forests were always prominent in the development of state conservation. Fish and game also were of major importance. Temporary commissions were established from time to time to examine the problems of state resources. In 1885 New York, California, Colorado, and Ohio created state forestry departments, but only the one in New York became permanent. Before the turn of the century, however, several other states set up, under various names, conservation commissions that have grown and become important parts of their state governments. But in general, the accomplishments before 1908 were of minor significance insofar as the state conservation movement as a whole was concerned.

As a result of the White House Conference of Governors in 1908 (p. 19), conservation commissions were established in forty-one states. During the past forty years these commissions have assumed increasing importance. Dealing in general with forests, waters, minerals, wildlife, grasslands, and the many problems incident to the handling of each, these state agencies are indispensable to the welfare of each commonwealth. Especially important in the handling of the resources are such matters as the provision of recreational developments through local and state parks, the control of water pollution, and the development of water supplies, and the solution of the many problems incident to a healthy and prosperous agriculture.

At present every state has one or more agencies to deal with its natural resources. Conservation departments, organized in a variety of ways, usually deal with forests, fish and game, and in some cases with other locally important natural resources. In addition to these departments, special ones often exist to deal with specific resources, for example with waters, soils, or minerals. Every state has its college of agriculture and its experiment station, both of which are immensely important in dealing with local agricultural problems. The complex and varied organization of the several agencies in the different states is in itself a matter of local development. The important fact is that these agencies exist for the constructive management of the individual state's natural resources.

Role of the states in conservation. State conservation activities have several major fields of action. In the first place, the state departments are charged with the administration of state-owned lands, including their forests and other natural resources. The development of these resources and the enforcement of regulatory laws applying to them are important parts of state government.

Then the states have many problems in relation to conservation on lands in private ownership. State agencies deal directly with private owners in matters of a regulatory nature. The state necessarily must assume major responsibility for instituting conservation measures in the development of privately owned resources. The states are better able than the federal government to acquire detailed information about the resources within their boundaries and find solutions to local problems. The taxation of property, an important issue in the management of many phases of natural wealth, is essentially a matter of state control.

In many states are found large areas of land owned by the federal government. Where federal lands are located within an individual state a number of problems must be adjusted to the satisfaction of both state and federal interests, and the state conservation commission is generally the agency which is charged with these activities. There are also certain federal co-operative arrangements whereby the state and federal government jointly contribute funds that are used for the promotion of various types of natural resource conservation, for example the control of forest fires, the development of forest-tree nurseries, and the protection and propagation of wildlife. The state conservation commissions have important responsibilities in working with the federal agency in the handling of these co-operative funds so that they are expended to maximum advantage.

Since resources seldom stop at state boundaries, the states of necessity are confronted with problems of an interstate nature. The need for co-ordination of the activities of the different states in dealing with their important resources is obvious. A constructive development is found in the establishment in the individual states of Commissions on Interstate Co-operation. These commissions, through their various committees, are giving serious study to all phases of state welfare, which obviously include the natural resources. When it seems advisable, legislation is recommended to the appropriate state bodies. Co-ordinating the work of the state commissions is the Council of State Governments, which is furnished data and service necessary to ensure the efficient operation of, and provide for the maximum of co-operation between, the state committees.

Another important development in state conservation is the formation of planning boards. More than forty states now have these boards to plan for the future. In their work they deal with every phase of state progress and in their planning natural resources occupy a prominent place.

PRIVATE INITIATIVE

Lack of conservation by private owners. Resources in private ownership were acquired with the primary aim of profitable exploitation. Farm lands and grasslands in the majority of instances were obtained for long-time operation, though in the early days there was little knowledge of the quality of much of the land or the techniques essential to the maintenance of continued productivity. Forests and minerals were acquired outright for logging and mining, and the income that would accrue as the resources were exploited. Waters and wildlife were in general public property to be used for the benefit and pleasure of those who would take advantage of them. Thus through intent, or lack of appreciation of the need for conservation, resources in private ownership were exploited rapidly and wastefully. Until recently, there has been, except in isolated instances, almost no interest on the part of private owners in natural resource conservation, the one major exception being that of progressive farmers who have maintained their crop and pasture lands in productive condition.

Present trends. During the past several decades, however, a number of trends have developed which indicate that progress is being made by private owners in using conservation techniques. These matters are discussed in detail in other parts of this book, but the more important developments may be summarized here.

The many problems in agriculture as a result of farming poor soils and of loss of soil through erosion focused the early attention of agricultural colleges and experiment stations on the important aspects of soil technology. As a result of the work of these agencies, many discoveries have been made and put into practice by large numbers of farmers. The problems of erosion were forcibly brought to the attention of the public by the Soil Conservation Service in the middle thirties. Conservation has made greater progress on farm lands than with any other privately owned natural resources. Yet the amount of farm land accorded the best forms of soil conservation is relatively small in contrast to the areas in need of such treatment.

Forests in private ownership are just beginning to be handled in a manner to obtain continuous yields of timber. A fair proportion of the large holdings are being placed under long-time management, but with the medium and smaller holdings the present status is still extremely discouraging.

The grasslands of the West have been robbed of much of their forage value. Many of the privately owned lands have been overgrazed badly. Years of constructive effort will be required for the rebuilding of range resources—a fact now recognized by progressive western stockmen. Some of the western agricultural colleges are engaged in training men in range management and in developing research programs aimed at the betterment of these great grassland areas.

Mineral exploitation has been so rapid that supplies of many of the important minerals have already reached a critical stage. Though

Figure 5. The Mahoning-Hull-Rust mine, Minnesota. This tremendous excavation for iron ore gives an idea of the great demand for the metal. (Hibbing Chamber of Commerce.)

more effective methods of extraction are constantly being developed, the need for minerals is also increasing. Efficient mining operations and the avoidance of waste are primary steps at present in mineral conservation. Since mineral wealth is nonreplaceable, the problem of future supplies must be attacked in ways entirely different from those employed in dealing with the renewable resources. The rapid exhaustion of our minerals is a matter of grave concern to those who must plan for the country's economic welfare and for its future national defense.

CONSERVATION PROBLEMS OF THE FUTURE

Although federal leadership has been responsible for many progressive developments in conservation on both the national and state levels, the accomplishments to the present are only the beginning of a program that must be expanded enormously. The major part of the soil of the country is yet to be brought under the techniques of soil conservation. Waters, in addition to being a primary cause of soil erosion, are still causing disastrous floods. Stream pollution is little short of a national scandal. The silting of river beds and of expensively constructed reservoirs is general. The greater part of the forests now under private ownership are being cut in ways that give no heed to the future; vast areas are unprotected from fire, and one-sixth of the forest-land area is idle or covered with inadequate and inferior growth. The majority of the western grazing lands are still deteriorating. Over most areas, wildlife populations are far below what they should be. Minerals have been exploited to the point where some have been virtually exhausted and some are nearing depletion, and only a small number remain in sufficiently large amounts to last a hundred years or more. These facts are known to those charged with the conservation of natural resources, but, in the face of general public unconcern and lack of the financial support essential to carry out adequate conservation measures, they can do relatively little.

Yet these are the problems to be solved, not in the distant but in the immediate future. The general principles of natural resource conservation are set forth in the pages that follow. Because of the national scope of most of the problems the federal government must continue to assume the leadership, but in dealing with many resources the individual states must also move rapidly. If they do not they may find federal authorities moving into areas that the states themselves should handle. And the private owners of natural wealth have heavy responsibilities. Unless they recognize and put into effect more progressive practices in handling their resources, they too may find federal and state governments regulating their operations for the benefit of the public generally. The trend toward public regulation of privately owned operations is certain to be intensified as the public becomes aware of the approaching exhaustion of the country's resources.

For the immediate future a number of important developments appear in which federal legislation and control in some form seem inevitable. The issue of the St. Lawrence Seaway project still remains to be settled by Congress. The problem of developing the Missouri River Basin with an over-all plan comparable to that of the Tennessee Valley Authority is an issue for the future. The extent to which other major river-valley authorities may be desirable and feasible will raise problems to be considered by Congress. The underwater oil resources of the tidelands and of the continental shelf will pose many questions relative to federal and state jurisdiction, the economic factors involved, and the effect on water and wildlife resources. Strong pressure on the part of private interests to alienate grazing and forest lands from the public areas and even from the national parks and monuments is frequently exerted on Congress. Attempts to exploit the resources of the parks may be expected to be made from time to time.

In some ways the most difficult of all problems for the future is the minerals, which are nonreplaceable and in some cases badly depleted. The question of how a country whose industrial greatness was built on the unlimited use of iron, coal, petroleum, and other essential minerals can continue to maintain its present level of economy on the basis of waning supplies, is one that cannot be answered—at least as yet.

The Secretary of the Interior recommends several steps for a partial solution of the problem of mineral resource conservation.[2] The first of these is a mineral inventory on a national scale, with the aim of making new discoveries and of determining the qualitative values of all mineral resources. It is estimated that this inventory would require twenty years for its completion. A second step is the construction of the St. Lawrence Seaway project so that ores from foreign countries can be delivered to the metal-fabricating industries of the Lake States area and thus sustain these industries as the native ores begin to give out. The third is the development of new processes for using low-grade domestic ores. And fourth is a step already taken by Congress, namely, the authorization of continued subsidy payments to producers of high-cost minerals, and the stock-piling of minerals for possible war needs.

As a final point, the issue of atomic energy must be considered. With the ingenuity common to American science and industry the possibilities inherent in the development of atomic power for peacetime uses are tremendous. Should research provide this form of energy, for commercial and domestic use, profound changes in the needs for mineral fuels are obvious. The form of its development, the time required to make it useful, and the services that it can supply are in the future. If atomic power is developed it will bring about changes in the country's present economy that cannot be visualized today.

[2] *Natural Resources Conservation* (Report of the Secretary, U.S. Department of the Interior; Washington, 1946).

CHAPTER II

The Soil

COAL, oil, metals, and minerals are all considered indispensable today, yet primitive man made little use of these materials. Although man could live without coal, iron, oil, or gold, it would be mere existence and not comfortable present-day living. The soil, on the other hand, has always been essential to man's life and probably always will be. Even though large quantities of food are obtained from streams, lakes, and oceans, man is directly or indirectly dependent on the soil for most of his food and clothing, and in a measure also for fuel and shelter.

Many processes were involved in the weathering of the rocks on the earth's surface and long geological ages were required for the formation of soils from rocks. The development of the lower animals, and of man as well, awaited the evolution of soils from which food might be produced. An appreciation of the time it takes to produce soils and of their importance as the source of many necessities of life should lead men to love the soil and to preserve it from deterioration and destruction.

SOIL MATERIALS PRODUCED BY THE WEATHERING OF ROCKS

The loose material that covers the surface of the earth was produced by the weathering, or breakdown, of the rocks in the outer part of the earth's crust. By *weathering* is meant the combined action of the physical and chemical agencies of climate on rocks. Often, indeed usually, both groups of agencies act upon rocks at the same time; the work of the physical agencies is termed *disintegration* and that of the chemical ones *decomposition*.

Disintegration. Changes in temperature, heating and cooling and freezing and thawing, and the action of glaciers, streams, winds, and waves over the centuries—yes, hundreds of centuries—tend to break rocks down into small particles. It matters little whether rocks are hard or soft, whether they disintegrate with ease or with difficulty, in time they all yield to these continually acting, irresistible, natural forces. During the thousands of years over which these forces have been acting on them, all kinds of rocks have broken down.

Changes in temperature. It is well known that many substances, including rocks and minerals, tend to expand when heated and to shrink when cooled. Many rocks are made up of different kinds of mineral grains that expand at different rates under the effect of the sun's heat.

Figure 6. The weathering of a granite boulder, New York. Note the roughness of the surface of this boulder. It was caused by the heating and cooling of its surface and the freezing of water in the cracks. Large cracks are visible on the left and smaller ones on the right. (A. F. Gustafson.)

Even though such alternate expansion and shrinkage is slight, if long continued such changes set up strains that tend to loosen the surface grains (Fig. 6).

In time small cracks develop between the grains. Water enters and, since it expands approximately one-eleventh upon freezing, it develops a force that is almost irresistible. Thus it widens the cracks still further. In fact, repeated alternate freezing and thawing may disintegrate the surface of such rocks as granites and coarse sandstones completely in a few years. Much soil material is produced in this way.

Glaciers. If the snow of winter fails to thaw during the following summer, a thick body of it accumulates over a long period of years. As the depth of the snow increases, it changes from the familiar flaky snow to granular ice. Ice fields accumulate on many mountains, and this glacial ice eventually moves downhill (Fig. 7).

The ice picks up and drags along with it soil, sand, and stones. In so doing the ice grinds them to finer particles. As rocks become frozen more or less rigidly into the ice mass, they act like great chisels or scrapers. They scratch and gouge material loose from the rock surface

Figure 7. Nisqually Glacier, Mt. Rainier. As the ice flows down the slope, it picks up much rock material. A thick, heavy mantle of ice is most effective in reducing rocks to fine material. (H. Ries.)

over which the ice moves. Sometimes the glacier loosens and picks up great masses of rock. In the forward movement these large pieces of rock, or boulders, rub against others and rasp and grind off the sharp, rough edges. As a result of this action the stones attain the rounded form so characteristic of boulders in heavily glaciated areas. Owing to its great thickness a large glacier has almost unbelievable weight and irresistible power and therefore is able to grind even the hardest boulders to rock flour. The fine soil material, gravel, and boulders are still further reduced in size as they are carried forward in and under the ice. Finally, however, thawing at the front becomes equal to the forward movement and the glacier comes to rest. Later, as thawing exceeds the advance, the glacier recedes and deposits its debris over the area it occupied.

Small glaciers are found on high elevations in our western mountains, as in Glacier and other national parks. Large ice fields occur in Alaska, Antarctica, and Greenland. By studying present-day glaciers one may learn of the work of the ancient ice sheets. Small glaciers, however, are much less effective in the formation of soil material than continental ice sheets.

Long ages ago great ice sheets covered the northern part of North America and the northwestern part of Europe at about the same time. These ice sheets are thought to have resembled the present Greenland and Antarctic glaciers. In North America the total area covered by the ice at different times, as shown in Figure 8, is estimated to have been about 4,000,000 square miles. Of the United States proper one-fifth was covered by ice at one period or another.

Figure 8. Glaciated area in North America. The total area covered by continental glaciers is shown, also the three centers of accumulation of ice. (Henry Holt and Co.)

The time that has passed since the ice thawed and disappeared from what is now the United States and adjacent Canada is variously estimated as 25,000 to 40,000 years. And a million years or more are believed to have elapsed since the earliest continental glacier from which deposits have been found and studied occupied large parts of the United States.

During the Glacial or Pleistocene Period, the ice advanced and retreated a number of times. Some advances covered a smaller area or an area different from that occupied during other glacial advances. These overlapping areas present an appearance somewhat like a shingle roof that is lying on a relatively level plane. Fortunately, the debris deposited by each glacial advance constitutes the present surface material somewhere in the glaciated area and therefore may readily be examined.

The ancient glaciers that covered Canada and the northern part of the United States apparently were several thousand feet thick in places and therefore had tremendous weight and grinding power. As evidence of this power we have noted the grinding to powder of hard rocks. In addition, glaciers gouged out and deepened valleys and wore down and leveled ridges of hard rocks.

Streams. Streams of all sizes, from mere wet-weather rivulets to great rivers, erode their beds and banks and shift the eroded material from place to place. At low-water stages the material removed from the banks may be deposited in the channel. At flood stage, on the other hand, streams erode their beds as well as their banks, and the channel is temporarily deepened. Thus eroded materials are constantly being shifted about from a stream's headwaters to its mouth. As this goes on, rocks, gravel, and sand particles that have been washed in grind each other and the sides and bottom of the stream as well. Such action produces immense quantities of fine soil material.

Waves. Waves are constantly at work on ocean and lake shores. Solid rock is being worn away with stones and pebbles as grinding tools. Sand and pebbles are rolled back and forth over the beach by the waves. As a result, pebbles on the seashore are well worn and smoothly polished, and their shape and appearance are characteristic of their mode of formation. Waves, therefore, produce large quantities of soil material, sand usually predominating because the finer material is carried out to sea. From there it may at length be elevated, become dry, and eventually be transformed into productive land.

Winds. As an agent for producing soil material the wind is effective in certain areas. The power of the wind may be better understood when it is stated that a single sandstorm may completely cut away the paint of an automobile in one hour. As sand is driven against rocks, both it and the rocks are in time reduced to a fine powder. When the lower part of a boulder is worn away, the boulder topples over and the new surface is then attacked by the wind's sand blast. As this action continues, boulders and solid rock are eventually worn away. An even more important function of the wind is to move materials from place to place.

Decomposition. Decomposition includes the work of all the chemical agencies of weathering. The chemical and the physical agencies act together and really aid each other in the breakdown of rocks.

A few examples may aid in obtaining a better understanding of the combined action of these agencies on rocks.

On exposure to the air, iron compounds in the surface of rocks may become oxidized and thus require additional space. As a consequence of the great force developed by this chemical action, the surface of iron-bearing rocks is cracked or shattered. Water enters these cracks and, upon freezing, pushes the loosened pieces of the rock farther apart. Such breaking up of the outer part of rocks greatly increases the surface area exposed and thus facilitates chemical action. The iron oxide, called *hematite,* is red and, if finely divided and present in sufficient quantities, gives soil materials a reddish color.

In common with some other substances in rocks, iron compounds take up and hold water loosely by means of the process called *hydration.* The hydrated iron oxide requires much more room than did the original iron compounds. Lines of weakness, therefore, are set up, and eventually cracks form in the surface of the rock. Upon hydration, red iron oxide becomes yellow and produces the yellow color so common in well-drained soil materials in our northern states.

Even though rocks contain no iron, the gases of the atmosphere in the presence of moisture and acids effect chemical changes in many minerals. Feldspars and other silicates are thus weathered to clay.

Carbon dioxide, which is always present in the atmosphere, dissolves in rain water and forms carbonic acid. This acid reacts with rock materials that contain compounds of calcium, potassium, sodium, or magnesium and thus forms new soluble compounds that may be readily washed out by rain water. In this way carbon dioxide removes the carbonates and leaves the impurities from the original limestone. It is these impurities that constitute the residual soil material from limestones.

Physical and chemical agencies act together in the formation of soil materials, but under some climatic conditions a single agency dominates the process. In humid tropical areas the chemical agencies together with heating and cooling produce the soil material. Under these conditions granites may weather to clay. In the cold areas, on the other hand, the physical agencies, freezing and thawing and heating and cooling, together with glaciers do most of the work. In the middle part of the temperate zone, with a humid climate, all agencies work together, none of them predominating. In the areas with low rainfall, the physical agencies are more important in the weathering process because sufficient water for chemical action is not present most of the time. In this situation granite is broken down to sand.

THE PLACING OF SOIL MATERIALS

The ways by which weathered rock or soil materials reached their present location are of interest and deserve attention. Numerous agencies played their respective parts in the placing of soil materials. **Sedentary or residual soil materials.** The soil materials that remain in the place where they were formed from the parent rock are called *sedentary* or *residual* materials. Such young or recently formed soil materials may bear some relationship to the parent rock. In extremely old soils, however, the effect of the parent rock is less evident and in places not discernible. In other words, in the course of thousands of years these materials tend to lose their relationship to the original rock, and all of them tend to become similar regardless of the kind of parent rock (Fig. 9).

On the basis of the area they occupy in this country, residual soil materials are most important. Outside the glaciated area, the river flood plains, the peat and muck lands, the coastal plains, and the area covered by materials moved by the wind, the soils of the United States were formed mainly from residual materials. In fact, more than half of the cultivated soils of this country were formed mainly from residual materials. Many of them are highly productive and of great agricultural importance.

Transported soil materials. Transported materials include all of those that were moved from their place of formation to their present location. Among the important transporting agencies are gravity, water, glaciers, and winds.

Colluvial materials. Colluvial materials, or those that were moved by gravity, consist of rocks of all sizes that have been broken from the faces of cliffs by heat and cold and freezing and thawing. Once loosened, gravity carried or rolled these materials to the bases of the cliffs or rock outcrops and spread them out there. Such materials may come from any kind of rock, but regardless of the parent rock, such materials usually are too coarse to form productive soils (Fig. 10). More soil material is moved by gravity on sloping lands than is generally realized. Such movement is most pronounced in wet, clayey soils when the frost is leaving the soil.

Glacial materials. As glaciers move forward, they pick up soil material, sand, gravel, and loose rocks. And as the glacier drags them along, great quantities of them are mixed with the ice. In addition, as previously stated, bits or blocks of solid rock are torn off and carried along by the ice. After ages of grinding these rock materials and mix-

Figure 9. Residual soil in North Carolina. The upper eight to ten feet is rather uniformly fine material. Below, coarser material is in evidence, and this lower zone passes downward into unweathered rock. Erosion is rapid after the surface has been cut through. (A. F. Gustafson.)

ing them with the ice, climatic conditions changed and the forward glacial movement ceased.

Wherever the margin of the ice remained relatively stationary over a considerable period, much of the debris dropped by the thawing ice accumulated as an indefinite ridge, called a *terminal moraine.* At length thawing became more rapid than the advance and the front of the ice receded. When this happened, the glacial load was deposited unevenly on the surface on which the ice had lain. The thickness of the resulting glacial deposit varied greatly with the depth of the ice and the quantity of material that it carried. This thoroughly mixed material, called *glacial till, drift, debris,* or *ground moraine,* because of the large area it covers, is by far the most important of the various

Figure 10. Colluvial or talus slopes, Levining Canyon in the Sierra Nevadas in California. The rock in these slopes is granite. As weathering proceeds, rock fragments of various sizes are loosened and roll to the base of the cliff. Fine soil material eventually covers the surface and holds enough water to support vegetation. (H. Ries.)

glacial deposits (Fig. 11). If a glacier paused several times during its retreat, it built up additional ridges that are referred to as *recessional moraines.*

In passing over rough, rocky areas glaciers rubbed off the higher points or crests of rock ridges and filled the valleys to varying degrees. Thus the general effect of the advance of a glacier over a region is to leave it smoother than it was in its preglacial condition. The bedrock, moreover, is generally covered to a fairly good depth with loose material, that is, a mixture of freshly ground and weathered rock. The effect of glaciation, therefore, was usually beneficial to agriculture.

Glacial stream materials. During the thawing of glaciers some streams

flow on the ice, others follow cracks in the ice, and still others flow
under the ice and out from the front of it. The streams in the ice are
credited with the formation of the long narrow ridges of stratified
gravel called *eskers.* These are well developed in Michigan and Wisconsin, and a few are found in New York, Maine, and Illinois. Rough,

Figure 11. Glacial till, debris, or boulder clay. This mixture of stones,
gravel, sand, and finer material is representative of unassorted glacial
deposits. (A. F. Gustafson.)

hummocky, irregularly stratified gravel deposits, called *kames,* are
formed in association with the front of the ice (Fig. 12).

Streams flowing from the front of a tongue of ice in a valley spread
sand and gravel over the bottom of the valley. Such deposits are of
common occurrence in the steep-sided valleys of the northeast states
and also in the wide-open valleys of the Midwest. Streams flowing
from the margin of the ice sheet assorted and transported the materials. Later, streams cut into these deposits producing a formation that
is often referred to as a *second bottom* or *terrace.* A huge glacier, such
as the great North American ice sheet with a front many miles in
length, had many streams flowing from its borders. These streams

spread a great sheet of sand and gravel over their respective valley bottoms. Such a deposit is called an *outwash plain,* a good example of which constitutes the greater part of Long Island, New York.

Lake deposit materials. In many places, the water that flowed from a glacier accumulated between the front of the ice and higher land. Thus lakes, sometimes of large extent, were formed. Great quantities of sediment were deposited in this water by streams from the thawing

Figure 12. Glacial stream material. In contrast to Figure 11, the material here is well stratified. Note that the deeper layers slope at various angles in comparison with the nearly level ones at the top. (A. F. Gustafson.)

ice or adjacent land. The coarser materials were deposited as *deltas* near shore, and the finer as the true *glacial-lake* material (Fig. 13).

In the United States these lake deposits are associated principally with the Great Lakes, which, today, are much smaller than they were during the latter part of the glacial period. Other glacial-lake deposits are located in Minnesota and the Dakotas, in Utah and Nevada, and in Canada, as is shown in Figure 14. In addition, many small lake deposits occur over the glaciated part of the country. Much of this material has developed into rich soils.

Stream-laid materials. Stream-laid or alluvial deposits occur as fans, flood plains, and deltas. Although these deposits do not occupy a large proportion of the total area of the United States, they are relatively important, the reason being that the soils formed from alluvial materials generally produce large crops under favorable conditions.

Wherever small streams with rather steep channels pass out onto the flood plains of larger streams, the slope of the small stream sud-

Figure 13. Lake deposit materials. Note the uniformly fine character of this material in contrast to that in Figures 11 and 12. Note, also, that this material slips and flows when the frost goes out. (A. F. Gustafson.)

denly flattens out. This flattening reduces the speed of the smaller streams, and this reduction in speed causes them to drop the coarser material carried in the water or rolled along on the stream bed. In time a fan-shaped area is built up that consists of coarse materials such as stones, gravel, and sand. Soils formed later on these fans are desirable for many uses, but because of the coarse material in them they are too dry for some crops.

The flood plain, or first bottom, is an important stream deposit from the standpoint of total acreage. The broad flood plain of the Missis-

sippi, particularly from the Ohio to the Gulf of Mexico, is a good example. Such a plain is usually well drained except in old stream channels. For centuries bottom lands have received plant-food materials
from the uplands; consequently they are very productive. Since the
white man plowed and planted the uplands, however, much coarse,
unproductive soil material has washed down onto rich bottom land
and made it less productive (Chap. IV).

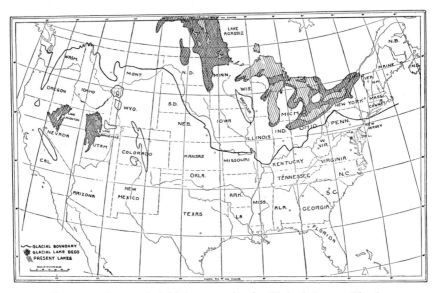

Figure 14. Large glacial-lake areas in the United States. The larger
glacial-lake areas in the United States, including Lakes Lahonton and
Bonneville, mainly in Utah and Nevada, are shown. (Compiled by A. F.
Gustafson.)

As already stated, delta deposits occur at the mouth of rivers in
lakes and at protected places in arms of the ocean. Much of the finer
material carried by streams is transported to lakes or all the way to
the sea. In time such deposits build up somewhat above the level of
the water and quickly develop into rich soils, which, however, are
often poorly drained. The delta of the Mississippi is one of the large
important delta formations of the world, as is also that of the Nile.
Coastal-plain materials. The material from which the coastal plains
were formed was in part carried into the sea by streams. It was partially weathered before reaching the sea, where it lay in the salt water

for many centuries. Eventually the land was elevated to a point where the coastal-plain material was washed by the waves for additional ages. The finer materials and some of the plant nutrients were removed by the waves and carried out to sea, leaving sand in many places. Upon further elevation, soils developed on the coastal plain of both the Atlantic Ocean and the Gulf of Mexico. Owing to their desirable texture and their favorable climatic location, soils formed from the coastal-plain materials, when heavily fertilized and well managed, produce excellent yields of a wide range of crops.

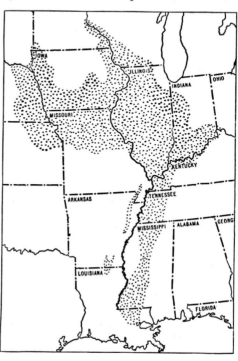

Wind-blown materials. Soil material deposited by the wind covers a large area in the lower Missouri and the upper Mississippi valleys. The deposition of this uni-form-sized soil material is associated with the later part of the glacial period. The lo-cation of this wind-blown material, called *loess,* may be seen in Figure 15. The deeper loess deposits of the United States are found in immediate association with the Mississippi and Missouri

Figure 15. Deep-loess deposits. The area in the United States that is covered by the deeper deposits of soil material transported by the wind is shown here. Excellent soils have developed from the windlaid deposits. (Redrawn from soil-material data.)

rivers. Often these deep-loess deposits occur as dunes or bluffs of rather hilly topography near the larger streams (Figs. 16, 17).

In addition to the loess deposits there are many areas of wind-blown sand. These are found on the Great Plains, on sea and lake shores, and in association with river bottoms and glacial outwash plains. In general, these sandy areas are of comparatively low agricultural value.

SOIL FORMATION

After soil materials were produced, weathering continued. At length low forms of plant life came into being and then higher forms. As plant life became established on the surface of the loose, unconsolidated rock covering the earth's surface, the weathered material may be said to have been slowly transformed into soil. More and more organic matter, largely the remains of plants (especially their roots), became mixed with the surface soil, on which vegetation became established. By the decay of their roots and the above-ground parts that fell back on the surface, plants contributed still further to the decomposition of the soil and to its improvement as a medium for the growth of plants.

Figure 16. Deep loess in western Illinois. These perpendicular walls are characteristic of the coarser deep-loess material near the Mississippi River. These walls stand in this condition for many years. The roadbed has been lowered mainly by erosion. (A. F. Gustafson.)

Burrowing animals made their homes in the soil and in so doing brought up material from below that became mixed with the surface soil. Also they carried plant materials into their burrows for food and for nesting purposes and thus mixed organic matter with the soil. As abandoned burrows became filled with surface soil, more organic matter was carried downward. When the animals died, their bodies returned to and became a part of the soil. Thus animals, as well as plants, are a source of the original organic matter of the soil.

No animal played a larger part in the development of the soil of humid areas than did the lowly earthworm. And this little animal is still working, improving the soil. It thrives in heavy, productive soils with a good supply of lime and organic matter. The latter serves the earthworm as food. It has been estimated that earthworms bring to the surface of productive, heavy soils from one-tenth to one-fifth of an inch of soil a year. In other words, the entire topsoil may be worked over by them in thirty-five to seventy years. In addition to earthworms, ants, and the larvae of insects, many other animals such as the gopher, ground squirrel, and woodchuck aid in the mixing of organic matter with the soil and in its general improvement for the benefit of crops.

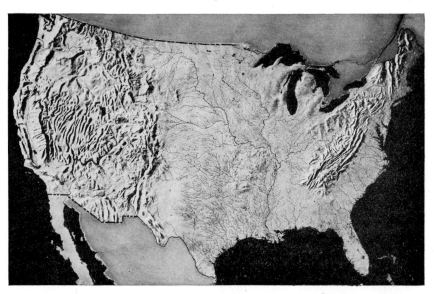

Figure 17. Relief map of the United States. A study of this map along with the soil-area map (Fig. 18) and the rainfall map of the United States (Fig. 23) reveals the reason for the location of the great agricultural regions of the country. The mountainous topography of some areas indicates why so large a proportion consists of nonagricultural land. (U.S. Geological Survey.)

THE SOILS OF THE UNITED STATES

According to the United States Department of Agriculture, our country consists of nine general soil areas or regions, which are shown in Figure 18. It is notable that in the eastern part of the United States the soil areas lie in belts running east and west. This section is well supplied with rainfall, which, however, is heavier in the South than in the North. First, temperature, and second, rainfall differences have caused the variations in the soils of the East.

In contrast with the East, the soil regions of central Iowa and Missouri and the Great Plains lie in distinct north-and-south belts. In

these belts the temperature varies greatly, from Montana and the Dakotas at the north to the Gulf Coast of Texas on the south. These
temperature differences had an influence on the development of these
soils, which vary somewhat between the North and the South. The
rainfall, also, varies greatly from central Iowa to western Kansas and
Nebraska, as may be noted in Figure 23 (p. 63). The amount of rainfall decreases rapidly from western Iowa to eastern Colorado. It is, in
fact, this difference in the amount of rainfall, first, and in tempera-

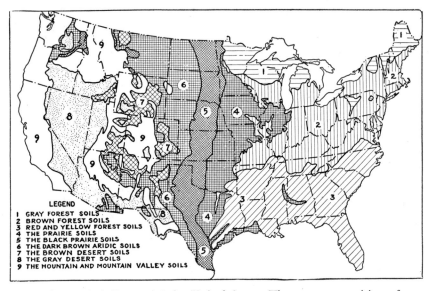

LEGEND
1 GRAY FOREST SOILS
2 BROWN FOREST SOILS
3 RED AND YELLOW FOREST SOILS
4 THE PRAIRIE SOILS
5 THE BLACK PRAIRIE SOILS
6 THE DARK BROWN ARIDIC SOILS
7 THE BROWN DESERT SOILS
8 THE GRAY DESERT SOILS
9 THE MOUNTAIN AND MOUNTAIN VALLEY SOILS

Figure 18. Soil areas of the United States. The east-west position of
the soil groups east of the Mississippi River contrasts sharply with the
north-south position of the soils to the westward. The latter corresponds
to rainfall zones. (U.S. Soil Survey.)

ture, second, that brought about the general differences between the
soils of these particular regions.

The nine general soil areas of the United States are (1) the gray
forest soils, (2) the brown forest soils, (3) the red and yellow forest
soils, (4) the prairie soils, (5) the black prairie soils, (6) the dark-brown
aridic soils, (7) the brown desert soils, (8) the gray desert soils, and (9)
the mountain and mountain valley soils (undifferentiated). Frequent
reference to the soil-area map (Fig. 18) will be found helpful in studying the soils of the United States.[1]

---

[1] Technical discussions on the formation and classification of the soils of the United
States are found in *Soils and Men: Yearbook of Agriculture,* 1938 (Washington: U.S. De-

The gray forest soils. The gray forest soils are located in the extreme northern part of the eastern half of the country. As might be expected from their name, the soils of this group are characteristically gray in color, partly because of the nature of the decomposition of the organic matter. Plant nutrients, or the substances in the soil that may be developed into plant food, have been washed out of these soils to a marked extent, the annual rainfall for points in this general region being from thirty to forty inches on the average. The productivity of these soils is rated as moderately low. The agriculture of the gray forest soil region consists of the production of forests and hay and, in addition, dairying (see Fig. 22, p. 59). It should be stated, however, that because of the favorable climatic conditions potatoes are grown intensively in Maine and some other local areas.

The brown forest soils. The brown forest soil area, which is located directly south of the gray forest soils, has higher temperatures and rainfalls than the latter. The range in elevation is fairly great, being from sea level on the Atlantic Coast to more than 5,000 feet in the Adirondack Mountains in New York, 6,700 feet in the Appalachians, and 2,000 feet in the Ozarks in Missouri. The east-and-west range is from eastern Maine to western Minnesota. The north-and-south distance covered is from central Maine, northern New York, and central Michigan and Minnesota to northern Arkansas and southern Tennessee. This is indeed a rather widespread territory, and it has many different soil conditions (Fig. 19).

A wide variety of crops is grown in this important soil area. Hay and milk in the northern and eastern, and corn and wheat in the southern, part of the region, however, are the leading products of the *extensive* agriculture of the area. The production of vegetables, apples, peaches, pears, grapes, and other fruits in specially favored sections constitutes the *intensive* agriculture of this great soil region.

The soils of the region are derived from a wide range of materials, but they were all subjected to much the same climatic influences. Such forest trees as pine, hemlock, spruce, oak, beech, maple, and birch covered much of the area when the white man came to this continent. The soils vary in productivity from moderate to high in this very important agricultural section.

The red and yellow forest soils. The red and yellow forest soils oc-

partment of Agriculture, n.d.), and also in various technical bulletins of the U.S. Department of Agriculture and in the more technical textbooks on soils.

cupy the middle and lower South as far west as southeastern Oklahoma and east central Texas. Except for the river flood plains and the loessial area on the east side of the Mississippi River from southern Illinois to the Gulf of Mexico, the soils of this region are residual.

There is a great difference in age between these southern soils and those in the glaciated area to the northward, the latter being young,

Figure 19. General view of the brown forest soils in the lake region of New York. Note the drumlins at the left, right, and central background. This rolling land produces excellent crops if supplied with sufficient phosphorus. (A. F. Gustafson.)

while the southern soils are very old. Although a wide variety of rocks has contributed the material for this soil area, the soils themselves are similar throughout the region. This similarity is the result of the action of the climatic forces on the rocks during thousands of centuries. The similarity is particularly marked in color. The red and yellow colors are imparted to these soils by iron compounds. Organic matter, which is so effective in giving color to soils in prairie areas, is all but completely masked by compounds of iron in the red and yellow forest soils (Fig. 20).

Cotton is the outstanding crop grown in the red and yellow soil belt.

Of only secondary importance is the production of tobacco and citrus fruits—oranges, lemons, and grapefruit. The growing of vegetables occupies a large acreage on the coastal plain. Texas and Florida produce winter vegetables. In addition, peaches and peanuts are rated as important crops.

Because of the climatic conditions discussed in Chapter IV, pages 101–134, the sloping soils of this region have suffered serious erosion during most of the two centuries since they were cleared and brought under cultivation. Even so, where erosion has not been too severe, these soils rank close to the brown forest soils in productivity.

Figure 20. A landscape in the area of red and yellow forest soils of the western part of Virginia. Here is seen the more gently rolling phase of this important soil area. This farm was the birthplace of Chief Justice John Marshall. (C. Vernon Eddy.)

The prairie soils. The prairie soil area extends from northwestern Indiana to eastern Nebraska. From the Missouri River southward, the western boundary of the prairie is practically that of the thirty-inch rainfall line (Fig. 23, p. 63). This area covers a much greater north-and-south range than do the eastern soil regions. It is the zone of change from the areas having abundant rainfall to those of the Great Plains that are decidedly deficient in moisture. The dark color of the prairie soils is due to the type of decomposition of the organic matter rather than to an especially high percentage of it in the soil. The organic matter consists mainly of the remains of grasses that covered the area until the white settler broke the prairie sod and planted the land to corn and wheat.

The corn belt crosses the north central part of the prairie area, and cotton occupies its southern portion. Generally speaking, this region receives sufficient rainfall for the production of the leading crops. Fruit and vegetables are grown in places, and in general the soils are of high productivity.

The brown and the red and yellow forest soils, together with the prairie soils, constitute a very important part of the most stable and dependable agricultural area of the country. The prairie soils are, of course, highly productive; and the brown and the red and yellow forest soils are of medium to high productivity. What the two latter soils lack in natural ability to produce large crop yields they make up in their stability, which is dependent in large measure on rather uniformly ample rainfall. In addition, fertilizers improve yields. The climate in these soil areas is favorable for a diversity of crops, and this land has attracted to itself a steady, thrifty, hard-working class of farmers. The nearby markets provide farmers an opportunity for making a good living in this vast area of good soils.

The black prairie soils. The black prairie soil region, which occupies the eastern part of the Great Plains, corresponds closely to the twenty-to-thirty-inch rainfall zone and is, therefore, a narrow north-and-south belt extending from Canada to Mexico. The low rainfall is the dominating climatic factor of the region. These treeless plains are covered with soils that are fairly rich in organic matter, to which the soil owes its dark-brown-to-black color. Because the rainfall in this region has always been low, plant nutrients have not been leached away. These soils, therefore, are capable of producing large crop yields, but because of the low, uncertain rainfall yields are frequently disappointing, especially in the western part of this soil belt (Fig. 21).

The leading crops are spring wheat in the Dakotas, corn in South Dakota and Nebraska, winter wheat in central Kansas, and cotton in Oklahoma and Texas.

The dark-brown aridic soils. The dark-brown aridic soils lie on the Great Plains to the west of the black prairie soils and east of the Rocky Mountains. Because of the low rainfall, which is less than twenty inches and in much of the region only a little more than ten inches, native plant growth was meager. In consequence, the soils are lower in organic matter than in those of the two soil areas immediately to the eastward.

The soils are rich in the mineral plant nutrients; but rainfall is insufficient for dependable crop production, and in dry years crops fail completely. However, spring wheat is grown at the north, and winter wheat in central and western Kansas and in northwestern Oklahoma.

The area in which intense blowing of the soil occurred in the 1930's is located in this soil region and in the black prairie region to the eastward. It centers in extreme western Oklahoma, the northern part of the Texas Panhandle, northeastern New Mexico, southeastern Colorado, and southwestern Kansas. Plowing the land for wheat de-

Figure 21. The Great Plains—black prairie soils. Beef-cattle production in western Kansas. (A. F. Gustafson.)

stroyed the native grass protection and exposed the soil to severe wind erosion (see pp. 114–117). Suggestions for controlling destructive blowing of the soil are given in Chapter V, pages 176–181.

The brown and the gray desert soils and the mountain and mountain valleys (undifferentiated). Together these three soil areas occupy the region between the dark-brown aridic soils and the Pacific Ocean. The rainfall of this vast region is highly variable. By far the greater part of the area (Fig. 23, p. 63) receives less than twenty inches, and a large area in the Great Basin receives less than ten inches of water a year. The soils are brown or gray in color, and because of low rainfall the plant nutrients and other soluble materials have not been removed by leaching. In fact, in some of these soils soluble materials have accumulated to such an extent that they are injurious to many crops.

Wherever the soils are suitable and a supply of fresh water can be obtained, irrigation (Chap. III, pp. 74–78) is carried on. When supplied with water under proper management, many of these soils produce large yields of a variety of crops. Wheat and hay are grown widely in eastern Oregon and Idaho. Forests thrive wherever the rainfall is sufficient for tree growth (see Chap. VI). On the coast of Washington, Oregon, and northern California, the annual rainfall is from 40 inches in California to 120 inches in Washington and Oregon. The northern part of this soil area extending into central California is the North Pacific hay, pasture, and forest region. Southwestern California, on the other hand, produces immense quantities of citrus fruits and vegetables. Irrigation is practiced generally in California and in other arid and semiarid areas that have available water.

THE PRODUCTIVITY OF LAND

The productivity of land depends on the character and the depth of the soil and the subsoil, the elevation and latitude, the temperature, the quantity and the distribution of rainfall, and the amount and availability of the plant nutrients in the soil. The soil may be very thin or even absent in places where streams, winds, or glaciers removed much or all of the original weathered material. Such areas generally cannot produce good yields of crops.

A minimum depth of four feet is desirable, and a much greater depth under many conditions improves the productivity of the soil. This is particularly true in the Great Plains and in other dry areas of the country where four feet of soil does not store enough water for good crop growth in long dry periods. Moreover, from the standpoint of wells, springs, and streams, four feet does not constitute a sufficient reservoir for water.

In the more heavily glaciated areas and in many residual soil regions, the thickness of the loose soil material on bedrock may vary from a few feet to ten or twenty feet over large areas, and is one hundred feet deep and even more in many places. An unusual depth of soil material occurs, as already mentioned, in the deep-loess area along the Mississippi and the Missouri rivers, in the glaciated area, in the bottom lands of some streams, and as lake and delta deposits. A good depth of soil and soil material is usually of distinct advantage to crops.

UTILIZATION OF LAND IN THE UNITED STATES

The total land area of the United States (exclusive of Alaska and the less closely affiliated areas) is 1,903,000,000 acres. According to the National Resources Board, as shown in Table 3, all except 130,000,000 acres, or about 7 per cent of this area, is used in some form of agriculture. This nonagricultural land is occupied by cities, golf courses, cemeteries, railroads, highways, parks, bird and game refuges, barren areas, nonirrigated parts of Indian reservations, beaches, and swamps and tidal marshes.

An area of 786,000,000 acres, or 41.2 per cent of the country, is rated as not being in farms, yet it contributes something to the total agricultural production of the nation. This area is divided into three classifications—grazing land (not forest or woodland), 329,000,000 acres or 17.3 per cent; forest and woodland, not grazed, 208,000,000 acres or 10.9 per cent; and 249,000,000 acres of grazed woodland or 13.1 per cent of the land area of this country.

Land classified as "in farms" consists of 987,000,000 acres or 51.8 per cent of the total area of the United States. Of this area in farms, 195,000,000 acres or 10.2 per cent are regarded as woodland, some of which is pastured, and some 45,000,000 acres rated as "all other land" (farm roads, farmstead, lanes). Of the farm land proper 379,000,000 acres, or 19.9 per cent, are devoted to the grazing of dairy and beef cattle, sheep, and other livestock. Of the remaining 413,000,000 acres, or 21.7 per cent of the area of this country, 359,000,000 acres, or 18.9 per cent, produced crops that were harvested in 1929. This area includes vegetables and fruits, grain and hay crops, cotton and flax, and all other food (human), feed (domestic animals), and fiber crops.

On the basis of the 1940 United States census data, there were 1,061,000,000 acres in farms in this country that year. Of this acreage, 301,000,000 acres were in crops that were harvested in 1939. An increase of 74,000,000 acres in farms had taken place during the preceding decade, but a decrease of 58,000,000 acres of harvested crops had occurred during the same period (Fig. 22).

The annual value per acre of the products of the crop land was about six times that of the nonforest pasture and range land and nearly eight times that of the forest land. As the productivity of crop land goes down because of depletion of plant nutrients or because of loss of surface soil by erosion, the land is rather generally used for

TABLE 3. MAJOR USES OF THE LAND IN THE CONTINENTAL
UNITED STATES, 1930 * †

Class of land	Area in millions of acres	Per cent of total land area
Total land area	1,903	100.0
AGRICULTURAL AND FOREST LANDS		
All land in farms	987	51.8
Crop land:		
Crop land harvested (1929)	359	18.9
Crop failure (1929)	13	.7
Idle or fallow land (1929)	41	2.1
Subtotal	413	21.7
Pasture land:		
Plowable	109	5.7
Not plowable	270	14.2
Subtotal	379	19.9
Woodland:		
Pastured	85	4.5
Not pastured	65	3.4
Subtotal	150	7.9
All other land	45	2.3
Land not in farms	786	41.2
Forest and woodland:		
Grazed:		
Public	106	5.6
Private	143	7.5
Subtotal	249	13.1
Not grazed:		
Public	57	3.0
Private	151	7.9
Subtotal	208	10.9
Grazing land (not in forest or woodland):		
Public	203	10.7
Private	126	6.6
Subtotal	329	17.3

* *National Resources Board Report*, 1934, p. 109.
† A Reappraisal of the Forest Situation, Report 1, by the Forest Service of the U.S. Department of Agriculture (Washington, 1946), gives 1,905,562,000 acres as the land area of the United States—not a significant variation from the acreage data in Table 3.

pasture. With the exception of rotation pastures, grazing lands are usually regarded as less productive than crop lands. As the returns from pasturing land become very low because of any or all of the usual causes of depletion, the land in the climatic areas suited to forests reverts to timber or may be planted to trees.

A large acreage of hay and pasture land has gone down in the agricultural scale because so many horses and mules have been displaced by the tractor and the automobile. When the oil supply becomes depleted or is required for other uses, or when the price becomes too

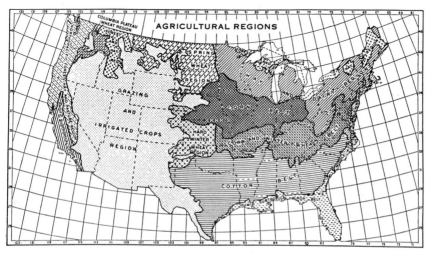

Figure 22. Agricultural regions of the United States. The major agricultural interests are shown for the entire United States. The relationship of crops to temperature and rainfall may be seen by referring to Figures 18 and 23. (U.S. Bureau of Agricultural Economics.)

high, a return to the use of animal power may take place. Lands retired to forest can then be brought back into the production of feed for draft animals.

During the decade 1919–1929, 33,000,000 acres, located mainly in the East and South, were retired from cultivation. In the same period about 30,000,000 acres in various places including the Great Plains were temporarily brought into cultivation. Because of recurrent droughts, much of the latter acreage has again dropped out of cultivation. Similar shifts in the utilization of land owing to changing conditions and varying requirements are likely to continue.

FUTURE SOIL NEEDS OF THE NATION

Rich soils, if conserved, well fertilized, and well managed, feed and clothe a large population. The United States proper has a land area of 1,903,000,000 acres, of which 1,061,000,000 are in farms. Of this area 301,000,000 acres were cropped in 1939. It has been estimated by the National Resources Board that an additional 30,000,000 acres of productive land will be needed for crops by 1960 in order to supply the needs of the people that are expected to be living in this country at that time.

Shifts from the use of horses and mules to tractors have a bearing on the situation. According to the latest United States census data, the number of horses and mules dropped from 18,737,000 in 1930, to 13,903,000 in 1940, a drop of fully 25 per cent. During the same decade, the number of cattle rose from 54,250,000 in 1930, to 60,675,000 in 1940, an increase of 6,000,000 head of cattle compared with a drop of 4,800,000 head of work animals. The net effect is a slight increase in demand for products of the land, which means a demand for additional land in production. Should this trend continue, even more than the 30,000,000 additional acres mentioned will be needed by 1960, particularly because of recent marked increases in population.

Other factors, however, affect the situation. Among them are the growing of improved, higher-producing strains and varieties of crops, of which high-yielding hybrid corn is an example; more efficient and higher-producing livestock, and improved feeding, management, and sanitation for farm animals; continuing mechanization of farms; changes in the dress of the people, generally in the direction of using less cotton and more of the synthetic fibers, of which rayon and nylon are representative; changes in diet, in part as a result of less walking and more riding in autos; and improved tillage of the soil, increased use of lime and fertilizers, and, to a small degree, supplemental irrigation in humid areas, particularly of vegetables and other high-return crops. In general, these changes are mainly in the direction of improvement in the productivity of the land or in decreased need for the products of the soil. How much production can be increased may not be accurately predicted at this time. Moreover, should the day come when it is necessary to grow crops for the production of fuel to replace gasoline (the known reserves of petroleum being regarded as exhaustible), what acreage will be needed for this purpose? Will animals for power return to farms permanently with the attendant requirement of large acreages for the production of feed for them? Exactly what acreage of land will be needed for the production of food and clothing for the population of the United States one or two centuries hence or a few thousand years from now cannot be accurately predicted. However, because of the probable need for the products of all the good land in the United States in both the near and the distant future, the conservation and maintenance of the land's productivity are the concern of every citizen.

CHAPTER III

Water: Its Uses
and Its Conservation

ALONG with soils, fuels, and metals water is an essential natural substance. Without water no plants or animals could exist on the earth.

THE IMPORTANCE OF WATER

In their green condition such common crop plants as grasses, grains, and vegetables consist of about three-fourths water and one-fourth dry matter. Woody plants, however, contain about half as much water as do green vegetables and correspondingly more dry matter. The water content of the bodies of living animals, including human beings, is somewhat higher than that of growing plants.

Plants and animals use large quantities of water directly in their development and growth. In humid areas crops require approximately 300 pounds of water for the production of one pound of dry matter and nearly 800 pounds in arid regions. For the production of one pound of beef between 30,000 and 60,000 pounds of water are said to be necessary. These quantities include all the water that is consumed directly by the animals and also that which crops use in the production of feed for them.

It has been estimated that a man who weighs about 150 pounds consumes annually 2,200 pounds of water in beverages, fruits, vegetables, and other solid foods. This quantity is equivalent to six pounds or approximately three quarts daily. Of this approximately two quarts are liquids—water, milk, tea, coffee. Even larger quantities of liquids are consumed in summer and in the warmer climates.

The quantities of water consumed by man as liquids are negligible compared with those that are required to produce his food. It has been estimated that in excess of 10,000,000 pounds of water are used in the production of the annual food requirements of an adult. This water amounts to nearly 44 acre-inches of water.[1] Although only approximate, these data emphasize the quantities of water that are required directly and indirectly by human beings.

SOURCES OF WATER

The oceans, which cover approximately three-fourths of the surface of the earth, are the ultimate source of water. From them all water comes and to them all water on the earth tends to return. (Hot springs,

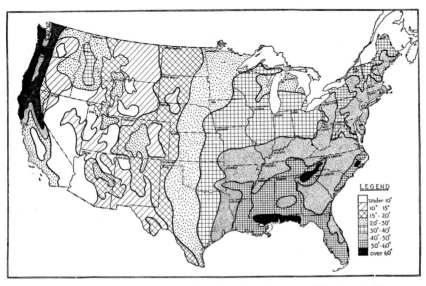

LEGEND

	under 10'
	10'- 15'
	15'- 20'
	20'-30'
	30'-40'
	40'-50'
	50'-60'
	over 60'

Figure 23. Precipitation over the United States. The different shadings show the precipitation (rain, snow, hail, sleet) in inches as an average over a period of years. (Redrawn from map by the U.S. Weather Bureau.)

however, supply small quantities from igneous sources.) Water evaporates from the surfaces of oceans, lakes, and streams, from the surface of the land, from the bodies of animals, and from the leaves and stems of plants. This water vapor forms clouds and is finally cooled and precipitated in the form of rain, snow, hail, or sleet upon the land and water surfaces of the earth (Fig. 23). Some water, however, evaporates on its way from the clouds to the earth, and important quantities are intercepted by plants and returned directly to the atmosphere by evaporation.

---

[1] An acre-inch is one inch of water over an acre.

Some of this water falls on rocks and other nonabsorptive surfaces, and frequently rain falls on the land faster than the soil can absorb it. Runoff then takes place, and the water flows back toward the ocean. On the whole, rain and the other forms of precipitation in varying degrees are taken up by the soil. In timbered areas or those heavily covered with grass or brush most of the water is absorbed by the soil. Areas that have impervious subsoils, however, are an exception. Here runoff accounts for large percentages of the total precipitation. Aside from the oceans and lakes, the *soil is the most important reservoir for the storage of water.* Certain rocks receive large quantities of water from the overlying soil materials. Particularly important among these are limestones and sandstones, which are dependable sources of underground water.

Springs. Under certain conditions water that entered the soil as precipitation comes back to the surface in springs. This return may occur wherever a water-bearing stratum is underlain by a layer of impervious material, such as clay or bedrock, that prevents further downward movement. In limestones and sandstones, water may flow along cracks or in larger passageways that have been dissolved out of limestones and come to the surface in valleys or other depressions.

On many northeastern farms springs are a very important source of water for domestic use and for livestock. Springs, large and small, are common in limestone regions. Silver Springs, near Ocala, Florida, is an example of a large spring or the emergence of an underground stream.

The flow from Silver Springs is about 368,000 gallons a minute.[2] Other large springs are Crystal Spring, Roanoke, Virginia, 35,000 gallons a minute; Comal Spring, Texas, 147,000; Warm Spring, Oregon, 116,000 gallons; and Giant Springs, Great Falls, Montana, 280,000 gallons a minute. Myriads of small springs help to maintain the flow of streams during periods of low rainfall.

Streams. Streams receive the runoff from the land and carry it to lakes and the oceans. During rapid thawing of snow and ice and after heavy rainstorms, streams carry large quantities of water, or flow at flood stage. At other times some streams are fed by thawing snow and ice in distant mountains, and others by springs. Much ground water is thus delivered directly into stream channels and helps to sustain their flow between periods of normal rainfall. And from the standpoint of water

---

[2] H. Ries and Thomas L. Watson, *Engineering Geology* (New York, 1936), p. 320.

for domestic use, for livestock, irrigation, power production, or navigation, streams are all-important.

In humid areas small streams, particularly, furnish the main supply of water for livestock, and in many of the drier regions they are the leading, if not the only, source of stock water. Smaller cities and some larger ones depend on streams for their supply of water. Among them are:

City	State	River
Bismarck	North Dakota	Missouri
Kansas City	Missouri	Missouri
Kansas City	Kansas	Missouri
Omaha	Nebraska	Missouri
Atlanta	Georgia	Chattahoochee
Cincinnati	Ohio	Ohio
Louisville	Kentucky	Ohio
New Orleans	Louisiana	Mississippi
St. Louis	Missouri	Mississippi
St. Paul	Minnesota	Mississippi
Minneapolis	Minnesota	Mississippi

In total, rivers furnish the domestic water supply for a large population.

Lakes. Lakes are a good source of water for both domestic and industrial purposes. This statement is particularly true of a glaciated area such as the region of the Great Lakes and of the more restricted Finger Lakes region in central New York. Syracuse draws its supply from Skaneateles Lake and Rochester obtains water from Hemlock and Canadice Lakes and also from Lake Ontario. Buffalo and Cleveland obtain water from Lake Erie, Detroit from Lake St. Clair, Chicago and Milwaukee from Lake Michigan, and Duluth from Lake Superior. Thus, lakes, like streams, supply water for many people in the United States.

Wells. With varying degrees of dependability, wells supply water for a wide range of uses. In years past and in some places today wells are dug to relatively shallow depths—only occasionally deeper than 50 feet. In general, however, as the work of man on the land caused a lowering of the water table, wells had to penetrate to greater depths in many places to obtain adequate supplies of water.

Drilled or driven wells of a diameter of 3 to 6 inches, which are used in many areas, usually go to depths of 50 to 200 feet. In some places wells penetrate to 400 or even 500 feet for a dependable supply of water. Such depths, however, are uncommon for farms and homes because of all but prohibitive expense, particularly under present-day costs of labor, tools, and materials. For city and industrial water supplies, wells are drilled to great depths, such as 1,000 to 3,000 feet or, more rarely, to over 4,000 feet. Not only is the initial outlay great for such deep wells, but unless the water stands relatively high in them, the cost of pumping is a heavy financial burden. Yet for domestic and industrial purposes adequate supplies of suitable water must be obtained almost without regard to costs.

Some cities obtain their supplies from the ground water by means of shallow wells. Dayton, Ohio, has wells about 60 feet deep; Schenectady, New York, 40 feet; Lowell, Massachusetts, about 40 feet; and Tacoma, Washington, from 30 to 75 feet. New York City obtains part of its supply from such wells. Wells in sand and gravel usually yield more dependable supplies of water than those in heavier materials such as clayey sands.

Among the 290 wells included in a report on the water table of central and western Long Island,[3] fourteen are deeper than 150 feet. In thirty-two of these wells, the distance from the surface of the land to the water table was more than 80 feet, which is the approximate distance that the water must be lifted for use. The variation in the location of the water table was from 34 feet below sea level to 118 feet above it. In two wells the water table was more than 100 feet above sea level; in fourteen wells it was between 80 and 100 feet; in fifty-seven wells between 60 and 80; in sixty wells between 40 and 60; in sixty-eight wells between 20 and 40 feet; and in fifty-eight wells between sea level and 20 feet above it. In thirty-one heavily pumped wells, mostly in Brooklyn, the water table was below sea level. These measurements were made in 1943, 1944, and 1945. The water table on Long Island in general slopes toward the Atlantic Ocean, and near the coast on the outwash plain is only a few feet above sea level.

Strictly speaking an artesian well is one that flows from the pressure in the water-bearing stratum. Such wells may be found where the water-bearing stratum lies between two impervious layers of clay or

3 C. E. Jacob, *The Water Table in the Western and Central Parts of Long Island, New York* (Department of Conservation, Water Power and Control Commission, Bull. GW-12; Albany, N.Y., 1945), pp. 17-24.

rock. The intake, or charging, area must be at an elevation higher than the mouth of these wells (Fig. 24). The northern Great Plains obtain water for domestic and farm purposes from water-bearing strata whose intake areas are located about the Black Hills in South Dakota and the eastern foothills of the Rocky Mountains. In addition, the condition, kind, and slope of the layers of rock on the Atlantic and Gulf coastal plains are favorable for artesian wells. Baton Rouge, Louisiana; San Antonio and Houston, Texas; Boise, Idaho; and Memphis, Tennessee, are supplied with water from artesian wells.

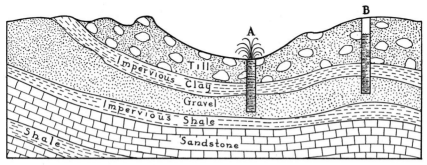

Figure 24. Flowing and ordinary wells. General conditions for flowing wells are shown. Water falling as rain or snow on the open gravel at the left permeates the gravel layer. The impervious clay above, and the shale below, the gravel hold the water and so develop the "head" in the higher gravel needed to produce the flowing well at *A*. Being on a higher elevation, *B* is an ordinary nonflowing well. Sandstone strata are also sources of water. (A. F. Gustafson.)

Deep wells are found at Aledo, Illinois, 3,114 feet deep; Galveston, Texas, 3,071 feet; St. Louis, Missouri, 3,843 feet; and Pittsburgh, Pennsylvania, 4,625 feet. Although often popularly referred to as artesian wells, deep ones like that at Aledo, Illinois, are not technically artesian wells.

Water from these deep wells is more likely to be charged with gas, salt, or other minerals than water from shallower wells. The Aledo well is representative. An abundance of good fresh water was obtained at approximately 1,600 feet, but in the hope of obtaining a flowing well drilling was continued to below 3,000 feet, and salt water was encountered. For years the salt water was pumped for medicinal purposes separate from the fresh water. But because the salt corroded the pipes, the salt water became mixed with the fresh to an undesirable degree. Later the salt water was shut out by filling the well with concrete up above the source of the salt water.

Reservoirs. Reservoirs range in size from small farm ponds to Lake Mead at Hoover Dam [4] (Fig. 25). Many small reservoirs are formed by earth dams, but the larger ones are made by concrete dams, whose foundations are in bedrock. Lake Mead, which has a capacity of

Figure 25. Hoover Dam, Arizona-Nevada, the world's highest dam. (U.S. Bureau of Reclamation.)

more than 31,000,000 acre-feet [5] of water, is the world's largest man-made reservoir. Other large reservoirs are formed by the Grand Coulee Dam (Fig. 26) in Washington, the Bonneville Dam in Oregon and Washington, and the Roosevelt Dam (Fig. 27) on the Salt River in Arizona. All of these are multiple-purpose reservoirs.

Boston obtains its supply of water from reservoirs that are located up to 100 miles from the city. New York City early obtained water from the Croton Reservoir, now a century old, on the east side of the Hudson River. Later as more water was required, the city constructed

---

[4] Hoover Dam on the Colorado River between Nevada and Arizona has a power-plant capacity of 1,835,000 horsepower.

[5] An acre-foot is one foot of water over an acre.

the Ashokan Reservoir, 90 miles from the city, in the southern part of the Catskill Mountains. More recently the Gilboa Dam was built on Schoharie Creek on the north slope of the Catskills. This reservoir is 125 miles from the city. Some water for the city is obtained from wells on Long Island. In order further to augment its water supply New York City has erected a dam on the Delaware River.

San Francisco obtains its water supply from the Hetch Hetchy Valley in the Sierra Nevada Mountains. At great cost the water is carried

Figure 26. Grand Coulee Dam, Washington. (U.S. Bureau of Reclamation.)

through pipes and tunnels from its source to the city, a distance of 170 miles. Thirteen cities, including Los Angeles, on the coastal plain of southern California organized the Metropolitan Water District. The district obtains part of its water from wells in Owens Valley, but the main supply is brought through an aqueduct 250 miles long from the reservoir at Parker Dam on the Colorado River, 150 miles downstream from Hoover Dam. The cost of this aqueduct, $220,000,000, is suggestive of the outlay that large cities must make to assure adequate supplies of suitable water. In addition, Los Angeles brings water 350 miles from the Mono Basin.

Many of the smaller cities of the country depend on local, nearby reservoirs for their water supplies. These surface supplies require filtering and chlorinating to render them safe for domestic use.

Figure 27. Roosevelt Dam. The famous Roosevelt Dam, which was completed more than twenty-five years ago, is estimated to have cost in all $6,500,000. It is the uppermost of a series of dams on the Salt River in Arizona. (U.S. Bureau of Reclamation.)

USES OF WATER

Few natural substances have such a wide range of uses as does water. Water in large quantities is used for (1) domestic purposes, (2) by industries, (3) for disposing of sewage and industrial wastes, (4) for livestock, (5) for irrigating crops, (6) for wildlife, (7) for producing water power, (8) for navigation, and (9) for recreation. Customs and requirements have established a fairly definite rating of these uses; the more important uses have the higher ratings. Domestic requirements always receive priority over the other uses, which are listed here in the approximate order of priority.

Competition for water supplies. In many areas keen competition for a major share of the available supply of water exists. The water may be needed for domestic use, for livestock, for irrigation, for industrial use, for wildlife in streams, for water power, for navigation, or for recreational uses. Domestic use usually wins, and the other uses may be expected to be served in the approximate order in which they are stated here. Livestock and irrigation are relatively high uses because of their bearing on food production and deserve high ratings. Navigation and recreation are likely to be served only after other uses have been satisfied.

The drainage of swamp lands on the moderate-to-high elevations lowers the water table under adjacent lands on lower elevations. The exploitation of agricultural lands usually leads to increased runoff and eventually a lessened ground-water supply for all uses. The withdrawal of water from moderate-sized streams in the quantities required by large cities disturbs natural stream conditions and lowers to that extent the total quantity of water available for all purposes between the point of withdrawal and the lake or sea into which the stream empties.

Such difficulties are more acute in the thickly settled areas of the East than in the Midwest or the Great Plains. A case in point is the Delaware River, which rises in the Catskill Mountains in New York. New York City planned an addition to its supply to be taken from the Delaware River. Residents of New Jersey claimed various types of injury from the withdrawal, but the court ruled in favor of New York City so long as no material injury was done to another state.

A similar difficulty arose when Boston planned to construct reservoirs on branches of the Connecticut River. The state of Connecticut argued that it would be damaged along the lower part of the river by this withholding of water from it. Nevertheless the reservoirs were built and Boston is using the water.

In the arid Southwest the Colorado River is an important source of supply both for domestic use and for irrigation. The quantity of water required for irrigation in the lower basin alone is nearly one-half greater than the total flow below Hoover Dam. Even so, the Metropolitan Water District requires and gets nearly 1,500,000 acre-feet of water annually. There simply is not enough water in the Colorado

River for all purposes. If the southern California cities are to have the water they need, some of the land suitable for irrigation cannot be watered and consequently must remain unproductive.

Domestic supplies. Cities require a completely dependable supply of pure, clean water for human consumption and other uses. The supply must be adequate at all times.

Quantities of water used. Eighty million people are served by public waterworks in this country. On the average, each person uses a little more than 105 gallons or 12 cubic feet of water daily. This is a total of approximately 7,500,000,000 gallons that are provided daily from these public water supplies. Small cities use less water per capita than do the larger ones. Five larger cities, on the average, use a little more than 300 gallons per capita, and five smaller municipalities about 60 gallons. It seems probable that greater industrial use in the larger centers accounts for part of this difference in the consumption of water. The present widespread use of air-conditioning may materially increase per capita consumption.

Beyond doubt, there is considerable wastage by the water departments themselves. In some cities all water passes through meters on its way to the consumer. In others, a flat rate is charged each householder. Under the flat-rate method of charging, a householder has little incentive to avoid leaky faucets or to report breaks in pipes. All this is reflected in the higher consumption under flat rates as compared with consumption where all water is definitely measured and the householder pays for all the water he uses.

Quality of water. Water should be clear, tasteless, odorless, and devoid of excessive quantities of sediment and dissolved materials that are detrimental to human beings. Water from sandstone areas or from regions of acid soils may be roily. Such water is often used for drinking purposes and except for appearance is not particularly objectionable. For laundry work, however, such water may be wholly unfit for use. Passing such water through desilting or settling basins may remove much of the objectionable suspended material. Much of the rest may be removed by treatments such as coagulation and filtration that cause sedimentation and thus clarify the water.

The best water is devoid of objectionable flavors and odors. In certain reservoirs algae grow during late summer and impart a distasteful flavor and odor to the water. Although such flavors and odors are harmless, they are unpleasant, particularly to people who are not ac-

customed to them. Treatment with copper kills algae and other organisms but does not make the water unwholesome for human use.
The presence of much sulfur is also objectionable from the standpoint
of flavor and odor.

Excessive hardness, or the presence of calcium bicarbonates, is objectionable, although moderate hardness is common in much of the
glaciated and limestone areas of this country. Soft water, however, is
generally desirable.

Surface waters are usually chlorinated for domestic use in order to
render them free of possible disease germs.

Industrial uses. Industry uses large quantities of water—in some
cities as much as 5 or 6 per cent of the entire municipal supply. Many
industries, however, obtain their supply independently of the city in
or near which they are located. For industrial use water may come
from any of the ordinary sources of supply. Water relatively free from
sediment and dissolved minerals is preferred. In some areas, however,
the more desirable waters are not available. Some waters are so
strongly charged with calcium bicarbonate that their use leads to serious scale formation in steamboiler pipes. Because this scale markedly reduces efficiency, such hard waters are treated to remove much of
the lime. This treatment causes some increase in costs of operation.
Ordinarily, less treatment is required to make water suitable for industrial use than for domestic consumption.

Fire protection. Fire protection in cities is an important use of water.
In most municipalities the ordinary city water is used for fire-protection purposes. In some cities separate mains carry water for fire protection. This is done where a material saving can be made by using
raw water for fire protection rather than water treated for domestic
use.

Disposing of wastes. Domestic sewage disposal requires large quantities of water. The water so used is a relatively high proportion of
the water used in homes.

In addition, the disposal of industrial wastes requires enormous
quantities of water. Large quantities of water are used in canneries to
wash vegetables and other products in preparation for processing.
Certain milk plants discharge wastes that need to be diluted with far
more water than is now being used to make the waste entirely harmless. Many food-processing plants and most manufacturing plants use
large quantities of water to dilute and carry away their waste products.

Irrigating crops. By irrigation is meant the application of water to land for producing food and feed crops (Figs. 28, 29). Additional water is needed by crops wherever the annual rainfall is much less than 20 inches, even though moderately well distributed throughout the year. The effect of temperature and relative humidity must also be recognized. A quantity of water that is adequate for good crop growth in the northern states is quite inadequate in southwestern Texas with its high temperature and low humidity.

Figure 28. Irrigation canals and irrigated land. (Union Pacific R.R.)

Irrigation has many advantages over ordinary dependence upon rainfall. One is that where water is plentiful it can be used when it is needed. Droughts and crop failures are usually a less serious problem in irrigated areas than in sections where natural rainfall is depended on entirely. Nevertheless, crops are sometimes badly injured or even ruined during hot, dry periods between irrigations. Because rainfall on these soils has been low for thousands of years, the natural plant nutrients in them have not been washed out as they have so largely been in humid regions. Consequently, once these soils are watered, they produce large yields. Multiple-crop agriculture is practiced, especially in the southern part of the irrigated area. From three to five or more cuttings of alfalfa are made in California in a single season.

In the irrigated area of the United States as a whole a wide range of crops is grown, including fruits, vegetables, nuts, hay, grain, and pasture crops (Figs. 30, 31).

Irrigation was carried on in various parts of the world before the Christian Era. Moreover, there is evidence that American Indians irrigated land in what is now Arizona and New Mexico long before Columbus made his first voyage to the Western Hemisphere. The

Figure 29. A main irrigation canal. This is a section of a typical large irrigation canal on the Salt River Project in Arizona. From a canal such as this, water is delivered to smaller canals and from these to the farm ditches. (U.S. Bureau of Reclamation.)

Mormons pioneered in modern irrigation in 1847 while Utah was still a part of Mexico. They diverted water from mountain streams for application to the rich unwatered lands of the eastern part of the Great Basin.

According to the 1944 census, more than 20,500,000 acres in this country are being cultivated under irrigation (Table 4). This area includes 1,000,000 acres in Louisiana, Arkansas, and Florida.

In the dry western part of this country are approximately 50,000,000 acres of rich soil that require only water to make them highly productive. Irrigation water is obtained in this area by diversion from streams and from reservoirs like those at Hoover, Coolidge, Roosevelt, Grand Coulee, Bonneville, and the many other dams, large and small, that have been built in the West in the past half-century. The water in many of these reservoirs comes from the thawing of snow in the mountains. Water from streams and reservoirs is carried in canals and ditches and in places through tunnels under mountains to the areas to be irrigated.

TABLE 4. ACREAGE OF LAND IRRIGATED IN THE UNITED STATES IN 1944 *

Geographic division	Acres irrigated
New England	12,153
Middle Atlantic	30,792
East North Central	12,795
West North Central	806,239
South Atlantic	224,446
East South Central	1,113
West South Central	2,146,737
Mountain	10,703,164
Pacific	6,602,031
Total	20,539,470

* *Bureau of the Census Release* (Washington: U.S. Commerce Department, 1945).

Snow water is, of course, fresh and perfectly good for crop production. Water from streams that flow for some distance through dry areas requires examination before expensive irrigation works are erected. Some waters carry salts in solution in quantities that may prove harmful to crops, and some salts are more harmful than others. Determination of the salts present, therefore, is essential. Not only the water but the soil also needs to be examined to determine whether harmful salts are present in quantities that may be detrimental to crops. If both water and soil are heavily charged with the more detrimental salts, crop production for any length of time is unlikely to be successful, except as the difficulty can be remedied by soil treatment.

Wells furnished water for 2,570,000 acres of land in California, Colorado, the Dakotas, Arkansas, Louisiana, Texas, Florida, New York, and other states in 1939. Of this acreage 1,500,000 was in California. Some of these are flowing wells, but many of them have to be pumped. The water may be carried in ditches like stream water, but

Figure 30. Distributing water on grassland. (Union Pacific R.R.)

Figure 31. Irrigating beans. (Union Pacific R.R.)

much well-water is applied to the land by means of sprinkling systems, the water being put under pressure by pumping.

Priority of use recognized. In irrigated areas, it is customary for priority in the use of water to be chronological. That is, regardless of where a farmer or group of farmers takes water from a stream, he who first withdrew water has a perpetual right to the quantity of water originally used. Water may later be withdrawn from the same stream by means of dams up the channel from the first farmer, yet the first man to use water for irrigation is protected. He has permanent water rights that go with his land, and newcomers do not have a right to take out so much water that an inadequate supply remains for those who have established legal priority. This system prevents the bringing into production on a given stream of more land than can be irrigated from the supply of water in that stream.

Wildlife needs. Fish, waterfowl, and certain fur bearers have a definite place in nature in this country. Fish and other animal and plant life in streams require a moderately uniform flow of clear, cool water. Deep, shaded pools of cool water are ideal for many fish. Many streams now drain areas of unprotected, clean-cultivated soils, with the result that streams remain muddy for days after each heavy rain. Flood waters cover with mud or wash away much of the plant life in the water on which some of the fish feed. In addition, industrial plants, mines, and cities and villages still dump detrimental wastes into streams. Some wastes destroy the food and others kill the fish themselves. The fish die or starve, and in either case disappear from badly polluted streams.

The drainage of swamps adversely affects waterfowl and some of the fur-bearing animals. The restoration of conditions favorable for water life is treated in Chapters XI–XIII.

Water power. Electric power may be produced wherever there is sufficient water and enough "fall." There must also be some demand for power to make the erection of a dam and the installation of generating equipment economically feasible. Sites having both the water and the demand are found in many parts of this country.

Small early water-power plants. In colonial days and soon thereafter many small dams were built to furnish power for local sawmills and grist mills (Fig. 32). Many of them were well located in areas where the catchment basins were largely in timber or grass. Here stream flow was fairly well maintained throughout a good part of the year.

Silting of the resulting reservoir was not too rapid, and the dam produced power over several decades. Sometimes the site was not so well chosen, the nearby land being cleared and planted to cultivated crops. In these places the reservoir soon filled with mud, and, because of the clearing of the forest, stream flow became extremely variable. In periods of low rainfall the water was insufficient to produce the power

Figure 32. An early type of water wheel. Water wheels still supply power for grist mills and sawmills in some places in this country. (U.S. Department of Agriculture.)

needed. So long as there was reservoir capacity, the stream flow could be accumulated overnight or for a few days and the mill operated for a short time as water permitted. The silting of the reservoirs, however, ended this practice.

With the advent of the steam engine, it was possible to operate mills regularly. This obviously was essential for many grist and flour mills. Eventually complete dependence was placed on the engine, and the dam and water-power equipment were allowed to deteriorate. In recent years electric power from steam or from large distant water-power installations has been used during dry periods or all the time. Thus, irregularity of stream flow because of the clearing of forests and the silting of reservoirs—and, in addition, the failure of dams—has led to the abandonment of many small water-power sites.

The larger installations of today. According to information supplied by the Bureau of Reclamation of the United States Department of the Interior, 202 medium-sized and large dams have been erected

Figure 33. Dam across Mississippi River between Keokuk, Iowa, and Hamilton, Illinois. (A. F. Gustafson.)

and the same number of reservoirs created in this country (Figs. 33–35). These dams are located in forty-one states; only Connecticut, Delaware, Florida, Indiana, Louisiana, and Minnesota are not represented. California leads with 44 dams; Washington has 14; Colorado, North Carolina, and Tennessee have 10 each; Texas, 8; Arizona and Idaho, 7 each; New York and Wyoming, 6 each; and New Mexico and Ohio, 5 each. The other twenty-nine states have from 1 to 4 dams each. Most of the states, if indeed not all of them, possess many other smaller dams. In New York, as an example, there are numerous power dams on the larger streams that flow out of the Adirondack Mountain area. On the Seneca River, the outlet of the Finger Lakes, there are

6 dams in a distance of about 11 miles, over which the water descends about 100 feet to Lake Ontario. In addition, there are sizable installations on the Genesee River. In total these smaller dams and the installations at Niagara Falls produce a large quantity of electric power.

From the standpoint of height, Hoover Dam leads, with 726 feet from the foundation to the top of the dam. Shasta in California fol-

Figure 34. Conowingo Dam on the Susquehanna River in Maryland, the largest dam on the eastern seaboard. Capacity 252,000 kilowatts. (Philadelphia Electric Co.)

lows with a height of 602 feet; Grand Coulee in Washington, 550; Ross, also in Washington, 545; and Fontana in North Carolina, in the TVA system, 480. Four other dams, Anderson Ranch in Idaho, O'Shaughnessy in California, Mud Mountain in Washington, and Owyhee in Oregon, vary in height from 456 down to 417 feet.

Sixty reservoirs have a storage capacity of more than 500,000 acre-feet; forty of them more than a million acre-feet, and five more than 6,000,000 acre-feet. Lake Mead at Hoover Dam leads with 31,142,000 acre-feet; Fort Peck Reservoir in Montana follows with 19,417,000; Roosevelt Lake, Grand Coulee Dam, in Washington has 9,517,000;

Wolf Creek Reservoir in Kentucky, 6,089,000; and Kentucky Reservoir, in Kentucky and Tennessee (dam in Kentucky), 6,003,000.

In length these 202 dams vary greatly, from a few hundred to 41,400 feet; the latter is given as the length of the concrete Santee Dam in South Carolina. Its height is 45 feet. Three additional dams exceed 20,000 feet in length: Santa Fe, an earthfill dam in California, 23,000 feet long; Buggs Island Dam of concrete in Virginia, 22,500 feet long and 144 feet high; and the Fort Peck, an earthfill dam on the Missouri River in Montana, 21,026 feet long and 250 feet high.

Figure 35. Wilson Dam on the Tennessee River. (A. F. Gustafson.)

In length, the Assuan reservoir in Egypt leads the world with 230 miles. The Fort Peck and Kentucky Reservoirs are, respectively, 189 and 184 miles in length. Roosevelt Lake (Grand Coulee) is 146 miles; Lake of the Ozarks in Missouri, 130; Lake Mead, 119; and Wolf Creek on the Cumberland River in Kentucky, 101.

Kentucky and Fort Peck Reservoirs and Lake Mead are the largest reservoirs in this country in terms of land area covered. They occupy, respectively, 261,000, 245,000, and 157,740 acres of land. Six other reservoirs occupy from 81,000 to 145,500 acres. When new dams are projected in areas which have productive soils, the fact that the soil covered by the reservoir will be taken out of agriculture for all time merits consideration.

Of the 202 dams, including 2 in the Panama Canal Zone, described by the Reclamation Service, 121 are single-purpose dams and 81 are multiple-purpose structures. Cities and water districts own or operate 41 of these dams; the Bureau of Reclamation and power companies, 40 each; Army Engineers, 36; Tennessee Valley Authority, 14; flood-control districts, 11; and irrigation districts, 11.

In the southeastern United States, the *fall line* occurs at the junction of the coastal plain and the Piedmont Plateau. In passing from the hard rocks of the plateau onto the softer rocks of the coastal plain waterfalls or rapids have developed. Washington, Richmond, Raleigh, and Columbia were built on the fall line to take advantage of the power available in the streams. Another point worthy of note is that in the early days boats navigated the rivers to the fall line.

A few dams have been built at rapids on the Mississippi River, one between Rock Island, Illinois, and Davenport, Iowa, the other between Keokuk, Iowa, and Hamilton, Illinois. The Keokuk Dam is 4,649 feet long and 53 feet high.

Figure 36. Transmission line. This line carries electric current from the Keokuk Dam (Fig. 33) to St. Louis and other industrial centers in the Mississippi Valley. (A. F. Gustafson.)

The lake that is formed extends 40 miles up the river. In Figure 33 (p. 80) the powerhouse is shown on the Iowa side of the river (Fig. 36). On that side also are the locks for steamboat and barge traffic on the river.

Water power from these widely distributed dams is a highly significant factor in the industrial development and progress of this country. In January, 1948, the water-power plants of the United States had a capacity of 22,663,000 horsepower.[6] The hydroelectric plants under construction have an additional capacity of 6,577,000 horsepower, or a total built and building of more than 20,000,000 kilowatts.

The Bureau of Reclamation is planning 236 new irrigation and

[6] Leon M. Fuquay, Secretary of the Federal Power Commission, letter to the writer, Dec. 5, 1947.

multiple-purpose dams in seventeen western states at an estimated cost of $3,000,000,000.[7] Forty of these projects have been authorized by Congress. Several years must pass in the building of dams and canals for distributing the water to irrigate crops on the thirsty land. New projects, therefore, can be of little or no assistance in the current world shortage of food. These projects include all the best sites for dams for their various uses. Other good sites are not available, and future generations will need reservoirs to store water for irrigation, for power, and for other uses. Remember that there has been great improvement in net production as a result of heavier fertilization, better weed, insect, and disease control, the progressive displacement of work animals by tractors, improved management and tillage of the soil, and the growing of hybrid corn and improved and better adapted strains and varieties of other crops. Granted that the rest of the world can use any surplus our farmers can produce, yet transportation and exchange of goods are difficult problems.

There is, to be sure, a temporary shortage of electric power, but once production has made up domestic and foreign deficits in goods resulting from World War II, our present supply will more nearly suffice.

Most of the best water-power sites are already in use. For this and other reasons costs have risen markedly since the early days of dam building. They are now eight or ten times what they were in the early part of the present century when the Keokuk Dam on the Mississippi was built. Inferior sites, the increased price of land, and the high general price level are important factors. In addition, the probable rapidity with which new reservoirs will be silted requires consideration.

To the degree that hydroelectric power is needed for purposes of defense, it should be developed without any question. European experience, however, shows that hydroelectric installations are vulnerable to bombing and might be destroyed by saboteurs. Steam-generating plants also are subject to similar attacks. Such plants, however, usually are not so large and are fairly well distributed. Moreover, steam plants can be restored to operation more quickly than can a large dam that has been partly destroyed.

Much government dam construction should be deferred because of excessive present-day and prospective costs and because of the enor-

---

[7] Carl B. Brown, "Aspects of Protecting Storage Reservoirs by Soil Conservation," *J. Soil and Water Conservation*, 1: 15–20, 43–45 (1946).

mous current government debt. A number of questions deserve consideration before a large-scale construction program is embarked upon. Is more irrigated land in the West needed for food production? Is there present, or immediately prospective, unsatisfied need for electric power from sites that are located at great distances from industry and centers of population? Is water power from high-cost or distant sites as economical as that which may be produced by improved steam-generating methods at the mouth of coal mines and then transmitted over relatively short distances to points of consumption? What about the silting problem and the possible period of usefulness of dams and reservoirs? Will their lives be long enough to repay costs of installation?

All undeveloped water-power sites must be preserved for ultimate use at some future date. The silting of existing reservoirs should be delayed in order to extend their usefulness as long as is economically feasible. Moreover, the possible development of adaptations of atomic energy for ordinary power uses might render water-power plants obsolete. Why not, therefore, defer dam building until the need for power or the products of irrigated land is definite?

Public control of water power. The Federal Power Commission, which is composed of the Secretaries of Defense (formerly War), Interior, and Agriculture, was established by Congressional enactment in 1920. The Federal Power Act became effective in 1935. The relationship of the Federal Power Commission with the production, distribution, and sale of power is similar to that of the Interstate Commerce Commission with transportation and transportation agencies. Whether or not transportation systems have been starved by low rates and tardy adjustment to increased costs may be open to debate. Similar conditions with respect to power, however, must not be allowed to develop because industry cannot function without an abundance of power at fair costs.

After complete investigation the Federal Power Commission can decide which water-power sites should be developed, when, and whether by private capital or by the government. If by industry, a definite long-term lease, but *not* a perpetual grant, can be arranged. The arrangement is to include a regular royalty per kilowatt-hour to the state or the federal treasury or to both.

There is good reason for federal control of water power. For one thing, the water in moderate-sized and large streams and lakes seldom comes from a single state. This is apparent from a glance at the map of this country. The TVA operates in seven states; seven states contribute water to the Great Lakes, water which is used for the production of power at Niagara Falls and may some day be so used in the St. Lawrence River. Five million horsepower are generated annually at Niagara Falls. The Colorado, Missouri, and Mississippi rivers all draw water from a number of states. The Illinois is one of the few large rivers that is wholly within a single state.

Navigation. The Great Lakes and the Mississippi River and its larger tributaries such as the Missouri, Ohio, and Illinois rivers constitute a large part of our natural inland water suitable for large-scale movement of freight. Far less use is made of the navigable rivers in this country than in the Orient or Europe.

The Great Lakes and the rivers. The Great Lakes are used for navigation to a large extent, but at far from capacity. During recent years, however, our rivers have not been widely used for navigation. The reason for this difference is apparent upon consideration. The water level in the lakes is essentially constant. In dry periods, however, the water in rivers becomes so shallow at many points that boats are forced to tie up at docks and wait for rainfall. Channel improvements in the larger rivers made by the federal government have undoubtedly bettered conditions for navigation to a marked degree. The deposition of sand and gravel bars by floods, however, will continue to hamper river navigation (Fig. 37).

The cost of river and harbor improvements in recent years has been enormous. To date $4,000,000,000 is the estimated cost of our waterways. Interest on the indebtedness has probably doubled this enormous amount. The United States Government has spent $288,000,000 for navigation between Pittsburgh and New Orleans.[8] The cost to the public is $8,000,000 to $10,000,000 a year greater than if the traffic were carried by the railroads that parallel the rivers. A nine-foot channel is under construction on the upper Mississippi that is expected to cost not less than $175,000,000. It is interesting to note that federal expenditures for the improvement of navigation on streams have greatly increased simultaneously with the steady decline in river-borne traffic.

The larger streams flow in broad curves which greatly increase the

8 A. E. Parkins and J. R. Whitaker, editors, *Our Natural Resources and Their Conservation* (2d ed.; New York, 1939), p. 355.

distance between traffic points, such, for example, as St. Louis and New Orleans. This markedly increased distance that boats must travel places river traffic at a distinct disadvantage because railroads and trucks follow comparatively direct lines.

The large movement of coal on the Ohio and Monongahela rivers is so timed that delivery is made at the desired season of the year. With coal and some other heavy materials speed is relatively unimportant. On the other hand, shippers demand quick delivery of many products. And since the larger streams are paralleled in general by railroads and

Figure 37. Transportation of coal on the Monongahela River. (A. F. Gustafson.)

highways, shippers use the latter because of their greater speed and uniform dependability even though the direct cost of water transportation may be lower than by rail or truck. The *total* cost of moving commodities on the rivers of the country clearly is greater than it is by rail.

Canals. Canals provided a method of transportation that was greatly needed in the days of early development in this country. Even the tiny early canal was a great improvement over oxcart transportation and profoundly affected the country's industry and agriculture. Previous to the completion of the early canals, wheat for the eastern seaboard cities was grown within oxcart haul of these populous centers. When the canals were opened, however, wheat was transported from the more favorable soil and climatic area of the Midwest to the eastern cities.

The Soo Canal between Lake Superior and Lake Huron and the Welland Canal between Lake Erie and Lake Ontario are indispensable links in the important Great Lakes waterway system. The Cape Cod Canal in Massachusetts shortens the route for shipping along the New England Coast. And of course the Panama Canal is indispensable in the movement of water-borne freight between the eastern and western parts of the United States. In addition to its great commercial value, the Panama Canal is essential for the defense of the entire Western Hemisphere.

The early smaller canals in this country served their purpose well for a time, but they were generally displaced by railroads when the latter were built. Two small inland canals of considerable length along with some shorter ones, including feeders and branches, are still operated in the United States. One is the federally owned Hennepin Canal that extends seventy-five miles from the Mississippi to the Illinois River in western Illinois. According to a recent report by the United States War Department, the cost of the canal was about $9,000,-000, and maintenance and operation totaled more than $176,000 a year.[9] The interest and amortization amounts to $700,000 a year,[10] or a total annual cost of $875,000. This amount is nearly four dollars for each dollar's worth of goods transported annually on this canal.

The other is the state-owned barge canal in New York (Figs. 38, 39) which was built in the second decade of this century. The cost of the barge canal has grown from the original $120,000,000 to about $231,-000,000. Maintenance and operation now costs $2,500,000 a year. The rated capacity of the canal is 20,000,000 tons of freight annually. In both 1936 and 1937 slightly more than 5,000,000 tons of freight passed through the canal. The tonnage carried in 1938, 1939, and 1940 varied slightly, but averaged about 4,700,000 tons annually for the three years. Petroleum products, pig iron, molasses, paper, vehicles, and implements showed a substantial increase in tonnage in 1937.[11]

Traffic on New York's Barge Canal dropped from 5,000,000 tons in

9 U.S. War Department, *Annual Report of the Chief of Engineers*, 1937 (Washington, 1938), p. 950.

10 Parkins and Whitaker, *op. cit.*, p. 361.

11 Harvey O. Shermerhorn, *Annual Report, Division of Canals and Waterways, State of New York* (Albany, 1938), pp. 28–33.

1937 to 2,000,000 tons of freight in 1944.[12] Decreased export of grain during this period and the demand for fast transportation of war materials led to the loss of tonnage. Pipe lines took traffic away, as did also the elimination of tankers from the eastern seaboard during World

Figure 38. A lock in the New York State barge canal system. At this point the Mohawk River is used as a canal, the level of the stream being controlled by dams. The boat in the lock is passing up stream. After the boat is in the lock, the gates are closed and the water allowed to enter from the canal. Then the gates at the other end of the lock (not shown) are opened and the boat passes on its way. In going in the opposite direction, a boat passes into the lock through the open upper gates which are then closed. The water is allowed to flow out, the boat lowered to the level of the water below, the gates opened, and the boat proceeds. Much time is consumed in passing a boat through locks. (Department of Public Works, Albany, N.Y.)

War II. Self-propelled barges with the capacity of a freight train should help in maintaining tonnage on the canal. When, and if, built the St. Lawrence Seaway may supply severe competition for the Barge Canal.

12 Maggie Weil, "Grain Exports Help to End Barge Canal's Slump," New York *Herald-Tribune*, sec. 9, pp. 7–8, Aug. 7, 1947.

It should be stated that some water power is produced in both the Mohawk and the Seneca sections of the canal (see p. 80). Since tolls are not charged, this power yields the only direct income produced by these canals. Because of lack of income the inland canals, other than those in the Great Lakes system, are a public problem in the country today. The cost of these canals, including interest, and the yearly outlay for their maintenance and operation constitute a burden on the taxpayer.

The city of Chicago operates the Sanitary and Ship Canal from Lake Michigan to Lockport, Illinois, a distance of about thirty-five miles.

Figure 39. Barges on canalized river. The four barges are being towed by the boat at the left. (Department of Public Works, Albany, N.Y.)

Disposal of sewage is, of course, the primary purpose of this canal. Within the city are fifty-four movable-span bridges that cost the city $37,000,000.[13] The interest on the investment plus the cost of operation and maintenance is approximately $50,000 a year for each bridge or about $2,700,000 a year for all of them. It was stated that the bridges were opened an average of four times a day in 1938. In other words, two barges or other craft make the equivalent of one round trip daily. This quantity of traffic is, of course, far less than the capacity of this canal. Sand has been the principal commodity transported on this waterway.

Sizable Great Lakes steamers were moved through the Sanitary and

---

[13] This information was transmitted by city officials in a personal letter to the author, July, 1941.

Ship Canal and down the Illinois and Mississippi rivers to the Gulf of Mexico for use on the open seas during World War II. Although this use was unusual, the canal was of real service to the country during the period of acute shortage of shipping.

Navigation on the Great Lakes and coast-wise shipping are firmly established, particularly for such products as ore, coal, limestone, sand, gravel, grain, and other products with which speed of delivery is relatively unimportant.

Recreation. Recreational uses of water are for fishing and hunting, swimming, skating, and boating. The fishing and hunting phases are fully covered in Chapters XI–XIII.

The facilities for swimming are the natural beaches on ocean and lake shores and the streams, both large and small. The beaches on the Great Lakes, on the Atlantic and Pacific Oceans, and on the Gulf Coast are especially well developed for bathing. The New Jersey coast line, including a strip of land one-half mile in width, is reported by the National Resources Board to be assessed for purposes of taxation at a figure in excess of the total valuation of the agricultural lands in that state. Such a valuation is a measure of the importance attached to adequate bathing facilities. This area is within easy reach of New York, Newark, Philadelphia, and the many smaller cities in New Jersey and the adjoining states. Other areas, such as the south shore of Long Island, also are highly popular. For winter use the beaches of Florida, of the Gulf Coast, and of southern California are of great value. The numerous lakes in Michigan, Minnesota, New England, New York, and other northern states, and in the Rocky Mountains are invaluable recreation centers for the population of these areas.

Because of fluctuations in height and muddy conditions after heavy rains, streams are somewhat less useful for recreational purposes than are the waters of ocean and lake shores. Many areas in the inland states need greatly expanded facilities for water recreation.

WATER PROBLEMS

Since water circulates through a definite cycle, as has already been stated (p. 64), it may appear at first that there are no water problems. One problem, however, is the uneven distribution of water, both as to seasons of the year and as to sections of the country. In some places the year's rainfall may be sufficient for crops, but too little of it comes during the period in which crops most need water. In large areas of our country the summer rainfall is sufficient for crops, but much of it falls in heavy showers of short duration. The result is that much badly needed water is lost as runoff and crops suffer as a consequence. In contrast, slow rains of moderate amount may be taken up completely by productive soils that are in a favorable condition for absorbing water. Under the latter conditions rainfall is relatively effective in crop production.

Not only is water lost to crops by runoff, but the floods that result from heavy, prolonged rains destroy homes, factories, bridges, roads, railroads, crops, fish and other water life and wash away rich soils. The annual loss from floods in the United States runs into hundreds of millions of dollars. Whatever is done to conserve water for agriculture tends to even up stream flow and, therefore, is helpful to fish and other water life. Any added flow in dry periods increases the potential production of power, aids in possible navigation, and improves the recreational value of streams. Moreover, holding water on the land helps to lower the crest of floods (pp. 185–195).

CONSERVATION OF WATER

The different ways of conserving water vary somewhat with the different uses of water. The methods of slowing up runoff water from heavy rains and from thawing snow need to be considered in connection with the use of the water.

For domestic and industrial uses. As long as the supply of water is ample for all domestic and industrial needs, its conservation receives little attention. During periods of less than normal rainfall, when the supply in reservoirs or from shallow wells is in danger of exhaustion, the individual householder can greatly reduce his daily consumption of water without serious inconvenience. Industrial consumers may already have curtailed waste because of the expense of purchased water, but perhaps even they may temporarily use less water without interfering with operations. Although these suggestions are so obvious as hardly to need statement, following them can lead to great savings.

Wherever water is obtained from wells in local deposits of sand and gravel, the supply is limited to the precipitation on the land and must not be pumped too low.

In Brooklyn, New York, water that has been used in air-conditioning buildings is run back into the underlying gravel. This returning of warmed water has raised the temperature of the ground water by as much as ten degrees Fahrenheit, according to a report by the United States Geological Survey. Even so, the return of the water is highly desirable.

Wherever water is obtained from underlying sands and gravels, as on Long Island, a problem arises. The supply of fresh ground water is limited to that entering the soil as precipitation. Water is needed by farmers for irrigating their vegetable crops during droughty periods. If too much water is pumped for domestic and industrial use in the villages and New York City, salt water may enter the gravel substratum from the Atlantic Ocean and Long Island Sound. In that event the farmer near these shores may pump salty water for his crops and livestock. In the matter of oil, gas, coal, and other minerals, the owner of the surface of the earth also owns the mineral resources that underlie the land. He is protected by law and by special provisions in the case of mobile materials such as oil and gas. In like manner a land-owner who needs water for domestic use or for the irrigation of crops requires protection against overpumping by others.[14] In an area such as Long Island, where water is needed for all three of the highest uses, a fine legal question may arise.

In some areas that are supplied by flowing wells, too many wells have been drilled and the water from some of them has been allowed to go to waste. After a drought in the intake area, such waste may cause not only inconvenience to householders but the loss of crops in areas that are irrigated with the well water. This has occurred in the vicinity of Roswell, New Mexico, where too many wells were drilled. The ground-water supply was insufficient for all of them and many wells had to be filled or stopped in order to maintain the supply in the others. Conservation of the supply by avoiding waste at all times is essential. Without in any sense contradicting this statement, it may be said that wells are justifiably allowed to flow in certain restricted areas. At Slaterville Springs, New York, small, shallow, strictly local flowing wells are allowed to flow to a limited extent in order to avoid clogging of the pipes with fine sand. The measures already suggested should be applied to wells flowing with clear water.

For the underground supply. All the methods of holding water on the land for crops help the water to percolate into the deep subsoil mate-

---

[14] A brief review of legal questions concerning underground waters, including those of Long Island, New York, is given in the *Louisiana Conservation Review,* Spring, 1938, by David G. Thompson and Albert G. Fielder of the Geological Survey, U.S. Department of the Interior.

rial and replenish the supply of ground water for springs and shallow wells. Some of the water goes on down into porous rocks and supplies deep wells that are drilled into those rocks. Between periods of runoff streams are sustained in some degree from this supply of ground water. Sustained flow is of the utmost importance for farm livestock, for fish and other stream life, and for water power and navigation.

As previously pointed out, the soil is the great invaluable reservoir; in total, soils hold truly immense quantities of water. Forest soils are particularly absorptive and retentive of water, partly because of the litter and leaf mold on the forest floor. This litter holds water against runoff until it goes into the soil. Moreover, this organic matter on and in the surface soil keeps it loose and open so it takes up water readily. Keeping land in forest or returning it to forest, if it is not needed for other purposes, therefore aids in maintaining the supply of ground water. Thrifty meadows and pastures under favorable conditions take up nearly as much water as forests. Poor meadows and overgrazed pastures, although better than bare land, are ineffective in holding water in comparison with thrifty ones. Contour tillage, seeding, cultivation, and harvesting, including contour furrows (Fig. 40), aid greatly in holding water for the ground-water supply.

When large acreages of land are taken out of production, as was done a few years ago and will probably be done again when similar conditions return, little if any additional swamp land should be drained. Natural swamp lands, particularly on the higher elevations, aid in maintaining the supply of ground water. Indeed, it is probable that many large and small areas of swamp land are of much greater value for maintaining the supply of ground water for wells, springs, and streams, and for breeding and feeding areas for wildlife (see Chap. XII) than for agricultural production. If at some future time swamp lands should be needed for food production, they can then be drained for that purpose. Thorough investigation of swamp lands by agronomists, economists, wildlife experts, and drainage engineers should precede drainage operations. Unless it is definitely agreed that the land is *needed* for food production, swamps should not be drained because of their great value for water supply and for wildlife.

For production of crops in humid areas. Almost every year some sections of this country, even those with ample average annual rainfall for good crop growth, suffer from droughts. During low-rainfall periods, more complete conservation of rain water would produce larger yields. Much can be done to hold the water on the land until it is taken up by the soil. Each acre can be managed so as to take up more of the water that falls on it than it ordinarily does. Storing much additional water in the soil is not only desirable but essential for many purposes.

Figure 40. Contour furrows, Texas. These lister furrows were made in the spring of 1935. Nearly two inches of rain fell the day before this picture was taken, yet the water was held evenly over the field. Without the furrows much of the water would have been lost. Being held, the water will be of great value to crops. (U.S. Soil Conservation Service.)

To conserve water, runoff must be greatly lessened if not prevented. Water readily runs off over smooth, bare, sloping land, particularly when rain comes in heavy showers. Remedies, therefore, are to keep uncropped land rough by means of suitable contour tillage and to maintain a crop cover during the time that the regular crops are not on the land. Grains, grasses, legume crops, and even the growth of weeds, and hay plants after harvest, delay runoff.

Except when the soil is frozen, such a cover enables it to take up much more water than it can if the soil is hard and bare. Any moisture thus retained improves the growth of crops in dry periods, particularly in the drier areas of the country. Conserving water for use by crops is more fully treated in Chapter V.

For irrigation in subhumid areas. Much of the water for irrigation in the western states, as previously stated, comes from snow and is collected and held in reservoirs. Accurate measurement of the total snowfall is now being made so that the quantity of water that may

Figure 41. Small farm or community dam. A small, inexpensive dam of this kind has many uses: swimming in summer and skating in winter. Such a dam may supply water for livestock and for vegetables and fruits in spring and summer. It may also help in the control of floods. (U.S. Soil Conservation Service.)

be available for the next growing season can be definitely predicted. Acreages to be planted and necessary measures for conserving the supply of water, therefore, can be determined in advance. In many areas the water supply for the entire growing season depends directly on the capacity of the local reservoir. Since only about one-tenth of the well-adapted land in the western part of this country can, because of the limited water supply, actually be irrigated, it is essential that all the available water be conserved and wisely used.

It has been common practice to supply water for irrigation *by the acre,* with the result that farmers sometimes used more water than crops required. Excessive use of water under some conditions has definitely proved to be detrimental to crops. It appears to be a better practice and a true conservation measure to meter water to the farmer for irrigation as cities meter water to the householder. Metering irrigation water would be expected to lead to its use only as needed for optimum growth of food, fiber, and feed crops.

Another cause of waste of precious irrigation water is leakage from the canals that carry the water from streams or reservoirs to fields.

Figure 42. Daugherty Dam, Walsh County, North Dakota. This earthen dam was built by a Soil Conservation Camp in the fall of 1935 and the spring of 1936. A reservoir of this size may be of even greater community service than the smaller one shown in Figure 41. (U.S. Soil Conservation Service.)

The loss through porous canal beds is estimated to be from one-tenth to one-third of the water carried. This water should be saved in order that a larger acreage of productive soil might be irrigated. The water thus lost makes a swamp of the land below the leak in the canal. The productivity of this land can be restored only by preventing leakage by proper lining of the canal or by expensive drainage operations and soil treatment.

For recreation. Many communities throughout the country lack facilities for water recreation. Dams on small streams, ponds and pools in open ravines, and ponds at the sites of springs associated with impervious soil may be developed in large numbers at small expense.

These small bodies of water may serve many purposes: (1) for watering livestock, (2) for possible fire protection, (3) for spraying fruits and vegetables, (4) for irrigating high-value crops, (5) for fishing after being fertilized and stocked, (6) for swimming and boating when sufficiently large, and (7) in the North, for skating. Moreover, if proper provision for drawing off part of the impounded water is made, these ponds can hold back water and thus aid in a small way in lowering the crests of local floods (Figs. 41–44).

Figure 43. Small pond of one acre in New York. A good growth of fish has been obtained in this farm pond. (A. F. Gustafson.)

POLLUTION OF WATERS MUST CEASE

For many years immense quantities of city sewage; industrial wastes; wastes from gas plants, milk plants, and cheese factories, from fruit, fish, and vegetable canneries; acid waters from mines; and other wastes both objectionable and poisonous have been dumped into streams, lakes, and coastal waters. The result has been inestimable damage to fish, waterfowl, and other water life.

The Interstate Commission on the Delaware River Basin, which is supported by Delaware, Pennsylvania, New Jersey, and New York, has shown that 2,500,000 people depend, in whole or in part, on the Delaware River for a living. For the cleanup of this river $100,000,000 has been earmarked.

The almost universal problem of river and harbor pollution is city sewage. About half of the country's sewage has been treated, yet more than 3,000 communities throughout this country discharge 2,500,000,-000 tons of raw, untreated sewage into inland and coastal waters every day.[15] Solid and liquid industrial wastes greatly augment the already immense total of wastes poured into these waters.

In certain areas wells have been drilled into the underlying rock to dispose of drainage water from farm lands, wastes from manufacturing plants and gas works, and even untreated sewage direct from toilet facilities in homes. This manner of disposing of underground field drainage water is not likely to be dangerous to human health. Its use in disposing of the other wastes mentioned must be eliminated at

Figure 44. Fishing in pond shown in Figure 43. (E. Van Alstine.)

the earliest possible moment. This is particularly vital in areas that are underlain by more or less cavernous limestone. Limestone is a water-bearing rock that is frequently tapped by wells for domestic water supplies; hence its pollution by sewage is particularly dangerous and without any justification.

Industrial wastes and sewage must be rendered harmless before being dumped into these public waters. Proper treatment of all sewage will obviously add something to city and village taxes. Some industrial wastes, however, can be turned into by-products of value. Unless this can be done, the cost of treatment must be added to over-

---

[15] "Water Pollution," editorial in the New York *Times,* Nov. 8, 1945.

all costs to the consumer. In any event, cities, industries, and individuals must be prevented from continued widespread pollution of any of the country's valuable surface and underground water resources.

Over a period of years there has been earnest agitation by public-spirited citizens and public and private conservation organizations for a federal law to control the pollution of coastal and inland waters. It was proposed to outlaw the discharge of any sewage or industrial waste into navigable streams or their tributaries and, after a reasonable period for necessary adjustments, to prohibit the discharge of any waste injurious to man or to waterfowl, fish, or other water life.

Finally, a law, the Taft-Barkley Act, was enacted in 1948 by the 80th Congress for the control of water pollution.[16] The act establishes a Water-Pollution Control Advisory Board. The board is to consist of the Surgeon General, or a sanitary engineer designated by him, as chairman, and representatives of the Federal Works Agency, the Departments of Agriculture and Defense, and six individuals to be appointed by the President. None of these six members shall have any connection with the federal government. One of them shall be an expert in the disposal of sewage and industrial wastes; one shall have an active interest in wildlife conservation; one shall represent state and another municipal governments; one shall represent affected industries; and there shall be one additional member.

The act gives wide authority for the abatement of pollution of coastal, interstate, and tributary waters to the Surgeon General and to the Federal Works Administrator. With full co-operation between federal, state, and local governmental agencies, industry, and the public, the pollution of waters can now be effectively prevented.

---

[16] Carl D. Shoemaker, "Shall We Have Water Pollution Control?" *Conservation News,* 13[4]: 1–2, 1948.

CHAPTER IV

Soil Depletion and Erosion

THE soil is the source of much of man's food and clothing, and of materials for shelter and fuel. Such food products as cereals, fruits, nuts, and vegetables are direct products of the soil. Man's meat comes from animals that feed upon the products of the soil. Materials for clothing, such as cotton and flax, and the plant materials from which rayon and other cellulose fabrics are made grow on the soil. Wool, furs, and silk come from animals that feed upon the immediate products of the soil. Moreover, many plant materials enter into the manufacture of numerous articles of everyday domestic and industrial use. In addition to the house itself may be mentioned such items as furniture, floor and wall coverings, draperies, and paints and varnishes, all direct products of the land.

It is well, therefore, to recognize our dependence upon the soil for food and clothing and in part for shelter and other necessities. Our dependence upon it is the reason for giving serious consideration to the depletion and erosion of the soil.

SOIL DEPLETION

For many years it was believed that ten simple chemical substances or *elements* were sufficient for plant growth. These elements were carbon, oxygen, hydrogen, nitrogen, phosphorus, calcium, magnesium, iron, potassium, and sulfur. Recently it has been found that at least four additional elements—manganese, copper, boron, and zinc —are needed in small amounts or traces for growth by many plants. In comparison with the amount needed of these *minor* or *trace* elements, relatively large quantities of phosphorus, calcium, nitrogen, sulfur, carbon, oxygen, hydrogen, and potassium are used by crops in their growth.

Sources of plant nutrients. The elements used for growth by plants are often referred to as *plant nutrients*. Water supplies plants with oxygen and hydrogen, and the air supplies oxygen directly and, in addition, both oxygen and carbon in the form of carbon dioxide. The latter is a product of the burning of coal and of the burning or the decay of wood and other organic matter. Moreover, carbon dioxide is thrown off, in breathing, from the lungs of animals, including man, and from the leaves of plants. Nitrogen, phosphorus, calcium, magnesium, sulfur, potassium, iron, manganese, zinc, copper, and boron are taken up by plants directly from the soil, usually in the form of solutions of various compounds of these elements.

Nutrient elements often lacking in soils. In much of the United States the soil is well supplied with all the plant nutrients except nitrogen, phosphorus, calcium, and potassium. In some areas soils lack sufficient iron, manganese, boron, copper, magnesium, sulfur, and zinc in usable form for good growth of certain crops. On very acid soils lime is needed for correcting soil acidity and other unfavorable conditions, as well as for supplying available calcium and magnesium (pp. 141–142). This is particularly true of alfalfa, clover, and other legumes, and of cauliflower, cabbage, and some other vegetables.

Supply of nitrogen inexhaustible. Nearly four-fifths of the air is nitrogen. The world supply of it, therefore, is ample for all time. The farmer's task is to manage soils and nitrogen-gathering crops (pp. 138–141) so as to use the nitrogen of the air over and over again.

Soils low in phosphorus. Many soils are naturally low in phosphorus, and this element is taken from the soil in substantial quantities by many crops. Even if the crops are fed to livestock on the farm, all the phosphorus cannot be returned to the soil, because all growing animals and meat animals retain phosphorus. Moreover, eggs, milk, and other animal products contain phosphorus. Consequently cropping results in a net loss of phosphorus to the soil.

Many soils rich in potassium. Often from 40,000 to 60,000 pounds of potassium an acre are present in the surface foot of average soil. Grain contains but little potassium in comparison with that in the stalks of corn or the straw of small grains. The quantity of potassium sold from the farm in the grain of a corn or wheat crop, therefore, is small in comparison with the total supply in the soil.

On the other hand, a shortage of potassium in both organic and mineral soils, particularly sandy and gravelly ones, often reduces the

yield of crops such as grains and vegetables. Many heavy soils, however, produce good yields of crops year after year without additions of
potassium.

How plant nutrients are lost. As plants grow, they take nutrients from
the soil and store them temporarily in their tissues. When wheat,
corn, flax, and cotton, including the seed, are harvested and sold from
the land, the mineral nutrients in these crops that came out of the soil
leave the farm. These nutrients are not returned to the land and therefore are lost *forever* to the particular soil from which the crops obtained them. On many farms in this country a smaller quantity of plant
nutrients is returned to the soil each year than crops took out of the
soil the year before. To that extent the soil is poorer than it was before
the crops were grown. Any single year's crop does not, of course, remove large quantities of plant nutrients. Nevertheless, as the decades
lengthen into centuries of cropping, the removal of plant nutrients
without corresponding returns to the soil leads ultimately to depletion or exhaustion of the soil.

Enough is known about the quantities of the different elements in
soils to give an idea of their ability to produce certain crops over a
period of years. An acre of the rich prairie soil of the Midwest contains
enough phosphorus to produce about 130 seventy-five-bushel crops of
corn. If corn is grown two years out of four, and lesser amounts of
phosphorus are used by the other crops, the productive life of such
rich soils is around 200 years. Under wheat two years out of four, the
life of this soil would be approximately 400 years. In comparison with
the many centuries of recorded agricultural history in the Orient two
or four centuries is indeed a brief period.

Except for parts of Tennessee, the famous blue-grass region of
Kentucky, and the dry areas of the West, our soils generally were not
richly supplied with native phosphorus. Many have become distinctly
deficient in this essential element in the short period during which
they have been cropped. Man cannot obtain sufficient food and materials for clothing from soils that have been depleted of their phosphorus.

Measurement of losses. The losses of potassium, calcium, sulfur, and
magnesium, as measured in the water from drainage tanks or *lysi-
meters,* are very high. The loss of calcium and magnesium is particularly high, and in part this explains why cultivated humid soils in
time become acid and require liming for good crop growth. In lysi-

meter experiments it has been found that only traces of phosphorus are usually lost in the drainage water. Even so the total loss of phosphorus in drainage from the field soils of the country over long periods is very great indeed, and leaching may be regarded as an important cause of loss of phosphorus and other plant nutrients as well.

Loss of organic matter. In their natural condition many soils contain a considerable amount of organic matter, that is, the remains of plants and animals. During the production of crops organic matter decays

Figure 45. Barn with heaps of manure. As manure lies under the eaves, it decays rapidly, with heavy losses of plant nutrients and organic matter. (A. F. Gustafson.)

in the soil. Part of the nitrogen and other plant nutrients thus made available is used by crops, but some of it is lost from the soil in drainage water and in other ways. Few farmers, except possibly some vegetable growers, keep up the supply of organic matter in the soil. Consequently, soils growing cotton, corn, wheat, flax, and many other crops lose organic matter year after year. This loss is usually accompanied by the development of many unfavorable soil conditions and results in a decrease in crop yields.

In many soils loss of organic matter causes poor tilth as a result of the breaking down of the natural granules or groups of soil particles.

These granules, which consist of myriads of particles, act somewhat as do fairly large sand particles. In other words, a well-granulated soil, or one in good tilth, is loose and more open or porous than is one that has lost its granular condition.

Losses of nutrients from farm manure. Farm manure, which consists of straw and various other absorptive materials mixed with animal excreta, is a valuable by-product of livestock farming. Larger quantities of plant nutrients are returned to the soil in manure than in all other fertilizers combined. As farm manure is generally handled in this country, heavy losses of nutrients occur. Part of the nitrogen and potash in it are soluble in water. For this reason rain water that falls on manure in an open pile, especially under the eaves of the barn, causes heavy loss of these elements (Fig. 45). Probably not more than half of the phosphorus and lower proportions of the other nutrients in crops are returned to the soil. Much of the nutrients leached from manure passes into streams and consequently is lost to the soil.

Plant-nutrient losses in the United States. The losses of important plant nutrients as estimated by the National Resources Board are given in Table 5.

TABLE 5. PLANT NUTRIENTS LOST ANNUALLY FROM 365,000,000 ACRES OF CROP LAND AND 1,000,000,000 ACRES OF PASTURE LAND IN THE UNITED STATES *

Losses	Nitrogen	Phosphorus	Potassium	Calcium	Magnesium	Sulfur	Organic matter
	Thousands of tons						
Harvested areas							
Crops	4,600	700	3,200	1,000	500	500	92,000
Erosion and leaching	6,500	900	21,600	39,600	19,000	8,200	130,000
Pastures							
Grazing	3,000	500	3,700	1,000	500	400	60,000
Erosion and leaching	2,000	400	7,700	12,000	3,800	2,200	40,000
Total losses	16,100	2,500	36,200	53,600	16,800	11,300	322,000
Total additions	11,830	1,100	4,800	13,800	4,600	8,700	100,000
Net losses	4,270	1,400	31,400	39,800	12,200	2,600	222,000

* *National Resources Board Report,* 1934, p. 163.

According to these estimates, the phosphorus lost annually by erosion and leaching, not including that used by crops, is sufficient to produce a 75-bushel crop of corn on 350,000,000 acres, or a 30-bushel crop of wheat on nearly 700,000,000 acres of land. Stated in another way, this quantity of phosphorus is equivalent to that in 15,000,000 tons of a phosphatic fertilizer such as 20-per-cent superphosphate. It would take 10,000 trains of 60 cars each, every car containing 25 tons of superphosphate, to carry as much phosphorus as is lost by erosion and leaching every year from the crop and pasture soils of the United States. Moreover, the phosphorus lost plus that used by crops is more than twice the quantity that is being returned annually in fertilizers to the soils of the United States.

The losses of potassium are large but less critical than those of phosphorus because many soils are well supplied with potassium. The losses of calcium, magnesium, sulfur, nitrogen, and organic matter are large and require attention in any program for the maintenance of the productivity of soils. Soils vary so widely in their native supplies of these elements that no general statement can be made regarding the necessity of returning them to any specific soil. Moreover, considerable acreages in this country are deficient in boron for alfalfa, apples, beets, turnips, cauliflower, and certain other crops. In some areas soils lack sufficient copper, zinc, or manganese for certain crops but not for all.

As a nation the United States is young, a mere infant, in comparison with China and other ancient countries that have cropped their soils for forty centuries or more. American soils have been farmed only one to three centuries. New as our soils are, their natural crop-producing power has already been considerably reduced. Unless plant nutrients and organic matter are returned to the soil, many additional acres will eventually be abandoned because it does not pay farmers to crop them.

Helpful experimental work. Long-term experimental work gives a fair indication of what the results of cropping the land without returning the phosphorus to it will be even on rich soils. At the Illinois Agricultural Experimental Station are plots that have produced the same crops in the same way for nearly three quarters of a century. One plot has grown corn every year since the spring of 1876. Another plot has alternated corn and oats and a third plot has grown corn, oats, and clover in rotation during this entire period.

Comparative yield data are available for more than half a century.

Since 1888 the yield of corn that was grown continuously on the same soil has dropped more than one-half. In the two-year rotation of corn and oats, the corn yield has fallen off by a little less than two-fifths. In the three-year rotation of corn, oats, and clover, the yield of corn during this half century has diminished by fully two-fifths or 40 per cent. In other words, less than half as much corn was produced at the end as at the beginning of this half century when corn was grown alone, and only about three-fifths as much in the two- and the three-year rotations.

The Ohio Agricultural Experimental Station has reported crop yields from 1894 to 1923. During these thirty years, wheat and oat yields on untreated land dropped one-fourth and corn yields fell off one-half. Such losses in thirty years and those at the Illinois Experimental Station in fifty years deserve serious consideration. Similar results have been obtained at other experiment stations, notably those of Missouri and Pennsylvania.

SOIL EROSION

Plant nutrients can be restored to the land but under present-day agricultural practices in this country soil that is once washed from a field is lost forever to that field. In some countries, soil is carried uphill on the backs of men and women and thus returned to the higher lands from which it came. In this country, however, the cost is usually too great, although some washed-off soil has been hauled back.

By soil erosion is meant the removal of soil by wind or water (Fig. 46). Differences between the erosion caused by winds and that brought about by water on slopes are shown later in this chapter.

Conditions found in this country by the white man. Three centuries ago, when white men came to this continent, the eastern part of the country was an unbroken forest. In the Midwest was a vast prairie of tall grasses, and westward were the short-grass area and the Great Plains country (Fig. 21, p. 55). In the virgin or natural condition a balance had developed between soils, vegetation, wild animals, and rainfall. Since the animals had plenty of feed they did not overgraze the short grass and expose the dry soil to wind and water erosion. The trees in the East and the Far West and the tall grass in the Midwest protected the soil perfectly against erosion. In the earliest days of American agriculture, therefore, the settler had no serious problem of soil erosion by either wind or water.

In the East and South where trees on slopes were cut or burned and the land converted into farms, erosion soon started. As the forest litter was plowed under, it and the tiny roots of the trees decayed and disappeared from the soil. The spongy, virgin organic matter soon vanished and with it the natural absorptive power of the soil. The soil became compact, and as heavy rains carried away the surface soil,

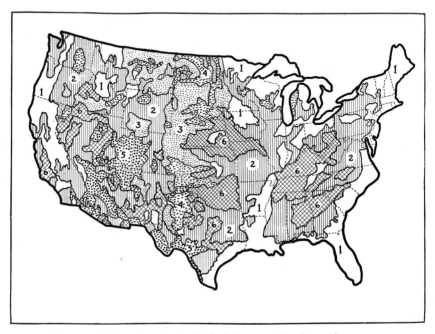

Figure 46. Soil erosion in the United States. 1. Erosion unimportant except locally. 2. Moderate sheet and gully erosion, serious locally. 3. Slight wind erosion, moderate sheet and gully erosion. 4. Moderate to severe wind erosion, some gullying locally. 5. Moderate to severe erosion, includes mountains, mesas, canyons, and badlands. 6. Severe sheet and gully erosion. (Drawn from data by the U.S. Soil Conservation Service.)

erosion was on in earnest, especially on the steeper slopes. In southern New York, for example, less than fifty years after lumbering operations cleared the slopes in the mid-nineteenth century, those lands were seriously eroded. In the years between 1900 and 1930 many farms in this area were abandoned.

On the prairie the story of the beginning of erosion was similar. The prairie grasses were plowed under and their decay and disappearance followed. Because the prairie soils of the Midwest contained much active organic matter and had gentle slopes, they resisted erosion longer than did the forest soils of the East. In time, however, even the rich prairie soils lost their fresh organic matter. The soil became compact; runoff and erosion followed.

The net annual loss of organic matter from the soils of the United States due to erosion and cropping has been estimated as 222,000,000 tons (Table 5). This loss occurs in spite of the return of organic matter to the soil by the farmer.

The easily available, virgin fertility of the soil was used up by crops in relatively few years. Consequently, crops grow less luxuriantly and protect the soil less completely now than when they were first planted. Fewer roots are present to hold the soil together, and less plant material is produced to help maintain the organic-matter content of the soil than in the early days of cropping these lands.

Early recognition of damage by soil erosion. Only a few years after the beginning of agriculture in some sections of this country, farmers noted serious loss of soil by washing.[1] Much space was devoted to this problem in early agricultural literature. George Washington recognized soil erosion on his lands at Mount Vernon as early as 1769. In 1817 Thomas Jefferson wrote that "fields were no sooner cleared than washed." Patrick Henry is credited with saying that "since the achievement of our independence, he is the greatest patriot, who *stops the most gullies.*"

About 1795 Washington wrote: "The soil . . . is a good loam. . . . From use, and I might add, abuse, it has become more and more consolidated, and, of course, heavier to work. . . . A husbandman's wish would not lay the farms more level than they are: and yet some of the fields . . . are washed into gullies, from which all of them have not yet been recovered." This letter was not wholly encouraging to prospective tenants, especially to English farmers whose homeland experience did not include farming among gullies.

In 1819 Madison advocated the adoption of soil-saving methods of cultivation. Otherwise ownership of the "red lands" (Piedmont soils), he said, was equivalent to a lease for a few years only. Damage by washing he believed was so serious and so general that "very little hilly land [in Prince Edward County, Virginia] cleared more than 20 or 30 years was of any value." Corn and tobacco had been grown gen-

---

[1] A. R. Hall, *Early Erosion Control Practices in Virginia* (U.S. Department of Agriculture, Misc. Pub. 256; Washington, 1938).

erally and, being soil-exposing crops, both had led to much erosion. The planting of corn without regard to slopes and frequent tillage contributed further to loss of surface soil and to gullying. Washington, Jefferson, and others noted the "ravages" of the soil by the growing of corn.

In those days crops were charged with causing loss of soil. In time, however, several prominent men came to recognize the real causes of "culturally induced" erosion. In 1801 Thomas Moore wrote: "Thus the land becomes sterile not so much from the vegetable nutriment being extracted from the soil by the growth of plants, as by the soil itself being removed; . . . it [depletion] is more from the manner of cultivation than from the exhausting properties of the crops. . . ."

All of this indicates that even in colonial times soil erosion was a serious problem in the Southeast. At the close of the eighteenth and early in the nineteenth centuries, agricultural writers showed deep concern over soil erosion. Instead of working out methods of controlling erosion, however, many farmers went west to new lands. An anonymous writer is credited with the statement, "The scratching [shallow-plowing] farmer's cares and anxieties are only relieved by his land soon washing away. As that goes down the rivers he goes over the mountains." In other words, after the land became seriously eroded, the farmer moved over the Allegheny Mountains to the fertile lands of the Midwest. The bare fields were left for nature to ruin completely or to cure by means of volunteer vegetation. The effect of this abandonment of land may still be clearly seen today.

Interest in the control of erosion was stimulated by offering prizes for "The best mode of restoring worn out land, filling gullies, and bringing it in order for the plough. The best rotation of crops in which Indian corn, wheat, and clover are included. . . . The best mode of preventing lands under the plough from washing." These practical questions are taken from a long list having to do with the restoration of washed land and the control of further washing on good, cultivated soils. As early as 1795 Washington said that establishing a cover of grass on washing land was the goal, rather than immediate profit. Gullied fields were smoothed and covered with weeds, straw, or other vegetable material to prevent further gullying and to encourage the growth of grass. In 1794 Jefferson made large use of clover in his cropping system. Redtop (*Agrostis alba*), which produced a good turf, was found to be effective against erosion because it thrived on eroded soils. "Horizontal" (contour) plowing was practiced by Jefferson in 1810. Hillside ditches and, later, narrow terraces came into use (pp. 162–164). Outlets for these hillside ditches gave much trouble and, through lack of engineering instruments and experience, terraces and ditches often caused gullying. Nevertheless, this early work led to the improved present-day methods of erosion control. The data just presented show that soil erosion in this country is far from being a new problem. In the older agricultural areas a solution has, in fact, been needed for more than a century and a half.

Figure 47. Gullying in loess in west-central Mississippi. This land, once in cotton, lost the top soil, was abandoned to pasture, and is now producing little; even the persimmon is struggling to live. (A. F. Gustafson.)

The Tennessee Experiment Station published a bulletin on *Practical Experiments in Reclaiming "Galled" or Washed Land* in 1890, and in 1894 the Arkansas Station published a bulletin on *Protection of Soil from Surface Washing* and other topics. Articles were published even earlier in the agricultural papers of the country. Many bulletins have been published by the United States Department of Agriculture and by individual states. The Soil Conservation Service has published an extensive bibliography on soil conservation.

Erosion by water. Soil erosion by water is of three more or less distinct types—sheet, rill, and gully erosion (Figs. 47, 48).

Sheet erosion. As already stated, heavy rain on bare soil brings soil particles into suspension in the water by means of the beating action of the drops. If the rain that falls on moderate-to-steep slopes is not taken up quickly by the soil, the water runs off and carries soil with it. The loss of soil is fairly uniform from all parts of a slope and is called *sheet* or *surface erosion*. Most of our sloping lands that are planted to such soil-exposing crops as corn, potatoes, beans, cotton, sorghum, and vegetables lose soil by sheet erosion during heavy rains. The actual loss often goes unnoticed for some years, yet the total damage to soil is greatest from this type of erosion.

Figure 48. Grass protects this long slope. Compare with Figure 49. (U.S. Soil Conservation Service.)

Rill erosion. The surface of plowed fields is seldom perfectly smooth. Small depressions are nearly always present. Water from a heavy rain that is not completely taken up by the soil may collect in depressions on its way down the slope. These tiny streams or rivulets cut narrow, shoestringlike channels. This type of erosion, called *rill washing,* is shown in Figure 49. Severe rill washing may carry away, on an average, from one-fourth to one-half inch or more of the surface of a sloping field during a single heavy downpour.

Seedbed preparation on a rill-washed field fills the little gullies and makes the surface smooth once more. Thus the real effect of rill washing is, in general, the same as that of sheet erosion. Much damage is being done by both sheet and rill erosion.

Gully erosion. If rill-washed soil is not smoothed and seeded, rills may grow into gullies. Depressions such as wheel tracks, ground-mole runs, plow furrows, and furrows by other implements often occur on hillsides. As rain water collects in such depressions, it carries soil downhill, and the stream becomes larger and larger, often cutting a large gully in a short time (Figs. 50–54).

Figure 49. Severe rill washing on summer-fallowed land. None is to be seen in the grass in Figure 48 under comparable conditions with respect to soil, slope, and rainfall. (U.S. Soil Conservation Service.)

In July, 1935, in southern New York a gully twelve feet deep and four feet wide was cut in a single night. The rain that made this gully was a succession of heavy thundershowers, not a cloudburst. Damage such as the formation of this gully cannot readily be repaired. Because farm implements cannot cross such gullies they increase greatly the time required to prepare for, plant, and harvest crops. Moreover, gullies actually reduce the area that can be cropped. In fact, large gullies increase the cost of producing crops in many ways and the formation of many gullies soon makes the farming of such land unprofitable. The farmer, unable to make a living for himself and his family, must go elsewhere. The land may be left to wash more and more with every heavy rain. This is the history of many farms in the Southeast, in the Southwest, in the Ohio Valley, and in the Midwest; of some areas in the northeastern states and on the Pacific Coast; and of a few in other parts of the United States.

In parts of the Far West are large areas of loose, dry soils that wash easily. Even though the total annual rainfall of the area is low, part of

Figure 50. Badly gullied land in the Tennessee Valley before treatment. Compare with Figure 93 (p. 171), which shows the same land after treatment. (Tennessee Valley Authority.)

it falls as heavy showers. Severe erosion of all types on these loose soils, especially the sandy ones, is the result (Fig. 55).

Wind erosion. Immense quantities of soil material are moved by the wind. In fact, it appears likely that winds in this country have moved far more soil material than have all kinds of streams combined. Wind is working continually in its zone of action, whereas water does little work except after heavy rains and during floods. Usually only dry soil is moved by the wind. Man's cultivation of land tends to make it drier. This is accomplished by drainage both by open ditches and by underdrains such as tile. Many crops encourage evaporation and permit

Figure 51. Gullying in deep loess in southern Iowa. (A. F. Gustafson.)

Figure 52. Gullying in dry, eastern Colorado. Close grazing is part of the cause of gullying in this area. Note the difference in vegetative cover on the two sides of the fence in the foreground. (A. F. Gustafson.)

much more loss of water by runoff than do native types of vegetation such as forests and prairie grasses. For these reasons, areas of low rainfall when placed under exploitative cultivation tend toward desert conditions and may encourage severe wind erosion.

On the Great Plains the native grass was plowed down and the land seeded to wheat. Excellent yields were produced during the years of normal and of heavier than average rainfall. After a period of dry

Figure 53. Gullies in a Wisconsin hog pasture. These slopes have been heavily stocked so that the vegetation is unable to hold the soil. Gullying has resulted. Note the absence of erosion on the right of the fence where the vegetation is undisturbed. (U.S. Soil Conservation Service.)

years, especially in the spring as in 1935 and 1937, strong dry winds blew away millions of tons of surface soil. The finest particles were carried to the Atlantic seaboard and even out to sea (Figs. 56, 57).

The wind acts most effectively on fine sands and on somewhat finer soils when these are broken down to dust during seedbed preparation or cultivation. The very finest particles are swirled up high in the air and thus carried long distances. Somewhat larger particles are picked up and carried considerable distances. Still larger particles are lifted only by the strongest winds and may be carried forward by means of a jumpy movement called *saltation*. Or they may be rolled along on the surface to be built up into dunes wherever a weed, fence, hedgerow

(Fig. 58), or other object checks the wind. In places small buildings have been nearly covered and from two or three to as much as eight or ten feet of sand has been deposited about houses and barns (Fig. 59). In many instances the entire plowed soil has been carried away.

In addition, bare sands and sandy soils on sea and lake shores and wherever they are not covered by vegetation are subject to blowing. In Dune Park in northern Indiana sand dunes have invaded and cov-

Figure 54. Severe erosion in Pennsylvania. Fumes from the beehive coke ovens have caused such high acidity in the soil as to retard and later prevent the growth of vegetation. Such conditions prevail also in the vicinity of smelters. Control of erosion there is difficult. Conservation demands the removal of the cause of such destructive erosion. This end may be accomplished by rendering such fumes harmless. (U.S. Soil Conservation Service.)

ered forests. Years later the dunes moved on and left behind the resurrected dead trees. Forests and even villages in northern Europe have been covered and later disinterred in this manner.

The burying of good, productive soil by unproductive sand causes heavy loss to many landowners. This takes place wherever sand is blown onto good soils. Soils so buried are not entirely uncovered when the dunes move on. Too often a foot or more of the coarser sand remains behind as a covering over good soils, and thus renders such land practically worthless.

Conditions influencing erosion. Among the conditions influencing erosion are the steepness and length of slopes, the relative amount of plant protection or the exposure of the soil, the amount and kind, and distribution of rainfall, the climate, the soil itself, and the farmer. *Slope of land.* Water flows faster on steep than on gentle slopes. Fast-flowing water cuts soil loose much more rapidly and carries far more of it than does slow-moving water. The steeper the slope, therefore, the faster the water runs off the land and the more soil it carries away.

Figure 55. Deposition of eroded material, Texas. Subsoil material from twelve to eighteen inches thick from an unprotected cotton field has been deposited on good soil. The productivity of the covered soil has been greatly reduced. (U.S. Soil Conservation Service.)

If the soil fails to absorb all of a heavy rain, the excess runs off. By the time it reaches the lower part of a long slope much water has accumulated. As the quantity of water increases, so also does its speed; and with the higher speed of flow comes greatly increased cutting and carrying power. It has been shown that doubling the speed of a stream multiplies its cutting power by 4 and the weight of the separate soil particles it can carry by 64. In other words, if the speed of a stream that is carrying particles weighing one milligram is doubled, it can then transport particles that weigh 64 milligrams. Further increases in velocity increase the size of particles that may be moved by stream currents to almost unbelievable proportions. These facts suggest the remedy: do something to reduce the speed of the flowing water.

Protection of the soil by vegetation. A bare soil suffers more loss than does one under thick grass or forest. A cover of grass or trees acts like an umbrella in that it protects the soil from the beating action of raindrops. Raindrops may churn bare soil into a thin mud, which flows into and fills the pores or other openings in the surface soil. This

Figure 56. A dust storm or black blizzard. This storm occurred on April 14, 1935. (U.S. Soil Conservation Service.)

prevents the water from entering the soil readily; consequently, it must run off, and in doing so carries soil with it. Under grass or trees, on the other hand, any water not taken up by the soil flows away clear and causes no erosion.

Virgin forest and prairie soils, being well supplied with organic matter, usually absorb rain water readily (Fig. 60). The organic matter itself takes up water and holds it. Less water, therefore, is lost from land that is covered with vegetation (Fig. 61).

Type, amount, and distribution of rainfall. In a section where rain falls slowly, the water is taken up by the soil as it falls. Or if the soil is already wet, the slow rain does not churn it into suspension to be lost in the runoff. In contrast, the heavy shower, which is the usual kind of summer rain in much of the United States, beats the smaller soil particles into suspension. Furthermore, heavy rains fall so rapidly that the soil cannot absorb all of the water. Much of it, therefore, runs off and carries away a great deal of soil, especially from bare fields. Wet soils suffer particularly severe losses.

Figure 57. Sand dunes in Death Valley. No vegetation is in sight to check the movement of the sand. (U.S. Department of the Interior.)

An inch of rain has been recorded in 10 minutes or even less in many places in the United States, two inches in 30 minutes, eight inches in 24 hours, and in 1935 as much as twelve inches in 48 hours in the East. During January, 1937, sixteen inches fell in the Ohio Valley. Such heavy rainfall on bare, sloping soils causes severe erosion, particularly if the soil is frozen but thawing on the surface.

Climate. Northern soils are usually frozen about four or five months each winter, and during this period little erosion takes place. During the open, rainy winter of 1936–1937 in the Midwest, much erosion occurred in corn fields as a result of rains on soil the surface of which had thawed a few inches. Upon thawing, the surface soil often becomes very wet, and rain falling on this mud makes it still thinner, and it runs off very easily. Because of alternate freezing and thawing, a middle zone across the country is subject to rather severe winter and early spring erosion.

In the extreme southern part of the country, little freezing occurs, and this section, therefore, escapes the erosion just described. The absence of freezing, however, means that the soil is subject to erosion

Figure 58. Sand drifts in the Northwest. The size of this sand drift in South Dakota is evident. Vegetation here checked the movement of the sand. (U.S. Soil Conservation Service.)

throughout the entire year. For this reason, erosion is usually more severe in the areas that are not protected by a period of freezing.

Kind of soil. Soils vary greatly in ease of washing, or erodibility. Coarse soils and those containing many stones do not wash readily. The loessial soils of the Midwest and other silt loam soils wash easily once the surface soil has been carried away. Heavy soils such as those formed from the glacial lake deposits in the northern part of the United States also wash easily on gentle slopes.

The residual soils of the Piedmont, owing to their heavy subsurface and coarse underlying material, wash readily. Another reason for the high erodibility of these soils is that their native organic matter has been largely lost, and consequently they take up water very slowly. The soils have become compact and, as a result, rain water runs off readily and takes soil with it. (See Fig. 51, p. 115.)

The farmer. The early American farmers came to this country mainly from Great Britain, Norway, Sweden, Denmark, and the northwestern part of Europe, particularly Germany and Holland. He was ac-

Figure 59. Sand dunes in a barn lot. Winds piled up large drifts of sand in this Kansas farm barn lot. (Farm Security Administration.)

customed to slow, light rains, and the homeland had produced largely grass and small grains. The cultivated crops were turnips, potatoes, and other vegetables. He was not prepared for the heavy, thundershower type of American summer rains. Nor was he accustomed to the production of large acreage of tobacco, corn, cotton, and other soil-exposing crops on all kinds of slopes. In the earlier days a tendency may have existed to think of heavy rains as unusual and the resulting erosion as unlikely to occur soon again, because ordinarily little erosion had taken place on the farms of the homeland.

RESULTS OF EROSION IN THIS COUNTRY

Erosion has been responsible in a measure for the abandonment of farm lands throughout the East. In New York, for example, abandonment has been at the rate of about 100,000 acres a year for several decades past. More recently, abandonment has been even more rapid. And because of erosion in the United States, more and more land is

Figure 60. Vegetation holding soil in the Muskingum Valley, Ohio. Vegetation has prevented erosion in this forested area. Note the complete cover of plants, together with fallen leaves and twigs. Cattle are not allowed to graze this woodlot. (U.S. Soil Conservation Service.)

destined for use other than agriculture. Much of it will return to forest. Because of the loss of the surface soil, the productivity of land has been lowered until now it does not pay to farm lands that produced a good living a few decades ago.

Results of erosion by water. Nearly a century ago United States Army engineers estimated that the Mississippi River annually dumped into the Gulf of Mexico soil material equal to a depth of 241 feet over one square mile. This quantity is equivalent to the surface soil six inches deep over 308,000 acres, or to the area of a good-sized county. In addition to the fine material carried, one-third as much coarser material was rolled and pushed along on the bottom of the river.

Much forest has been cleared and much prairie sod broken so that

Figure 61. Kudzu holding soil in Georgia. Kudzu, a trailing legume introduced from the Orient, has caused the filling of a gully in the foreground. (U.S. Soil Conservation Service.)

erosion is far greater now than in 1861 when the engineers made their studies. T. C. Chamberlin, late Professor of Geology of the University of Chicago, made a later and higher estimate, his being equivalent to the surface soil over approximately a million acres. If these figures fix in the mind of the reader the heavy losses of soil every year by erosion, they will have served their purpose. The actual loss of soil from fields is many times as great as that which is carried into the sea, for much valuable material is left in grass, brush, or forest on the lower part of slopes below cultivated fields and on the flood plains of small streams and rivers.

The finest soil particles are carried first from the fields by heavy rains. It is from the fine material that crops can most easily obtain nutrients for growth. Some of this material is so fine that, once in suspension, it is carried all the way to the sea. As the loss of fine soil continues from year to year, from decade to decade, or from century to century, only stones are left as a sort of stone pavement. This occurs on fields that were originally covered with loams that contained some stones. Such soil, having lost its fine material, is far less productive than it was before the loss occurred.

Losses from soil erosion. The acreage and the percentage of land in the United States (not including city areas) affected by different kinds of erosion are given in Table 6.

According to these figures nearly one-third of the total acreage of this country shows little or no erosion. This area includes the level-to-very-gently-undulating prairies of the Midwest, the various glacial-lake beds in the northern part of the United States, and other fairly level areas. Nearly one-third of the United States has lost from one-fourth to three-fourths of its surface soil as a result of sheet erosion. More than one-tenth of it has lost more than three-fourths of its surface soil and in places some of the subsoil.

Wind has damaged one-sixth of the country's land acreage, and 9,000,000 acres have been damaged severely. Gullying and sheet erosion have damaged some 4,000,000 acres to the extent of practical ruin. Figure 46 (p. 108) gives a general idea of the parts of the United States where erosion losses have been most severe, as well as where they have been slight or moderate.

In the Piedmont area, in Virginia and southward, fields often lost all the surface soil in thirty years, and farmers are cropping what was originally subsoil. In order to produce fair yields on these lands, more than twice as much fertilizer is required as before the surface soil was washed away. The loss of soil, therefore, has materially increased the cost of producing crops—or, in other words, has impoverished the man who is farming such land.

In many sloping areas the surface soil is being lost slowly, in others

TABLE 6. RESULTS OF WIND AND WATER EROSION IN THE UNITED STATES *
More than one-quarter of the land affected as indicated

Erosion condition	Acres affected	Percentage of area of the United States
Mountain lands, canyons, rock	144,768,315	7.6
Areas with little or no erosion	576,236,371	30.3
Total area affected by sheet erosion	855,260,347	44.9
One-fourth to three-fourths topsoil lost	663,199,473	34.8
More than three-fourths, topsoil, some subsoil lost	192,060,874	10.1
Total area affected by wind erosion	322,181,740	16.9
Moderate wind erosion (some gullying)	233,321,336	12.2
Severe wind erosion (some gullying)	79,659,052	4.2
Destroyed by wind erosion (some gullying)	9,201,352	0.5
Total area affected by gullying	864,818,281	45.4
Occasional gullies (with sheet erosion)	523,351,168	27.5
Severe gullying (with sheet erosion)	337,305,021	17.7
Destroyed by gullies (with sheet erosion)	4,162,092	0.2
Total area exclusive of large cities and water	1,903,176,620	100.0

* *Erosion Survey Data* (U.S. Department of Agriculture, Soil Conservation Service, 1943, revised 1935).

rapidly. Each heavy rain takes its toll from bare soil and from that growing soil-exposing crops on appreciable slopes. Three-fourths of the state of Missouri, for example, is said to be in danger of more or less serious loss of soil by erosion when cropped. Erosion has been especially critical on loess soils along the Mississippi and Missouri rivers. The writer spent his early years in this region of deep loess and has observed and mapped it for 500 miles along the Mississippi River. Once erosion begins on these soils, gullies grow rapidly. Much unproductive subsoil material is carried into the valleys, where it buries productive soils. Moreover, this eroded material often clogs stream channels and may create swampy conditions in some locations.

In some areas cultivated apple and peach orchards have been washed so badly as to leave the trees standing on dry ridges. The roots are exposed and the trees are unable to get the food and water they need. As a result they produce poor yields and eventually die.

People sometimes think of the northern Mississippi Valley states as the "boundless" *level* prairies. Yet much destructive erosion has taken place and is still going on in Illinois, Iowa, Indiana, Minnesota, Missouri, and Wisconsin (Fig. 53, p. 116).

Deposits of eroded material usually destructive. Small streams usually have rather steep channels in the hills; upon passing onto the valley land, the channel suddenly becomes almost level. The largest stones transported are dropped there because the stream can no longer move them, and the smaller material is deposited farther on. The coarse material is of little agricultural value. In fact, worthless stones have buried a large acreage of productive land in this way.

Thousands of acres of productive vegetable soils occupy this sort of valley position. Over these soils, streams from the uplands hold a constant threat, both from the standpoint of overflowing them and of burying them under coarse, unproductive, stony material. In Figure 55, p. 118 is shown material that covered productive soil.

Deposits sometimes valuable. In 1905 and 1906 the writer mapped soils in Illinois counties along the Mississippi River. In one area a farmer had changed the course of a stream and, by means of low levees, caught the wash and thus covered an area of heavy clay land with good loessial soil. Since the loess had already been weathered, the wash at once became a productive soil.

Farther south in Illinois a lake had been receiving similar wash since the forest was cleared from the upland loess. Several hundred acres of productive land had been formed in this lake where the Indian had fished scarcely a century before. Ordinarily, however, beneficial results are rare from the washing of soil from the uplands into the valleys.

Results of wind erosion. As already indicated, wind erosion has caused untold damage to the soils of the Great Plains and other dry areas. Parts of the Dakotas, California, Utah, Oregon, Nevada, Minnesota, and Wisconsin are subject to considerable damage from wind action during dry, windy periods (Figs. 57–59, pp. 120–122). Sandy ocean and lake shores and sandy outwash plains suffer much from wind action.

During moderately dry periods in winter exposed heavy soils become granular and, like sand, are subject to wind action. The granules drift onto roads and into ditches and sometimes are blown onto crops. All in all, such blowing of heavy soil causes considerable damage.

In some areas of sandy soils during dry days in late spring, the wind picks up and hurls sharp sand grains against rapidly growing plants whose tender stems are easily injured killing the plants. This makes reseeding necessary in order to produce a crop. A second planting is costly and the crop, being late, may fail to mature, or the yield may be

Figure 62. Wind damage on muck land in New York. The onions along the fence were blown out by wind from the right. A new crop has been planted in place of the onions. In strong winds as in 1945, windbreaks afford far less protection than they do in moderate ones. (A. F. Gustafson.)

considerably reduced. In either case the farmer suffers considerable loss.

Cleared muck or peat is usually planted to vegetables or other high-yielding crops (Fig. 62). During dry periods in late spring strong winds pick up sharp, light bits of wood or granules of muck and drive them against the plants. The tender plants are seriously injured or killed. Onions grown from seed are particularly sensitive to such injury. In addition, the soil is sometimes blown away from the roots of crops, and this causes further injury.

Results of wave erosion. Waves on ocean, lake, and river shores carry away valuable land. Most serious financial loss occurs when recreational, municipal, or transportation facilities are destroyed. The clogging of canals or harbors by sand carried by shore currents necessitates large expenditures for dredging operations. In other places farm land is being worn away by the waves. It has been estimated that 64,000 acres of land have been worn away by wave action during the past 1,900 years and that New Jersey alone lost 2,200 acres between 1840 and 1920. But even if all this acreage were farm land, the loss would be insignificant in comparison with the losses brought about by either wind or water erosion on cropped lands.

SEDIMENTATION OF RESERVOIRS

Society suffers great loss from the filling of reservoirs with sand, silt, and stones. Because of the importance of the silting of reservoirs, this topic is treated here instead of in its logical position under the effects of soil erosion.

Man-made reservoirs are the result of building dams of various kinds. Reservoirs are used for six principal purposes: (1) for storing water for domestic and industrial use, (2) for the irrigation of land, (3) for the production of electric power, (4) for the regulation of stream flow for the benefit of navigation, (5) for the protection of fish and other water life, and (6) for detaining water for the purpose of lowering the extreme height of floods.

General considerations. If a dam is built across a stream in a forest, or one that is flowing from a heavily timbered area, it may serve from the beginning mainly as a diversion dam. This is because such woodland streams have a relatively even flow throughout the year and reservoir capacity is not of first importance.

On the other hand, consider a reservoir whose purpose is to furnish water over long periods of low rainfall for cities, manufacturing, or irrigation. Every cubic foot of silt deposited reduces the capacity of the reservoir to that extent. It will, therefore, have less value for the purposes it was intended to serve. In irrigated areas silted reservoirs may fail to water crops during periods of great need, and crop failure is the result. Silting, therefore, in storage reservoirs in time destroys their value.

The destruction of a dam built at great expense is nothing compared with the destruction of the site for the use of future generations. In some situations, to be sure, a number of small reservoirs may be constructed in tributaries of the main valley. Although costly, these tributary reservoirs may serve to feed the original reservoir to some extent and thus make some use of the original site in perpetuity.

Streams run clear or free of sediment from natural woodland areas, as they do from undisturbed virgin-grass areas. These two facts explain the slow rate of silting of reservoirs in such areas in the early days. As already pointed out, clearing the forest, plowing the prairie sod, and then growing clean-cultivated crops on sloping lands have brought about soil erosion. The severity of the erosion and the rapidity of consequent silting of reservoirs have varied with the degree of protection that man has given the land.

Agriculture and reservoirs. Over the years more than twenty dams have been built in the immediate vicinity of Ithaca, New York. Four of them have been washed away and twelve filled with silt, sand, and stones. Only four of them are still in use. Two divert water to electric generators, and one diverts it to a filter plant. The fourth was built in 1910 to form the reservoir for Ithaca's water supply. By 1935, or during the first twenty-five years, 23 per cent of the water capacity of this reservoir had been filled with eroded material. At this rate the total life of the reservoir can be only about 110 years. Moreover, after the reservoir is filled to the extent of 60 or 70 per cent, it will no longer hold sufficient water for the city during long periods of low rainfall. Then another site must be found and a new dam built because it is usually too costly to remove silt from a reservoir. To take out and haul away the silt washed into the Ithaca reservoir up to 1935 would then, it was estimated, have cost more than $100,000, or at the rate of about $4,000 a year for the twenty-five years. It is less expensive to build another dam if a site is available.

In the early days of settlement the forest was cleared from the land surrounding Ithaca. The land was plowed and seeded to grain and cultivated crops. Much of the land has considerable slope, but the danger of erosion was not recognized until after some years of cropping a part of the land to corn, potatoes, and buckwheat. None of these crops protect the soil, and, as a consequence, valuable soil from the fields found its way directly into the streams and filled the reservoirs.

A treble loss is the result. Valuable soil washed from fields that may be needed some day for growing crops to feed the growing human family. This possibility appears remote at the present time, since in this country governmental agencies are now taking land out of production and reducing the acreage of crops by various means. At the same time, however, several European nations have lately spent large sums to bring a few additional acres into production.

A second loss was suffered by those who built these dams. Whereas the life of reservoirs should be several hundred years, many were filled completely in from fifty to seventy-five years or even less.

A third loss is to society. When a reservoir has been filled with silt, its site has been destroyed for future use. Its value is gone. With all our mechanical skill and inventive genius we do not have means for

Figure 63. Reservoir at Schoolfield, Virginia, filled. This reservoir has been drained temporarily. Note the silt and the island in the reservoir. (U.S. Soil Conservation Service.)

clearing these reservoirs of deposited silt at anything approaching a feasible cost (Fig. 63).

Consider the effect on irrigation projects of the filling of reservoirs that supply water for the land. In some places other sites may be found and new dams built at great expense. Seldom, however, are many dam sites found in any one drainage area. When new ones cannot be located, the land once irrigated must be abandoned. The farmers and their families must move away because the agriculture of the area, their source of livelihood, has been destroyed.

In other places the silting of reservoirs reduces the amount of power available to a point where a factory or mill must seek additional power. This may increase costs of production to such an extent that the manufacturing plant must move to a more favorable location. Such a move results in great loss in the value of workers' homes, and many workers, being unable to follow the factory, are left stranded in the familiar "ghost" village. These are sad but familiar sights in areas where water power has failed or where a coal, copper, gold, or other mine has been worked out or abandoned.

Forests and reservoirs. Dams in the Adirondack and other mountain areas are still serving their purposes. Some of them are 100 to 150 years old or even more. This is a different situation from that already described in central New York. The difference is that the watersheds of the Adirondack reservoirs were and still are in forest, and those near Ithaca were in cultivated crops during the life of the reservoirs. The movement of silt in forests is very slow. In fact, it has been estimated that reservoirs under natural forest conditions may be filled at the rate of only about one foot of silt in 300 years. This is in marked contrast to the rapid silting of reservoirs in regions having even a moderate proportion of cultivated crops in their drainage areas.

Rate of sedimentation of reservoirs. Data about reservoirs in various parts of the United States under different soil, rainfall, and cropping conditions are given in Table 7.

Wide variation may be noted in the indicated life of these reservoirs. As improvement is made in control measures, the life of reservoirs will be increased accordingly. On the basis of these figures a reservoir life of more than 250 years may be regarded as fairly substantial. Surely, however, a reservoir life of less than 100 years is costly to society. The effective life of reservoirs is much shorter than the figures in the final column of Table 7 indicate. This is because a storage reservoir, the capacity of which has been reduced one-half or three-fourths by silt, may no longer be adequate for its purpose.

It is notable that with one exception the Texas reservoirs are silting very rapidly; two of them will be completely filled in fourteen years.

A study has been made of the rate of sedimentation in 27 small reservoirs in Maryland, Pennsylvania, and Virginia.[2] Silting rates were highly variable; one reservoir in Pennsylvania and one in Virginia have an indicated life of 1,000 years; one in Pennsylvania has only 17

---

[2] L. C. Gottschalk, *Report on Loch Raven and Prettyboy Reservoirs* (Soil Conservation Service, Sedimentation Section, Sp. Report 5, Baltimore, Md., 1943).

TABLE 7. LOCATION AND RATE OF SEDIMENTATION OF RESERVOIRS *

Reservoir	Location	Period	Average percentage of original water capacity filled with silt a year	Years needed to fill reservoir completely at this rate of silting†
White Rock	Dallas, Tex.	1923–28	0.69	145
		1910–35	0.86	115
Elephant Butte	Hot Springs, N.M.	1915–35	0.68	147
Roosevelt	Roosevelt, Ariz.	1911–25	0.41	244
Lake Michie	Durham, N.C.	1926–30	0.24	417
		1926–35	0.36	277
Lake Worth	Fort Worth, Tex.	1915–28	2.26	44
Lake McMillan	Carlsbad, N.M.	1894–1915	2.14	47
		1915–25	0.38	263
Zuñi	Black Rock, N.M.	1925–32	0.31	323
		1906–17	3.03	33
		1917–27	3.83	26
Sweetwater	Sunnyside, Calif.	1916–27	0.56	178
Lake Chabot	Oakland, Calif.	1875–1923	0.43	232
Gibraltar	Santa Barbara, Calif.	1920–31	1.06	94
		1931–34	4.82	21
		1934–36	2.06	49
University Lake	Chapel Hill, N.C.	1932–35	1.14	88
Greensboro	Greensboro, N.C.	1923–34	0.79	126
High Point	High Point, N.C.	1927–34	0.84	120
Lake Concord	Concord, N.C.	1925–35	0.65	154
Spartanburg	Spartanburg, S.C.	1926–34	2.10	46
Lloyd Shoals	Jackson, Ga.	1910–35	0.51	196
Rogers	Rogers, Tex.	1922–34	1.91	52
Lake Waco	Waco, Tex.	1930–35	2.48	40
Guthrie	Guthrie, Okla.	1920–35	1.03	97
Boomer Lake	Stillwater, Okla.	1925–35	0.59	169

* Henry M. Eakin, *Silting of Reservoirs* (U.S. Department of Agriculture, Technical Bull. 524; Washington, 1939), pp. 9, 25, 120–123.

† Calculations in final column made by the writer to show comparisons more strikingly.

TABLE 7. LOCATION AND RATE OF SEDIMENTATION OF RESERVOIRS (*Cont.*)

Reservoir	Location	Period	Average percentage of original water capacity filled with silt a year	Years needed to fill reservoir completely at this rate of silting†
San Carlos	Coolidge Dam, Ariz.	1928–35	0.47	213
Coon Rapids Pond	Anoka, Minn.	1899–1931	1.08	93
Lake Austin (new)	Austin, Tex.	1913–26	7.35	14
Lake Austin (old)	Austin, Tex.	1893–1900	7.10	14
Lake Pemick	Lueders, Tex.	1920–27	4.47	22
La Grange	La Grange, Calif.	1895–1931	2.31	43
Sterling Pond	Sterling, Ill.	1912–30	0.82	122
Boysen	Fremont Co., Wyo.	1911–24	6.25	16
Keokuk	Keokuk, Ia.	1911–28	2.02	50
Lower Salt Creek	Natrona Co., Wyo.	1924–33	10.79	9
Furnish	Pendleton, Ore.	1909–31	3.73	27
Hales Bar	Guild, Tenn.	1913–30	1.72	58
Cheoah	Fairfax, N.C.	1918–30	0.88	114
Parksville	Parksville, Tenn.	1912–30	1.14	87
Buckhorn	Loveland, Colo.	1907–25	2.64	38
Schoolfield	Danville, Va.	1904–15	7.32	14

years. Seventeen have a life of 300 years or more, the others from 33 to 300 years. Most of these reservoirs may be regarded as having fairly good prospects for a goodly period of usefulness.

CHAPTER V

Soil Conservation

IN 1910, Charles R. Van Hise, late President of the University of Wisconsin, wrote: "The conservation of the soil is the greatest of all the problems of conservation; because upon its products we depend for food and clothing, the basal necessities of man." [1] There is great need for a fuller realization of the truth of this statement. The pages that follow deal with the problem of conserving and maintaining the productivity of our soils.

THE RETURN OF PLANT NUTRIENTS TO THE SOIL

As shown in Chapter IV, all crops remove plant nutrients from the soil. Some plants take up relatively large amounts of certain nutrients when compared with the quantity of them naturally present in the soil. This is true with respect to nitrogen and phosphorus in most mineral soils. Potassium, on the other hand, is present in grain in quantities that are relatively small in comparison with the supply in many mineral soils. Organic soils, such as peat and muck, contain much nitrogen, a moderate supply of phosphorus, and potassium only in very small quantities.

Because crops are often unable to obtain from the soil as much nitrogen, phosphorus, and potassium as they need for thrifty growth and large yields, these materials have been added in commercial form, called *fertilizers*. Since fertilizers supply mainly these three materials, nitrogen, phosphorus, and potassium, they are referred to as the *fertilizer elements*. The industry, however, uses the term *phosphoric acid* instead of *phosphorus,* and *potash* instead of *potassium.*

The return of organic matter. Many fertilizers contain small quantities of organic matter, but in the main organic matter for returning to the soil must be grown on the land. The beneficial effects of plant materials on the soil were discussed in Chapter IV. The principal

---

[1] *The Conservation of Natural Resources in the United States* (New York, 1910), p. 361.

sources of organic matter that may be economically returned to the soil are farm manure, crop residues, and green manures.

Farm manure. Farm manure is a valuable by-product of livestock farming. Animals, however, retain some nutrients from the feed eaten for growth, and for such purposes as egg, wool, or milk production.

Manure contains organic matter, nitrogen, phosphorus, potash, sulfur, calcium, and small amounts of other plant-nutrient elements. Manure is a particularly unstable or perishable material. A single ton of manure does not contain large quantities of plant nutrients, but the total quantity of manure produced every year contains enormous amounts of them. Their conservation is, therefore, of real importance in the maintenance of the nitrogen and organic-matter content and the productivity of soils. Early return of manure to the soil and protection of it from weathering during storage aid in conserving the nutrients.

Crop residues. Under the term *crop residues* are grouped such materials as stalks of cotton, corn, sorghum, and broomcorn, stubble and straw of wheat, oats, and rye, and the trimmings and leftovers of vegetables. It is not long since corn and broomcorn stalks and small grain straw and stubble were burned regularly, and some farmers still burn them. Some years ago a sky lighted at night by cornstalk fires was a common April sight in the Midwest (Fig. 64). In the Northwest straw was burned as soon as the threshing machine had been moved a safe distance from the straw. Severe blowing of soil is partly the result of this wholesale destruction of organic matter. Moreover, the burning of straw in the Dakotas has lowered wheat yields by liberating the nitrogen in the straw. The crop, deprived of this nitrogen, makes poorer and poorer growth, and affords less and less protection to the soil from both wind and water as the decades pass. Crops, even on the rich corn-belt soils of Illinois, are producing lower yields than formerly, in part because of the loss of organic matter.

The Illinois Agricultural Experiment Station operates a number of outlying fields in various sections of the state. After crop residues had been turned under for five years on an experiment field near Bloomington, wheat produced 4.4 bushels and corn 7 bushels to the acre more on it than on land from which the residues had been removed. In the southern part of the state the return of residues to gray prairie soils, low in active organic matter, markedly increased crop yields.

Except where crop diseases or insect pests are a serious problem, crop residues should not be burned but should be turned under, both for their direct benefit to crops and for their aid in holding the soil against washing and blowing.

Green manures. Some crops are grown to be plowed under in the green state and are referred to as *green manures* or *green-manure crops.* Usually green-manure crops are grown before, after, or between the regular crops of the season. Areas such as the South and Southeast

Figure 64. Burning cornstalks in Illinois. This was a common practice thirty years ago, and such residues as stalks and straw are all too frequently burned today. (Illinois Agricultural Experiment Station.)

that have a long growing season are much favored with respect to the growing of these soil-improving crops in addition to the regular ones. Rye, winter vetch, wheat, and many grasses may be seeded in the early fall after cotton, corn (Fig. 65), or other intertilled or cultivated crops have been harvested. These green-manure crops grow throughout the fall and during mild weather in winter and in early spring. Not only do these crops add fresh organic matter to the soil upon being turned under, but they take up and hold plant nutrients that would otherwise be lost from the soil in the drainage during the nongrowing season.

In vegetable production in an area having a short growing season, early vegetables may be followed by green-manure crops. In the same way late vegetables may follow the turning under of green-manure crops. Midseason vegetables may be followed by a winter green-manure crop such as rye to be turned under the following spring.

Organic matter from any of these sources aids in producing good tilth, which is beneficial to crops. The organic matter itself and the

Figure 65. Rye in cornfield. Seeding rye with soil-exposing crops for the purpose of controlling erosion is a good practice. Four and a quarter inches of rain in two hours caused very little erosion in this field. Protection of the soil by the rye during winter and spring is important. Moreover, the rye produces considerable pasturage. (U.S. Soil Conservation Service.)

improved tilth it produces aid in the absorption of water, so that less of it is lost by runoff. Morever, the plant nutrients held in the organic matter enable crops to produce larger yields and in turn to protect the soil better against erosion.

The addition of nitrogen. Often the natural supply of nitrogen is not great, and crops draw heavily on the soil for this element. Additions of nitrogen, therefore, must be made regularly in order that lack of it may not reduce crop yields. Nitrogen may be added to soil in a number of ways.

Nitrogen-gathering plants. The family of plants called *legumes* includes such well-known crops as garden peas and beans, clovers and alfalfa, cowpeas, soybeans, crotalaria, peanuts, lespedeza; such shrubs as *Amorpha fruticosa,* rose acacia (*Robinia hispida*), and Scotch broom (*Cytisus scoparius*); and such trees as the black or common locust (*Robinia Pseudo-Acacia*) and others (Fig. 66). Under favorable conditions, with the right legume organism present, this group of plants produces irregular-shaped, soft, whitish bodies called *nodules* on its roots. Tiny plants called *bacilli* live and work within the nodules. The legume, called the *host* plant, supplies the organisms with certain

Figure 66. Effect of clover on growth of grain. The grain on the left followed a crop of clover and that on the right followed timothy. The yield after clover was more than double that after timothy. (A. F. Gustafson.)

food materials. The organisms take nitrogen from the air and furnish it to the host plant. This association is referred to as a *symbiotic* relationship. The legume helps to feed the organisms, and they, in return, supply the legume with nitrogen that it could not otherwise obtain. Few people realize how largely dependent man, the lower animals, and even other plants are on legumes.

Man is making wide use of these valuable plants. Clover and timothy are seeded together in order to make full use of the legume. White clover and grasses are grown together for pasturage. Alfalfa and grass grown together produce excellent yields of hay. Crotalaria in Florida and adjacent states and cowpeas, soybeans, vetch, and other legumes are grown over a wide area to be turned under as green manure. Other than crotalaria, these legumes may be fed to livestock and some of the nitrogen in the feed returned to the soil in animal manures. Nitrogen thus added to the soil aids nonlegumes in their growth (Fig. 67).

Other organisms fix nitrogen in the soil under favorable conditions, and in addition small quantities of nitrogen are brought to the soil in rain water.

Chemical fixation of nitrogen. During recent years chemists have de-

Figure 67. Plowing under a green-manure crop. Here is shown a field of thirty-two acres of soybeans that is being plowed, September 16, for the following season's corn crop. Although this is rather early for fall plowing in Illinois, the turning under of soybeans and weeds is good farm practice. (U.S. Soil Conservation Service.)

veloped a number of ways of combining nitrogen with other elements. Once combined, this nitrogen may be converted into a large number of products, many of which are used in fertilizers.

Nitrogen from other sources. Among other sources of nitrogen are the *caliche* beds in Chile on the west coast of South America. From these beds nitrogen is refined as nitrate of soda and shipped to all parts of the world. Other important sources of commercial nitrogen are the coke ovens of the steel industry and city gas works. This nitrogen occurs in commerce as sulfate of ammonia.

The pulp left after the removal of the oil from cotton seed, linseed or flaxseed, and soybeans is used for livestock feed and in fertilizers mainly because of the nitrogen it contains. Since castor meal, from which castor oil has been removed, is unfit for feed, it is used in fertilizers. Various wastes from the processing of tobacco, meat, and fish carry some nitrogen and serve a useful purpose as an ingredient of fertilizers. Many other wastes and by-products carry some useful nitrogen and other plant nutrients.

The use of lime to correct soil acidity. Soils formed from acid shales and sandstones often are acid or sour. Other soils were formed from mixtures of the acid rocks and limestones. Such soils may still contain various proportions of limestone, which is sometimes referred to as basic material. In nature the basic material leaches out of soils in the drainage. For this reason many soils that contained limestone as part of their original material have become acid.

Strongly acid soils do not support satisfactory growth of such legumes as red clover, alfalfa, sweet clover, and garden peas. A feasible way of correcting the condition ordinarily called *soil acidity* is by the use of lime or finely ground limestone, blast-furnace slag, and certain other by-products. Because ground limestone is often the least expensive liming material, it is widely used. In addition to correcting unfavorable soil conditions, liming materials supply calcium and magnesium, which in some soils are needed as nutrients (Fig. 68).

The addition of potassium. Potassium is present in many soils in relatively large quantities, but often it is not readily available to crops. The problem, therefore, is either to render potassium available to plants by additions of organic matter or to add potash directly (Fig. 69.) Potassium is found in wastes, salt lakes, and underground beds.

Industrial wastes. Various industrial wastes contain much valuable potash. Low grades of molasses remain from the manufacture of sugar. Some molasses is fed to livestock and thus its potassium may be returned to the soil. Much molasses of low grade is used in the production of industrial alcohol, and the residues, which are rich in potassium, are used in fertilizers. Cement-kiln fumes and flue dusts are other possible sources from which much potassium may be recovered. Tobacco stems and wastes and wood ashes also contain potassium of value.

Saline lakes. Potassium was recovered from the saline or salt lakes of Nebraska during World War I. Production of potassium from Searles Lake in California was begun at that time and has been continued.

This lake now supplies large quantities of high-grade potash and other valuable products. Potash is also being recovered near Great Salt Lake in Utah.

Underground deposits. Studies begun in 1905 resulted twenty years later in the discovery of underground deposits of high-quality potash-bearing salts in Texas and New Mexico. Three corporations are now actively mining potash near Carlsbad, New Mexico. These domestic

Figure 68. Lime spreader in action. Lime is being applied for the benefit of clover or other crops. (Deere and Co.)

sources supply the potash needed for the soils of the United States at the present time. Before 1940, however, this country imported approximately half of the potash used in fertilizers (Figs. 249, 252, pp. 502, 506).

The addition of phosphorus. Phosphorus, because of the general need for it in soils, is the most important fertilizer element. In fact, phosphorus is often referred to as the *limiting* element in crop production because it is frequently lacking or unavailable and, therefore, limits yields. The low phosphorus content of many soils and the rapidity with which phosphorus is being lost from the normal cropped soil have been mentioned in Chapter IV.

The importance of the phosphorus problem is evident when it is considered what a tremendous amount of experimental work has been done on fertilization with phosphorus in this country. The long-time work in Illinois is representative. There plots that had been cropped continuously for nearly thirty years were divided so that one-half of

Figure 69. Potassium deficiency for cotton. The cotton at the left was fertilized with insufficient potash. That at the right was more adequately supplied with it. (American Potash Institute, Inc.)

each plot was cropped without treatment as before. The other half of each plot was treated with moderate amounts of farm manure, limestone, and phosphorus. In thirty-four years this treatment nearly doubled the yield of the continuous corn plot and also that of the plot on which corn and oats were alternated. Likewise, this treatment increased the yield of corn by one-half of the plot on which corn, oats, and clover were rotated. The phosphorus used played an important role in the restoration of the productivity of this prairie soil (Figs. 70–72).

Ways of maintaining the active phosphorus content of soils have been developed and must be put into general practice very soon. Unless phosphorus is returned to the soil, the latter cannot be expected to feed and clothe our present population over a period of centuries. *Phosphate deposits.* Phosphate deposits in Florida and Tennessee are being worked intensively. The reserves in Florida are sufficient for many years at current rates of use. Large deposits of phosphate rock are located also in Idaho, Utah, Wyoming, and Montana. The United

Figure 70. Fertilizer factory, Eastern States Farmers' Exchange. In this factory fertilizer materials are mixed for use as complete fertilizers on vegetables, grains, and other crops. (Eastern States Farmers' Exchange.)

States is fortunate indeed to have such large reserves of high-grade phosphate rock.

Up to 1910 the federal government had withdrawn from entry more than 2,500,000 acres of known phosphate land. Detailed data on phosphate reserves in the United States are given in Chapter XVIII. When needed, these federally owned phosphate lands may be worked under lease or royalty by private citizens. Government control, however, must be retained. Government agencies subject to political control, however, do not suffice. What is needed is an intelligent, independent conservation commission of good size, having real authority, whose members are appointed for long terms. Moreover, it has been seriously urged that the exportation of high-grade phosphate rock from the eastern, privately owned deposits be definitely prohibited. A number of foreign countries fortunately have large supplies of their own.

Recent improvements in manufacturing processes have led to the making of superphosphate of three or four times the usual strength. This development is equivalent to a large reduction in the cost of transportation and has made possible the use of western phosphorus

Figure 71. Old fertilizer plots, Illinois. At the far end is a plot that has grown seventy-three consecutive corn crops. In the middle, corn and oats have been alternated, and in the immediate foreground a rotation of corn, oats, and clover has been followed. Note that the nearer part of each plot has larger corn than does the far side. This difference was brought about by the application of phosphorus, limestone, and manure on the nearer half; the far half of each plot has received no treatment for more than seventy-five years. (Illinois Agricultural Experiment Station.)

over a wider area. Furthermore, these methods may be modified so as to employ in the future the lower grades of phosphate rock in the East.

Animal bones. Animal bones were the earliest commercial carrier of phosphorus for use on the soil. Buffalo bones were collected in the early days and bones are now being saved in the packing houses and rendering plants. These are returned to the land in the form of bone meal. The need for conserving the phosphorus in bones is apparent when it is realized that the bones of a beef animal contain twenty, and an average hog two and a half, pounds of phosphorus and that other animals contain phosphorus in similar proportions. By the return of animal bones to the soil phosphorus may be used over and over many times.

The need for co-operation. Co-operation on a wide basis is needed to solve so large a problem as keeping up the phosphorus content of the soil. The farmer, the city dweller, the phosphate producer, and the

Figure 72. Crop response to soil treatment. The treatments indicated were given to this representative soil on which red clover was seeded. It is notable that in the second acid pot, phosphorus and potash produced almost no increased growth of clover. Limestone in addition (Pot 3), however, enabled the clover to make good growth. Phosphorus and limestone (Pot 4) made nearly as good growth without as with potash. Without the addition of phosphorus, however, limestone and potash (Pot 5) did not greatly increase the yield over no treatment. This is representative of crop response to phosphorus on many soils. (A. F. Gustafson.)

government, both state and national, can well work together. The problem requires the best efforts of all. The farmer can do much to reduce losses from manures. Present information is to the effect that seldom is more than one-half of the phosphorus in feed returned to the land. By reducing these preventable losses the farmer can use phosphorus over and over. In this way phosphorus can be kept working for man throughout the ages.

City people can work out new means of sewage disposal that will be less wasteful of the plant nutrients in sewage than the present methods are. Material now being discarded by phosphorus producers as too poor for use should be separated from wholly useless materials because such rock may conceivably be needed in future years. When workings are abandoned, they should, insofar as possible, be left in such a condition that they can be reopened if needed (Figs. 253, 254, pp. 508, 509).

The addition of minor elements. Some of the essential plant nutrient elements, as already indicated, are used by plants only in minute quantities. These minor elements include boron, copper, zinc, and manganese. Wherever these are lacking, they may easily be added in fertilizers. The return of residues and farm manures often supplies enough of some minor elements. A deficiency of boron for vegetables, alfalfa, fruits, and other crops is often encountered.

Crop rotation. Many advantages are derived from growing crops in regular sequence or rotation. The control of crop diseases, insects, and weeds is more difficult in single cropping systems than in rotations. The residues from one crop are especially beneficial to another. These benefits of growing crops in rotation are obtained in addition to those from liming and fertilization.

Remedies for farm-tenancy problems. Farm-tenancy problems exist in many sections of this country. In some areas, and particularly with the poorer tenants or renters, land often is leased on a year-to-year basis. In other words, the tenant does not know until late in the crop year or perhaps after the season is over whether he may stay on the farm another year. Under these conditions the tenant must do all he can to produce the largest total yield of crops for the year with the least possible outlay for soil treatment. He does not feel justified in making any expenditures except as they may increase returns for him during that particular season. Moreover, a one-year tenant has little interest in the land and, therefore, may do little work and make no outlay to control soil erosion. Such a tenant cannot make the necessary expenditures for lime, fertilizers, and seed of the desired legumes because of the uncertainties involved. Productivity is not maintained and erosion is almost certain to occur on sloping lands of tenant farms. Society as well as the landowner sustains a permanent, yet unnecessary, loss from these conditions.

Some provisions for the conservation of the soil can be made in state laws and others can be arranged by agreement between landowners and tenants. Among the remedies are relatively long-term written leases. A tenant who is a good farmer deserves such a lease. It may run for a definite term of from three to five years or longer, or it may be made automatically renewable over a term of years by mutual agreement between the owner and the tenant. Notice of termination of such leases should be given by either party one year, or at least six months, prior to actual termination of the lease. Under many conditions a period of only four months, as provided in the Iowa law, is rather too short for the best interests of both parties. When competition between tenants is keen, a livestock farmer may need plenty of time to find a new farm of the right size, or he will need time to adjust the number of his livestock to the size of the new farm. If competition for good tenants is keen, landlords may need more than four months in which to find the right man.

In the Midwest moving time on farms is March first and four months' notice means that November first is the date on which a tenant may be certain concerning his operations for the ensuing year. Obviously a period longer than four months is often desirable both for the owner and the tenant. In most cases, no doubt, the decision to terminate the lease is announced at an earlier date, with benefit to both parties.

For the good of the land, state laws are needed to provide for reimbursement of retiring tenants for improvements they have made on a farm. Improvements such as the enlargement of buildings, or the erection of new ones, and the putting up of fences are normally provided for by written agreements. Legal provision is needed everywhere for the reimbursement of tenants for the unexhausted part of soil treatment with such materials as lime, fertilizer, and manure.[2] Improvements that are of continuing benefit to a farm, such as draining land, building farm ponds, and making outlays for the control of erosion, are in the same category as fertilizers.

Wherever state laws do not take into consideration payments to tenants for unexhausted soil treatments and improvements of lasting benefit, the owner and tenant should make mutually satisfactory arrangements. Under such laws or arrangements, any good farmer will follow practices that will both give him adequate returns and conserve the soil. Laws providing for such reimbursement of tenants have been

---

[2] Under certain conditions, such as when the tenant brings purchased or other feed onto the farm, reimbursement for the unused or residual part of manures resulting from this feed and subsequently applied, as well as payment for manures accumulating later, should be legally required.

in effect for many years in Great Britain, and they have resulted in distinct benefits to the land.

Remedies for soil depletion. The remedies for soil depletion or loss in productivity are as follows: (1) Build up and maintain the organic matter content at a good level. The proper organic matter level varies, however, with the soil, climate, and cropping conditions. (2) Maintain the nitrogen supply by growing legumes, by returning crop residues and farm and green manures, and by applying nitrogen in fertilizers when needed. (3) Apply potassium to soils wherever crops will pay for it. (4) Make frequent, liberal applications of phosphorus. (5) Put on lime as needed to grow the desired leguminous and other crops. (6) Apply the minor elements wherever these are needed. (7) Practice systematic crop rotation. (8) Keep the land protected by a crop to reduce losses of nutrients by leaching.

CONTROL OF SOIL EROSION

Controlling erosion is of utmost importance on upwards of one-half of the cultivated soils of the United States. In fact, another century of uncontrolled soil erosion might reduce the acreage of productive soil to a point where the land could not feed well our present population. Even casual observation of the more seriously eroded sections reveals the damage that has already been done. Once erosion is well under way, it tends to become worse with increasing rapidity.

If the surface soil washes away, it is gone forever. Although phosphorus and potash may be restored to soils, there is no feasible way of collecting and returning soil to the field from which it came. It is imperative in the interest of the nation as a whole, therefore, that soil erosion be brought under control as completely and as early as possible.

A recent development is provision for soil conservation districts. These districts are legal, administrative units that are established under state laws. In some states the districts are identical with counties. This arrangement has the advantage of functioning within established boundaries, as do the farm bureau and the county agricultural agent in most cases. In some states, however, a watershed constitutes a soil conservation district.

Districts are established by vote of the landowners of the area, and land utilization is regulated by the residents of the district. Through this organization technical assistance and the necessary machinery for building the various mechanical erosion-control structures can be provided. In some states the district is permitted to rent heavy machinery from the state and county highway authorities as an economy measure. Other districts purchase the machinery needed.

The organization of soil conservation districts appears to be a distinct forward step in furthering the widespread adoption of recognized methods of soil-erosion control and of rational, long-term soil utilization. The organization and functioning of the district produces co-operation between the private landowner and the public treasury. Within reasonable limits, this relationship has a sound basis because the public has a deep interest in the conservation of the soil. Soil conservation constitutes defense against a future lack of food and clothing and, in a measure, of fuel and shelter for the people.

Research in soil-erosion control. The Illinois Agricultural Experiment Station began field work on the control of soil erosion in 1907 under the direction of the late Professor J. G. Mosier. The writer supervised much of this experimental work. The results of the first ten years were published in *Washing of Soils and Methods of Prevention* (Illinois Agricultural Experiment Station, Bulletin 207) in 1918.

Pioneer measurements of losses of soil and water from sloping lands were started by F. L. Duley and M. F. Miller at the Missouri Agricultural Experiment Station in 1917. The data for the first six years were reported in 1923 by Duley and Miller in *Erosion and Surface Runoff under Different Soil Conditions* (Research Bulletin 63). These data and those for eight additional years were published in 1932 in *The Influence of Systems of Cropping and Methods of Culture on Runoff and Erosion* (Research Bulletin 177), by Miller and H. F. Krusekopf.

On the basis of these average yearly losses, erosion would carry away the surface seven inches of soil from a fallow field in 25 years, from continuous corn in 50 years, from continuous wheat in 100 years, from a rotation of corn, wheat, and clover in 370 years, and from blue grass in 3,000 years.

In order to determine the losses of soil and water that take place under a wide range of soil and cropping conditions the United States Department of Agriculture established a number of experiment stations in 1931. One of them is located at Clarinda, Iowa, on good productive soil that the nation cannot afford to lose by erosion. The land in this experiment has a slope of 9 per cent (that is, it drops 9 feet in each 100 feet of horizontal distance). According to the progress report by G. W. Musgrave and R. A. Norton (*Soil and Water Investigations,* U.S. Department of Agriculture, Technical Bulletin 558, 1937) the land in corn year after year lost nearly 25 tons of soil an acre annually. A rotation of corn the first year, oats the second, and clover the third suffered an average annual loss of 6 tons of soil an acre. Under similar conditions, land under alfalfa lost 0.3 ton of soil a year. In blue grass (*Poa pratensis*), land like that in alfalfa lost almost no soil.

Figure 73. Measurement of losses of soil and water, U.S. Soil-Erosion Control Experiment Station near Marcellus, New York. The water and soil are first caught in the long boxlike tank at the right. By means of an accurate divisor, a definite fraction of the water with soil in suspension is conducted into the large round tank after the boxlike one is full of water. In like manner, a definite fraction is caught in the smaller round tank after the larger one has been filled. The water and soil are measured to determine the extent of loss of soil and water from the experimental area. A similar setup is used on each plot from which losses are measured. (A. F. Gustafson.)

Figure 73 shows the type of equipment used for measuring losses of soil and water. At the rate of erosion on the continuous corn land, the surface seven inches of soil would be lost entirely in about 40 years. From the land in a three-year rotation, 160 years would be required for the complete removal of the top seven inches. From the land in alfalfa and blue grass the loss is so slight that 3,000 years would be taken for washing away the surface seven inches of soil. Although these figures are preliminary, they are valuable. These results are strikingly similar to and thus tend to confirm those reported by the Missouri investigators.

A mass of valuable data on losses of soil and water have been accumulated and additional measurements are being made at erosion-control experimental stations. These results, together with those from state experimental stations, and the experiences of farmers point the way to practical means of controlling soil erosion.

Productivity and protection of the soil. Plants on a productive soil grow large root systems whose rootlets occupy the soil completely and hold it together. Moreover, plants on such soils grow large tops,

Figure 74. Gullying, resulting from plowing up-and-downhill. (Source unknown.)

which protect the soil against washing. Such annual crops as sorghum, corn, and spring grains leave a large quantity of residues on productive soils. In addition, the after-growth of hay plants aids greatly in the protection of the soil against the beating action of raindrops and also against the action of alternate freezing and thawing, and on the lighter soils against wind action. The organic matter from these residues is helpful in all of the ways stated in the previous chapter. The specific ways of building up and keeping up the organic matter in soils were discussed at the opening of this chapter.

Tillage in relation to soil erosion. Under the term *tillage* are included plowing, all kinds of harrowing, and any other methods of seedbed preparation, seeding, and cultivation. Depressions, however tiny, are left in the surface of the soil by the different tillage implements. If tillage is done up-and-down slopes, the depressions may lead to gully erosion. If, however, tillage is on the contour or across slopes on the level, the depressions catch and hold water which soaks into the soil and consequently no erosion results (Figs. 74–76).

Plowing on rolling lands may well be done a little deeper than ordinarily. Thus, temporarily, more water is absorbed and less erosion

Figure 75. Up-and-downhill planting of corn. (U.S. Soil Conservation Service.)

is the result. Dead furrows, the final open furrow left in plowing, up- and downhill are the direct cause of many gullies. The tiny sloping furrows left by harrows frequently lead to the formation of rills. If these unite, a sizable gully may easily form. Seedbed preparation seldom needs to be done up- and downhill for the purpose of smoothing the surface. Later stirring that is to be left untouched for any length of time must be done on the contour to hold the soil. And for these reasons all cultivation of such crops as vegetables, corn, cotton, beans, and potatoes ought to be done on the contour.

Trashy cultivation may be practiced for the purpose of leaving much of the stubble or other coarse organic matter on the surface or in the immediate surface part of the soil. Coarse material in that position aids in the control of blowing as well as of erosion by water.

Crops in relation to soil erosion. Crops vary greatly in the degree to which they permit or prevent erosion. Most of the regular crops fall into one of two classifications, *soil-protecting* or *close-growing* (Fig. 77) and *soil-exposing* or *clean-tilled* crops (Fig. 78).

Most of the crops grown for hay, small grain, and pasture are classed as soil-protecting. Among them are wheat, oats, rye, barley, alfalfa,

Figure 76. Contour planting of potatoes in Maine. This practice is easier on the team, or requires less tractor power, than if planting is done up-and-downhill (see Fig. 75). The potato ridges hold rain water until it soaks into the soil and thus reduce runoff and erosion. Note also the sodded waterway; the grass helps to prevent gullying throughout the year. (U.S. Soil Conservation Service.)

clovers, lespedezas, hay and pasture grasses, and such annual hay crops as millet and sudan grass. The individual plants of these crops are so close together that they protect the soil rather completely against beating by raindrops. Buckwheat, although a somewhat close-growing crop, fails to protect the soil against erosion. This crop occupies the soil only about two months, and leaves it bare and exposed to erosion the rest of the year. It should not be seeded on steep slopes. Much of the American commercial supply of this grain, however, is grown on land with slopes steep enough to be susceptible to severe erosion under unfavorable conditions. Closely seeded cowpeas, soybeans, and flax protect the soil during the latter part of the growing period about the same as buckwheat does. After harvest, however, all these crops expose the soil to erosion.

Crops that are to be cultivated are planted in rows from less than two to more than four feet apart. Considerable soil between the rows,

Figure 77. Oats, a soil-protecting crop. Soil-protecting crops such as the small grains prevent raindrops from striking and beating the soil into suspension. In addition, the plants grow so close together and their roots are so interwoven that the crop holds the soil against washing. (American Potash Institute, Inc.)

therefore, has no crop protection. Moreover, cultivation keeps the surface inch or two of soil in a loose condition that washes easily indeed on relatively steep slopes. Soil-exposing crops include most garden vegetables, field-grown beans, cabbage, and potatoes, and corn, cotton, and sorghum. Erosion is often severe in late potatoes in the northern states. The washing takes place not so much while the crop is growing as it does after it has been harvested. In New York, Maine, and other northern states it is usually too late to obtain any appreciable growth of a cover crop for the purpose of protection after the potatoes are harvested. Machine digging, in particular, leaves the soil soft and so smooth that sheet washing may readily take place. On such potato land any treatment that produces contour ridges would be beneficial and should usually not be too costly. Somewhat earlier strains of late potatoes have been introduced recently. Following the digging of them with a seeding of rye aids materially in the control of erosion.

In some areas erosion is less serious on corn than on potato land. For

Fig. 78. Cotton rows on the contour, Alabama. Contour planting and cultivation are particularly essential because of soil conditions and the type of rainfall in the cotton belt. This slope of 20 per cent is a very steep one for cultivated crops in the Piedmont. (U.S. Soil Conservation Service.)

this there are a number of reasons. The soil becomes compacted more or less in corn and thus does not wash very readily. The residues from the crop afford some protection to the soil. Moreover, the final cultivation is given the crop in early to mid-summer, after which some cover of weeds may develop. In wet seasons weed growth is rather luxuriant and protects the soil to a considerable extent. Not only do corn and weed roots hold the soil together, but the above-ground growth protects it against the action of the rain. Most of the other soil-exposing crops are similar in erosiveness to corn.

The seeding of a cover crop such as rye, or rye and vetch, in clean-tilled crops is feasible under many soil, cropping, and climatic conditions (Fig. 79). Wherever the cover crop can make fair growth in the fall and early spring, it will aid materially in holding the soil and in reducing the loss of plant nutrients.

Crop rotations. The beneficial effects of growing crops in regular rotation have been discussed (p. 147). The growing of soil-exposing

Figure 79. Rye in cotton stalks, Tennessee. Here is a fine growth of rye seeded in cotton. This practice aids greatly in holding water and in reducing the loss of soil by erosion. The rye, moreover, may be used for early spring pasturage. (U.S. Soil Conservation Service, Tennessee.)

crops year after year on erosive soils with moderate to steep slopes usually leads to severe erosion. Soil-protecting crops, especially the turf-forming grasses, on the other hand, control erosion almost completely. It is clear that farmers cannot produce the vegetables, cotton, wheat, and other grains that are needed for food and feed and at the same time keep the soil covered with grasses and close growing legumes. A compromise that alternates soil-protecting with soil-exposing crops is therefore necessary.

In the corn belt a typical rotation is corn the first year, oats the second, and clover the third. A second year of corn is often grown on the richer corn soils, thus making a four-year rotation. In the East, corn, potatoes, cabbage, or beans the first year; oats or barley the second; clover the third; and timothy the fourth is a common rotation. In the South, cotton the first year; spring grain the second; and corn the third are grown, legumes being used to some extent for winter cover

Figure 80. Erosion down lister rows, Oklahoma. Erosion in the Southwest is particularly severe down lister rows. Note the gullying and silting in the foreground, resulting from the collection of water from the furrows. (U.S. Soil Conservation Service.)

of the soil. Cowpeas for hay may be added as a fourth year. In the Southwest, a grain sorghum such as kafir or milo (Fig. 105, p. 181) may be grown the first year, barley or oats the second, and wheat the third and the fourth years. The addition of sweet clover or lespedeza is highly desirable in the areas to which they are adapted. The rotation should be such as to aid in the maintenance of high crop yields and high organic-matter content of the soil, and at the same time to aid in the protection of the soil against washing.

Seeding across slopes essential. Seeding crops across slopes or on the contour aids in holding and absorbing rainfall (Fig. 78). If the rainfall is all absorbed, no runoff and, therefore, no soil erosion take place. Up-and-downhill rows, in contrast, permit unimpeded runoff, but contour crop rows check the flow of water down slopes. More water is absorbed with contour rows than with up-and-downhill rows (Fig. 80). Moreover, the crop plants themselves check the speed of runoff water and thus reduce its cutting and carrying power. Contour seeding, therefore, largely eliminates rill washing and controls gullying in a large measure.

Figure 81. Strip cropping, New York. Here is a good example of the strip-cropping method of controlling erosion. Potatoes, corn, beans, vegetables, or other soil-exposing crops are grown on relatively narrow strips that are alternated with strips of such soil-protecting crops as clovers or alfalfa and grasses grown for hay. (A. F. Gustafson.)

All intertilled crops and even close-growing, soil-protecting ones are best seeded on the contour. Contour-ridged potato rows on gentle to moderate slopes may hold two inches or more of rain without any loss of water. Not only is the soil held against erosion, but the water is all taken up by the soil for use of the crop later in the season. In dry years contour planting of potatoes may make the difference between a good crop and a poor one. Even in seasons of average rainfall the water thus held increases crop yields. Grain with meadow mixtures should be sown on the contour. When this is done, the meadow plants are in more or less definite contour rows. Such rows aid in reducing the loss of water from sloping meadows.

Strip cropping on the contour. By strip cropping is meant the growing of crops in belts or bands across slopes (Fig. 81). By this means a long slope is broken into a number of strips. No two adjacent strips are planted to soil-exposing crops at the same time. In fact, it is common practice to alternate clean-tilled with soil-protecting crops such as legumes, hay grasses, or small grains. In this way only half of a slope is planted to the more erosive crops at any one time. Any water that is

Figure 82. A diversion channel. This diversion channel is in every sense a terrace. The wheelbarrow and man at the left stand in the broad, flat water channel. The middle man stands on the crest of the terrace embankment, and the man on the right at its base. The whole area is being fertilized and limed in preparation for seeding grasses and legumes. This channel diverts the water coming from a ten-acre field above and empties it on thrifty, erosion-resistant pasture in the background. (A. F. Gustafson.)

not absorbed on the cultivated strip may be caught, held, and absorbed by the meadow strip immediately below it. In case of ridged potatoes or corn, these crops may catch and hold water coming from the strips of close-growing crops.

For the best control of erosion, strips must be kept definitely on the contour and the crop rows planted on the level without many low spots in them. Unless this is done, water collects between the rows and flows toward such low spots. As a number of rows cross an up-and-downhill depression, such as an old gully, sufficient water may collect to start a new gully or to reopen an old one.

A distinct advantage of contour strip cropping is that crop rows are kept on the level year after year. All of the advantages of contour tillage, contour seeding, and contour cultivation that are enumerated in the previous section are attained by means of strip cropping. Although

Figure 83. **Outlet for diversion terrace channels.** This broad, open, sodded channel serves as outlet for a series of terraces up the slope to the right. Because of the danger of gullying by the water collected in diversion terraces, it is particularly essential that such outlets be well protected. Protection can be accomplished by means of vegetation, as it is done here, or by means of various types of engineering structures. Vegetation has the advantage that, under proper conditions, its protection improves with the years of growth. (U.S. Soil Conservation Service.)

strip cropping cannot control sheet erosion completely, it is a definite aid in the prevention of both gully formation and sheet washing.

The best width of strip to use varies with the length and steepness of slope, the rate of absorption of water by the soil, the type of rainfall —slow or heavy showers—the value of the land, and the value and nature of the crops grown.

Diversion channels. As strip cropping breaks one area into a number, so diversion channels make a number of narrow drainage areas out of a large one on a long slope (Fig. 82). Channels are laid out with a slight fall from one end to the other. The water from the land directly above each channel flows slowly around the hill to a prepared outlet (Fig. 83). Safe outlets that do not wash may be developed in pasture or meadow, in brush, or in forest.

Small diversion channels may be placed at the lower edge of each

Figure 84. Building a terrace. Here a terrace is being built with a heavy tractor and a blade terracer. The soil is being moved from the channel on the upper side of the embankment. (Caterpillar Tractor Company, Peoria, Ill.)

contour strip. More often, however, they are placed below each third or fourth strip, depending on local soil and slope conditions. Sometimes these channels drain a wet area or to protect a steep part of the slope. Once water is collected, it must be managed so that gullying will not result from its concentration.

Terraces. Terraces are a refinement and a great improvement over the hillside ditch. A crude terrace had been used for some years in the Southeast, but it was Priestly H. Mangum who first built the terrace that bears his name. This first terrace was built by him more than sixty years ago and was still in use in 1936. The Mangum terrace is a broad-base ridge from fifteen to twenty-four inches high with a wide water channel above it. The water that collects in the channel from its drainage area is carried at a slight slope around the hill to the prepared outlet (Figs. 84–85). A slightly different form of terrace, the Nichols terrace,[3] is rapidly coming into general use. Terraces are used more generally in the South, Southwest, and Midwest than in other sections of the United States. To a lesser extent terraces are used in the Northeast and in the upper Mississippi Valley. Contour farming and contour strip cropping are sometimes practiced on terraced land.

Figure 85. Terraces in Missouri. Wheat has been drilled on the contour on these terraces. Deposition of soil in the channel may be noted on the extreme left. (U.S. Soil Conservation Service.)

Contour furrows. The contour furrow is laid out on the exact contour or level for the purpose of holding water (Fig. 86). Such furrows must be level; otherwise the collection of water in them may cause washing where there was none before. Pastures are benefited by the water held by these small elongated ponds. One or two inches of rain may thus be held against runoff and, by entering the soil, increase the growth of pasture grasses during dry periods. When a sufficient area is contour-furrowed, springs that have long been dry may flow again.

In the West, contour furrows have reduced floods by holding water

---

[3] The Mangum terrace is formed by building up the terrace ridge with soil from both sides. The Nichols terrace is made from soil moved out of the channel on the upper sides of the ridge only.

until it soaks into the soil. The quantity of water, mud, and stones that washed down long slopes into some cities in that area has been greatly reduced by contour furrowing. Because of the protection from flooding that contour furrows may afford, people in cities that are located at the base of long slopes in areas of high-intensity rains are enthusiastic about contour furrows.

The use of grasses and trees. In this country land has been taken out of production because, temporarily, more food, forage, and fiber (flax,

Figure 86. Contour furrows in Idaho. These contour furrows built on the slopes of the watershed greatly reduce the flood hazard in the city of Pocatello. They decrease the amount of water, silt, and rock carried down into the city during cloudbursts. Moreover, holding water on the land aids in the re-establishment of grasses on bare slopes. (E. M. Rowalt.)

cotton) were grown than could be sold at a fair price. In order to control erosion on such land the less productive, steeper areas may be seeded to grasses or planted to trees. Land taken out of production by whatever agency, private or governmental, should immediately be protected from erosion. Otherwise such land may contribute unduly to floods and to the silting of reservoirs and the clogging of streams (Figs. 87, 88).

Gully control. Contour strip cropping on terraced land largely prevents gully formation. Much land, however, is not so protected and therefore is subject to gullying. It is always advisable to fill or to bring gullies under control as soon as possible after they are formed. In gully control, use is made of the knowledge that reducing the speed of the current lowers its cutting and carrying power. Placing in gullies materials that reduce the velocity of the water aids in gully control. Straw, fine brush, and trash of various kinds are especially effective in small gullies. The trash used is staked down to prevent heavy rains from

Figure 87. Forest plantation protecting the soil. This plantation of Scotch pines on rolling lands in the Catskill Mountain area of New York holds rain water against runoff and affords complete protection to the soil against erosion. (A. F. Gustafson.)

washing it away. As brush or straw checks the current, the coarser soil material is deposited and in time fills the gully (Figs. 89–95).

Seeding with various grasses and legumes and planting with ordinary native shrubs or with leguminous shrubs such as *Amorpha fruticosa,* Scotch broom (*Cytisus Scoparius*), and rose acacia (*Robinia hispida*), and with the black locust (*Robinia Pseudo-Acacia*) and other trees in areas to which they are adapted, help to control gullies. Shrubs bearing food for man or for wildlife are preferred. Representative of these are blackberries, raspberries, and hazelnuts. Nut or fruit trees may be used as well as leguminous trees (Figs. 96, 97). Covering the bottom of gullies with large stones checks washing. Earthen, log, stone, and concrete check dams are sometimes used, but unless they are rightly placed and correctly built, dams may do harm rather than good.

Figure 88. Hardwoods protecting the soil, Virginia. Note the fine cover and the complete absence of erosion under the trees. The litter slows runoff and helps much of the water from rain and snow to soak into the soil for the benefit of vegetation and for wells and springs. This is beneficial for stream life, for power production, and for recreation. (U.S. Soil Conservation Service.)

HAULING AWAY SURFACE SOIL BAD PUBLIC POLICY

In some areas the surface soil from large areas is stripped off, sold, and hauled away. Such surface soil is used for the lawns of homes, in cemeteries, on exposition grounds, and on the slopes of fills and cuts and on the shoulders of highways and parkways. Taking off all the darker colored surface-soil material, which usually contains the natural and added organic matter and is most productive of crops, leaves behind distinctly unproductive land. In areas of sandy soils such as are found on Long Island, New York, blowing follows removal of the surface. In the frequent periods of strong winds in winter and spring nearby residents suffer considerable inconvenience and loss from the sand that sifts into their homes. Health also may be endangered.

In places the surface soil has been sold and removed. Later homes are built on the desurfaced land. To produce a lawn, surface soil is taken from other areas and an inch or two is spread over the subsoil. If the underlying material is sandy or gravelly, that depth of surface soil

Figure 89. Brush dam of the Nebraska type in Iowa. Control is accomplished here by means of a series of dams. The brush dam in the foreground is effective. The brush below acts as an apron that prevents erosion by water falling over the dam. The use of some live brush and stakes of willow, elderberry, cottonwood, or other adapted woods that root from cuttings makes the control relatively permanent. (G. W. Musgrave and R. A. Norton, U.S. Department of Agriculture.)

seldom produces a good lawn or garden even with frequent watering throughout the growing season.

On Long Island some towns have been empowered to prohibit the removed of topsoil from fields for any purpose. Although such laws are difficult to enforce, restrictions are essential in many places to protect homes from dust storms and to conserve and maintain the productivity of land for the future.

The material deposited in millponds and reservoirs, however, may be used to good advantage for surfacing purposes. Some surface soil may be taken without permanent damage from bottom lands that are subject to overflow and which, therefore, receive frequent deposits.

New York State highway officials, who now recognize the value of surface soil, recently began stock-piling the topsoil from new sections of the right of way. This saving of topsoil is a commendable conservation measure. No longer need farm lands be robbed of surface soil to produce a suitable protective cover of grass on highway cuts, fills, and shoulders.

Figure 90. Log check dams, South Carolina. Stones are used as an apron below the dam to prevent washing where the water spills over the dam. Also, unless other means have produced permanent control, erosion may begin again when the logs have decayed. In this instance the black locust and other vegetation should bring about complete permanent control (see Figures 50 and 93). (U.S. Soil Conservation Service.)

RECLAMATION AND DEVELOPMENT OF STRIP-MINED AREAS

Strip, open-pit, or open-cut mining of coal, phosphate, stone, sand, gravel, and iron ores is practiced generally throughout this country (Figs. 5, 98, 99). Strip mining of coal was begun in Illinois in 1866.[4] At first the overburden was removed with a spade and wheelbarrow, later came the horse- or mule-drawn slip scraper. Little development of the industry, however, took place until the invention of the revolving

[4] W. C. Croxton, "Revegetation of Illinois Coal Stripped Lands," *Ecology*, 9: 155–175 (1928).

steam shovel in 1911. Since then the industry has expanded with the production of necessary shovels and loading and other equipment. Shovels today have booms 100 to 200 feet in length that move many cubic yards of overburden in each dipperful. The reduction in the cost of coal by almost complete mechanization placed strip mining in a position to produce 16 per cent of this country's entire coal production (or nearly 101,000,000 short tons [5]) in 1944.

Figure 91. Straw used in gully control. Further erosion in this gully is being controlled by filling the gully with straw for the purpose of slowing the speed of flow and causing silting. Brush at the end of the gully holds the straw in place. It is often necessary to drive stakes through the straw or fine brush to hold it against being washed away. (A. F. Gustafson.)

The area mined and the strip-minable coal in Illinois are about 65,000 acres and in Ohio about 62,000 acres. These are, respectively, about 0.22 per cent of the area of Illinois and less than 0.25 per cent of Ohio. Generally speaking the acreages are smaller in the other states.

Sand, gravel, stone, and ores for many years have been recovered by means that are essentially strip mining. These operations raised no particular complaint on the part of the public. The strip mining of coal is somewhat different in that enormous shovels are used that turn

---

[5] W. H. Young, R. L. Anderson, and L. H. Isaac, "Bituminous Coal and Lignite," preprint from U.S. Bureau of Mines, *Minerals Yearbook*, 1945 p. 41.

over large acreages in a short time. The spoil material is left in such rough, raw, unproductive, unsightly ridges that strip mining of coal has aroused public criticism. The resulting spoil banks are much less productive than high-priced corn land, which some of these lands were before strip mining began. On the other hand, strip mining in a few years has improved the productivity of some lands that had previously been abandoned. Other lands, where the final surface spoil is largely rock, will produce little, even of worthless brush and shrubs, until

Figure 92. Brush giving protection to the soil. Brush scattered over badly surface-washed spots protects the soil against further erosion and helps seedlings of trees and other plants to bring about permanent control of erosion. (U.S. Soil Conservation Service.)

after many, many years of weathering and until some organic matter has been supplied by the growth of weeds and legumes.

It has been claimed that strip-mined lands are a menace to health, pollute streams and injure water life, fill stream channels and reservoirs, contribute to erosion, are unsightly, break up community life, interrupt highway communications, remove lands from production, and lower the total tax base of the local governmental units. Seldom are all of these damaging factors found in any one community. On the other hand, there is no better way of recovering this coal. The roof is too weak for ordinary underground, or deep, mining, and it is essen-

Figure 93. Badly gullied land after treatment. Note the small check dam at the right. Black locusts (*Robinia Pseudo-Acacia*) are making fine growth. This bad erosion is rapidly being brought under control. Black locusts should be equally helpful in the northern states for this purpose. This gully before treatment is shown in Figure 50 (p. 114). (Tennessee Valley Authority.)

Figure 94. Gullied land in southwestern Illinois. (W. R. Mattoon, U.S. Department of Agriculture.)

tial that the coal be gotten out for industrial and home use. Between this economic need and the damage done to the land and the local community, a compromise must be worked out. This arrangement must be equitable and to the economic benefit of the people of the state and of the local governmental units both now and in the future.

Because of the public feeling about the consequences of strip mining, Illinois, Indiana, Ohio, Pennsylvania, and West Virginia have enacted laws to ensure a measure of reclamation and improvement of

Figure 95. The same gullies as in Figure 94, slopes eased and planted. (W. R. Mattoon, U.S. Department of Agriculture.)

strip-mined lands. The Ohio statute is, in general, representative of these state enactments. Its purposes are stated to be as follows: aiding in the protection of game, birds, and wildlife; decreasing soil erosion and flood hazards; aiding in the prevention of pollution of lakes, rivers, and streams; and improving the use and enjoyment of strip-mined lands.

Its requirements are as follows: (1) A permit to operate must be obtained and an annual registration fee of $50 must be paid to the chief of the Division of Mines. (2) Each operator must file with the chief of the Division of Mines a bond of $100 for each acre of land to be mined during the year, with a minimum of $1,000, for faithful performance of requirements. (3) Within 30 days after beginning operations the operator must furnish the chief of the Division of Mines the following information: (a) the name and number of the operation, (b) the location of the operation, county, township, and nearest public road, (c) a legal description of the area to be mined, and (d) the name and address of the landowner.

When an area is mined out, the operator is required to (1) cover the exposed face of coal with three feet of soil and bury all roof coal and pyritic shales; (2) seal off with earth fill any break-through to under-

Figure 96. Gullies under control. This picture was taken one year after Figure 95 was. The black locust (*Robinia Pseudo-Acacia*) already has controlled the gullies and is now producing valuable timber. (W. R. Mattoon.)

ground workings; (3) provide roads and fire lanes in accordance with plans approved by the state forester; and (4) level off crests of all ridges of spoil banks to a minimum width of fifteen feet.

The operator is required to plant trees, shrubs, and grasses at a cost of not more than $50 an acre within one year after completion of operations. Planting shall be in accordance with a plan prescribed by the director of the Ohio Agricultural Experiment Station. When finished the operator is required to file a report on planting. Failure of operators to obtain a permit or to plant as required subjects them to fines and to forfeiture of bonds.

There are some differences in the laws in the various states. The main one with respect to performance bonds is that Illinois requires $400 an acre. There are other but less important differences in these laws such as variations in registration fees.

Figure 97. Black locusts of fence-post size, Kentucky. These trees eight years old are from twenty-five to thirty-five feet high. A wornout field was planted to locusts six feet apart each way. Note how completely the leaves and other litter cover the soil and protect it from erosion. (W. R. Mattoon.)

There seems to be fairly general agreement that it is uneconomical to level the spoil banks completely. It does appear, however, that the fifteen feet required in Ohio will prove too narrow for roadways for fire-control purposes and for hauling out timber products. This is for the reason that unless an erosion-resistant cover is quickly established, washing will materially reduce the width of the top of the leveled ridges.

The principal economic uses of strip-minded areas are for (1) pasture that may be seeded by airplane at low cost, (2) forest, (3) wildlife, (4) parks for recreation, and (5) fishing and water sports in the lake that is easily produced in the final cut of a strip-mining operation. Game will feed on adjacent farm lands and use the strip-mined lands for cover.

These uses should help to maintain the tax base, or its equivalent in recreational values, for the benefit of the local people and their governmental units. Millions of trees have already been planted, and they grow well on good sites. Important acreages have also been seeded by airplane to adapted legumes and grasses, and are producing good returns in pasture. It should be borne in mind, however, that only the

Figure 98. Spoil banks from strip-mining coal in Kansas. (A. F. Gustafson.)

Figure 99. Trees on strip-mined land in Alabama. Near Jasper, trees two years old are making excellent growth. (Robert L. Eikum.)

better situations quickly develop a cover of grass or trees. The steepness of the spoil-bank ridges makes it impossible to apply lime or fertilizer for pasture with the usual spreaders. The slopes are entirely too steep for making hay of the grass by anything but primitive methods. Also, they are so steep as to make it difficult to harvest timber when it has reached the desired size (Fig. 100).

Figure 100. Reclaimed strip-mined land in Illinois. Afforestation by the United Electric Coal Corporation near Cuba. Trees planted in 1931, photographed in 1938. Lakes like this one occupy the final cut in mining operations. (J. W. Bristow.)

Whatever else is done, spoil, whether from strip mining of coal or from the recovery of gravel, phosphate, stone, or ores, must be so managed as to prevent erosion and consequent covering of productive land, clogging of streams, silting of reservoirs, and pollution of streams or other water supplies.

CONTROL OF WIND EROSION

That much damage has been done to the soils of the United States by wind erosion has already been shown. The wind may act on dry soils over long periods, whereas water erosion is active only for a short time during and following heavy rains. Some of the principles of the control of erosion by water are applicable also in the control of wind erosion.

Organic matter and vegetative cover of the soil. Organic matter is helpful in keeping sandy soils from blowing because it absorbs and holds water. A moist soil usually does not blow; the addition of organic matter, therefore, is highly important for soils that are subject to blowing.

Figure 101. Beach grass on Long Island, New York. American beach grass has been planted to prevent the sand from blowing over the road and from covering valuable property. (A. F. Gustafson.)

A relatively thick cover of vegetation keeps the wind from direct action on the soil. The wind is unable to pick up the fine soil particles or to roll the larger ones along on the surface. Plant roots also hold the soil and thus retard its movement by the wind. On seashores and other sandy areas, American beach grass is planted to hold the sand in place (Fig. 101). Seeding a long-lived legume or an annual legume that reseeds itself is helpful. Long-leaved reed grass grows wild in central Illinois and adjacent states and serves the same purpose. Often it is most important to hold sand in place in order to avoid its covering good soil or other valuable property.

Keeping soil cloddy. On dry areas that are subject to blowing, implements that leave the surface soil rough and cloddy aid in the control of wind erosion.

Furrows. Various kinds of furrows may be used to advantage (Figs. 102, 103). Small grain is seeded in furrows made by a special furrowing drill, and corn is planted in deep, wide furrows. One advantage of these furrows is that they keep the surface of the soil rough. As soil particles are rolled along, they drop into the furrow and stay there

Figure 102. Furrows holding soil, central Illinois. These furrows on sandy soil used for growing watermelons have been made with an ordinary plow. The previous furrows had been nearly filled with sand and the new ones were made at right angles to them. (A. F. Gustafson.)

until the furrow is filled. When this happens, new furrows may be made, and protection thus renewed on uncropped land. In dry areas wheat and other crops may be grown in alternate years only. During the uncropped year the land is cultivated in order to accumulate sufficient moisture to produce a crop the succeeding year. This is called *fallowing,* or the land is said to be *fallow* during this year of cultivation without crop and furrows may be useful here.

Direction of tillage and seeding. In humid areas tillage and seeding are done at right angles to the slope in order to conserve soil and water. For the same purpose tillage, especially furrowing and seeding, is done at right angles to the direction of the prevailing wind in areas

subject to blowing. Because the wind often shifts its direction, an occasional furrow or drill width of grain across the main direction of
seeding or furrowing improves the protection that these methods
afford.

On comparatively level land these furrows hold rain and snow as
well as soil. On slopes, however, the furrows might cause erosion, but
this is controlled by means of small cross dams in the furrows. The re-

Figure 103. Lister furrows holding water for crops, Oklahoma. Furrows
are on the contour and hold all of the water from a heavy rain where it
falls. The water so conserved not only helps vegetation to protect the soil
against water erosion but keeps the soil moist and thus prevents wind
erosion. (U.S. Soil Conservation Service.)

tention of water in furrows is of great service. Moreover, if water can
be held during the growing season, grasses and other crops produce
more cover, which in turn further protects the soil against blowing.
Strip cropping. Strip cropping is used to help hold the soil against the
wind. As with the furrows and seeding, crop strips are planted at right
angles to the general direction of the wind. Thick, tall, soil-protecting
crops are alternated with small grain or intertilled crops where these
are grown. If soil is blown from a cultivated strip, some of it is caught
and held in the soil-protecting crop (Fig. 104).

The grain sorghums are capable of growth in areas of low rainfall and are, therefore, regarded as drought-enduring crops (Fig. 105). For this reason sorghum is grown on a large acreage in the Great Plains. This is particularly fortunate because it is resistant also to wind erosion. Even the dwarf varieties serve somewhat as windbreaks. The stubble and residues protect the soil over winter.

Windbreaks. Windbreaks check the wind on the leeward side to an estimated distance of about twenty times their height. Thus a windbreak ten feet high affords protection over a distance of about two hundred feet or somewhat less (Figs. 106, 107).

Figure 104. Strip cropping for control of wind erosion, North Dakota. A three-year rotation of wheat, oats, and corn is practiced on this 160-acre field. The strips are kept on the contour for the control of losses of soil and water by runoff. The regular crop strips are separated by so-called buffer strips of grass. By this method of cropping only one-third of a field is in an intertilled crop (corn) at any one time and thus exposed to either wind or water erosion. The strips of wheat and oats control erosion and tend to control it on the corn strip. (U.S. Soil Conservation Service.)

Shrubs, trees, and, in some instances, crops that are adapted to the locality serve well as windbreaks. Thick-growing or dense-topped trees are naturally more effective than are thin-growing ones. Checking the wind reduces loss of water from soil and crop. Thus windbreaks reduce soil movement directly as well as by enabling crops to make larger growth. And such larger growth further protects the soil against wind movement. A leguminous tree, such as the black locust, makes good growth under conditions moderately favorable for it. Its top, however, is thin, and it needs to be supplemented with thicket-topped trees. Evergreens are especially helpful in this respect in areas to which they are adapted. Permanent willow windbreaks are grown on muck lands in New York, and they afford a good measure of protection. Woven picket or snow fences and single rows of oats are also used with distinct benefits (Fig. 62, p. 128). In some areas there is a tendency to rely on temporary windbreaks of the picket-fence variety.

Figure 105. Kafir, a grain sorghum, Texas. Kafir is adapted to the drier and hotter areas of the Southwest and the Great Plains. Not only does the growing crop protect the soil against erosion, but the stalks and stubble are effective in holding the soil after harvest. (U.S. Soil Conservation Service.)

CONTROL OF WAVE EROSION

Waves cut away the land on ocean and lake shores and to a lesser extent on the banks of the larger rivers. Public works, cities, or resorts must be protected by engineering structures, even at great cost, because of the high value of such properties. On individual farms wave erosion may be a serious problem, but it is often extremely difficult to control at reasonable costs (Figs. 108, 109). Because of the relatively low value of farm land, little expenditure can be made for its protection. The seeding of grasses and legumes and the planting of adapted,

Figure 106. Windbreak in Nebraska. This windbreak is of sufficient height to afford protection over an area of considerable width. Conifers are equally effective in all seasons of the year, but the deciduous trees, like those on the right, are only partly effective during late autumn, winter, and early spring, a time during which the soil and the farmstead are in greatest need of protection. (U.S. Soil Conservation Service.)

Figure 107. A deciduous windbreak on Long Island, New York. Windbreaks of this type help check winds even in winter and spring when the trees have no leaves. (A. F. Gustafson.)

native vines, shrubs, and trees may aid in stabilizing shore lines if cutting is not too rapid. Because of their ability to fix nitrogen and to make good growth on raw unproductive subsoil material, legumes always deserve first consideration in connection with wave and other erosion-control problems.

Figure 108. Atlantic Coast of Long Island, New York. These large boulders break the force of the waves to some extent, but the shore line is still being cut rapidly. Eventually the accumulation of boulders will protect the higher land. (A. F. Gustafson.)

CONTROL OF SEDIMENTATION IN RESERVOIRS

In Table 7 (p. 133) it was shown that sedimentation in many reservoirs has been rapid. Reservoirs in more protected areas may have much longer lives.

There are three types of reservoirs with respect to usefulness and replacement value.[6] (1) Some reservoirs may be replaced by new ones at less expense than the cost of materially delaying complete sedimentation. Many stock ponds and small reservoirs are in this group. Other sites are generally available, so that a new reservoir can be built when

[6] Carl B. Brown, "Aspects of Protecting Storage Reservoirs by Soil Conservation," *J. Soil and Water Conservation*, 1: 15–20, 43–45 (1946).

sedimentation has seriously reduced water capacity. (2) New sites for reservoirs in this group will be costly. It is desirable to put the water-shed under protective soil conservation as quickly as possible at moderate costs. (3) In the third group reservoirs may be classed as "indispensable, irreplaceable, nonsubstitutable natural resources." This group must be protected as fully as possible. Irrigation reservoirs in this group are undergoing sedimentation, and when it is complete, irrigation will no longer be possible unless other sources of water can

Figure 109. Vegetation resistant to wave action. Natural shrubbery here protects the north shore of Long Island. Wave action is less severe than on the Atlantic Ocean side. (A. F. Gustafson.)

be found. The land that has been watered from such a reservoir will become essentially valueless, and the people must find other land on which to make a livelihood. In the case of power reservoirs, electricity will no longer be produced and any aid in flood control will be lost.

In the control of sedimentation it is well to bear in mind that the finer particles from agricultural lands may be drawn off and sent downstream in the newer-type dams. It is the coarser material or the stream-bed load that fills reservoirs. Wherever there are alternative sites, heavy expenditure to delay sedimentation does not appear to be warranted. The demand for the power or irrigation water a reservoir can supply will influence the degree of control of sedimentation that may be applied with profit.

Every effort, however, must be made with little regard to cost to protect the indispensable, nonsubstitutable reservoirs. For these reservoirs, control measures ought to be developed before the gates are closed and filling begins. Water conservation measures are needed on every acre of the watershed in order to reduce the rate of stream flow into the reservoir. Here, as elsewhere, the more water is concentrated in a channel, the faster it flows. And the faster the current, the more material, such as sand, gravel, and stones, is rolled and pushed into the storage area of the reservoir.

Many city reservoirs are practically irreplaceable because of the shortage of alternative sites. The better sites in most localities are already in use, and new ones will be costly. In contrast, little needs to be done to control sedimentation in stock ponds and other easily replaceable reservoirs. For these, the cost of sedimentation control exceeds the cost of replacement.

CONTROL OF FLOODS

Floods in this country are not a new or a man-made phenomenon. They occurred before the white man felled and burned the forest or plowed the prairie sod. The destruction of much of the natural vegetative cover has hastened runoff from the hilltops into the valleys. Moreover, putting the land into cultivation has undoubtedly raised the crests of floods (Figs. 110–113).

Floods occurred in the upper Mississippi Valley [7] in 1785, 1811, 1823, 1826, 1844, 1851, 1855, 1858, 1862, 1881, 1883, 1892, 1903, and 1909 (an average of about once every nine years)—also in 1912 and 1913. The flood of 1844 was the highest up to that time, but it was exceeded by those of both 1912 and 1913. The most notable floods on the lower Mississippi River [8] occurred in 1815, 1828, 1844, 1849, 1850, 1851, 1858, 1859, 1862, 1865, 1867, 1874, 1882, 1884, 1890, 1893, 1897, 1903, 1912, 1913, 1916, 1922, 1927, 1929, 1937, 1944, and 1947 (an average of once every five years). The flood of 1912 was the worst up

[7] H. C. Frankenfield, *The Ohio and Mississippi Floods of 1912* (U.S. Department of Agriculture, Weather Bureau, Bull. Y; Washington, 1913), p. 11.

[8] Bennett Swenson, *The Ohio and Mississippi River Floods of January–February 1937* (U.S. Department of Agriculture, Weather Bureau Monthly Weather Review, Suppl. 37; Washington, 1938), p. 50.

to 1913. Great floods on the Ohio River occurred in 1882, 1883, 1884, 1897, 1898, 1907, 1913, and 1937. Those of 1884, 1907, 1913, and 1937 were higher than the others.

The damage done by floods in recent years is appalling. The estimated flood damage in this country from 1900 to 1908 was $850,000,-000, or nearly $100,000,000 a year.[9] The 1913 flood caused $100,000,-000 of damage in the Miami Valley in Ohio and $180,000,000 of dam-

Figure 110. Damage by a flood in a California orange grove, 1938. The damage to the grove was great and the cost of removing the sand, gravel, and other debris will be prohibitive. (U.S. Soil Conservation Service.)

age in the Ohio Valley the same year. In 1927 losses caused by floods in the Mississippi Valley and in New England were $330,000,000 and $40,000,000 respectively. The damage in Texas in 1935 was $128,000,-000. In 1936 New England again had serious floods that caused damage of $70,000,000. The previous high-water mark in the Ohio River at Cincinnati was about 70 feet, and that was the occasion of a disastrous flood. In 1937 when the water rose above 80 feet, calamity struck the city and the whole middle and lower Ohio Valley and caused heavy property damage. Pittsburgh suffered flood losses of $200,000,000. In

[9] George W. Pickels, *Drainage and Flood-Control Engineering* (2d ed.; New York, 1941), pp. 10–11.

Figure 111. Bridge destroyed by a flood in California. The same flood damaged the grove shown in Figure 110. (U.S. Soil Conservation Service.)

Figure 112. Railroad tracks washed out near Ravenna, Nebraska, June, 1947. Severe damage resulted during this flood period on the smaller rivers as well as on the Missouri and Mississippi rivers. (Jack Bailey.)

1947 the damage done by record floods in the Missouri and upper Mississippi Valleys reached the estimated total of more than $165,000,000.[10] Both flood heights and flood losses appear to be increasing. Nearly every year some section of this country suffers heavy property damage and often loss of life from floods.

It is unlikely that floods in this country can be prevented; improved control, however, is possible. The crest of floods can be lowered some-

Figure 113. Work of a flood. This is one of three houses within two miles destroyed by a flood on a small stream in southern New York in August, 1937. One house was washed away completely. (A. F. Gustafson.)

what. The cost of control is certain to be high, but even a moderate lowering of flood crests would save millions of dollars' worth of property.[11]

According to the *National Resources Board Report, 1934,* flood-control works are of four types:

1. Storage reservoirs to impound flood waters for later release.
2. Retarding basins automatically to smooth out peaks (of stream flow).
3. Channel improvements to increase capacity or facilitate flow.
4. Levees to protect from overflow the bottom lands behind them.

---

[10] H. C. Gee, Lt. Col., Corps of Engineers, War Department, Washington, letter to author, Jan. 7, 1948.

[11] A brief discussion of flood control is found in *Land Economics* (New York, 1940), pp. 351–361, by Richard T. Ely and George S. Wehrwein.

Reservoirs. Water is collected and stored in reservoirs during heavy rains and thawing of snow to be released gradually after the crest of the flood has moved well down the valley of the main stream. The time to release water depends on downstream flood conditions and on the prospect of an immediate heavy rain. Obviously a reservoir must be empty, or nearly so, before the next big rain or it will have little capacity to impound flood water. Human judgment will be the determining factor.

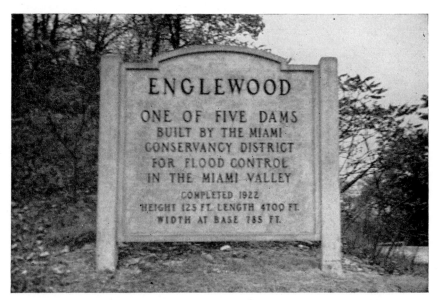

Figure 114. Information about a Miami Conservancy District dam.

Detention dams. Detention dams are open at all times to the capacity of the channel below the dams. They simply detain the water that otherwise would flood the valley below, allowing it to flow out at channel capacity until the basin is empty and ready to receive the waters of the next heavy rainfall. Two million dollars does not build and equip a very large earthen dam of the detention type.

The dams of the Miami Conservancy District (Figs. 114–117) are of the retarding-basin type. The basins on the Muskingum River in southeastern Ohio are of the same type, but one of the latter is made of concrete. Some detention dams are equipped with gates to control the flow of water through them. The cost of the dams on the Muskingum River and its tributaries was about $50,000,000. Similar retarding basins are in use in New York and in other parts of the country. The basins on the Muskingum River are said to have little effect on the crest of floods, except for a relatively short distance down the Ohio from the mouth of the Muskingum River.

Reservoirs on the upper Mississippi have a capacity for nearly 100,-000,000,000 cubic feet of water. The impounding of this quantity of water lowers flood crests there but has a negligible effect on floods 100 miles downstream. Many large dams are of the multiple-purpose type in that they supply water for irrigation and hydroelectric power pro-

Figure 115. Outlet and spillway of the Englewood Dam. Flood waters are detained by the dam but allowed to flow away to the capacity of the outlet. (A. F. Gustafson.)

duction and at the same time have considerable capacity for the detention of water. The Hoover Dam serves all three purposes and collects silt in addition. The Norris Dam produces power primarily, but it also has considerable capacity to detain and slowly release flood water. To be effective flood discharge needs to be reduced by one-third.[12] Flood-control reservoirs are seldom economical in comparison with water-supply, irrigation, or power reservoirs. Enormous numbers of dams would be needed to reduce the quantity of flood water in the larger valleys by one-third or even by one-sixth.

The United States Army Engineers in 1945 announced a list of flood-control and river-improvement projects that had been author-

---

12 Pickels, *op. cit.,* p. 383.

ized by Congress.[13] Work was to begin the following year and the "estimated" cost was $1,500,000,000. Many additional projects are under investigation. These should be carefully studied, not only because of the great cost of dams, but also because of the limited area protected. One acre of reservoir protects only three or four acres of land downstream. It might be wise to defer the building of more dams until their effects in lessening floods in at least one major stream valley can be determined. Wherever feasible, the multiple-purpose dam is desirable because the power produced can pay most of the costs of operation and amortization.

Figure 116. The Englewood Dam with a roadway on its crest. (A. F. Gustafson.)

Sedimentation occurs whenever the velocity of a stream is reduced. Deposition of coarse materials—the bed load—therefore occurs when a stream enters a reservoir or detention basin that contains water. Loss of capacity is inevitable over the years, although the finer material will largely go out through detention dams or the spillway of reservoirs. As already shown, sedimentation is relatively rapid in many reservoirs. There is danger that at some future time the capacity of detention basins or reservoirs for flood water may be too small to give the expected protection downstream. Disaster may result because of dependence on these structures for protection.

Channel improvements. Channel improvements consist of straighten-

---

[13] Brown, *op. cit.,* p. 15.

ing, widening, and smoothing the channel and removing obstacles. Straightening a channel shortens it and gives it greater fall, and consequently increased capacity for removing flood waters. Widening, deepening, and smoothing likewise increase capacity and hasten the flowaway of larger quantities of water than before improvement was effected. The clearing of trees from channels and the removal of abandoned bridge piers allows freer, faster flow of water, aids it in getting

Figure 117. Dam checking a flood, Miami Conservancy District, Dayton, Ohio. This earthen dam is one of five erected in the Miami Conservancy District, to control floods. When this picture was taken the retarding basin formed by the dam held 37 feet of water. In 1929 the water was 54.5 feet deep, 21 per cent of its capacity. The dam holds back the flood water over and above the capacity of the stream channel or the opening through the dam. (Miami Conservancy District.)

to sea quicker, and, therefore, lowers the crests of floods. At times of very high floods, even bridges obstruct the flow. It may even be necessary to rebuild bridges whose piers are so close together as to seriously impede river flow. When this checking of flow occurs, the water piles up above the obstruction and flood conditions there are aggravated.

Channel improvement should be largely confined to the lower reaches of streams where it will help to rush the water out to sea. On small tributary streams this type of improvement merely hastens the delivery of water into the principal outlet or terminal stream and consequently materially raises the crests of floods there. Channel improvement of headwater streams is costly because flood waters clog the new channels with coarse debris, which must soon be removed to restore their capacity. In the terminal section of rivers acceleration of the rate of flow into the sea by means of channel improvement is desirable if not too costly.

Levees. Levees have long been employed for the control of floods. For a time after their construction levees confine flood waters. The building of additional levees, however, reduces the storage space for water so that the crest of floods is raised. Eventually, high floods overtop the lower, older levees, with great damage as the result. Levees on the middle Mississippi River failed in this manner in 1947, with unusual loss on crop lands. In most places the water did not subside in time to plant the year's corn crop, and wheat was a complete loss on inundated lands.

The big, new government levees on the lower Mississippi held in 1937 and again in 1947. It has at times, however, been found necessary to open the levees and fill the floodways, which had been provided for that very purpose.

Levees should be located well back from the banks of streams in order to provide a considerable capacity for flood water. Levees, by confining the water, increase its depth by as much as eight feet at Memphis and therefore its velocity and scouring capacity. In contrast, the jetties placed in stream beds for improving navigation in periods of low water actually hinder the flow of flood waters.

Holding water on farm land and at the headwaters of streams by means of erosion-control and water-conservation measures such as maintaining a thrifty vegetative cover on sloping cropped lands and forests on the rougher lands will aid in making flood-control works effective.

In the case of levee and drainage districts, costs are assessed against landowners on the basis of benefits derived from the improvements. The question arises whether the cost of flood-control works should be assessed on the same principle, that is, the costs charged in part directly to the owners of the property protected. Works financed wholly by the federal government, however, are paid for by the entire nation. Owners of hill property far above floods pay just as heavy taxes for such control projects as do the owners of business or residence property in the flood zone.

REPORT OF WATER PLANNING COMMITTEE

The Water Planning Committee of the National Resources Board was aware of the possible waste that might follow the employment of the old-fashioned "pork barrel" method of appropriations for local purposes. As a result of their deliberations this committee recommended the appropriation of federal government funds under the following conditions: "(1) only where there is reasonable protection against maximum floods; (2) only where the total benefits justify the expense; (3) only where there are responsible and legally constituted authorities with which to deal; (4) to an extent not greater than 30 per cent of the cost of labor and materials where the benefits are chiefly local; (5) to an extent greater than 30 per cent only in proportion to benefits definitely applicable to recognized national interests; (6) to a full 100 per cent only where the benefits are almost wholly of national interest."

These provisions are wise and liberal. Some completed projects and others under construction do not appear to meet them in whole and some projects not at all. The latter may possibly have been justifiable purely on the basis of "relief" work. However, in the consideration of future control projects, great care should be exercised to determine whether *"the total benefits justify the expense"* before work is undertaken. Along with benefits must be considered the numerous nonbenefits, such as the abandonment and moving of public highways, railroads, schools, churches, villages, and farm homes and the flooding of agricultural land. Except for decreased agricultural production in certain areas, these nonbenefits may be regarded as costs. Any real attack on the problem of flood control in the United States must be a comprehensive one if it is to have even a fair chance of success.

NEED FOR GOVERNMENTAL ACTION

The utmost should be done to educate the farmer and the general public in the control of soil erosion and in the conservation of water— that is, holding as much water as possible on the land on which it falls, Reforestation of steep or idle land is essential also. Doing these things will aid in lowering the crest of floods and in reducing the damage to all kinds of property in the valleys. If after a reasonable period of education the desired control is not attained, it may be necessary for a government agency to take steps toward this end. Such an agency should have authority and be entirely beyond political influence. Its efforts need to be directed toward complete conservation of soil and water so that ample food and clothing for the population may be produced and so that flood damage and the silting of reservoirs may be reduced to a minimum.

The erection of new dams of any considerable size for the purpose of producing water power or for storing water for irrigation or other purposes should be deferred until soil erosion on the drainage areas of the dams can be brought under control. Only thus can the value of reservoir sites be preserved and guaranteed for future generations.

CHAPTER VI

Forests and Forest Lands

THE PRESERVATION and restoration of the country's forests have always occupied a prominent place in the nation's conservation program. The original forests, vast in area and widely distributed geographically, were composed of the most varied and magnificent collections of valuable tree species in the entire world. Now only a remnant of the old-growth forest remains.

Much of the original forest naturally gave way to agricultural development; but millions of acres that should be coming back into thrifty forests of valuable second-growth timber are, today, because of destructive logging and severe fires, covered with trees of inferior quality or are idle and nonproductive. The nation's forest heritage has been used in a prodigal manner.

During the past sixty years notable progress in forest conservation has been made, but the efforts to the present are far short of what is needed if the nation is to be assured of ample timber supplies and to receive the benefits that extensive forest cover provides. The old-growth timber supplies in private ownership are going all too rapidly. Ample supplies of second growth are the only replacements possible. These supplies can be grown, but only through a far more intensified effort in the future than has been made to the present. Directly or indirectly, forest conservation is a matter of concern to every citizen of the country. Individual comfort and national security rest in part on continuing supplies of forests and their products. That the people of the United States with its potential forest wealth will fail to adopt progressive measures to make all of its forest lands continuously productive seems incredible. Yet these developments will not come about until the public as a whole gains a far better appreciation of the value of its forests than it has at the present time and demands, through adequate legislation, that all the country's forests be placed under management techniques that will ensure their protection and continuous productivity.

SIGNIFICANCE OF FOREST CONSERVATION

Necessity of forest conservation. The land area of continental United States as now constituted aggregates 1,905,000,000 acres. Originally, superb forests containing an incomparable wealth of many kinds of old-growth timber covered 822,000,000 acres, or 43 per cent of the total land area. Composed of diverse species of trees, each valuable for varied and specific uses, these forests were unrivaled anywhere in the world for the heavy volumes per acre, or the valuable types of products that they could supply.

Great areas of forest growing on potentially valuable soils were cleared to create much of the rich farm land of the nation, a natural and thoroughly justifiable development. Vast areas were also cleared on lands later found to be unsuited to agricultural use. Such lands were in many cases abandoned and are now again reverting to forest growth. Land abandonment is still continuing.

But the land taken for agricultural use is only a small proportion of the total original forest area. The nation's forests have been cut over with incredible speed. Enormous volumes of timber have been cut to provide housing, fuel, and innumerable physical conveniences for a rapidly growing population; to create vast industries that occupy an important place in national and international commerce and trade; and to furnish enormous quantities of materials critically needed in national defense and war.

Insofar as forests have contributed to national welfare and security they have served the nation well. But with full recognition of this fact, the forests were cut and used in a highly destructive manner. Only the best materials were removed. Waste and destruction during logging operations were the rule. Vast areas of fine timber were ruined by fires. And even today the level of technical practice in handling most of the nation's forests and forest lands is comparatively low.

To show the extent to which forest depletion has gone a few figures are given. These statistics and what they signify will be developed in the pages to follow.

Commercial and noncommercial forests. Of the 822,000,000 acres of original forest, 198,000,000 acres have been cleared for agricultural, industrial, and urban development. The remainder of 624,000,000 acres represents the present forest-land area of the United States, an area that is not expected to change to any great extent in the foreseeable future.

Of this forest-land area, 163,000,000 acres are of a type unsuited to the growing of forest crops for commercial use. These forests are termed *noncommercial forests.* Some have been withdrawn from timber-growing use for parks; others are alpine forests where climatic and physiographic conditions make timber production impossible; and still others are in the more arid sections where only a sparse tree and shrub growth can develop.

These noncommercial forests, though unsuited to the production of commerical tree crops, are none the less highly important for other services, namely, watershed protection, recreational use, wildlife development, and, in many parts of the West, grazing resources for great numbers of cattle, sheep, and other domestic livestock. These areas must be adequately protected and managed even though timber is not the main crop.

The area of land on which the nation's future timber supply must be grown aggregates 461,000,000 acres. These are termed *commercial forest lands,* and are the lands capable of producing timber of commercial quantity and quality, available now or prospectively for commercial use. Of this total area there now remain only 45,000,000 acres or 10 per cent of old-growth timber. Seventy-five million acres or 16 per cent, because of destructive logging and forest fires, are denuded or poorly stocked with young seedling and sapling growth; 160,000,000 acres or 35 per cent are growing back into second-growth and saw-timber stands; 95,000,000 acres or 20 per cent are covered with forests of pole-timber size (trees from 4 to 12 inches in diameter); and 86,000,-000 acres or 19 per cent are covered with a fairly adequate stocking of new seedling or sapling growth.

This is the over-all picture today. It highlights the problems of forest conservation.

Forest conservation defined. The problems of conservation fall into several broad groups. First, they involve the continued use of the mature forests for the products that they will furnish, but use in a manner that will avoid waste and destruction and make provision for successive future crops. In other words, these forests must be used but they must also be kept continuously productive. Secondly, there is the important task of restoring the idle, poorly stocked, and nonproductive lands to a new forest growth of valuable tree species, and then protecting and properly managing these growing forests so that they will ultimately be continuously productive. Third, there are the problems that must be solved of properly developing the great areas of land now covered with second growth in various stages of immaturity.

As the first step in forest conservation all types of forest land must be fully protected from fire and other destructive agencies. Some areas must be restored to a new forest growth. Others, now mature, require a conservative form of cutting to maintain them in a continuously productive condition. And still other vast areas, at present immature, must be managed so that they will grow into maturity with well-stocked stands of valuable trees and gradually assume their role in supplying useful products.

In summary, forest conservation means complete protection, wise and continued use of mature timber, the rehabilitation of idle and nonproductive forest lands, and the practice of forest management techniques so that all the nation's forest lands will bear a productive, continuously renewed cover of timber growth.

SERVICES OF FORESTS

Forests and their products. From colonial times to the present the products of the forest have been indispensable to the welfare of the people. The first settlers found an unbroken expanse of forest before them, and from these forests came the material that built their homes and provided their fuel, as well as their ships, bridges, agricultural implements, and furniture. As the pioneers left the early centers of colonization and spread to the west and south, it was always the forest from which they obtained the wood for dwellings and fuel. In the early communities the two primary essential industrial establishments were the sawmill and the grist mill. Once the new settlement was past the pioneering state, the development of industries and trade, based on lumber and other forest products, gradually but steadily took place. In every section of the country where great areas of forest existed, the forest and wood-working industries developed rapidly into positions of great economic importance.

The forests of the country with their heavy stands per acre and their great variety of trees were ideal as a source of supply for pioneer and industry alike. Wood is an extremely adaptable and easily worked material and is suited to a great variety of uses. Some of the softwoods were best for building and construction purposes. The hardwoods of many kinds supplied woods with special qualities of beauty, hardness, strength, and durability. With the wealth of diverse kinds of forest trees it became a simple matter to select those woods that were easily adapted to specialized uses.

The forest products that were essential to the life of the early settler have continued to be indispensable to modern civilization. The emphasis on the types of products needed has shifted somewhat as the country has grown, but not too greatly. Although competing materials

Figure 118. The forest as a source of lumber. The logs in this picture have been collected at a central point and are being loaded on railroad cars to be taken to the mill. Sometimes the logs must be transported from 50 to 60 miles. At the mill the logs will be sawed into lumber for building purposes and many other uses. (C. H. Guise.)

often supplant wood for certain uses, new developments constantly take place and, as a result, create continuing demands of enormous proportions on the nation's forests. Especially important and even critical are the demands for forest products in time of war and national emergency. During the Second World War more than three-quarters of all lumber produced was allocated to the war effort, and even with these huge allotments forest products could not be furnished in adequate amounts. The difficulty of obtaining wood for civilian use and the drives for waste paper (a forest product) are recent reminders of the scarcity of this valuable material.

The outstanding use of wood, past and present, is for the construction of homes and other buildings. Four-fifths of the existing dwellings of the United States, occupied by some 90,000,000 people, are of wood construction. Although other materials are used for this important purpose, wood still is the principal material for house construction for families of moderate income.[1]

In 1944, 12,000,000,000 cubic feet of timber were cut from the forests of the United States. In terms of the 12,000,000,000 of cubic feet cut, 55 per cent went into lumber, 18 per cent into fuelwood, 10 per cent into pulpwood, and the remainder, 17 per cent, into other products, including railroad ties, poles, piling, veneer logs, barrels, shingles, handles, and many other products.

The individual products for which wood is used are almost innumerable. An investigation some years ago indicated almost 5,000 individual uses, and even then the study was not complete. New uses for wood are constantly being found. Of special interest are the developments in plywood whereby large sheets of veneers are glued together into built-up boards of varying thickness. For these sheets, which are extremely easy to handle, a wide future use is certain, since plywood is adapted to interior finish, panels, furniture, boats, airplanes, motor trailers, house prefabrication, and concrete forms.

Products of great commercial importance other than lumber and wood are obtained from forest trees. Especially well known are the resins from some of the southern yellow pines, from which are obtained turpentine, rosin, pitch, and tar. Also familiar to everyone are the sirup and sugar obtained from the sugar maple. Likewise important are the products of wood conversion. The cellulose of wood is used in the manufacture not only of pulp and paper, but in the cellulose derivatives that supply the synthetic fabrics for rayon and other materials, for explosives, photographic film, and various plastics. Research has shown that wood can be treated with various chemicals and subjected to heat and pressure treatments so that its form is changed completely. Softwoods can be made hard and strong, and though this type of use may be relatively insignificant in the over-all consumption of wood, modified wood will be important in industry.[2]

---

[1] J. Alfred Hall and T. J. Mosley, *Products of American Forests* (U.S. Department of Agriculture, Forest Service, Forest Products Laboratory; Washington, 1944).

[2] *Problems and Progress of Forestry in the United States* (Report of the Joint Committee on Forestry of the National Research Council and the Society of American Foresters, Henry S. Graves, Chairman; Washington, 1947).

Another development is extracting cellulose from wood chips and sawdust by treating this wood waste with mineral acids. By chemical processes the cellulose is converted to sugar, and by further treatment to ethyl alcohol, a product used in tremendous quantities by industry. It is also possible to produce from this sugar a form of yeast that has a high nutritive value for cattle feed.

The economic importance of forest products has been and is very great. The ability of wood to supply many basic needs and the possibility of adapting it to many uses probably now unknown make certain that forests will continue to be of vital importance to the welfare of the citizens of this country.

Table 8, which shows how wood is classified with respect to use, indicates some of the many ways in which wood and wood products are used.

TABLE 8. PRINCIPAL PRODUCTS OF AMERICAN FOREST TREES

Logs
  Lumber
    Rough construction material
    Planing-mill products
    General mill work
  Manufactured articles
    Boxes, crates
    Furniture
    Handles
    Woodenware and novelties
  Veneer
    Furniture
    Plywood
    Shipping containers
  Bolts
    Barrel staves
    Shingles
    Handles
  Timbers
    Beams
    Stringers
    Joints
  Railroad ties
Poles, piling, posts, mine timbers
Cordwood

Fuel
Tannin
Excelsior
Distillation products
  From hardwood
    Charcoal
    Acetate of lime
    Acetic acid
    Wood alcohol
  From softwood
    Oils
Pulpwood
  Lignin
    Plastics
    Fertilizers
  Cellulose
    Fiber products
      Paper
      Pulp and paper products
      Wall boards
    Chemical products
      Rayon
      Cellophane
      Explosives
      Photographic films

TABLE 8. PRINCIPAL PRODUCTS OF AMERICAN FOREST TREES (*Cont.*)

Celluloid	Cleaning fluids
Imitation leather	Soaps
Phonograph records	Drugs
Gums	Synthetic rubber
Balsam, heptane, and storax	Printing ink
Drugs	Bark
Adhesives	Tannins
Resins	Drugs
Gum rosin	Dyes
Varnishes and lacquers	Sap
Paper sizes	Sugar and sirup
Scaling wax	Foliage
Disinfectants	Oils
Gum turpentine	Decorations
Paints, varnishes, stains	Extracts
Floor and furniture polishes	Nuts and Fruit

The forest as a protective influence. Unwise clearing of forests has exposed valuable topsoils to the direct washing effect of surface water, with the result that these soils, built up through thousands of years, have often been washed away within a decade after clearing. Where forests cover hillsides and mountain slopes, the crowns of the trees break the force of falling rain. The porous forest soils, with their cover of litter and organic matter, absorb and hold back in great volumes surface and ground waters. Some of this ground water is absorbed by the roots of the trees and later transported and evaporated from the leaves. Much of the water seeps through underground passages and gradually is furnished clear and pure to springs and streams. Where a forest cover exists, there is little if any loss of soil through erosion. Streams in forested mountains and hills run clear, in contrast to the muddy, silt-filled creeks and rivers traversing agricultural and nonforested regions.

Since, on forest-covered country, surface runoff is retarded and much of the rain that falls reaches the streams indirectly, the danger of extremes in stream levels is reduced. Under normal conditions of rainfall the stream flow is more even, and, though periods of low and high water are bound to occur, the dangers from disastrous floods or complete drying up are greatly reduced. In the early spring, when melting snows are likely to produce flood stages, extensive areas of forest cover will likewise tend to reduce the danger. The slow melting of snow in the forest and the absorptive power of forest soils cause the water to be supplied gradually to the rivers and brooks. In the open country the rapid runoff of melting snows frequently causes disastrous spring floods.

Floods cannot be eliminated by means of forests alone. Long periods of rainfall or extraordinarily heavy storms will sometimes supply so much water in such a short period of time that bad floods are inevitable unless proper engineering devices are installed to assist in the problem of control.

The relation of the forest to climate is extremely complex. The size of the forest area, its geographic location, and the topographic character of the land are all interrelated. Forest regions are always popular as summer resorts and recreational centers. A cooler and more even temperature prevails, though often this is due primarily to high elevations or to the presence of lakes and other bodies of water. Certainly the temperature is influenced locally by the forests in that they break the force of hot, drying winds. Likewise they exert a protective influence against the cold winds of winter. Many homes in rural regions have retained or planted small woods for this essential purpose. Wind erosion, a serious problem in many of the states west of the Mississippi River as well as in some of the eastern states, can be controlled in part by the planting of trees. Rows or strips of forest growth planted for this purpose are termed *shelter belts*. In 1933 the establishment of a great shelter belt extending from Canada south through the prairie states was undertaken, and it is being continued in modified form today.

Small areas of woods have no effect on rainfall. Over large areas, however, the forests may exert a strong influence. Forests transpire enormous quantities of water. This transpiration of moisture from the trees is accompanied by the cooling process of evaporation. When warm air, completely laden with moisture, passes over the cooling air currents arising from the forests, the moisture-holding capacity of the air is decreased, and consequently rain may result. This condition, of course, holds only for extensive areas.

The value of forests in regulating stream flow and in preventing the erosion of soil may on some areas equal or even exceed their importance in the production of usable wood. Yet relatively little forest land need be withheld from timber use for watershed protection.

Well-managed forests can supply wood and at the same time serve protective purposes. Nearly three-quarters of all forest land in the United States exerts a major or a moderate influence in protecting watersheds.

The recreational use of forests. The forest has always been used extensively for recreational purposes. Great numbers of people spend their vacations and weekends in forested areas for camping, hunting, and other forms of relaxation (Fig. 119). The intensive development

Figure 119. Forests and recreation—Gallatin National Forest, Montana. Millions of people from all parts of the United States make use of the national forests for recreational purposes. Camping, riding, exploring, hunting, fishing, and other forms of relaxation are available to any citizen in the country's wilderness areas. (U.S. Forest Service.)

of city life and the desire for periods of complete rest have created a demand for forest recreation, a need that has been supplied through the extensive development of national, state, and municipal parks. The desirability of these areas, highly developed for recreational use, is due largely to their forest cover. There are now millions of acres of forest land in various parts of the United States given over primarily to recreation. Well known for their scenic and playtime values are the White Mountains, the Adirondacks, the northern Lake States, the southern Appalachians, and the famous forest regions of the West.

Great numbers of people prefer forests not developed for parks, because they can find in them more seclusion and less restriction of their activities, particularly with respect to hunting. Annually many millions of people are spending huge sums for the pleasure of visiting forests and parks in the United States. Authorities in national planning estimate that, in all, four times as much land as is now in use should be set aside primarily for recreational purposes.

In addition, other forest areas of vast extent should be managed so that they, too, may be used for recreation as well as for the production of forest products. Practically all forest land has recreational value. In European countries the recreational use of forests has for generations gone hand in hand with the growing and the conservative cutting of timber.

Forests and wildlife. The forests and the waters in them are preeminently the home of wildlife (Fig. 120). Most of the big game, such as deer, bear, elk, and moose, is now found in the forested areas and their borders, for it is in the forest that this wildlife finds food and a protective cover. Whether one wishes to hunt or merely to observe the habits of wild animals, one usually goes to forested regions. In keeping streams and lakes clean and cool the forest cover exerts a strong influence on the numbers and kinds of fish that can be raised and maintained. The best trout fishing occurs in woodland streams. If the forests are cut, the cover and the food supply of many of the game animals are destroyed. Further, the removal of the trees results in rapid erosion of soil; streams become muddy and warm and are ruined for many kinds of game fish.

So important is this phase of forestry that conservationists and sportsmen have used their influence to have many forest areas set aside permanently as game refuges and sanctuaries and have vigorously supported forestry and forest conservation. Almost all the forest land in the United States is usable for game management. Except in a few areas and in a few states, however, the wildlife population is far below what it should be.

Forests and grazing. More than one-half of all the forest lands of this country supply pasturage for domestic livestock (Fig. 121). In the West some 160,000,000 acres of forest range are in use, with the result that they provide directly an income to thousands of stockmen, benefit greatly western agriculture as a whole, and contribute largely to the national meat, leather, and wool supply. Many stockmen depend almost exclusively on the high mountain summer ranges for feeding their livestock. The western range resources are discussed in Chapter X, but it may be mentioned here that in many instances they are badly depleted and that as a whole they have a capacity of less than two-thirds of what is possible with their restoration and conservative management.

In the South millions of cattle and hogs graze on some 125,000,000

Figure 120. Forests and wildlife. Swift-flowing streams like these in a forest wilderness create a fisherman's paradise. (U.S. Forest Service.)

acres of forest range. The forage values are negligible. Most serious is the widespread practice of burning forest lands annually, a custom that originates in the belief that such treatment improves the grass-growing possibilities of these forest ranges.

In the eastern central regions approximately one-half of the farm woodlands are grazed. In general, the forage is poor in amount and quality, and the primary benefit to stock is that of shade. The concentration of stock in small areas of woodlands results in great damage to tree growth and seriously reduces watershed benefits.

Although pasturage for grazing animals is an important product of the western and southern forests, many problems exist in relation to control and conservation. The ranges must be properly managed. Otherwise they become overgrazed, the forage resources are reduced or destroyed, soil erosion sets in, and these areas cease to serve for watershed protection. Yet, wisely handled, the grazing resources of forest lands in the West and South may be perpetuated and maintained with great economic benefit.

Forests and agriculture. The two principal forms of permanent land use are forestry and agriculture, the interrelation of which is vital to

Figure 121. Forests and grazing—Lewis and Clark National Forest, Montana. The grazing lands in the forests of the West provide forage for millions of head of livestock and contribute in large measure to the prosperity of the western livestock industry. (U.S. Forest Service.)

national welfare. A sound forest economy promotes the prosperity of agriculture and rural life. Agriculture has always drawn heavily on the forest. Material for buildings, fuel, containers, equipment, and posts annually runs into many millions of dollars. In the western country water is a precious commodity, and in some regions farming is not possible without irrigation. The beneficial effect of the forest in holding back water from rains and melting snows and in supplying it evenly and regularly is of great importance in all agricultural regions, particularly in those where irrigation farming is practiced. Again, the forest, as previously explained, is a valuable agency in preventing the loss of surface soil, through its influence in preventing erosion. In many regions farm income is supplemented by winter employment in the woods or in the wood-using industries, or by the sale of surplus material from the farmer's woodlands (Figs. 122, 123). Many forest industries depend in large part on the wood brought to them in small amounts by the farm owner. Land economists stress the need of farming only the lands that will pay and advise the use for forestry of the poorer lands. A thrifty woods of valuable trees increases the general value of a farm. Forests and forest industries pay heavily in commu-

Figure 122. Sugar-maple logs from a farm woodland. Many farm woods contain mature trees that are ready for harvesting. Logs like those shown in this picture are of high quality and will sell for a good price. (H. W. Hobbs.)

nity taxes and share with the farmer the expenses of maintaining schools and roads. When the forest is gone, the taxes stop and the burden of building and maintaining these services and of operating the local government falls on other property owners. This means that the farmer along with others must pay higher personal taxes or be prepared to have less in the way of public service than he has had heretofore.

Forests and economic values. Many once-prosperous communities are now bankrupt, or have virtually ceased to exist, primarily because of the exhaustion of forest resources. Particularly is this true in certain re-

gions in the Lake States and the South. When forests and forest industries flourish, large numbers of men are employed and steady payrolls contribute to general prosperity.

The adoption of a system of permanent forest management to ensure a steady supply of raw materials to wood-using industries will sustain the prosperity of those communities that are now dependent on
the manufacture and distribution of forest products. Unless the practice of continuous forestry is adopted in those regions that still have

Figure 123. Pulpwood from an improvement cutting in a farm woods.
The farm forest can supply considerable amounts of wood for use and
sale. From this woods a large amount of aspen has been cut for pulpwood.
(C. H. Guise.)

ample supplies of standing timber, there will inevitably follow the old
story of exhaustion of supply, the sudden appearance and rapid increase of tax-delinquent lands, and finally the economic breakdown of
what were formerly flourishing communities. The renewal of forests
and their conservative management will again bring prosperous conditions to many localities where the forest stands are now exhausted.

For years prior to the Second World War a sustained flow of forest
supplies to the forest industries was maintained in the central European countries and in Scandinavia. There the forests and the products

that they provide have long been recognized as indispensable to national economy.

THE FOREST RESOURCES OF THE UNITED STATES

The original forests. At the time of the discovery of America virgin forests covered, as previously stated, an estimated 822,000,000 acres, approximately 43 per cent of the total land area of the present continental United States, excluding Alaska. Forests of vast extent covered almost solidly all portions of the country east of the prairies, and in addition blanketed the great territories dominated by the western mountains, the Rockies, the Sierra Nevadas, the Cascades, and the Coast Ranges. Over the prairies, plains, and many of the nonforested intermountain areas were heavy stands of grasses and other plants that later were to become extremely valuable as grazing resources.

Nowhere in the world has there been, within a comparable area, such a wealth of valuable tree species, from the standpoints of abundance, density of volume, economic utility, and ease of exploitation. Today only 45,000,000 acres of the original old-growth forest areas remain for commercial use, and of this 90 per cent are in the West. Vast forests, once thought to be inexhaustible, disappeared before the axe and saw. Great areas were destroyed by fire. It is appalling that the magnificent old-growth forests have been depleted so speedily and heavily.

The natural forest regions. Because of great variations in climate, soils, and physiography the original forests were of many diverse types, which were available to supply products to meet a wide variety of needs. Although the original forests have disappeared for the most part, except in the West, the second growth that has followed is, and will continue to be, characterized by the same kinds of trees that grew originally, though the proportions in which they now appear may differ widely from those in the first-growth stands.

The forest regions of the country have been classified in various ways, but for this discussion the divisions most recently adopted by the United States Forest Service in its 1945 reappraisal study are used.[3] This classification takes into account economic and industrial factors as well as those of climate, soil, and physiography. The kinds of trees

---

[3] *Gaging the Timber Resources of the United States* (U.S. Department of Agriculture, Forest Service, Reappraisal of the Forest Situation, Report 1; Washington, 1946). All statistics used in this and succeeding chapters are taken from the Reappraisal Reports, 1 to 6.

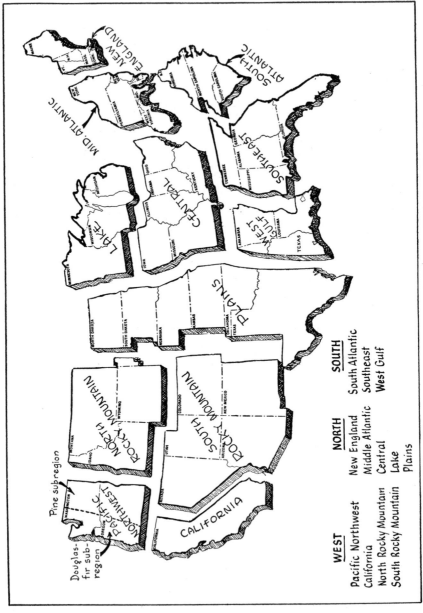

Figure 124. Forest regions of the United States. (U.S. Forest Service.)

WEST
Pacific Northwest
California
North Rocky Mountain
South Rocky Mountain

NORTH
New England
Middle Atlantic
Central
Lake
Plains

SOUTH
South Atlantic
Southeast
West Gulf

native to the various regions are many; in the present discussion only the more prominent ones will be mentioned. Certain species often occur in pure stands, but more often they associate themselves in distinctive groupings or mixtures, primarily as a result of climatic and soil conditions. The limits of the several regions are not sharply defined by the types of tree growth, and there are usually broad zones in which the key species of one region merge with those of the region adjoining.

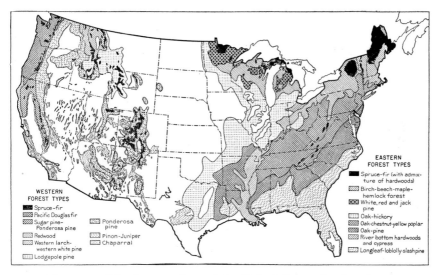

EASTERN
FOREST TYPES

■ Spruce-fir (with admixture of hardwoods)
Birch-beech-maple-hemlock forest
White, red and jack pine
Oak-hickory
Oak-chestnut-yellow poplar
Oak-pine
River bottom hardwoods and cypress
Longleaf-loblolly-slash pine

WESTERN
FOREST TYPES

■ Spruce-fir
Pacific Douglas fir
Sugar pine-Ponderosa pine
Redwood
Western larch-western white pine
Lodgepole pine
Ponderosa pine
Piñon-Juniper
Chaparral

Figure 125. The forest regions of the United States, showing the geographic location of the principal types of forest growth. (U.S. Forest Service.)

Twelve principal regions are recognized: the New England, Middle Atlantic, Lake, Central, and Plains regions, grouped together as the forest regions of the North; the South Atlantic, Southeast, and West Gulf, grouped together as the regions of the South; and the Pacific Northwest, with its two Douglas fir and pine subregions, California, North Rocky Mountain, and South Rocky Mountain regions, brought together as the forest regions of the West.

Reference to Fig. 124 will show the location and the states comprising each region.

The northern forest regions. The forests of the United States that lie east of the prairies are of many types, and they are extremely complex in their composition (Fig. 125). The forests of the East are characterized by both the evergreen and the deciduous species. Evergreen species, with such representatives as pine, spruce, fir, and hemlock, are frequently termed *conifers* or *softwoods*. Deciduous trees, of which maple, oak, ash, and gum are examples, are commonly spoken of as *broad-leaved trees* or *hardwoods*. The terms *softwoods* and *hardwoods* have established themselves by usage, though neither is strictly accu-

Figure 126. Forests of the Adirondacks—a small lake with Mount McIntyre in the background. Note the spruce and fir around the edges of the lake, the beech, birch, and maple forests at the lower elevations, and softwood forests of spruce and fir on the upper slopes. This section is famous for its recreational use. (U.S. Forest Service.)

rate as a descriptive term. In the colder regions to the north and in the warmer regions to the south, the forests are often composed almost solidly of evergreen species. In the great central regions the broad-leaved trees predominate. Many extensive overlapping zones occur where both evergreens and deciduous trees grow together in varying degrees of mixture.

In the northern forest regions spruce, fir, and pine predominate where the climate is most severe. These trees are found, often in pure stands, in the northern parts of Maine, New Hampshire, and Vermont, in the Adirondacks of New York, and in the northern parts of the three Lake States, Michigan, Wisconsin, and Minnesota (Fig. 126).

Special mention should be made of the superb and famous virgin forests of white and Norway pine that originally grew on great areas

Figure 127. White pine in northern Minnesota. Vast areas of white pine in the northern Lake States were the basis of a gigantic lumber industry. Since the 1860's this region has been important as a producer of lumber. (U.S. Forest Service.)

of sandy land in the Lake States (Fig. 127). These areas today, heavily cut and burned, now tend to come back to a growth of aspens and jack pine along with the more valuable white and Norway pines.

Where the climate is less severe, the evergreens give way to the northern hardwoods, beech, birch, and maple. Commonly mixed with these hardwoods are white pine and hemlock. Farther south where still milder climatic conditions prevail, central hardwood trees, including the oaks, ash, basswood, black cherry, elm, and others, enter into mixture with the northern hardwoods.

Where the forest growth extends into the central region (Ohio, Indiana, Illinois, Iowa, Missouri, and Kentucky) and the southern part of the Middle Atlantic region, the hardwoods predominate. Magnificent forests of the famous central hardwood species, including the oaks, ash, hickory, black walnut, black cherry, yellow poplar, beech, birch, maple, locust, basswood, and elm, once covered this region. In some sections were also evergreen species, including various pines, hemlock, and cedars. Chestnut was once present in abundance, but the chestnut bark disease has almost completely eliminated this valuable tree from all the forests in which it originally grew. The hardwoods were especially valuable for construction, interior finish, furniture, flooring, cabinet work, and a multitude of other uses where woods of special beauty and high quality were essential.

The original central forests covered, in large part, lands that were destined to become rich farming country; hence the forests gave way to farms, and today, in the agricultural regions, only cut-over remnants of these once grand forests remain as small parcels of wood attached to farms. Many of the richest farm lands in the nation are in the region that once grew the magnificent stands of central hardwood timber.

The southern forest regions. The South Atlantic, Southeast, and West Gulf regions, grouped together in the southern region, make up the largest area of commercially useful forest land in the United States. The area includes the states of Virginia, North Carolina, South Carolina, Georgia, Florida, Alabama, Mississippi, Tennessee, Louisiana, Arkansas, and eastern Texas.

A wide variety of physiographic features is included in the southern region. The flat, sandy coastal plains of the Atlantic and Gulf States are characterized by extensive forests of the southern yellow pines (longleaf, loblolly, and slash pines, Fig. 128). In the swamps, rich river bottoms, and deltas are found forests of cypress, gum, oaks, cottonwood, and sycamore. Successively inward from the flat coastal plains are the lands of higher elevation, the Piedmont Plateau and the Appalachian Mountain system. In the Piedmont country loblolly and shortleaf pines are mixed with the oaks, yellow poplar, ash, hickory, and other hardwoods. In the higher mountains the pines give way to the hardwoods (Fig. 129); at the highest elevations spruce and fir are abundant.

With a wealth of valuable tree species, easy conditions of logging, and nearness to centers of population, it was inevitable that the southern forests would be exploited extensively. Yet the climatic and soil conditions are so favorable for rapid tree growth and the species re-

Figure 128. Old-growth longleaf pine in Florida. Many millions of acres in the coastal plain areas of the southern states were covered with forests like these. Note the open forest and the flat land. This is one of our greatest forest regions. For over fifty years forests like these have been supplying great quantities of timber. These are the forests which supply most of our rosin and turpentine. (U.S. Forest Service.)

new themselves so vigorously that the South will always be one of the country's most important regions for timber production.

The western forest regions. The forests of the western part of the United States, in contrast to those of the East, are composed almost entirely of evergreen species. In general, these forests cover the rugged mountain ranges of the West, the Rocky Mountains, the Sierra Nevadas, the Cascades, the Pacific Coast Ranges, and their outlying spurs (Fig. 125, p. 213).

Figure 129. Mixed hardwood and spruce. A virgin forest in the mountains of West Virginia. (U.S. Forest Service.)

The North Rocky Mountain region, including the forests in Idaho, Montana, and Wyoming, is characterized by rough topography and high peaks, many of which extend far beyond the line of timber growth. At the highest elevations at which tree growth occurs are spruce and fir. Lower down are extensive forests in which western

Figure 130. Virgin white pine in northern Idaho. Idaho white pine is one of the country's most valuable timber trees. Many of these trees are from 4 to 5 feet in diameter and over 150 feet in height. (U.S. Forest Service.)

larch, Douglas fir, and western white pines are associated (Fig. 130). Where drier conditions prevail, ponderosa pine is abundant. On lands severely burned by forest fires, great areas are covered with forests of lodgepole pine. Of greatest commercial value are the ponderosa and western white pines, although lodgepole pine also is used extensively for certain purposes.

The forests of the South Rocky Mountain region are located in the

Figure 131. Old-growth Douglas fir in the Pacific Northwest. The giant firs in the Pacific Northwest forests make up 27 per cent of the remaining saw-timber supply. Many of these trees are 10 feet in diameter and 250 feet tall. These are typical of the world's heaviest stands of timber. (*The Timberman.*)

states of Colorado, Utah, Nevada, Arizona, and New Mexico. In general, these forests are found on the mountain slopes and great plateaus. In many parts of this region extremely dry conditions exist, and in such sections the tree growth gives way to low scrubby vegetation and to deserts.

As in the North, forests of spruce and fir occur at the higher elevations. Where climatic conditions are more favorable, extensive forests of the valuable ponderosa pine are found. Lodgepole pine is common in the northern sections. Where the moisture is insufficient for even the pines, open forests of piñon and juniper cover large areas. Vast stretches of the southern Rocky Mountain region are grazing land.

Although the forest industries have made heavy inroads and fire has been a serious problem in the forests of the Rockies, particularly in the northern sections, large virgin stands still exist. Extensive areas are now included in the national forests, and in the Rockies are some of the best-known national parks, including Glacier, Yellowstone, Rocky Mountain, and the Grand Canyon.

The Pacific Coast forest regions include the states of Washington, Oregon, and California. For magnificence in respect to size of trees and heavy stands per acre, these forests are unequaled anywhere in the world. The forests are found on both the east and west slopes of the several mountain ranges, the Sierra Nevadas and Cascades to the east, and farther west the Coast Ranges, which rise immediately from the Pacific Ocean. The Pacific Northwest region lies in Washington and Oregon. On the Coast Ranges and western slopes of the Cascades is the Douglas fir subregion, with its wonderful forests of Douglas fir, western red cedar, Sitka spruce, and western hemlock (Fig. 131). Individual trees are often from 6 to 10 feet in diameter and from 200 to 250 feet tall, and they form some of the heaviest timber stands in the world. In this respect they are equaled only by the coast redwoods of California. On the eastern slopes of the Cascades and in the other mountain regions of Oregon and Washington is the pine subregion. Here drier conditions prevail, and the forests are predominantly composed of ponderosa pine and Douglas fir.

The California forests are found in the Sierra Nevadas and the Coast Ranges. On the eastern slopes of the Sierras the forests run heavily to ponderosa pine. On the western slopes of the Sierras ponderosa pine is associated with sugar pine, incense cedar, and the various firs (Fig. 132). World-famous big trees (*Sequoia gigantea*) occur in the western Sierras in scattered groves. In a narrow strip bordering the Pacific Ocean along the northern half of California and extending into southern Oregon are the equally famous forests of redwoods

(*Sequoia sempervirens*). Some of these trees are over 300 feet in height (Fig. 133). The Coast Ranges of southern California bear forests of pines and other species, but to a large extent they are covered with a complex growth of shrubs that collectively are called *chaparral*. Chaparral is also found on the slopes of the southern Sierras.

Figure 132. Ponderosa pine and sugar pine. Forests of valuable ponderosa pine and sugar pine cover large areas on the western slopes of the Sierra Nevada Mountains. The tree in the foreground with the bark in large plates is ponderosa pine; the tree with heavily ridged bark is sugar pine. (*The Timberman.*)

Particularly valuable commercially among the Pacific Coast trees are Douglas fir, Sitka spruce, western red cedar, redwood, ponderosa pine, and sugar pine. In the Pacific Coast region also are located many national forests and some of the most famous national parks, including Rainier, Crater Lake, Yosemite, Mount Lassen Volcanic, and Sequoia.

Basic information needed. Forest conservation involves the initiation of effective policies that will control the wise use of existing forest resources and at the same time make long-range plans for the future. To formulate intelligently these policies requires basic information on the amounts of forest-growing land available, the volumes of timber remaining, the present condition of the country's forested areas, and the extent to which these forest lands are publicly and privately owned. Likewise essential are the best estimates that can be made of the country's future needs of forests and their products.

Only by having information on these points is it possible to approach intelligently the problems of present and future needs, and to make the plans that will enable both public and private forest-land owners to contribute most effectively to the solution of these intricate problems.

Forest-land areas of the United States. A detailed presentation of the location and extent of the forest-land areas of the United States is given in Table 9.

An examination of the figures in Table 9 shows that, of the total land area of the country, 624,000,000 acres or 32.8 per cent are forest land. Of this great area, 212,000,-000 acres or 34 per cent are in the northern forest regions; 187,000,000 acres or 30 per cent are in the southern forest regions; and 225,000,000 acres or 36 per cent are in the western forest regions. Throughout the North, South, and West the distribution is reasonably even, a fact of importance, signifying that each of the twelve regions grouped into the northern, southern, and western forests has great areas that can be used and developed for supplies of timber and the other essential services that forests can render.

Of the 461,000,000 acres of commercial land, 37 per cent are in the northern forest regions, 40 per cent are in the

Figure 133. Redwoods (*Sequoia sempervirens*). The redwoods exist in a narrow belt of forest on the Pacific Coast in the northern half of California and extend into southern Oregon. Some of these trees are over 300 feet tall. Redwood burls can be seen on one of the trees. The heavy growth of ferns is typical of redwood forests. Many forests like these have been saved through efforts of the Save-the-Redwoods League. (U.S. Forest Service.)

South, and 23 per cent are in the West. As in the case of the total forest-land areas, the distribution of the commercial areas is reasonably even, and every section of the country has ample land for its future forests. One feature of interest is the percentage of commercial land found in those regions that have the heaviest stands of timber remaining in this country. The Pacific Northwest region includes only 10 per cent, California 4.4 per cent, and the north Rocky Mountains 6.3 per cent.

TABLE 9. FOREST LAND AREAS OF THE UNITED STATES BY REGION

Region	Total land area	Forest land				
		Total	Com-mercial	Noncommercial		
				Total	With-drawn	Other values
	thousand acres	*thousand acres*	*thousand acres*	*thousand acres*	*thousand acres*	*thousand acres*
New England	40,451	31,092	30,851	241	165	76
Middle Atlantic	80,369	44,214	41,586	2,628	2,489	139
Lake	122,718	55,700	50,345	5,355	1,138	4,217
Central	191,129	44,919	44,213	706	432	274
Plains	380,016	35,828	3,326	32,502	54	32,448
North	821,683	211,753	170,321	41,432	4,278	37,154
South Atlantic	76,566	43,843	43,923	920	639	281
Southeast	162,074	91,842	89,390	2,452	671	1,781
West Gulf	87,403	51,119	50,953	166	37	129
South	326,043	186,804	183,266	3,538	1,347	2,191
Pacific Northwest Douglas fir subregion	35,119	29,145	26,027	3,118	1,032	2,086
Pine subregion	69,410	24,710	20,177	4,533	472	4,061
Total	104,529	53,855	46,204	7,651	1,504	6,147
California	100,354	45,515	16,405	29,110	705	28,405
North Rocky Mountain	212,782	53,246	29,066	24,180	2,876	21,304
South Rocky Mountain	339,971	72,655	15,782	56,873	1,883	54,990
West	757,636	225,271	107,457	117,814	6,968	110,846
All regions	1,905,362	623,828 100%	461,044 73.9%	162,784 26.1%	12,593 2.0%	150,191 24.1%

Noncommercial forest lands aggregate 163,000,000 acres, or 26 per cent of the total forest area. Some 12,000,000 acres bear commercially valuable timber, but these lands have been withdrawn from timber use and placed in parks, refuges, and preserves of various types; the remainder, 151,000,000 acres, includes land of low productivity, extreme inaccessibility, and general unsuitability to the growing of timber crops.

Of the noncommercial forest lands, 72 per cent lie in the forest regions of the West, 26 per cent in the regions of the North, and only 2 per cent in the regions of the South. Actually the Plains region, included in the North, makes up 20 per cent of the total. Thus the Plains, Rocky Mountain, and Pacific Coast forest regions include 92 per cent of all the noncommercial forest land.

In the discussions that follow, primary attention will be given to the commercial forest lands, since it is on these that forest management for timber production will be developed. Nevertheless the noncommercial forest lands are of the greatest importance in an integrated plan of natural resource conservation. These lands must be protected and given the attention that is essential to maintaining them so that they will be of maximum benefit.

Conditions of forest growth. In dealing with the commercial forest lands, five principal classes of cover or condition are recognized. The virgin forests are those that are scarcely touched by axe or saw. Next are the areas formerly cut over but now bearing a second growth of trees of saw-timber size. In the third class are the pole-timber areas, which are characterized by timber too small for saw-log operations but large enough for cordwood. Fourth are the more recently cut-over lands that bear only young seedling and sapling growth, but which in future years, if protected, will grow into new stands of larger trees. And fifth are the areas that have been cut and burned so severely that they are either denuded of forest growth, or covered with an entirely inadequate stand of young seedlings or sprouts.

In Table 10 the area of commercial forest land of the United States is classified by the condition of the forest growth in each region. For the entire country, 9.6 per cent of the area is still covered with old growth and 34.9 per cent with second growth of saw-timber size; 44.5 per cent bears forests that can now produce saw logs. The areas covered with pole-sized trees make up 20.6 per cent of the total, the seedling and sapling areas 18.6 per cent, and the poorly stocked and denuded areas 16.3 per cent. All these figures are significant, but the last figure particularly so, for it indicates that one-sixth of the commercial forest-land area of the entire United States is little more than idle and waste land.

Of the areas of virgin timber 42 per cent are in the Pacific Northwest, 19 per cent in California, 16 per cent in the northern Rocky Mountains, and 16 per cent in the southern Rocky Mountains. In all, 93 per cent of the areas containing virgin timber are in the four western forest regions.

Of all lands bearing saw timber, 61 per cent are found in the South. In this region climatic and soil conditions are favorable and tree growth is rapid, with the result that large areas of second growth are now attaining saw-timber size. The pole-timber areas are well distributed, as are those with a sapling and seedling growth.

Of the areas that are not restocking or at best have an inadequate cover of young trees, 42 per cent are in the North, 43 per cent in the South, and 15 per cent in the West. Attention is called to the large areas of this class in the Lake region and in the Southeast. In the Lake region is 18 per cent of this land and in the Southeast 28 per cent. While these two regions contain 46 per cent of the poorly stocked and denuded land, the other regions each include areas that are far too large. Some way must be found to make these lands produce.

Volumes of timber. The total stand of saw timber in the United States is estimated to be 1,600,000,000,000 board feet.[4] Of this vast amount, 81 per cent is softwood timber and 19 per cent hardwood. Western species, almost entirely softwoods, make up 65 per cent of the total, eastern softwoods 16 per cent, and eastern hardwoods 19 per cent.

Of the entire stand of saw timber, 40 per cent is in the Pacific Northwest, 21 per cent in the South, and 14 per cent in California. Although the Pacific Northwest has 40 per cent of the nation's supply, the forest land involved makes up only 10 per cent of the total area of commercial land. What is even more striking is the fact that the Douglas fir subregion makes up only 6 per cent of the land area but contains 31 per cent of the volume of the saw-timber stands of the country. Figures of this type reveal clearly the density of the forests of the West Coast.

Other facts are important. Virgin timber in the amount of 840,000,-000,000 board feet makes up 52.5 per cent of the country's present supply of saw timber. Of the 840,000,000,000 board feet, 97 per cent is in the West, 513,000,000,000 feet or 61 per cent being in the Pacific

---

[4] The board foot is the most common unit of measuring forest products. A board foot is a unit one foot square and one inch thick. Lumber and standing timber are bought, sold, and measured on the basis of thousands of board feet.

TABLE 10. TOTAL COMMERCIAL FOREST AREA OF THE UNITED STATES BY CONDITIONS OF GROWTH AND BY REGION

Region	Total		Saw-timber area			Pole-timber area	Seedling and sapling area	Poorly stocked seedling and sapling, and denuded area
	thousand acres	per cent	Total	Virgin growth	Second growth			
			thousand acres	thousand acres	thousand acres	thousand acres	thousand acres	thousand acres
New England	30,851	6.69	13,895	188	13,707	8,116	5,503	3,337
Middle Atlantic	41,586	9.02	14,813	161	14,652	12,714	8,200	5,859
Lake	50,345	10.92	6,470	1,510	4,960	9,502	20,480	13,890
Central	44,213	9.59	11,936	230	11,706	10,049	14,642	7,586
Plains	3,326	.72	1,082	200	882	1,061	545	638
North	170,321	36.94	48,196	2,289	45,907	41,445	49,370	31,310
South Atlantic	42,923	9.31	22,854		22,854	7,195	9,155	3,719
Southeast	89,390	19.39	43,537	436	43,101	15,869	8,992	20,992
West Gulf	50,953	11.05	31,986	537	31,449	6,258	4,726	7,983
South	183,266	39.75	98,377	973	97,404	29,322	22,873	32,694
Pacific Northwest Douglas fir subregion	26,027	5.64	13,158	9,348	3,810	4,394	3,040	5,435
Pine subregion	20,177	4.38	13,140	9,171	3,969	3,107	3,115	815
Total	46,204	10.02	26,298	18,519	7,779	7,501	6,155	6,250
California	16,405	3.56	10,897	8,400	2,497	3,398	53	2,057
North Rocky Mountain	29,066	6.31	11,991	7,292	4,699	9,913	5,524	1,638
South Rocky Mountain	15,782	3.42	9,417	7,145	2,272	3,454	1,577	1,354
West	107,457	23.31	58,603	41,356	17,247	24,246	13,309	11,299
All regions	461,044 100%	100.00	205,176 44.5%	44,618 9.6%	160,558 34.9%	95,013 20.6%	85,552 18.6%	75,303 16.3%

Northwest, 180,000,000,000 feet or 22 per cent in the California forests, and 113,000,000,000 feet or 14 per cent in the Rocky Mountains. Of second-growth saw timber, which aggregates 760,000,000,000 board feet or 47.5 per cent of the total existing supply, the South leads with 326,000,000,000 feet or 43 per cent. The West is second with 235,000,000 or 31 per cent, and the North is third with 199,000,000,000 board feet or 26 per cent.

The softwoods aggregate 1,296,000,000,000 board feet and 80 per cent is in the West. One-half of the latter is in the Douglas fir subregion. Of all hardwoods, which amount to 304,000,000,000 board feet, 51 per cent is in the North, 47 per cent is in the South, and only 2 per cent is in the West.

The major part of the country's existing supplies of saw timber consists of a relatively small number of species. Ten groups of trees make up over 80 per cent of the entire volume. These are shown in the following tabulation:

Species	Per cent of volume	Species	Per cent of volume
Douglas fir	27	Beech, birch, maple	4.2
Ponderosa pine	12	Sugar and western white	
Southern yellow pine	12	pines	2.5
True firs	7	Western spruce	2.2
Western hemlock	6.1	Redwood	2.4
Oaks	6.3	Others	18.3
			100.0

The miscellaneous species that account for 18.3 per cent are principally western larch, lodgepole pine, eastern spruce and fir, eastern white pine, Norway pine, hemlock, cypress, red gum, tupelo, yellow poplar, cottonwood, and aspen.

The ownership of forest lands. Some of the most complex problems of forest conservation have their origin in the status of land ownership. Basically, two broad classes of forest-land ownership exist, public and private. Publicly owned lands include, first, those in the possession of the federal government, including the national forests, grazing districts, Indian reservations, national parks and monuments, and other lands; second, those of the individual states; and, third, those of the counties, municipalities, and other smaller governmental units. In private ownership are, first, the lands of the lumber companies, pulp and paper companies, and other industrial units, and, second, those woodlands that are parts of farms. The former are termed *industrially owned forests,* and the latter *farm woodlands.*

Fundamentally, the rate at which the depletion of the country's existing timber supplies will take place and the extent to which the practice of forest management will develop depends upon the type of ownership by which the nation's forest lands are held.

The privately owned industrial forests must be operated to produce income. The financial structure and obligations of an industry, the amounts of land and timber that it owns, and the size of plant that must be operated in order to remain solvent are factors that the management of an industry must weigh carefully if it is to embark successfully on a long-time forestry program. In many instances private owners are in positions where they must, in order to sustain their present investments, cut more heavily than would in theory be desirable from the standpoint of good forest management. Particularly disturbing from the standpoint of forest conservation is the lack of interest in forestry on the part of many of the private owners of small and medium-sized forest properties. Some industrial owners manage their lands admirably, others do what is economically possible, and still others have no interest in any policy other than that of early liquidation.

Farm woodlands are in an entirely different category. Whereas the industrial forest is a unit of property owned and operated for the sole purpose of cutting and selling timber for profit, the farm woods is only one part, usually a small one, of an operating farm. The farm woods cannot be treated as an independent unit, but instead must of necessity be handled as one phase of an integrated farm enterprise.

This aspect has distinct advantages. As a part of the farm unit the woods can be operated at a time when other farm duties are not pressing; it can supply fuel and materials for the farm as well as material for sale. Yet these woods are small and obviously will continue to be treated in diverse ways to meet the needs of the individual farms. Farm woods cannot be subjected to centralized control or to any generalized plan of management. Each is an individual case. Farm woods in the main have received little intelligent care. On the contrary most of them have had little but abuse. Overcutting, grazing, and burning have been the rule—forms of abuse that have been due either to ignorance of the damage being done or to sheer inertia and lack of interest on the part of the owner.

Forests in public ownership need not measure up to a balance-sheet type of accounting, as is the case with the industrially owned lands. Hence the pressure to cut heavily is not so great. Other uses and values can be given full recognition, and a more conservative form of management can be practiced.

The areas of commercial and noncommercial forest lands in various forms of ownership are shown in summary in Table 11. Statistics show-

TABLE 11. OWNERSHIP OF THE COMMERCIAL AND NONCOMMERCIAL FOREST LANDS OF THE UNITED STATES EXCLUSIVE OF ALASKA

Class of ownership	Total	Commercial	Non-commercial
		million acres	
Private			
Farm woodland	184.5	139.0	45.5
Industrial and other	224.6	205.9	18.7
Total	409.1	344.9	64.2
Public			
Community	10.4	9.2	1.2
State	27.4	17.9	9.5
Indian reservations	16.4	6.6	9.8
Grazing districts	17.0	1.0	16.0
National forests	123.2	73.6	49.6
Other federal	20.3	7.8	12.5
Total	214.7	116.1	98.6
All classes	623.8	461.0	162.8

ing for each of the forest regions the commercial forest-land areas, classified by major forms of ownership, are presented in Table 12.

Four hundred and nine million acres or 66 per cent of the total 624,000,000 acres of forest land are privately owned; 177,000,000 acres, 28 per cent, are federally owned; and 38,000,000 acres, 6 per cent, are in the ownership of states, counties, and communities. Of the commercial forest lands aggregating 461,000,000 acres, private ownership accounts for 345,000,000 acres, 75 per cent; federal ownership for 89,000,000 acres, 19 per cent; and state and local ownership for 27,000,000 acres, 6 per cent. Of the 163,000,000 acres of noncom-

TABLE 12. OWNERSHIP OF COMMERCIAL FOREST LAND OF THE UNITED STATES, BY REGION *

Region	All ownerships	Federally owned or managed			State, county, and municipal	Private		
		Total	National forest	Other		Total	Farm	Industrial and other
	thousand acres	thousand acres	thousand acres	thousand acres	thousand acres	thousand acres	thousand acres	thousand acres
New England	30,851	891	822	69	666	29,294	6,477	22,817
Middle Atlantic	41,586	1,476	1,265	211	3,613	36,497	11,854	24,643
Lake	50,345	6,495	5,455	1,040	14,805	29,045	13,930	15,115
Central	44,213	2,117	1,951	166	326	41,770	25,789	15,981
Plains	3,326	332	30	302	4	2,990	2,960	30
North	170,321	11,311	9,523	1,788	19,414	139,596	61,010	78,586
South Atlantic	42,923	3,485	2,775	710	536	38,902	23,377	15,525
Southeast	89,390	5,909	3,802	2,107	1,216	82,265	33,134	49,131
West Gulf	50,953	4,684	3,561	1,123	408	45,861	12,549	33,312
South	183,266	14,078	10,138	3,940	2,160	167,028	69,060	97,968
Pacific Northwest								
Douglas fir subregion	26,027	10,201	7,682	2,519	2,616	13,210	1,951	11,259
Pine subregion	20,177	12,811	9,659	3,152	819	6,547	1,383	5,164
Total	46,204	23,012	17,341	5,671	3,435	19,757	3,334	16,423
California	16,405	8,099	7,684	415	23	8,283	1,309	6,974
North Rocky Mountain	29,066	20,012	18,061	1,951	1,702	7,352	2,847	4,505
South Rocky Mountain	15,782	12,445	10,765	1,680	380	2,957	1,498	1,459
West	107,457	63,568	53,851	9,717	5,540	38,349	8,988	29,361
All regions	461,044 100%	88,957 19%	73,512 16%	15,445 3%	27,114 6%	344,973 75%	139,058 30%	205,915 45%

* Prepared by the Forest Service, U.S. Department of Agriculture. Includes land capable of producing timber of commercial quantity and quality, and available now or prospectively, for commercial use. Status beginning of 1945.

mercial forest land, private ownership includes 64,000,000 acres, 39 per cent; federally owned lands cover 88,000,000 acres, 54 per cent; and state and local lands make up 11,000,000 acres, 7 per cent.

Of all forest lands in private ownership, 84 per cent are commercial in type; of those in state and local ownership, 70 per cent are commercial; and in federal ownership only 50 per cent of the lands fall in this category.

Federal ownership. Federally owned forest lands aggregate 177,000,-000 acres. Most of these lands are in the West, being located in the regions dominated by the great mountain chains and the intermountain regions. Of this total area, more than 123,000,000 acres, 70 per cent, are included in the national forests. The balance is found in the Indian reservations, grazing districts, national parks, and other lands in various forms of federal ownership.

As shown in Table 12, almost 89,000,000 acres are classified as commercial forest land. Of this area, 72 per cent is in the West. These federal lands bear 39 per cent of the country's existing supply of saw timber, almost all of it being in the West. The federally owned lands in the eastern United States have, for the most part, been cut over.

Of the federally owned commercial forest lands, 83 per cent are included in the national forests. These national forests include within their boundaries 74,000,000 acres of timberland, occupy 16 per cent of the nation's commercial forest-land area, and contain 32 per cent of its existing supply of saw timber.

Commercial forest lands included within the Indian reservations, grazing districts, and other areas in federal ownership aggregate more than 15,000,000 acres. They comprise only 3 per cent of all commercial timberland areas, and bear only 7 per cent of the country's total volume of standing saw timber.

The major parts of the forest lands in both the Indian reservations and the grazing districts are classified as noncommercial. All of the timberland in the national parks is noncommercial since the forests are not available for exploitation.

State, county and municipal ownership. State forests and parks amount to 27,000,000 acres, of which 18,000,000 are commercial forest land. County and other local units own 10,000,000 acres, of which almost all is commercial land. Together the state and local forest lands include 6 per cent of the country's total forest-land area. Of these lands

80 per cent are in the eastern United States, with 55 per cent being found in the Lake region. This relationship is entirely different from that existing with the federally owned lands, of which 72 per cent are located in the West and only 28 per cent in the East.

State and county forest lands bear only 4 per cent of the country's supply of saw timber.

Privately owned forests. Three hundred and forty-five million acres, or three-fourths of the total commercial forest land, are privately owned. These lands contain almost three-fifths of the remaining supply of saw timber and provide from 80 to 90 per cent of the current annual timber cut. They include the best and most accessible forest land, and it is estimated that they represent 90 per cent of the potential timber-growing capacity of the entire country. With 64,000,000 acres of noncommercial land also privately owned, these lands in total cover nearly two-thirds of the country's watersheds. Because of the vast areas included, the types of cutting practices in the past, the conditions of the lands today, and the limited extent to which forestry is practiced on them at present, the lands in private ownership and their future management constitute the crux of the nation's forestry problem. This is true of the areas in industrial ownership and in farm woodlands.

INDUSTRIAL OWNERSHIP. The industrially owned commercial forest lands total 206,000,000 acres, 45 per cent of the nation's commercial forest land area. Of these 206,000,000 acres, 48 per cent are in the South, 38 per cent in the North, and 14 per cent in the West.

Industrial holdings account for 42 per cent of the country's remaining supply of saw timber, a total of 670,000,000,000 board feet. More than half of this timber, 54 per cent, is in the West, 28 per cent is in the South, and 18 per cent is in the North. Of special interest are the industrial holdings in the Pacific Northwest. In this area industrial holdings include 8 per cent of the country's total forest-land area and 33 per cent of its standing saw timber.

FARM WOODLANDS. Woodlands that are integral parts of farms total some 185,000,000 acres, of which 139,000,000 are classed as commercial forest land. This is a great area, making up 30 per cent of the country's commercial forest lands. Almost 94 per cent lies east of the Plains region. These woodlands are scattered about on more than 3,000,000 farms.

The amount of saw timber in farm woodlands is not inconsiderable,

15 per cent of the country's entire supply being found there. Almost 55 per cent of this timber is in the South, 31 per cent is in the North, and 14 per cent is in the West.

The existing volumes of standing saw timber, classified by major regions and principal forms of ownership, are presented in Table 13.

TABLE 13. OWNERSHIP OF SAW TIMBER IN THE UNITED STATES, 1945

Class of ownership	North	South	West	United States
	billion board feet			
Farm	76	134	34	244
Other private	124	183	363	670
All private	200	317	397	914
National forest	8	14	496	518
Other federal	2	4	98	104
State and local	10	3	52	65
All public	20	21	646	687
All owners	220	338	1,043	1,601

A further breakdown of the pattern of forest-land ownership emphasizes a problem that will be extremely difficult of solution. The major part of the privately owned holdings is in small parcels, including not only farm woods but individual forest properties of fewer than 5,000 acres each. Such properties make up 57 per cent of the entire area of commercial forest land in the country and 76 per cent of the privately owned commercial forest lands. Medium-sized, privately owned properties, from 5,000 to 50,000 acres, amount to 33,000,000 acres or 7 per cent of the total commercial forest area; large holdings, over 50,000 acres in extent, total 51,000,000 acres or 11 per cent of the commercial forest lands (Table 15, p. 269).

Studies show that the types of cutting practices, while far from satisfactory on most lands in private ownership and on many of those in public ownership, are particularly bad on the smaller privately owned areas. Because of their vast extent and the over-all difficulties in establishing long-time programs of sound forest management on them, these lands cause some of the most serious of all problems in forest-land management.

CHAPTER VII

The Development and Status of Forest Conservation

FOR more than three centuries forest industries operated at the nation's frontiers and served an ever-growing and migrating population. Immense quantities of timber were cut and used. Vast amounts were needlessly wasted and destroyed. In the wake of the industries, as they shifted from one section to another, there remained all too often a desolate land, ruined by logging and fire. A pioneer industry in a pioneer country gave little heed to conserving the forests for future generations. The problems of conservation were created by the practices of the past.

The ways in which the major part of the forest lands of the country passed into private ownership are discussed in Chapter I. Also presented in that chapter are the major steps in the development of the conservation movement in this country. This chapter is a brief account of the manner in which the forests have been used and destroyed, a review of the history of the forest conservation movement, and a summary of its progress.

UTILIZATION AND THE FOREST INDUSTRIES

The forest industries in the East. The utilization of the country's forests began more than three hundred years ago. The start naturally took place in New England, one of the early centers of colonization. Moreover, the forests there were characterized by great quantities of valuable white pine, a tree that was a dominating influence in the industry for more than two centuries.

The first timbers, planks, and boards were hewed by hand. Yet as early as 1625 a sawmill was reported at Jamestown, Virginia. Another mill was built in 1631 at Berwick, Maine. Other mills followed in rapid succession in various parts of the eastern seaboard. All of these early mills were small, crude, and driven by natural water power.

An export trade in masts, spars, cooperage stock, shingles, and clapboards developed with England almost immediately. Particularly valuable for export and shipbuilding were sawed lumber and large timbers, also the naval stores from the southern forests. With forest supplies accessible and abundant, the shipbuilding industry took root, and before the end of the seventeenth century was in a flourishing condition. As the population increased, the demands on the forest became greater. Industries that drew upon the forests for their raw material naturally brought about their rapid exploitation, but at the same time contributed greatly to the prosperity of many communities. The New England States held the lead as a lumber-producing region until 1840.

During this period the lumber industry was developing in other sections of the country. Shipyards and sawmills appeared all along the Atlantic Coast from Maine to Virginia. The forests of New York and of other eastern states were being cut in order to supply lumber at low prices to an expanding population. White pine was still the principal commercial timber, though other valuable trees were cut in large numbers for local use and long-distance shipment. The water-driven mill was being replaced by the mill powered with steam, and by 1850 high-speed circular saws were producing in single mills more than 100,000 board feet daily. Every effort was made to speed up production of both logs and lumber.

As time went on, the leading role in the production of lumber passed from Maine, and New England generally, to New York and, later, to other states. The industry grew rapidly in all parts of the United States. In 1860 the lead went to Pennsylvania, and ten years later to the Lake States. Michigan was the leading lumber-producing state from the Civil War period to 1890, Wisconsin from 1890 to 1904. The high point in production of white pine and other associated species was reached in 1892, when 9,000,000,000 board feet were produced. Lumbering had reached gigantic proportions. The West was being settled, railroad expansion was making it possible to transport forest products in large amounts at low cost, and the demands for construction materials were ever on the increase. After 1892 the amounts cut in the Lake States region started to decline, and by 1900 the lead shifted to the South. Extensive operations in forests of southern yellow pine and other valuable trees had started in the eighteen seventies and gradually increased until they reached their peak in 1909, when 17,000,000,000 board feet were produced. Production has declined appreciably since 1909, but the South still continues as one of the most active forest regions.

Figure 134. Starting the undercut on a large western yellow pine with an electric saw. Saws powered by electricity or gasoline motors are used extensively in felling trees and in making logs. (U.S. Forest Service.)

The forest industries in the West. The lumber industry on the Pacific Coast started in a small way more than a century ago, but it was not until 1850 that lumber in large quantities began to be produced from steam-powered mills. With large supplies of accessible timber, the industry grew rapidly and by the turn of the century was producing enormous amounts of lumber, timbers, and other products for domestic consumption and for export to all parts of the world. Great mills, some of which could saw as many as a million board feet in a day, were established throughout the coast and in the mountain forests to the west, wherever dense stands of timber were available to provide the vast quantities of logs required. The largest concentration of mills was in the Douglas fir region. Although the Rocky Mountain forests, particularly in the North, produced large quantities of lumber for local use and for shipment to other sections of the United States, the total amounts cut were not comparable to the volumes coming from the mills in Washington, Oregon, and California.

In 1905 Washington became the leading state in the production of

Figure 135. Logged-over Douglas fir. The areas of heavy timber are completely cut. Nothing remains except slash and other debris. Unless protected, such areas are dangerous fire traps. (C. H. Guise.)

lumber, but it was not until 1926 that the West as a whole took the lead from the South. Fir, spruce, cedar, redwood, sugar pine, ponderosa pine, and other western species have been, and still are being (Fig. 134), logged and sawed in great quantities.

The West Coast forests are composed of the largest trees that grow in the United States. Consequently special methods of logging and powerful types of equipment are required to handle the logs. Since great areas of forest must be cut to keep the mills supplied with logs, and because logging in the past was of a highly destructive nature, regions of wide extent have been cut over in a manner that has left little tree growth (Figs. 135, 136). A great reservoir of timber remains in the western forests, but heavy demands are made upon it by great industrial activity.

The economic importance of the forest industries. Lumbering is the oldest of the great American industries. From a modest start it grew gradually for two centuries, and then developed rapidly into gigantic proportions. In 1907 the nation's output was 47,000,000,000 board feet of lumber from some 50,000 mills. This was the peak year of lumber production in the United States.

Figure 136. Logging in the redwoods. Heavy machinery, hoists, and cables are required for handling the large Pacific Coast timbers. When these areas are logged over in this way, little, if any, live timber is left standing. (C. H. Guise.)

During the decade 1904–1913 the annual production of lumber never fell below 42,000,000,000 board feet. After 1913 the figures fluctuated irregularly, but the trend was generally downward, though in the middle 1920's the cut went up to 40,000,000,000 feet. During the depression year of 1932 production fell to 10,000,000,000 feet, then gradually increased during the prewar years, and during the war years rose to 35,000,000,000 board feet annually. More lumber would have been cut had labor and supplies been available. In 1945 production declined to 27,500,000,000 feet. Contingent on the availability of labor and accessible timber, the annual production during the postwar years will be high. The amounts to be produced, once postwar needs are met, are then a matter of conjecture. However, the public will probably demand all that the dwindling forest resources can possibly supply.

In all sections of the country the forest industries created small settlements and were instrumental in developing many of them into towns and cities. In each principal forest region these industries developed, reached a peak, and, as the supply of raw material gave out, declined. Progressively they shifted from one region to another, tapping new supplies of timber and serving the changing centers of population.

The forest industries have left behind them in the shape of wrecked lands and ghost towns much that is to be deplored, but on the other side of the ledger is the fact that in many places they have been the backbone of industrial development from pioneer times to the present. Forests contribute to prosperity since they provide directly and indirectly large sums of money that bring in taxes to the government, freight revenue to the railroads, wages and salaries to thousands of workers, and income to businessmen for large amounts of industrial supplies.

Much of the business done by bankers, merchants, professional workers, and farmers is possible because of the distribution and turnover of income derived in the first place from the manufacture and distribution of material cut from the forest. Wherever forest industries operate, they support, to a large degree, the economic and social life of the region. If the forest industries are maintained, or if they are renewed where they have for the most part disappeared, they will create economic benefits of major importance, both to communities and to entire regions.

DESTRUCTION AND DEPLETION

Logging and forest destruction. The cutting of the country's virgin forests was inevitable and necessary. But it is undeniable that incredible amounts of valuable forest growth were destroyed as the forest industries operated with almost reckless abandon. Whether the utilization of the forests could have proceeded without their destruction in a pioneer country in which the supplies were thought to be inexhaustible, the competition severe, and the margin of operating profit small is extremely doubtful. In the light of present-day knowledge of the damage done, it is easy to see how beneficial more conservative practices would have been. But the lumberman operated under conditions that existed then, and under conditions of fact and not theory. The concept of conservation was scarcely formulated in those times. Even if the need for more conservative operation of timberlands had been appreciated, such operation could not have been undertaken in view of the abundant supply and the heavy demands. The public was uninformed and indifferent. It wanted wood, and the lumberman provided it.

Figure 137. The result of a severe crown fire. Formerly a dense softwood forest, this area is now completely ruined because of destructive crown fires. Areas like this are subject to soil erosion and may never be productive again. (U.S. Forest Service.)

The fact does remain, however, that the lands were badly handled, and vast quantities of forests were destructively logged and severely burned (Fig. 137). The amount of waste that took place, as judged by present-day standards, is almost incredible. Business competition was severe, and in mixed stands only the then currently valuable species were cut. The operations dealt with the present. Seldom, if ever, was care taken to provide for a second stand or to protect the trees left standing. Slash and other logging wastes were everywhere, setting the scenes for the destructive fires that were certain to follow.

From every standpoint deplorable conditions have followed the reckless cutting of the forests, and the industries involved were directly responsible for creating them. Whether the owners of these industries should be censured, working under the conditions that then prevailed, is another matter. Nevertheless, the forest industries have destroyed untold amounts of forest, caused the deterioration of vast areas of land, and created the forest-land problems that are among the most baffling in forest conservation.

Forest fires and destruction. First among all agencies destructive to the forest is fire. Had it not been for the fires that invariably followed the first logging operations, destructive as they in themselves were, the majority of the cut-over lands would now be bearing valuable second-growth stands, many of which would be ready for a second cutting.

Forest fires destroy or damage almost irreparably mature timber, stands of second growth, the young cover of seedlings and sprouts, and the soil that supports tree growth. A severe fire burns the rich organic content of surface soil and in a few hours can destroy the soils that were built during centuries of time. There are countless examples of soils so badly damaged that they are incapable of growing a second crop of timber. Burned-over forests scar what would otherwise be an attractive landscape; they destroy the value of property for recreational use and bring about the loss of great numbers of wildlife that depend on the forest for shelter and food. The beneficial value of forests in preventing the eroding of surface soil and in regulating stream flow is lost (Fig. 138). Once trees are killed or injured by fire, it is a simple matter for destructive insects and fungous diseases to gain a foothold and, in a few years thereafter, ruin whatever value the remaining timber may have had for commercial use.

From an economic standpoint forest fires are ruinous because they destroy timber, the utilization of which would provide income to wage earners and many others, taxes to communities, and profits to business and industry. There are tragic examples, all too numerous, of severe fires that have completely wiped out villages and towns, and resulted in a heavy loss of human life.

Kinds and causes of fires. Forest fires are of several types. First and most spectacular are the crown fires that occur in coniferous forests. When fires of this kind start, they spread in a wall of flame with almost unbelievable speed, killing and destroying everything in their path (Figs. 139, 140). The country's great forest fires, which have been so destructive of human life as well as of timber and other resources, were invariably those which, with a strong wind back of them, swept through the crowns of thousands of acres of evergreen forests.

Many crown fires covering great areas have been extremely destructive in both human life and property. Records show that in the Miramichi fire of 1825 in Maine, 3,000,000 acres were burned and 160 people killed. Twenty years later occurred the Yaquina fire in Oregon

Figure 138. Timber loss and watershed destruction—Cabinet National Forest, Idaho. Severe forest fires destroy timber, denude mountain slopes, and ruin watersheds. The area pictured above was burned in 1910 and, after 30 years, is still without a forest cover. Without a protective forest, runoff is rapid, surface soil is washed away, bridges are destroyed, and stream channels are filled with silt and gravel. (U.S. Forest Service.)

destroying 500,000 acres of West Coast forest, and in 1853 the Nestucca fire, also in Oregon, which burned over 320,000 acres. The historic Peshtigo fire in Wisconsin took place in 1871; in it 1,500 people perished and 1,280,000 acres of forest were destroyed. Also famous in the Lake States is the Hinckley fire of 1894, which laid waste to millions of acres, destroyed 12 towns, and brought about the death of 418 people. In 1903 severe fires in the Adirondack forests covered 450,000 acres. The severe fires of 1910 covered millions of acres in the Lake States northern Rockies, and the Pacific Northwest. In the Cloquet fire of northern Minnesota in 1918, a large town was destroyed, and damage done to the extent of $30,000,000, though the loss of life was held to seven. The most recent of the bad fires are the Tillamook burns in Oregon. The first of these occurred in 1933, covered an area of 245,000 acres, and destroyed in eleven days enough timber to equal the entire timber cut of the United States for that year. This same area burned again in 1939. And in the summer of 1945 it was on fire again.

The list of the big fires could be expanded to great length, but the few examples given indicate that the severe crown fires are still taking place. The problem of preventing and controlling them is far from solution. The destruction and loss have been so great that they can scarcely be evaluated.

Second and most common of all are the surface fires that burn on the top of the soil and destroy the leaf litter, shrubs, young trees, and other surface vegetation. Almost all forest fires start as surface fires. They are not as spectacular as crown fires, and for this reason are regarded without

Figure 139. A crown fire and forest destruction—Flathead National Forest, Montana. Crown fires that gain headway are extremely difficult to control; they usually cover great areas and ruin irreparably the lands they burn. (U.S. Forest Service.)

concern by many who live in the forested regions. Actually the damage done by surface fires is enormous. In some cases the flames spread to tree crowns and start crown fires. But even as surface fires they destroy the young growth, which must be the basis for a new crop of larger trees. Also, they damage the larger trees, enable insects and diseases to gain their footholds, and greatly impair the fertility of the soil.

Third and less common are ground fires. These fires burn through the soil, usually at a slow rate, and destroy completely all organic matter in the soil, along with the valuable decayed humus and leaf mold on top of it (Fig. 141). It is difficult to extinguish ground fires, and they usually burn for long periods.

The majority of forest fires are caused by men and can be prevented. Studies of forest fires and their causes, for the United States as a whole, show that the average annual number of fires is 175,000 and

Figure 140. The interior of a forest after a severe crown fire. Almost every tree in the path of the flames has been killed. Many trees have been entirely consumed. Formerly a valuable property, it is now waste land only. (U.S. Forest Service.)

the annual area burned is over 25,000,000 acres. When the causes are broken down into percentages, it is found that incendiarism accounts for 25 per cent; smokers, 24 per cent; debris burning, 14 per cent; miscellaneous causes, 9 per cent; lightning, 9 per cent; unknown causes, 7 per cent; campers, 6 per cent; railroads, 4 per cent; and lumbering, 2 per cent. Of the total number, some 90 per cent are caused by man, a shocking state of affairs. Incendiarism has many causes and its cure demands forceful measures. Hunters, smokers, campers, fishermen, recreationists, brush burners, and others who use the woods are directly responsible for most of the forest land burned each year. Naturally fires will always occur because of lightning and from accidental causes, and fire-protective organizations must always be prepared to fight them. Yet care on the part of all users of the forest would immeasurably reduce the number of fires started annually and the areas

Figure 141. Burned-over peat lands. Ground fires have completely destroyed the organic material in the soil and rendered this land a total loss as far as producing another crop of forest trees is concerned. (U.S. Forest Service.)

burned over. What is needed more than anything else is a better-developed sense of social responsibility than that which now exists.

Insect enemies of forests. Insects rank next to fires as destroyers of large quantities of mature timber, of young growth, and of forest products. The destruction of forest products can be prevented without great difficulty, but the control of insects working in growing timber is exceedingly difficult. Insects work slowly at first, are hard to see, and often get such a start that they cannot be controlled with any reasonable expenditure of money.

Various kinds of insects carry on their injurious work in different ways. The numerous bark beetles are extremely destructive (Fig. 142). In the West bark beetles destroy annually many millions of board feet of standing timber. The gypsy moth and brown-tail moth of the Northeast have killed thousands of acres of trees. Forty years ago the tamarack sawfly destroyed most of the tamarack throughout its natural range. The spruce budworm of recent prominence has already brought about the loss of millions of cords of valuable spruce and fir in eastern North America and threatens much of that still standing. The white pine weevil and the locust borer are examples of insects that, while they do not kill trees outright, deform them so badly that, unless control measures are effective, these species can scarcely be grown for good timber. Insect-killed timber soon becomes a serious fire menace.

Figure 142. Damage by insects. Insects of various types work quietly but destructively in many forests; a forest of ponderosa pine in which great quantities of commercially valuable trees have been killed. (U.S. Forest Service.)

Foresters and forest entomologists are well aware of the problem and are attacking it vigorously. The most promising measures of control lie in proper methods of forest management, the introduction of insect parasites, and airplane spraying with effective insecticides. Birds and small mammals are also useful in the control of forest insects.

Diseases of forest trees. As with forest insects, forest-tree diseases are difficult to control and appraise. It is known, however, that the damage caused annually by fungi is very extensive. Within two decades the chestnut bark disease, identified in this country in 1904, had destroyed virtually all of the valuable chestnut in the eastern United States (Fig. 143). The white pine blister rust is a serious menace to both eastern and western white pines. Numerous fungi gain entrance to living trees, often through fire scars, and cause interior wood decay, damaging much of the valuable heartwood.

Figure 143. Trees killed by the chestnut-bark disease. The chestnut-bark disease has within a few years killed almost all of the chestnut trees in the eastern United States. (U.S. Forest Service.)

Diseases of forest trees cannot be controlled unless the conditions that make it possible for them to attack trees and develop on them are prevented. This means growing healthy trees, eliminating forest fires, and using eradication measures and quarantine where feasible. Foresters and forest pathologists are doing their best to combat this forest enemy. Sometimes it is impossible to prevent epidemics of forest-tree diseases. When these occur, the timber that is attacked must be utilized if it is not to become a total loss.

Other destructive agencies. In general, wildlife has not been a serious factor in forest destruction. In some localities, however, certain animals have created distinct problems. In the Northeast beavers by their dams have frequently caused the overflow of much valuable spruce and fir land, killing all the trees on the flooded areas. In other regions deer have multiplied so rapidly that the natural food supplies have been exhausted. As a result these animals have been forced to browse on young trees and have thus destroyed young forest growth over considerable areas. Rodents are sometimes destructive to immature forest growths. But these are usually local problems and by no means serious in comparison with other forces of destruction.

DEVELOPMENTS IN FOREST CONSERVATION

A review of federal legislation. As stated earlier (p. 196), the forests have always occupied a leading and prominent part in the conservation movement. In Chapter I are listed the major steps by which the conservation movement progressed; some of these deal specifically with forests, others with associated resources. The appointment of a forestry agent in the Department of Agriculture in 1876, the Law of 1891 that gave the President authority to withdraw the forest reserves, the Act of 1897 providing for the administration of these reserves, the transfer of the forest reserves to the Department of Agriculture in 1905, the changing of the Bureau of Forestry to the Forest Service also in 1905, the renaming of the forest reserves as the national forests in 1907 were all matters of great importance in national forest conservation. The White House Conference of Governors in 1908, dealing with other resources as well as forests, was a highly significant development, since it brought the issue of natural resource conservation to the public generally and caused the governors of most of the states to establish conservation commissions. The Weeks Law of 1911, providing for the purchase of national forest lands in eastern United States and for co-operative aid with the states in fire protection, has had far-reaching results. The Clark-McNary Act of 1924 increased the financial support granted in the Weeks Law, as well as provided for new developments in co-operation with the states.

Other laws and events not heretofore mentioned that have had significant effects on the forest conservation movement will be discussed briefly.

The congresses of the American Forestry Association. In each of the years 1882, 1905, and 1946 an American Forest Congress has been held under the auspices of the American Forestry Association. The meetings have all been of national importance. As a result of the first two congresses public support of progressive conservation measures had much to do in bringing about the more important legislative acts heretofore mentioned. At the 1946 Congress, attended by leaders in all branches of conservation in government, industry, labor, and other fields, the opportunity was presented for an open discussion on a prepared program aiming to assure an adequate and continuing supply of forest products and to provide ample protection to the allied resources of soil, water, wildlife, and recreation.[1] As is usual with meetings of this type, there was a wide diversity of opinion as to details, but general agreement on the major objectives. As time passes, many of the proposals made for the furthering of the conservation movement will undoubtedly be put into practice. National gatherings are important in forest conservation, since they inform and influence a large segment of the general public, which could scarcely be reached in any other way.

The United States Forest Products Laboratory. Established in 1910 at Madison, Wisconsin, the Forest Products Laboratory early attained prominence as the world's outstanding research organization dealing with wood and wood products. This laboratory is one unit of the research organization of the Forest Service. Splendidly equipped for its research activities, the laboratory directs its studies to the mechanical properties and structure of wood, the seasoning of wood, the preservative treatment and fireproofing of wood, pulp and paper manufacture, wood lamination including the making of plywood, and the chemical derivatives and other phases of wood chemistry. The services of the laboratory have been invaluable to everyone concerned with the use of wood and timber products. Especially outstanding have been the contributions of this laboratory to the efforts in both World War I and II.

Federal forest experiment stations. Since 1928 as a result of the federal McNary-McSweeney Act, a number of federal forest experiment stations have been located regionally throughout the United States. At these stations research in all phases of the management of forests has been undertaken. The investigations deal with the many aspects of the growth of forests and the utilization of their products, with pro-

---

1 *Proceedings of the American Forest Congress* (Washington, 1946).

tection from fire, insects, diseases, and other injurious agencies, with forest wildlife, with the relation of the forest to watershed management and to climate, and with the proper handling of the forest ranges.

Education in forestry. Education in forestry has kept pace with developments in practice. The first college of forestry in the United States was established at Cornell University in 1898. This was followed in 1900 by the establishment of the Yale School of Forestry. Other schools of collegiate grade followed rapidly. There are now in existence twenty-two colleges or departments of forestry accredited by the Society of American Foresters. Since 1900 more than 14,000 foresters have been trained. Without the professionally trained foresters it would have been impossible to have placed the nation's forests under administration and management. These men are today in charge of forests and forestry problems and are the leaders in forest conservation. Most of the state colleges of agriculture provide courses of study designed to teach the elements of farm forestry and to acquaint the student with the problems of forest conservation.

The National Industrial Recovery Act. An extremely important development in industrial forestry occurred in 1933 and 1934 which, although of brief duration, influenced a number of timberland owners to adopt better practices of handling their timberlands and, in addition, indicated the success that might attend new efforts along similar lines. Under the National Industrial Recovery Act of 1933 the timber and timber-products industries adopted a code of regulations, one of which committed the industries to keeping their lands in productive condition provided certain forms of public co-operation were extended. In 1935, however, the United States Supreme Court declared the act unconstitutional. Nevertheless the effect on the industries as a result of the studies, discussions, and meetings and the realization of the probable advantages of such a co-operative arrangement were far-reaching. Many industries continued some of the forestry practices included in their codes, and the National Lumber Manufacturers Association urged its members to follow the constructive provisions of its code. These dealt with protection from fire, prevention of damage to young trees during logging, provision for replanting where necessary, leaving of part of the merchantable timber for a second crop, and in general partial cutting or selective logging.

The report of the Joint Committee of Congress on Forestry. On March 14, 1938, President Roosevelt sent to the Congress of the

United States a message recommending a study of the forest-land problem of this country. Stressing the importance of the forest as a natural resource, he said:

Forests are intimately tied into our whole social and economic life. They grow on more than one-third the land area of the continental United States. Wages from forest industries support five or six million people each year. Forests give us building materials and thousands of other things in everyday use. Forest lands furnish food and shelter for much of our remaining game, and healthful recreation for millions of our people. Forests help prevent erosion and floods. They conserve water and regulate its use for navigation, for power, for domestic use, and for irrigation. Woodlands occupy more acreage than any other crop on American farms, and help support two and one-half million farm families.

Our forest problem is essentially one of land use. It is a part of the broad problem of modern agriculture that is common to every part of the country.

The forest problem is, therefore, a matter of vital national concern, and some way must be found to make forest lands and forest reserves contribute their full share to the social and economic structures of this country, and to the security and stability of all our people.

As a result of the President's request a joint committee of ten men from the Senate and the House of Representatives was appointed to study the problems set forth and to make recommendations for the advancement of a policy of forestry on the nation's timber-growing lands, both in private and public ownership. This joint committee after three years of intensive study, which included public hearings held in various parts of the United States, submitted its report on March 24, 1941.[2]

The report was relatively brief. It included statistics assembled by the United States Forest Service and presented condensed but important statements of fact and their analyses bearing on the forest-land problems, the existing resources, the services the forests yield, the problems raised by the issues of public and private ownership, the obligations that must be assumed by each class of owner, the need for more adequate protection of forest lands, and in general the necessity for a rational plan of future management of all forest resources.

[2] *Forest Lands of the United States* (Report of the Joint Committee on Forestry, Congress of the United States, Senate Document 32, 77th Congress, 1st Session; Washington, 1941).

The findings of fact were followed by sixteen specific recommendations. The first recommendation dealt with the protection of forest lands from fire, and advocated an extension of co-operative protection on private and state-owned forest lands by increasing the authorization of the Clark-McNary Act for this purpose from $2,500,000 to $10,000,000 adding $2,500,000 annually to the current appropriation until the total authorization had been reached. This was a highly significant proposal.

The other recommendations were presented briefly. They provided for co-operative protection against insects and diseases on private and state-owned forest lands and for constructive developments in reforestation, in forest extension, in the establishment of co-operative sustained-yield units, in forest credits, in farm-forest co-operatives, in leases and co-operative agreements, in research in forest products and forest management, in state and federal forest-land acquisition, in tax contributions to local governments, in national forest protection and management, in the completion of the forest survey of the United States, and in investigations dealing with the supplies, production, and distribution of pulpwood.

Some of the recommendations of the Joint Committee met with unanimous approval and have been enacted into law. Federal contributions under the Clark-McNary Act have been increased to $9,000,-000 annually. Co-operative sustained yield units have been authorized, as have been increased funds for farm-forestry activities, for research, and for the continuation of the forest survey in the United States. A number of recommendations have received no action. As would be expected, some provoked extended controversy. This important study of the forest problems of the United States made by a joint committee of Congress presented concrete evidence of the need for much immediate and constructive legislation.

The Forest Service reappraisal. During the years 1945 and 1946 the Forest Service made a reappraisal of the nation's forest situation, with the aim of bringing up to date previous analyses of a similar nature. Reports have been issued containing information on timber resources of the United States, the potential requirements for timber products in the United States, the management status of the country's forest lands, wood waste, protection against forest insects and diseases, and on other important plans of forestry. The statistical material is in great

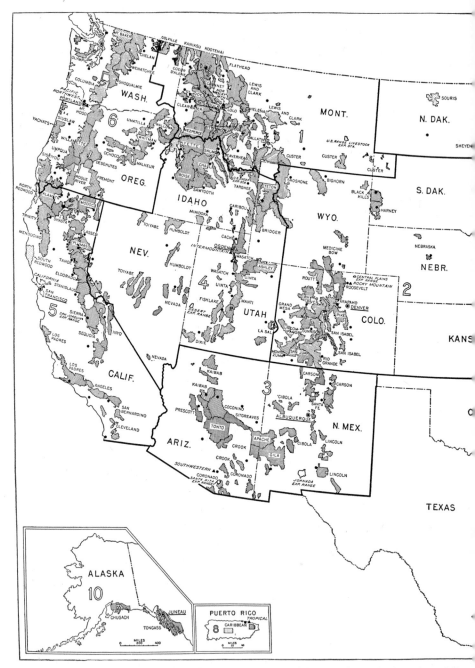

Figure 144. National forests of the United States. This map shows the location of the large areas are found in the mountain regions of the western United States. In all

NATIONAL FORESTS
AND RELATED DATA

PREPARED IN THE DIVISION OF ENGINEERING

MILES
0   50   100   150   200

▨ NATIONAL FORESTS
☐ PURCHASE UNITS
⬧ REGIONAL BOUNDARIES AND NUMBERS
◉ REGIONAL HEADQUARTERS
• SUPERVISOR'S HEADQUARTERS
▲ FOREST AND RANGE EXPERIMENT STATIONS
✳ LABORATORY (MADISON, WIS.)

▲ FOREST AND RANGE EXPERIMENT STATIONS

ALLEGHENY, PHILADELPHIA, PA.
APPALACHIAN, ASHEVILLE, N.C.
CALIFORNIA, BERKELEY, CALIF.   NORTHERN ROCKY MOUNTAIN, MISSOULA, MONT.
CENTRAL STATES, COLUMBUS, OHIO   PACIFIC NORTHWEST, PORTLAND, OREG.
INTERMOUNTAIN, OGDEN, UTAH   ROCKY MOUNTAIN, FT COLLINS, COLO
LAKE STATES, ST PAUL, MINN.   SOUTHERN, NEW ORLEANS, LA.
                                      SOUTHWESTERN, TUCSON, ARIZ.
        TROPICAL, RIO PIEDRAS, PUERTO RICO

national forests and the ten geographic regions in which they are administered. The
here are 152 national forests, aggregating more than 158,000,000 acres.

volume and detail and supersedes the figures presented in the report of the joint committee of Congress.[3]

THE STATUS OF FOREST CONSERVATION

The national forests. The national forests of the United States, though largely confined to the Rocky Mountain and Pacific Coast regions, are located in forty states, in Alaska, and in Puerto Rico. In all, there are 152 national forests, administered by the Forest Service in the United States Department of Agriculture. Central headquarters are at Washington, but the administration is decentralized into ten geographic regions, nine of which are in continental United States and one in Alaska (Fig. 144).

The federal lands included within the national forests in continental United States, Alaska, and Puerto Rico aggregate 180,000,000 acres. Excluding 21,000,000 acres in Alaska and Puerto Rico, the national forest lands in continental United States total 159,000,000 acres. Of these 159,000,000 acres, 123,000,000 acres are in forest, 36,000,000 acres are grasslands and high mountain country. Within the exterior boundaries of the national forests 49,000,000 acres of land in both private and other forms of public ownership are intermingled with the national forest lands.

The creation and development of the national forest system is the major advance, up to the present, in forest conservation. The establishment of these areas has profoundly influenced the entire movement of natural resource conservation. Prodigal disposal of public lands was traditional policy prior to the withdrawal of the national forest reserves. The establishment of these reserves initiated a major change in policy. A new point of view began to make itself felt, with the result that more and more the unappropriated public lands were retained in federal ownership. Natural resources of untold value, including forest, grazing, and mineral wealth, have now been placed under national control.

By a carefully planned program of management that includes protection, forest planting, controlled cuttings, and timber-stand improvement, the national forests are being maintained and built up to serve a variety of purposes, such as timber supply, watershed protec-

---

[3] Reappraisal of the Forest Situation, Reports 1 to 6 (U.S. Department of Agriculture, Forest Service; Washington, 1946).

tion, wildlife development, recreational use, and forage production for livestock.

From the national forests timber sales to industry currently provide between 2,500,000,000 and 3,000,000,000 board feet of timber, cut in a manner that provides adequately for successive crops of trees (Fig. 145). Special emphasis is placed on maintaining the stability of local communities and privately owned industries dependent on timber supplies to be obtained in part, or in whole, from the national forests.

Figure 145. Timber-sale area on a national forest after cutting—a scene in the Plumas National Forest in the Sierra Nevada Mountains in California. The areas shown have been logged for mature timber by methods that leave the land well stocked for another crop of trees. (C. H. Guise.)

National forest stumpage is becoming increasingly important in maintaining industries and communities as the supplies of privately owned timber diminish. Highly important in this connection will be the development, which is now starting, of co-operative sustained-yield units, which provide for the joint operation of public and private timberlands under sustained-yield management plans.

The national forest lands are protected, both from wasteful cutting and from fire; and in most of them provision is made for a continuous forest growth. Seventy-one per cent of the forest lands are being cut on a sustained-yield basis. The lands not being so operated are remote. The areas that receive the most intensive forms of management are relatively small, but this in the present stage of American forestry is not too important.[4] It is significant, however, to note that all lands are protected, and on most of them a form of cutting is being followed which provides for a continuous forest growth. The intensity of management can be stepped up as the need arises and the economic factors permit.

In the West most of the important rivers have their sources in national forest areas; many of the large eastern rivers likewise start in national forests. By means of protection, controlled cutting, range management, and other forestry practices, the watershed volumes are being materially improved.

Wildlife resources are being protected and increased (Fig. 146). The national forests support one-third of the country's big game animals as well as great populations of small game. Included in the forests are 90,000 miles of fishing streams, and one and a half million acres of lakes. The national forests are particularly well suited for supplying wildlife with food and shelter. Wildlife production is co-ordinated with the management of the forests for timber, forage, and other resources. Between three and four million hunters and fishermen are visiting the national forests annually.

Recreational use is highly developed and one of the major management policies (Fig. 147). Plans for all forms of recreational use during all seasons of the year looking to an extension of existing facilities have been prepared, to be developed as funds and materials become available.

More than 80,000,000 acres of national forest land are suitable for grazing livestock. These areas include the meadows and other non-forested lands as well as the grasslands in the more open forests. More than 30,000 owners of stock are grazing, during from three to six months of each year, some 9,000,000 head of livestock. Thousands of stockmen depend to a great extent upon the national forest ranges for the feeding of their stock during certain seasons. The successful operation of 26,000,000 acres of ranch properties, representing investments

---

[4] Intensive forest management involves the highest standards of technical practice, so that the maximum yield of forest products may be obtained. Extensive forest management includes protection and other measures designed to keep forest lands continuously productive, though they may not produce the highest yields of wood. These items are discussed more fully later in the next chapter.

of some $330,000,000, is largely dependent on part-time grazing in the national forests.[5] By control of the stock that is allowed to use the ranges and by protection and care, the ranges are being built up steadily.

Splendid results have been achieved by the Forest Service. Yet the building up of the national forest system has, in the opinion of some, not been sufficiently rapid. If it has been too slow, there can be no

Figure 146. A wild turkey in a West Virginia forest. Forests are essential if the cover and food supplies of many of the wild animals of this country are to be brought back and conserved. (U.S. Forest Service.)

criticism, but only hope that the excellent work of the past will be accelerated. Early opposition to the establishment of the forests, their remoteness, the serious problems created by the presence of private interior holdings, and the lack of a sufficiently large personnel to handle the work raised many difficult obstacles to the most effective management.

Indian forests and others in national ownership. The forests of the

---

[5] U.S. Department of Agriculture, *Report of the Chief of the Forest Service* (Washington, 1946).

Indian lands are under the forestry branch of the Indian Service in the United States Department of the Interior. The Indian Service has its own staff of foresters. A federal law enacted in 1934 requires that the Indian forests be managed on a permanent, sustained-yield basis. Their management is similar to that of the national forests. The forests of the national parks, also under the United States Department of

Figure 147. Winter sports in Wasatch National Forest, Utah. Skiing and other forms of winter sports are attracting increasing numbers each year to the national forests. As winter playgrounds, the forests are providing a form of recreational use that is destined to become increasingly popular. (U.S. Forest Service.)

the Interior, are carefully administered and protected. The forests in the national parks are parts of lands reserved for scenic, scientific, and recreational purposes, and obviously not subject to exploitation. In addition to the primary purposes for which they were created, they are invaluable as game refuges and exceedingly useful for watershed protection.

The forest lands of the grazing districts, although they include relatively little commercial timberland, are all important for protecting watersheds, and many of them have distinct values for forage production and wildlife perpetuation. Certain forest areas included within the grazing districts are under management. To other areas little attention is given, although a certain amount of protection from fire is provided. Much more administrative care is needed for these lands if they are to be brought back to productive condition.

Other forest lands in national ownership are under administration. Some of the areas, including the important Oregon and California Revested Lands, are intensively developed for timber production.

State forests and forestry. The major part of state-owned forest lands are included within a relatively small number of states. Minnesota leads with more than 5,000,000 acres, New York is second with 2,700,-000 acres, Pennsylvania is third with 1,700,000 acres, and Michigan is fourth with 1,000,000 acres. Montana, Idaho, Washington, New Mexico, Massachusetts, and Wisconsin, with areas ranging between 170,-000 acres and 520,000 acres, are the other states that own large areas of forest land. State forests and forestry occupy an important place in the nation's forestry program.

In point of time state forestry developed along with the federal program, though obviously it had no stimulus comparable to the creation of the forest reserves. Between the years 1867 and 1891 a number of states established commissions or organizations of one type or another to study the local problems of forest depletion, but most of these were short-lived. The first of the states to undertake permanent public forest-land administration was New York, where legislation was enacted in 1885. Pennsylvania initiated her forestry work ten years later. Other states began to create forestry organizations, and by 1900 twelve states had embarked upon this work. Prior to 1910 ten additional states inaugurated forestry programs. The Weeks Law, enacted in 1911, included, with other provisions, one whereby the federal government would co-operate with the individual states in protecting forest lands from fire. This gave an impetus to a number of additional states to create departments to deal with their forest resources. The Clark-McNary Law of 1924 contained provisions for federal and state co-operation that not only took the place of the fire-protection clauses in the Weeks Law, but also authorized extensive developments in growing and distributing to state residents trees for reforestation, and in increasing farm-forestry extension activities. Other federal laws affecting state forestry are the Fulmer Act of 1936 which authorizes federal funds for the purchase of state forest properties, and the Norris-Doxey Farm Forestry Act of 1937, a co-operative act that furthers many of the provisions of the Clark-McNary Act but specifically strengthens the work of state forestry agencies in assisting farm woodland owners in the marketing of their forest products.

As a result of the early initiative of some states, and the encouragement given by federal laws, state forestry has grown to a status where all states in which forest lands are important now have official organizations for administering these properties.

The state departments of forestry are engaged in diverse types of work. Land acquisition and administration, protection of property from fire and other injurious agencies, reforesting idle state lands, growing forest nursery stock for distribution to private landowners, supplying technical service in forestry to individuals, and selling timber are the principal types of activities in which state forestry organizations are engaged.

Of primary importance in administering the state forest lands are the developments for recreational use and for maintaining and increasing wildlife (Fig. 148). In many states the conservation commissions are organized so that they will specifically provide for the development of these resources.

State forests can serve the public in diverse ways, and there is general agreement that many of the states should greatly increase their areas of forest land. By so doing they will create forest wealth on lands now relatively unproductive and, in addition, further extend to their citizens the advantages that result from hunting, fishing, and other recreational activities. The extension of state forests is of particular importance in the eastern United States where national forest areas are relatively limited in size.

County and municipal forests. County, municipal, school, and institutional forest lands total more than 10,000,000 acres. Of this area approximately 3,000,000 acres in more than 2,300 separate locations are being developed as community forests for the primary purposes of recreation, protection of local water supplies, and for wood. Forests of this type offer an excellent opportunity for counties, cities, towns, and other municipal organizations to establish enterprises that will lead to civic betterment in a variety of ways. In addition to the benefits they create, they can produce income and provide work for local citizens. Wisconsin is far ahead of all other states in establishing county forests and now has, in twenty-five counties, forests that aggregate more than 1,700,000 acres.

In central European countries the communal forest, which corresponds roughly to the county and municipal forest, is of great importance for recreational and protection purposes as well as for the production of an annual income to help meet the expenses of local government. Many of these communal forests are old and famous. An

Figure 148. State forests. Many state forests are developed for recreational use. Extensive areas with lakes, mountains, forests, and streams are similar to this one in the Adirondacks. (U.S. Forest Service.)

extensive development of the county and municipal forest system is desirable in this country.

Industrially owned forests. Many forests are owned by lumber, pulp and paper, mining, and land companies, by railroads, and by other miscellaneous agencies. On these lands the dominating aim is successful financial operation. Timber is the primary product to be removed, and the industrial operators cannot be expected voluntarily to manage their properties for watershed protection, recreational use, wildlife management, or what are to them secondary benefits.

The industrially owned forests have, for the most part, been cut over for the immediately available crops of mature timber, with entire disregard for future growth. The demand for immediate profits, the intense competition that has served to keep prices low, the danger from fire, increasing taxes, and the long periods of time required to grow trees have all been important factors in discouraging the private owner from practicing forestry. The decline in the per capita consumption of wood and the fact that the lands were acquired for liquidation instead of sustained operation have also influenced industrial operators in the courses that they have taken. Further, they have never been forced by laws to control their methods of cutting. Many of these lands have been so badly cut and burned that the expense of rehabilitation is prohibitive. All too commonly the pressure is to continue to liquidate and either to sell the lands that remain or let them revert to states and counties for nonpayment of taxes.

In spite of all the discouraging factors controlling their practice, many in the industrial field have pioneered and made distinct progress in using, and at the same time conserving, their forests (Figs. 149, 150). As a result of their efforts, and with federal and state co-operation, distinct gains in fire protection have been made. The effect of the National Recovery Administration Act of 1933, short-lived as the act was, and the general impact of the conservation movement have also helped to create a progressive point of view on the part of many industrial owners.

Encouraging is the fact that more than two-thirds of the 15,000,000 acres owned by pulp companies are under either intensive or extensive forest management. More than one-third of the 37,000,000 acres of the forest lands controlled by lumber companies are under similar levels of management. However, with the 154,000,000 acres in other forms of industrial ownership, only 21 per cent are under extensive management and practically none are intensively managed. Of the total area of privately owned forest lands in the country in industrial ownership less than one-quarter is today being accorded even a crude form of forest management. One bright spot in this picture is the fact that an increasing number of owners of the larger forest properties are planning to handle their lands on a long-time basis. Yet the small areas, which on the aggregate make up the bulk of the industrial holdings, have as a whole shown relatively little interest in sustained-yield forestry.

Tree Farms. A relatively new development in the practice of forest management on privately owned lands is the Tree Farm movement. Started in 1941 on an extensive property owned by one of the larger timber operating companies in the Northwest, the Tree Farm idea

Figure 149. Forest management on the lands of an industrially owned pulp and paper company in Arkansas. The trees removed in this selective cutting amount to 16 cords per acre. In the remaining stand are 20.6 cords per acre. The wood removed will be chemically reduced and manufactured into paper. (U.S. Forest Service.)

attracted favorable attention nationally with the result that the National Lumber Manufacturers Association initiated a nation-wide Tree Farm movement to encourage the protection and permanent productive use of private forest lands.

A Tree Farm is simply an area of privately owned forest land ded-

icated to the growing of forest crops for commercial purposes, protected, and managed for continuous production. The name Tree
Farm is awarded by the American Forest Products Industries, Inc., a
subdivision of the National Lumber Manufacturers Association, after
the area has been certified by a state committee as meeting specified
requirements. For registration with the American Tree Farm system

Figure 150. Selectively logged forest of mixed sugar pine and western
yellow pine, with residual stand for a future harvest—California. (Western Pine Association.)

the owner must assure his willingness to use the land under his control
for the production of forest crops; provide reasonable protection from
fire, insects, and disease and from damage by excessive grazing; and
harvest forest crops from his Tree Farm in a manner that will ensure
future crops.

The common feature of all Tree Farms is the protection and management that assures a continuously growing forest and repeated forest crops for commercial purposes. The term may be applied to the

farmer's small woodlot of only ten acres from which is cut for sale no more than a cord of wood per year, or to the large industrial holding of several hundred thousand acres from which millions of board feet are taken annually.

More than 1,000 individual holdings aggregating some 12,000,000 acres, largely in the West and South, have been certified as Tree Farms. This development is constructive and an important factor in bringing privately owned forest lands under management.

Farm woodlands. Farm woodlands constitute an important national forest resource. If properly managed and developed, these woods can contribute to the stability and prosperity of local communities, and add appreciably to the country's supply of forest products. They are estimated to contain 15 per cent of the saw timber of the country, but much of it is inferior in quality. Though the income-producing potentialities have never been appreciated, the farm woods have many advantages for timber growing. Ownership is stable, costs of holding are small, and forestry activities require but a small part of the owner's time. Yet the farm woodlands as a class have received more abuse and less constructive attention than any other farm crop.

The farm owner has seldom been able to sell his product to best advantage because of his lack of bargaining power and his inability, usually, to sell to well-equipped manufacturing plants. Extension assistance in farm forestry has never been supported to the extent that it has been in agriculture. Furthermore, the farmer has seldom regarded the farm woods as a growing crop. He has all too often cut the salable timber without regard for the remaining stand, pastured his woods heavily, and let fire go through it indiscriminately.

Available statistics indicate that on only 27 per cent of the farm areas is a type of cutting being done that can be characterized as fair or good. Most farm woods are in a state of deterioration and in need of rehabilitation. A vast amount of constructive work is needed in the field of farm woodland management.

The status of protection from fire. The extent to which the commercial forest lands of the country, in the several forms of ownership, receive protection from fire is presented in Table 14. An analysis of the figures in this table shows that 327,000,000 acres or 71 per cent of the total of 461,000,000 acres are receiving a degree of protection that rates fair or good; that 88,000,000 acres or 19 per cent receive poor protection, and 46,000,000 acres or 10 per cent receive none.

TABLE 14. EXTENT OF FIRE PROTECTION ON COMMERCIAL FOREST LANDS

Ownership class	Area, million acres	Extent of fire protection by percentage of area			
		Good	Fair	Poor	None
All lands	461	36	35	19	10
Private	345	19	44	24	13
North	140	22	60	12	6
South	167	7	35	37	21
West	38	64	27	9	0
Public	116	84	11	4	1
National forests	74	98	1	1	0
Other federal	15	54	25	17	4
State and local	27	66	28	4	2

On the 345,000,000 acres of privately owned lands, 217,000,000 acres or 63 per cent are receiving fair and better fire protection, 83,-000,000 acres or 24 per cent get poor protection, and 45,000,000 acres or 13 per cent receive none.

On the publicly owned lands, 116,000,000 acres in all, fair or better protection is given to 110,000,000 acres or 95 per cent and poor protection to 5,000,000 acres or 4 per cent. Only 1,000,000 acres or 1 per cent are without protection.

In general, the public lands are well protected. On the private lands considerable effort must still be made. The problem areas where lack of adequate protection is most critical are in the South. Breaking down the 345,000,000 acres of private land into regions, the North contains 140,000,000 acres of forest land of which 82 per cent receive fair or better protection; the West contains 38,000,000 acres of which 91 per cent receive protection that rates fair or better; but in the South with 167,000,000 acres, only 42 per cent are similarly protected. In the latter region 37 per cent of the lands receive poor protection and 21 per cent receive none. Thus in the South alone 97,000,000 acres or 58 per cent of its forest area receive little or no protection. These 97,000,000 acres in the South are 76 per cent of the 128,000,000 acres of privately owned forest land in the entire country receiving little or no protection.

The extent to which the forest lands of the country are protected is not satisfactory. Adequate protection from fire must be accorded all forest lands if they are to grow continuous crops of timber.

The status of cutting practices. Without adequate protection from fire, timber crops cannot be grown. Yet protection is only the first step. The cutting must be done in a way that provides for a second crop, and it is therefore of interest to examine the extent to which conservative cutting practices are followed on lands in the various forms of ownership.

Figures showing the types of cutting practice on the several classes of land are presented in Table 15. In this table the privately owned properties are broken down into four groups, including farm woodlands and three classes of industrial lands; the latter are subdivided into areas under 5,000 acres in size, from 5,000 to 50,000 acres, and over 50,000 acres. This breakdown is essential since there is a wide difference in the types of cutting practice taking place in the larger holdings as contrasted with the smaller areas.

TABLE 15. TYPES OF TIMBER CUTTING PRACTICE ON LANDS IN OWNERSHIP CLASSES

Ownership class	Area of forest land			Types of cutting practice		
	Total		Operating	High order and good	Fair	Poor and destructive
	million acres	per cent	million acres	per cent	per cent	per cent
Private						
Farm woods	139	30	123	4	23	73
Under 5,000 acres	122	27	100	4	25	71
5,000 to 50,000 acres	33	7	30	8	31	61
Over 50,000 acres	51	11	49	29	39	32
All private	345	75	302	8	28	64
Public						
National forests	73	16	65	80	19	1
Other federal	16	3	13	43	32	25
State and local	27	6	23	47	10	43
All public	116	25	101	67	19	14
All lands	461	100	403	23	25	52

Good and high-order cutting practices require that timber be cut in accordance with sound silvicultural techniques and that the land be left in possession of desirable tree species in condition for vigorous growth in the immediate future. Intensive treatment of the forest, as has been followed in Europe for decades, necessitates high-order cutting practice, but this type of treatment is only in the initial stages in the United States. By fair cutting practice is meant the methods that will maintain at least a reasonable stock of desirable and marketable species. Poor and destructive cutting practice leaves the land in unsatisfactory condition for future growth. Possibilities for reproducing new stands are limited or completely removed. The land is left either without timber or with limited stocking of inferior species.

Of the 461,000,000 acres, some 58,000,000 acres or 13 per cent are, for various reasons, classed as *nonoperating* lands. The remainder of 403,000,000 acres is termed *operating* forest land. The percentages of land listed by types of cutting practice apply only to the areas listed as operating acreages.

As a whole, the public lands are being well handled, with 67 per cent of the area rated with cutting practices that are good or better. National forests are far ahead of other federal and state and local lands in this respect. As time goes on these percentages on the public lands will all change for the better.

In the case of the privately owned lands, the farm woods together with the small industrial holdings present a discouraging picture. These two types of ownership, aggregating 261,000,000 acres, or 57 per cent of all privately owned forest land, are in an estimated 4,200,000 individual properties. In each class only 4 per cent of the lands are cut with a type of practice that rates good or of high order; on from 23 to 25 per cent of them there is only a fair type of cutting practiced, and on 71 to 73 per cent the cutting is poor or destructive.

On only 8 per cent of the 33,000,000 acres of land held in blocks of from 5,000 to 50,000 acres each are cutting practices good or better. On 31 per cent of these areas cutting practices are fair, and on 61 per cent they are poor and destructive. These lands are in the hands of 3,200 owners.

The 51,000,000 acres in blocks of 50,000 acres and larger are held by 400 owners. These large holdings rate higher than any of the other classes in private ownership. On 29 per cent of the operating area, cutting practices are good or better, on 39 per cent they are fair, and on only 32 per cent are they poor and destructive.

Because of the weight of the great area in the smaller privately owned units, the total percentages for the 345,000,000 acres present a dismal record. On only 8 per cent of the land area is the cutting practice good or better; on 28 per cent it is fair, and on 64 per cent it is poor or worse.

When statistics show that poor and destructive cutting practice still is the rule on more than half of all the commercial forest lands in the United States, the evidence is at hand that improved forest practices are imperative.

CHAPTER VIII

Forest Conservation:
A Program for the Future

THE GOAL of forest conservation is the practice of forestry on the forest lands of the country so that these lands will be of maximum use in growing timber, in protecting watersheds, in providing food and shelter for wildlife, in serving recreational needs, in furnishing forage for domestic livestock, and in otherwise serving to best advantage the owner and the public.

Forestry aims to protect all lands, to maintain in productive condition those lands that now bear forests, and to make suitable provisions for a second crop on forest lands when harvesting of timber takes place. It proposes to rehabilitate with a new tree growth those lands that are now idle and unproductive, and otherwise to institute and carry out those policies and practices that will both permit the use of forests and, at the same time, plan adequately for the country's future needs.

The extent to which the practice of forestry is essential varies widely. On some lands protection from fires and other destructive agencies is all that is needed; at the other extreme are forests in which the most intensive practice of forestry looking to a sustained yield is desirable; in between are lands of diverse types on which the form of forest management must be adjusted to meet the existing conditions of ownership, growth possibilities, and the services that the specific forests can provide.

The issues involved are complex. They are also widely different and must be solved for a great variety of conditions. National, state, communal, industrial, and farm forest lands each present their peculiar problems. The geographical location of the forest lands, the regional occurrence of the volumes and kinds of remaining timber supplies, and the general condition of the existing forest cover create situations that can be met only by practices designed for specific regions. Also important are social and economic considerations. Programs of forest conservation undertaken for the future must be consistent with economic as well as social progress.

As is evident from preceding pages, distinct progress in forest conservation has been made. There still remains much to be accomplished, and many gaps exist that must be filled. The immediate needs are discussed in a generalized manner in this chapter.

PROTECTION OF FORESTS

Without qualifications, the fundamental requirement in forest conservation is the protection of forests from fire and other destructive agencies. This protection must include lands in both public and private ownership and must be developed to a degree that will ensure, insofar as it is humanly possible, the prevention of fires, the suppression of those that occur, and, in addition, the control of damaging insects and fungous diseases.

Forest lands regardless of ownership, present type of forest growth, or potential growing capacity must all be brought under a system of organized fire protection. Fires can start on any type of forest land; where they begin on areas at present regarded as of little or no value, they may and usually do spread rapidly to the more valuable forests.

Systematic forest fire control in the national forests started more than forty years ago. Prior to that time efforts had been made in a small way by some states and private owners to control the fire menace. The start of a broad-scale protection system, however, came with the enactment of legislation by the federal government in 1911.

Recognizing that forest fires are in large part caused by the general public and that their control is beyond the power of the individual landowner unless he is assisted by federal and state governments, Congress in 1911 enacted the Weeks Act. This law granted the sum of $200,000 annually to the Secretary of Agriculture for use, in co-operation with those states that match the federal funds dollar for dollar, in protecting forested watersheds on navigable streams from fire. The Weeks Act was followed by the Clark-McNary Act of 1924, which also contained legislation for co-operative fire protection, with amounts considerably in excess of those authorized under the Weeks Act. In 1924 the federal appropriations were $660,000 annually. These funds have been increased over the years, and at the present time annual federal authorizations amount to $9,000,000 dollars. With more than an equal amount being appropriated by the states, and some $2,000,-000 being expended by private owners of timberland, over $25,000,-000 is now being expended annually. A decade ago it was thought that the $9,000,000 from federal sources would be adequate to provide coverage for all forest lands. At present this sum is not ample, and efforts are being made to obtain federal authorization for $16,000,000. If this sum can be obtained, the total spent by federal, state, and private agencies would range between $35,000,000 to $40,000,000 each year, an amount believed to be adequate to provide protection to all forest lands. At present approximately 130,000,000 acres, or more than 20 per cent of the total forest-land area of the United States, does not receive organized protection.

That organized protection brings effective results is well illustrated by estimates submitted by the states for the year 1945. For that year the estimates show that on lands with total protection less than 1 per cent of the areas was burned, whereas on the unprotected lands fires burned over almost 12 per cent of the areas. Other studies in the past have shown comparable relationships.

The American Forest Products Industries, mentioned in connection with the Tree Farm movement, has pushed vigorously its "Keep Green" program, a plan of public education in forest-fire prevention. Committees develop the program through publicity channels, including news releases, motion pictures, radio talks, posters, and divers other ways of bringing forest-fire protection before the public. The "Keep Green" program has been adopted and supported in a number of states. This form of activity by an association of industrial timberland owners is an indication of a progressive point of view and is a concrete effort on the part of industry to aid in controlling forest fires.

To ensure proper protection from fire requires an extension of the methods that have already been brought to a high state of efficiency in prevention, early detection, and suppression. This means extending the systems of fire wardens, patrols, lookout towers, and communication by radio and telephone; it demands that an adequate force of men be instantly available with proper fire-fighting equipment (Fig. 151); and it makes necessary more complete systems of roads and airplane delivery of men and supplies, so that men can get to fires as quickly as possible and have favorable positions from which to fight them.

Fires can be put out if they are attacked before they develop. But when forest fires, often driven by strong winds, start to spread over inflammable areas, it is frequently impossible to check them. Many thousands of acres of nonforested lands, if protected from fire, will slowly be covered by nature with another crop of trees.

The individual citizen must understand the serious and destructive nature of forest fires, the small fires as well as the large ones; and

Figure 151. Fighting forest fires. There are many ways of attacking forest fires, one of which is clearing trenches down to the mineral soil and attempting to prevent the fires from crossing the cleared strips of land. (U.S. Forest Service.)

when in the woods he must make every effort to keep them from starting. He should do his part in creating a public opinion that will demand adequate leadership and support by the various governmental agencies in bringing about a nation-wide protective system.

The excellent protection that is now being provided to more than three-quarters of the country's forest lands should be extended to all parts of all regions of the United States. Additional co-operation between federal and state governments and the individual owners will be required if full coverage is to be obtained. The need for more adequate protection is particularly acute in the South. An enlightened public opinion can bring about a great reduction in the man-made fires. With an adequate protective organization, fires that do start can be extinguished before they get out of control.

The prevention and control of forest fires is of primary importance, but destructive insects and tree diseases must also be checked, for they destroy great quantities of timber. While a forest fire is spectacular, the insects and diseases work quietly, but they often do great damage before they are discovered. They are particularly difficult to fight; yet it is none the less essential that an adequate force of trained men be constantly on guard against these pests.

Grazing and fires must be kept out of farm woodlands if they are to be made productive. Keeping stock and fire from these woods should be a relatively simple matter, but in practice it will be brought about only when the owner appreciates the value of his woods and the damage that unrestricted grazing and burning create.

IMPROVED CUTTING PRACTICES

The great majority of cut-over stands were logged in a manner that did not entail conscious effort either to save the smaller or unmerchantable trees or to ensure a succeeding second growth (Fig. 152). Such lands were acquired only for the liquidation of the mature timber. Large areas of saw timber remain to be logged in the future. In many of these forests operations are now under way. Steps should be taken to ensure that they are logged in a fashion that will make provision for a second crop and otherwise keep these forests continuously productive.

In the eastern forests and those of the Rocky Mountains the trees, even though fully mature, are of sizes that permit of relatively easy handling and that do not require for their extraction the high-powered machinery that, in the past, has wrecked so much forested land.

In the Pacific Coast forests, where most of the old-growth timber remains, the trees, especially Douglas fir and redwood, are so large and the logs so heavy that they can be logged only by means of powerful engines, cables, hoists, and tractors. Terrific destruction has resulted from the logging of these timberlands, and it has by no means ceased. Today the operators are fully aware of the fire problem and are spending large sums of money for fire control. They are also trying, in many instances, new methods of logging designed to leave the lands in productive condition. Particularly progressive is the use of heavy tractors (Fig. 153). More conservative practices are still needed in the far-western forests, but the encouraging feature is that many of the lumbermen are aware of the need and anxious to meet it. However, much waste and destruction still occur. On 52 per cent of all commercial operating forest lands in the United States cutting practices are poor or destructive; on 14 per cent of publicly owned lands and on

Figure 152. Heavily logged and repeatedly burned. This land was once covered with a fine forest. Now, as a result of destructive logging and severe forest fires, it is waste land. In this country there are 75,000,000 acres of land in similar condition. (U.S. Forest Service.)

64 per cent of privately owned lands poor or destructive cutting practice prevails. It is evident that continuous forest production is impossible unless these figures change greatly for the better. The present situation is thoroughly unsatisfactory, and the public is almost certain to demand, possibly through compulsory legislation, more conservative cutting methods.

The initiation of cutting practices that protect uncut timber and make full provision for an adequate second growth on the major part of all operating forest lands is, along with adequate protective measures, a fundamental and essential step in a national conservation program.

SUSTAINED-YIELD MANAGEMENT

When a forest property is organized and administered so that a steady and continuous supply of forest products is obtained, the property is managed on a sustained-yield basis. Sustained yield is the ultimate goal in the management of forest properties that are maintained for the production of wood materials. The practice of sustained-yield management in most of the country's forests is essential if the future needs of the people are to be adequately met.

Figure 153. Skidding logs in the western pine region of southern Oregon with a Diesel-driven tractor with arch. Tractor skidding is common in logging operations in all parts of the United States. (Western Pine Association.)

Sustained-yield management implies a high type of technical practice; it includes and co-ordinates all phases of forestry techniques. It deals with protection, the restoration of denuded lands by planting or encouraging natural reproduction, the cultural care of forests in every stage of development, and the methods of cutting that will ensure future growth and continuous yields (Fig. 154).

The ideal unit of forest property contains a reasonably even distribution of age or size classes. From such a forest there can and should be cut periodically an amount of wood that is the approximate equivalent of the volume of wood being grown elsewhere in the forest during the same period of time. Relatively few forest units in the United States meet the conditions whereby the cut can be balanced with the growth.

On lands that have been heavily cut over, are badly depleted, or contain a poor distribution of age classes, the periodic cut must be less

Figure 154. Silviculture in a lodgepole pine forest. Only a part of the trees have been removed in this operation. The timber cut will be used for poles, railroad ties, or lumber. The trees left standing will grow at a more rapid rate than before thinning. This is good forestry and the ideal way to manage forests of this type. (U.S. Forest Service.)

than the increment so that an ample growing stock may accumulate. Much of the cut-over forest land in the United States is at present in this stage.

On lands bearing an excess of overmature timber, volume growth is low and the periodic cut will of necessity be far in excess of the increment until the surplus volumes are removed. The problem of management in these old-growth forests, located mostly in the western

United States, is that of regulating the volume of the cut so that a gradual conversion to sustained-yield practice may be effected.

In the present stage of forestry practice in the United States and in planning for the future, forest management of both intensive and extensive forms is recognized. Intensive forest management concerns itself with long-term plans based on high standards of cutting practice, cultural measures, protection, and planting, where necessary, so that the ultimate yield will approach the productive capacity of the land. Forestry of this type with its planning for a carefully regulated sustained yield is possible only on those lands that are characterized by good soil, favorable ownership, and strategic location with respect to consuming centers, and on lands otherwise available for the most intensive use. It is estimated that some 100,000,000 acres of forest land in the United States will ultimately be suited to intensive forest management.

Extensive forest management involves complete protection and other phases of cultural measures and cutting practice that are less intensive in nature but nevertheless designed to keep the lands in a condition so that they will provide a steady flow of products, though not to the full capacity of the forest. Economic and physical factors make impossible the most intensive care of such forest lands. There are approximately 300,000,000 acres of forest land in this country on which an extensive form of forest management will be advisable.

In addition, 60,000,000 acres are so remote and the growth possibilities so low that they justify, as far as can now be foreseen, merely adequate protection.

If these great areas are brought to the stages of management indicated, there will be no question about an ample and perpetual supply of timber to serve the country's future needs, and in addition a large supply for export to other countries. Furthermore, the management of the forests for a sustained supply of products will stabilize and keep prosperous thousands of communities and industries that depend on forest supplies for their existence.

On the basis of estimates by Forest Service economists on current drain from the forests, on current growth, and on future requirements to meet the needs of a population that may ultimately reach 185,-000,000 people, Table 16 is developed. Though estimates only, these figures show some interesting relationships. The current cubic feet drain and growth approximately balance. The saw-timber drain exceeds the saw-timber growth by 50 per cent. The figures indicate that the present growth of saw timber must be stepped up by 100 per cent to meet the estimated future needs of the country. Such an increase is well within the limits of possibility if sustained-yield forestry is practiced. On 400,000,000 acres of forest land an average annual growth of 50 cubic feet per acre would provide the 20,000,-000,000 cubic feet estimated as necessary; or an average annual growth of 180 board feet per acre would furnish the 72,000,000,000 board feet required. These average annual growth figures are not high; in fact they should be attained easily if all lands were accorded even an extensive form of management.

TABLE 16. DRAIN, GROWTH, AND POTENTIAL TIMBER REQUIREMENTS

	All timber, including saw timber	Saw timber only
	billion cu. ft.	*billion bd. ft.*
Current drain	13.7	53.9
Current growth	13.4	35.3
Future needs	20	72

A significant development in sustained-yield forestry is the establishment of co-operative sustained-yield units (see p. 253). Under the authority of a federal law of 1944, the Departments of Agriculture and of Interior may enter into co-operative arrangements with private timberland owners for the joint sustained-yield management of public and private forest resources. The object of this program is to stabilize forest industries and communities dependent upon them by working out jointly plans whereby public and private properties will each agree to supply, on a long-time basis, timber in sufficient quantities to maintain production and payrolls. Under this plan co-operating properties must be managed for sustained yield. Several co-operative units have been authorized and additional ones are being planned. This form of federal-private co-operation is an important step in the development of sustained-yield forestry on both private and public lands.

REHABILITATION OF IDLE LANDS

Of the commercially useful forest lands of the country, 75,000,000 acres, or one-sixth of the entire area, are in nonproductive condition. Some of these lands bear an inadequate cover of young growth, and others are entirely without restocking (Fig. 155). For the most part lands of this type have been brought to their present condition by destructive logging and severe forest fires. Approximately 43 per cent of this area is in the South, and 18 per cent more is in the Lake States.

In addition to these idle lands are great areas of abandoned farm lands. Some 50,000,000 acres have already been abandoned, and the

Figure 155. Forest destruction. Rapid and high-powered logging has not only removed all of the mature timber but at the same time destroyed the small trees that should have been left to grow into a future stand. Lands of this type will be nonproductive for many years. (U.S. Forest Service.)

process is continuing. While inferior for successful farming these lands are capable of producing forests, and the only solution for their use is to restore the nonforested sections to trees.

Many of the nonproductive lands will in time restock themselves with tree growth through natural seeding, provided they are protected from fire. Others, estimated to aggregate 25,000,000 acres, can be restored only by means of planting (Fig. 156). Because of the expense involved the industrial owner is seldom interested in undertaking extensive reforestation operations. On farm areas, the establishment of new forests is entirely practicable; individual parcels of land are not likely to be large, and a gradual program of reforesting the idle farm lands is to be encouraged.

The nonrestocking areas are now completely useless. They produce nothing and fail to render services for watershed protection, recreation, or wildlife development. The lands in public ownership should be rehabilitated by protection and by planting where necessary, and

Figure 156. A plantation of Norway pine, 30 years old, in central New York. Planted in 1915 at the rate of 1,200 trees per acre, all but approximately 500 trees per acre have been removed in thinnings. The trees average 7.5 inches in diameter and 45 feet in height. (C. H. Guise.)

the costs should be borne by the various governmental owners. Those that are parts of farms can in large part be restored to forest growth. But those in industrial holdings present a more vexing problem. They should be given full protection. Probably the only effective solution to the restoration of a suitable forest cover lies in transferring much of this land to public ownership.

To the present only about 5,000,000 acres in the United States have been successfully planted, a fact that indicates the enormous problem ahead of restoring the idle and poorly stocked lands to a healthy forest cover. Mechanical tree-planting machines greatly speed up the rate of forest planting, and undoubtedly these will be used more and more in the reforestation programs in all sections of the country. Even with the extensive use of these machines many years must elapse before the major part of these vast land areas can be restored to productive condition. Yet these lands must ultimately bear forests if they are to contribute to the country's economic welfare. Extensive reforestation is essential in the development of a nation-wide plan of forest conservation.

INCREASE IN PUBLIC OWNERSHIP OF FOREST LANDS

At present one-third of the forest-land area of the country is in public ownership. Provided the forest lands in private ownership are suitably managed, there will be no special need of large-scale additions to the areas now publicly owned. If, however, there are privately owned lands where forestry cannot pay its way or for other reasons will not be practiced, the only solution is public acquisition. Only in this manner can these lands be permanently administered for the welfare of the people. There will always be instances where it will be advisable to purchase lands in order to straighten boundaries, block up key areas, and otherwise obtain land required for the most effective administration. If major acquisitions to the publicly owned lands are to be made, it is generally recognized that they should be added to the national and state forest systems in the East.

The extent to which publicly owned forests should be increased through the acquisition of privately owned land is subject to vigorous debate. Those who are against such a program feel that the cost will be too great, that if vast areas are removed from privately owned holdings a great sum in taxes will be lost, and that it is unwise to have the government become too large a factor in industrial enterprise.

On the other hand, those in favor of this plan feel that private ownership has been largely responsible for exhaustion of the forest resources and that conditions will not improve unless the governments take over large areas of property for addition to their present forest system. They believe that the means can be found with which to carry out this program of land acquisition, although they admit that the cost will be high and the period of time required for it long.

They feel that the long-term benefits resulting from additional forest-land areas in public ownership will repay the costs.

The forest areas in state and municipal ownership may well be increased many times. Particularly is this increase important in the eastern United States, where the areas of forest are large but those in public ownership comparatively small. Actually, through purchase and the acquisition of abandoned, tax-delinquent lands, additions are now being made constantly to the publicly owned areas. This is, however, a slow process.

Certainly a reasonable increase is justified. The forest resources must be renewed and maintained, and governmental agencies are best able to spend the time and money for this great conservation enterprise. A reasonable and steady increase in the public ownership of forest lands is another foundation stone in a permanent program of forest conservation.

PUBLIC CO-OPERATION

For many years the principle of federal and state responsibility for the permanence and security of the nation's forest lands has been recognized by these governments. This principle rests on the facts that the benefits derived from forest growth accrue to all citizens and that many of the problems connected with privately owned forests are created by the general public. As a result of the recognition of public responsibility the government has enacted from time to time various laws whereby financial and other co-operation is extended to the private timberland and farm-woods owner.

This co-operation is provided the individual owner either indirectly by the federal government through the states or directly by the states. The assistance furnished under the co-operative laws has been favored by the individual because it has given him financial help and has not involved burdensome regulatory restrictions. The acceptance of the provisions has been entirely voluntary on the part of the owner to be benefited.

Public co-operation has taken diverse forms, the most important being assistance in protecting forest lands from fire. In this field the first steps in federal action were taken as a result of the provisions of the previously mentioned Weeks and Clark-McNary Laws. Funds are allotted to states that by legislation have established a fire-protective system, and co-operation between the states and the private owner is handled directly by delegated state officials. The funds to be granted do not exceed those made by both the state and the individual. As a result of these laws 303,000,000 acres of land have been placed under protection. The importance of these co-operative measures cannot be overestimated, for without them only a small fraction of this area would have been given the protection that it is now receiving.

Other phases of public co-operation take the form of the establishment of co-operative sustained-yield forest units (see above, p. 281), extension education in farm forestry, research for the benefit of growers and manufacturers of timber, and assistance in producing in forest nurseries trees for forest planting. The several states, colleges, experiment stations, farmers, industrial owners, and the public as a whole, all benefit directly from the co-operative measures.

Considerable pressure is being exerted to have the co-operative acts extended, both to increase present benefits and to explore new fields. The future may see new developments in such fields as forest insurance and forest credits and in more equitable forms of forest taxation. Whatever may develop, the co-operative measures thus far undertaken have been highly beneficial. Their continuation is essential and their expansion in some fields highly desirable.

REDUCTION IN WASTE

Of the total volume of timber currently cut from American forests only 50 per cent is ultimately used in the products for which the trees were felled.

Of the other 50 per cent, which is left in the woods as logging waste or at the mills as sawdust, trimmings, and edgings, one-third is used as fuel. Thus 50 per cent goes into primary products, 16 per cent goes into fuel, and the remainder, 34 per cent or one-third of the total stand, is not utilized. Obviously the extent to which waste can be reduced is primarily a matter of economic operation in woods and mill.

If, however, a part of this material now wasted could profitably be used, there would inevitably be a saving in the amount of timber that has to be cut to supply current demands. In the heavy stands of old-growth timber in the Pacific Northwest, logged-over areas often contain as much as 10,000 board feet per acre of abandoned logs and damaged trees. Current trends indicate that small mill operators could profitably use much of this timber. Mill wastes may also be used to some extent in the manufacture of ethyl alcohol, various cellulose derivatives, plastics, and other products. Under prevailing economic conditions, it is probable that only a part of the woods and mill waste can be utilized in the immediate future. Nevertheless all action that tends to reduce this loss is a gain in forest conservation.

REGULATION OF PRIVATELY OWNED FORESTS

Whether or not regulatory measures should be adopted by the federal or by the state governments to control in various ways the woods practices of the individual timberland owners is one of the most controversial issues in forestry. On this question all shades of opinion exist.

The advocates of compulsory regulation say that it is essential, for the reason that public co-operation and acquisition are inadequate and too slow. They believe that restrictive measures will not be unduly burdensome, that they will include only the minimum requirements needed to keep forest lands productive, and that only this process can prevent continued destructive liquidation on many forest properties. It is pointed out that regulatory laws are in force in every country in which forestry is practiced successfully on a nation-wide scale. They argue that many states today have restrictive legislation dealing with the protection of forest lands and that some states have enacted laws that control other phases of forestry practice as well.

Those opposed to restrictive regulation point out that a progressive point of view is now held by many timberland operators, and that this attitude is gradually bringing about the woods practices that the more reasonable proponents of regulation desire. Opponents further state that studies of existing supplies, growth, and drain indicate no urgency or need of precipitant haste in enacting restrictive laws, and that it is wiser to defer such action until it has been proved to be absolutely essential. Regulatory laws are costly to administer, disturbing to normal economy, and detrimental to business generally. Further, there is frank distrust of the bureaucratic control that will inevitably follow the enactment of such legislation.

Undoubtedly there are extremists among the industrial owners who want no interference of any description by governmental agencies and who, furthermore, wish to operate in a manner that suits only their own interests. These men fail to realize that times have changed since pioneer days, that they have an obligation to the public, and that, even in a democratic country, it is no longer permissible to deplete natural resources in a way that is injurious to the nation as a whole.

Fortunately many industrial owners are now subscribing to the principle that their timberlands must be managed so that they will continue to produce successive crops of wood. They understand that certain types of forestry practice must be undertaken, that this practice entails certain changes from past methods, and that they have distinct responsibilities to the public. Yet they feel that these changes should be instituted by themselves and not superimposed by federal law.

It is impossible to say what the final outcome of this controversy will be. Probably regulation in some form will eventuate, if not on a voluntary basis, then on a compulsory one. There is merit in the arguments of both sides. Certainly voluntary action is to be preferred. If regulation by law comes, its success will depend upon the type of restrictions enforced, the justice of administration, and the extent to which the individual owner can still continue profitably to handle his forests and the industries dependent on them.

FOREST CONSERVATION IN SUMMARY

In this and the two preceding chapters the attempt has been made to describe briefly the country's original forest resources, to trace the steps by which they were utilized and depleted, and to describe the conditions that exist at present. In dealing with the depletion of the forests no effort has been made to excuse those responsible for their disappearance, but the point has been brought out that during their exploitation no other course was possible. The forests helped build the nation, although they were used ruthlessly in the process; now because of destruction, fire, and dislocations of a social and economic nature, their depletion has created a host of baffling problems for this and future generations to solve. Forest conservation today must take the conditions that exist, recognize fully the causes of past abuse and destruction, and plan constructively for the future.

It has been shown that the forest is a valuable natural resource that serves mankind in many ways; that only a remnant of the original forest remains; that great areas of land are now covered with a second growth of trees, much of which is inferior in quality; that one-sixth of the commercial forest-land area is now idle and nonproductive; that many acute problems exist in relation to the character of ownership of forest land; and that the forestry problems of this country have far-reaching economic and social implications. All of these facts must be considered in an effective program of forest conservation. It is apparent that a problem of tremendous size and great difficulty lies ahead if the forests that remain are to be conserved, the denuded lands to be reforested, and all forest lands to be placed and maintained in productive condition so that they will serve perpetually the needs of mankind.

In bringing together the various steps essential to a well-rounded program of forest conservation it should be emphasized that the suggestions have been presented for the country as a whole, and not for regions in detail. The problems vary in intensity, they differ by region and by condition of land, and they are affected by the form of land ownership. If all forest lands are adequately protected from fire, if more conservative cutting practices are followed, if sustained-yield forest management in either intensive or extensive form is generally adopted, if the unproductive lands are restored to forest growth, if the public forest areas are enlarged to a reasonable extent, if public co-operation is further extended to the private timberland owners, and if the waste in forest and wood utilization is materially reduced, then forest conservation will be an accomplished fact.

To attain this goal will require a long period of time and careful planning in advance. The cost will be large, but small in relation to the benefits received. Trees grow slowly and great areas of land are involved. All forms of ownership must play their parts in this great undertaking. Every conservation agency must co-operate if the forests are to flourish once more as they did in the past and if they are to be useful in providing a continuous flow of forest products and in solving the varied problems of soil erosion, stream-flow regulation, wildlife management, forage production, and forest recreation.

CHAPTER IX

Parks: National and State

UNIQUE in the field of conservation are the park systems that have been established and developed by the federal and various state governments. Classified in detail the areas are of many kinds, but broadly they can be placed in three major groups.

First and outstanding in importance are the national parks, set aside by acts of Congress in order to preserve forever, in a natural state, the country's areas of superlative scenic and scientific value. Because of their marvelous scenery, including mountains, glaciers, canyons, lakes, waterfalls, caverns, and hot springs, their forests and other plant life, their varied collections of wild animals, and their relics of prehistoric days, they are visited by millions of people yearly, who observe and study their unusual plant and animal life and their many features of geologic and historic interest.

Second are the numerous reservations, other than national parks, that are also owned by the federal government and administered by the National Park Service. Most numerous are the national monuments, but in addition there are many other areas set aside for their historic and general scientific value. These areas are created directly by Presidential proclamation and not by acts of Congress.

Third are the parks that have been established by the individual states for the purpose of preserving their own areas of outstanding beauty and scientific importance.

The national and state park systems are invaluable in a program of conservation, since they preserve for all time various classes of animal and plant life that otherwise would almost inevitably face extinction. They likewise protect the country's geological and archeological wonders and the other scientific and historic resources that might be lost or ruined through exploitation. These parks afford unlimited opportunity for public recreation. And what is highly important, they bring to great numbers of citizens a realization of the character and scope of the country's natural resources and stimulate interest in their perpetual maintenance. They serve on a grand scale as out-of-door museums of natural history.

NATIONAL PARKS

The national park system. In 1872 the lands now making up the famous Yellowstone were set aside as a public park for the benefit and enjoyment of the people of the country. This was the first national park and the forerunner in a system that was subsequently to expand to include the majority of the nation's areas of superlative scenery and scientific importance. The law of 1872 creating the Yellowstone National Park was not in itself the act that set up the national park system as it now exists, but it did embody a bill of rights that made mandatory the preservation from injury or exploitation of all timber, mineral deposits, natural curiosities, or wonders within the park, and the retention in their natural condition and the protection of fish and game against wanton killing or against capture or destruction for the purpose of sale or profit. The Yellowstone Act is sometimes referred to as a Magna Carta for national parks. The provisions embodied in the act are, with some modifications, those that guide the National Park Service in its administration of the parks today, and this law may clearly be regarded as the cornerstone of the present system.

In 1890 three more parks were created, Sequoia, Yosemite, and General Grant. The latter was a national park until 1940 when it was incorporated as a detached unit in the Kings Canyon National Park. At varying intervals of time additional lands have been reserved by Congress in order to maintain them forever against commercial development or spoilation. The park system is not static, and some additions and changes have been made within the past several years, but as a whole the national park system is almost complete, and further changes of an extensive nature are improbable.

In 1916 the National Park Service was created, placed in the United States Department of the Interior, and charged with the administration of the parks and some of the then existing national monuments. Prior to 1933 the federal park system included many different types of areas, administered by various federal departments, with no one of them responsible for the system in its entirety. In 1933 all the federal parks, monuments, and related historical reservations administered by the several agencies of the federal government were made the responsibility of the National Park Service.

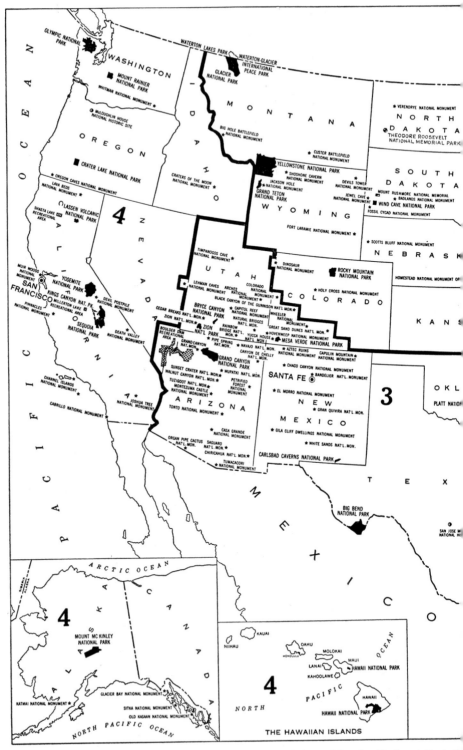

Figure 157. Areas administered by the National Park S[ervice]

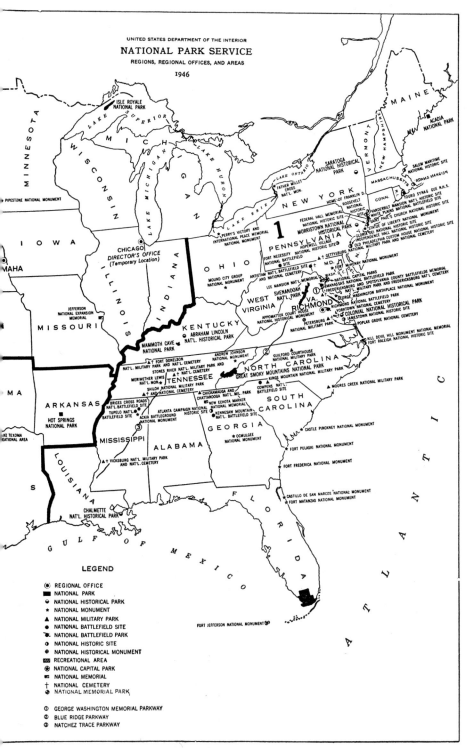

UNITED STATES DEPARTMENT OF THE INTERIOR

NATIONAL PARK SERVICE

REGIONS, REGIONAL OFFICES, AND AREAS

1946

LEGEND

- ◉ REGIONAL OFFICE
- ■ NATIONAL PARK
- ◓ NATIONAL HISTORICAL PARK
- ★ NATIONAL MONUMENT
- ▲ NATIONAL MILITARY PARK
- ● NATIONAL BATTLEFIELD SITE
- ✺ NATIONAL BATTLEFIELD PARK
- ○ NATIONAL HISTORIC SITE
- ◐ NATIONAL HISTORICAL MONUMENT
- ▦ RECREATIONAL AREA
- ✪ NATIONAL CAPITAL PARK
- ▭ NATIONAL MEMORIAL
- † NATIONAL CEMETERY
- ◑ NATIONAL MEMORIAL PARK

- ① GEORGE WASHINGTON MEMORIAL PARKWAY
- ② BLUE RIDGE PARKWAY
- ③ NATCHEZ TRACE PARKWAY

d projected developments. (U.S. Department of the Interior.)

Today the national park system consists of 171 nationally important areas, totaling more than 21,000,000 acres, set apart for the benefit of the people (Fig. 157).

The policy controlling the activities of the National Park Service was succinctly stated as follows in 1925 by Hubert Work, then Secretary of the United States Department of the Interior. This policy rests on three broad principles:

The national parks and national monuments must be maintained untouched by inroads of modern civilization in order that unspoiled bits of native America may be preserved to be enjoyed by future generations as well as our own.

They are set apart for the use, education, health, and pleasure of all the people.

The national interest must take precedence in all decisions affecting public or private enterprise in the parks and monuments.

Thus the national parks are maintained in a purely natural state for the use of present and future generations. In this way, the policy of control differs from that of the national forests, which are used for commercial development, although they, too, contain many features of great beauty and scientific interest. In the parks logging, mining, and hunting are strictly prohibited. Fishing is permitted under regulations that prevent the depletion of streams and lakes. Camping is encouraged. Commercial grazing still exists in some of the national parks, but is gradually being eliminated. Every effort is made to protect and ensure the perpetuation of the varied forms of existing animal and plant life (Fig. 158).

Size and location. The national parks, now twenty-eight in number, aggregate in area over 11,000,000 acres. Within the parks' boundaries are some 6,000,000 acres of forest, which add immeasurably to their beauty and attractiveness. Moreover, since these forests are maintained in a natural state, visitors to the parks will always have the opportunity of seeing forest lands representative of the different sections of the United States. The parks vary greatly in size, as is seen from Table 17.

Seventeen of the national parks are located in the western states, nine are in other parts of the United States, one is in Alaska, and one is in Hawaii.

Inasmuch as each park represents the highest type of scenic or scientific phenomena to be found in the country, and as very few, if any, unreserved areas meet this high requirement, it is not likely that the Congress will authorize more than limited additions to the national park system as now constituted.

TABLE 17. A LIST OF NATIONAL PARKS, GIVING THE LOCATION, AREA, AND DATE OF ESTABLISHMENT OF EACH

Name of park	Location	Area in square miles	Date of establish-ment
1 Yellowstone	Wyoming	3,458	1872
2 Sequoia	California	600	1890
3 Yosemite	California	1,182	1890
4 Mount Rainier	Washington	378	1899
5 Crater Lake	Oregon	251	1902
6 Platt	Oklahoma	1	1902
7 Wind Cave	South Dakota	18	1903
8 Mesa Verde	Colorado	80	1906
9 Glacier	Montana	1,558	1910
10 Rocky Mountain	Colorado	405	1915
11 Hawaii	Hawaii	271	1916
12 Lassen Volcanic	California	161	1916
13 Mount McKinley	Alaska	3,030	1917
14 Acadia	Maine	44	1919
15 Grand Canyon	Arizona	1,008	1919
16 Zion	Utah	148	1919
17 Hot Springs	Arkansas	2	1921
18 Bryce Canyon	Utah	56	1928
19 Grand Teton	Wyoming	150	1929
20 Great Smoky Mountains ...	North Carolina Tennessee	720	1930
21 Carlsbad Caverns	New Mexico	71	1930
22 Shenandoah	Virginia	302	1935
23 Mammoth Cave	Kentucky	79	1936
24 Olympic	Washington	1,325	1938
25 Kings Canyon	California	710	1940
26 Isle Royale	Lake Superior	209	1940
27 Big Bend	Texas	1,080	1944
28 Everglades	Florida	710	1947

Character of parks. For lack of space it is impossible to comment on all of the parks, but it is of interest to point out the important features of some of the better-known ones.[1]

Yellowstone is perhaps the most famous of the national parks. It contains more geysers than are found in all the rest of the world, a canyon of great beauty for its delicate coloring, majestic waterfalls, in-

Figure 158. Wildlife in Yosemite National Park. As a result of the protection afforded the wild animals in the national parks, they become exceedingly tame. Some of the animals, particularly the bears, learn early in life to beg for food, and in a few of the parks are becoming something of a problem in their lack of respect for property rights. (U.S. Department of the Interior.)

numerable hot springs, mud volcanoes, and a rich and varied assortment of animal life (Figs. 159, 160). The Yellowstone, 3,458 square miles in area, is in itself a huge game preserve; grizzly, black, and brown bears, bison, deer, elk, moose, mountain sheep, and antelope all live here. Some 200 species of birds find this park a natural refuge.

---

[1] Detailed information describing the individual parks and the national park system is available from the National Park Service, U.S. Department of the Interior, Washington.

Figure 159. The Lower Falls and Grand Canyon of the Yellowstone. The majestic waterfall, over 300 feet high, and the walls of the great canyon with its beautiful coloring are outstanding scenic features of Yellowstone Park. (C. H. Guise.)

Figure 160. Old Faithful, Yellowstone. Old Faithful is the world's most famous geyser. It plays regularly at intervals of approximately one hour, and rises to a height of from 80 to 100 feet. The surrounding country is a high plateau covered with forests which run heavily to lodgepole pine. (U.S. Department of the Interior.)

The streams and lakes are well stocked with fish. Old Faithful is one of its best-known landmarks.

Yosemite is noted for its beautiful valley, set in the midst of towering peaks and cliffs, its spectacular waterfalls, its forests of sugar pine and ponderosa pine, three groves of big trees, and its superb mountain scenery. The famous valley, over seven miles long and approximately

Figure 161. Yosemite National Park. The beautiful valley of Yosemite with its granite cliffs and lofty waterfalls is one of the most popular national parks. The famous El Capitan, Half Dome, and Bridal Veil Falls are familiar to millions of people. (U.S. Department of the Interior.)

one mile wide, is only a small part of more than a thousand square miles of magnificent mountain wilderness (Fig. 161).

Sequoia has great collections of big trees, wonderful pine and fir forests, impressive mountain scenery, and innumerable lakes. Here are thousands of the trees for which the park is named (Fig. 162). In Sequoia is the General Sherman Tree, probably the largest in the world. It is 272.4 feet high, 36.5 feet in diameter at the base, and 17 feet in diameter at a distance of 120 feet from the ground. It is estimated to be over 3,000 years old. Sequoia also includes representative areas of the rugged Sierra Nevada Mountains. In this park is Mount Whitney, 14,496 feet in elevation, the highest peak in the United States, excluding Alaska, and numerous other peaks exceeding elevations of 13,000 feet. This park is also rich in animal life.

Mount Rainier, in the Cascade Range, snow-capped the year around, is the starting point for a number of individual glaciers (Fig.

Figure 162. Big trees in Sequoia National Park. Great numbers of big trees, *Sequoia gigantea,* are found in Sequoia National Park. These great trees, many of which reach a height of more than 250 feet, are the oldest and largest living things in the world. (U.S. Department of the Interior.)

163). An extinct volcano, it towers to an elevation of 14,408 feet, rising almost two miles directly from its surrounding base. At the higher elevations are mountain meadows and broad fields of unusual subalpine wild flowers; at the lower elevations are magnificent virgin forests of giant Douglas fir, western hemlock, western red cedar, and other species.

Crater Lake National Park, also in the Cascades, is an area of 251 square miles in rugged, mountainous country. It is noted for a circular lake of sapphire blue, six miles across, which rests in the crater of an extinct volcano. Volcanic cliffs tower from 1,000 to 2,000 feet above the water. The entire surrounding area is covered with heavy forests of pine, hemlock, and fir.

Glacier National Park, at the Continental Divide in the northern Rockies, is noted for its rugged mountains, lofty, sharp-pointed peaks,

Figure 163. Mount Rainier and the Nisqually Glacier. Mount Rainier rises to a height of 14,408 feet above sea level, and almost two miles above its surrounding base. From the upper slopes a number of individual glaciers start on their downward courses. (U.S. Department of the Interior.)

great valleys, steep precipices, beautiful lakes, and swift-flowing streams (Fig. 164). This is a wilderness country of the first order, containing some of the finest mountain scenery in America.

Rocky Mountain National Park, in the heart of the Colorado Rockies at the Continental Divide, is another region of magnificent mountain scenery with numerous lakes and rushing streams. Longs Peak rises to a height of 14,255 feet. Valleys, meadows, peaks, lakes, and streams combine to make this one of the most famous national parks.

Mesa Verde National Park in southern Colorado contains the most famous and best-preserved prehistoric cliff dwellings in the United States, if not in the world.

In Lassen Volcanic National Park is the most recently active volcano in this country. Also in this park are hot springs, mud geysers, and other evidences of recent volcanic activity.

Figure 164. Glacier National Park—Upper St. Mary Lake. Glacier National Park at the Continental Divide in the northern Rockies is a region of rugged, sharp-pointed mountains, steep precipices, lakes, and swift-flowing streams. Going-to-the-Sun Mountain, to the right of the lake, is one of the famous peaks in the park. (U.S. Department of the Interior.)

The Grand Canyon in Arizona is regarded by many as the world's most sublime spectacle (Fig. 165). Nowhere else can be seen such a combination of river erosion and brilliant coloring. It is approximately one mile from the rim of the canyon to the depths where the Colorado River flows. In width the canyon varies from four to eighteen miles. The sides of the canyon and the fantastically eroded cliffs are brilliantly colored in blues, tans, reds, grays, and purples. The Grand Canyon is a park of unbelievable beauty and grandeur.

Zion and Bryce Canyon National Parks, both in Utah, are also examples of spectacular coloring and extensive erosion. Fantastic are the temples, pinnacles, spires, cliffs, and amphitheaters, brilliantly colored in various shades of reds and whites. These parks of the Southwest are unequaled for their erosion effects and rich coloring.

The Great Smoky National Park in Tennessee and North Carolina includes the most massive mountain uplift in the eastern United

Figure 165. The Grand Canyon. The Grand Canyon, from 4 to 18 miles in width, is the world's most spectacular example of river erosion. The Colorado River flows through a granite gorge at a distance of one mile below the canyon's rim. The coloring of the eroded cliffs is unsurpassed for grandeur and beauty. (U.S. Department of the Interior.)

States. Especially noteworthy is the grand scenery of the southern Appalachians and wonderful reservations of remaining old-growth hardwood forests. This park is particularly rich in its animal and plant life. There are 152 varieties of trees, including spruce, balsam, hemlock, and pine, at the higher elevations, and a great variety of deciduous trees at the intermediate and lower levels (Fig. 166). The park abounds in fish and game.

The Everglades National Park, located in the subtropical area of Florida, is characterized by extensive watercourses, saw-grass prairies, and large forest areas in which mangrove, cypress, and palm trees are common. Numerous other species of southern trees also occur. The park is outstanding for the variety and abundance of its animal life. In addition to the many well-known animals inhabiting the forests and waters of this region are some species which occur in no other part of the United States. It is the only place in this country where the American crocodile is found. In the waterways leading in from the west coast of the peninsula is the aquatic manatee or sea cow. The

Figure 166. Great Smoky National Park. The Great Smoky National Park in Tennessee and North Carolina contains magnificent scenery and rich collections of forests and wildlife. (Asheville Photo Co., Asheville, N.C.)

wealth of birdlife is extraordinary. Herons, cranes, ibis, and egrets are present in large numbers. The subtropical wildness of the Everglades is, because of its beauty and its unique plant and animal resources, an important addition to the national park system.

Each park, with its diverse and distinctive features, is worthy of extended comment. Yet any discussion, however complete and detailed it might be, is a poor substitute for the inspiration that comes from actually viewing the brilliantly colored canyons of the Southwest, the geysers and other natural phenomena of the Yellowstone, the majestic peaks and waterfalls of Yosemite, the glaciers, forests, and flowers of

Rainier, or the Continental Divide at Glacier. It is only by living in the parks that one can gain a realization of their scope and beauty and appreciate the true significance of the role that they play in national conservation.

Recreational features. In order that the public may enjoy the wonderful scenery, observe wildlife in its natural habitat, and live for a brief period in primitive areas, the recreational features of the parks have been highly developed. Accommodations for visitors at hotels, lodges, and camps are provided to meet the needs or desires of every class of tourist. Facilities are available for those who wish to pitch their own tents.

A great increase in tourist travel has taken place since 1916, the year when the National Park Service was created. In 1915 the number of visitors amounted to more than 300,000. Now more than 15,000,000 people are visiting the parks annually to see and enjoy these wonderlands for their scenery, forests, animal and plant life, and other natural marvels. Lakes and streams attract great numbers whose primary interest is in fishing. Rest and simple forms of recreation appeal to many. Winter sports are now being developed extensively in some of the national parks. Park naturalists, museums, and guides aid the visitor in becoming acquainted with his surroundings.

Excellent road systems give access to the more important centers. Trails for walking and horseback travel are generally available for those who wish to penetrate even the most remote sections. By using these trails the visitor really gets to know the parks.

Conservation problems. From the standpoint of conservation, the parks are carefully protected and administered. Several recent developments, however, have caused uneasiness among those best informed about the national parks. The first of these is the rather rapid development of the park system. Constant pressure, local and political, is being exerted to create new parks from areas that are not generally deemed to be of national park stature. Such areas are no doubt worthy of being reserved and developed as state parks, but not as national parks. In fact, there are few areas remaining in the United States of sufficient scientific interest or value to warrant their addition to the national park system. To add to this system reservations that properly should be set aside as state or local parks will inevitably lower the prestige that the national parks now hold.

Equally serious is the pressure for commercial developments and for extensive improvements. A heated controversy took place before the Colorado–Big Thompson water diversion project in Rocky Mountain National Park was approved. When this project is completed, a thirteen-mile tunnel through the Rocky Mountains will tap the waters on the western side of the Continental Divide and carry them to the farms and ranches in the eastern part of Colorado. In some of the other national parks pressure for the use of water resources has created problems of major proportions.

There is also some controversy over the manner in which the parks are being opened up by roads and trails. Many think that the wilderness features are being impaired by these developments. Others hold that only roads that are essential for access are being built. Certainly the parks should be accessible to the public, but road and trail systems should not be too extensive.

During the war years intense pressure was exerted to open various parks to logging, mining, and a wider use of the grazing resources. In some parks these efforts still continue. A vigorous attempt is being made at the present time to eliminate some ninety square miles of heavily timbered areas from the western lowland sections of Olympic National Park so that these lands can be exploited for their heavy stands of timber.

If the logging of Douglas fir and Sitka spruce is permitted in Olympic National Park, these great areas will cease to exist as virgin forests of superlative quality. The income to be received from those who come year after year to visit these old-growth forests may well exceed the immediate returns which would accrue to a limited number of persons who would profit by cutting this timber. Tourists will not be interested in visiting and spending money to see large areas of slash and stumps or of young second growth. With such an invasion as an entering wedge, when and where will the next demands appear? They will be certain to come and will be backed with strong support.

Likewise if the grazing interests are allowed free access to the parks, will it be possible to eliminate or control this use at a later date?

Proposals to mine certain critical minerals in the parks and monuments have been followed by studies showing that the minerals are seldom of sufficient quantity or economic value to justify extraction.

As a general policy the Park Service gives careful study to the demands for commercial exploitation, if the needs seem critical, but so far almost all requests have been denied.

The use of the natural resources in the parks must be held to a minimum. Emergencies may occur which will require some changes in policy, but each request for entry into the parks for the utilization of their resources must be given the most thorough consideration. The parks belong to the citizens of the country and their interests as a whole must come first.

NATIONAL MONUMENTS AND OTHER RESERVATIONS

The national monuments are areas of prehistoric, historic, scenic, or scientific interest, usually too limited in size or character of attraction to meet the standards required of a national park. Whereas national parks are established by acts of Congress, national monuments are created by Presidential proclamation, a power that was granted to the President by a federal law known as the Antiquities Act, passed in 1906. This important legislation was enacted as a result of widespread interest in the preservation of the country's archeological phenomena, particularly the cliff dwellings in the Southwest; it was subsequently broadened in scope to include other features of national historic and scientific importance, both natural and man-made.

As a result of the Antiquities Act, a number of national monuments were reserved prior to the creation of the National Park Service in 1916. Some were administered by the War Department, some by the Department of Agriculture, and some by the Department of the Interior. As stated previously, all national monuments and other historical areas were placed under the National Park Service in 1933. There are at present 143 of these reservations.

Though the national parks and monuments differ in the method of their establishment, it is not always easy to define in a conclusive way the exact differences between them. Numerous examples can be cited of parks and monuments that preserve the same types of phenomena. In some instances areas were first reserved as national monuments and subsequently created national parks, as was the case with the Grand Canyon, Olympic, and Zion.

Two of the national monuments are larger than any of the national parks, these being the Katmai and Glacier Bay monuments in Alaska. Death Valley National Monument is exceeded in size only by the Yellowstone and Mount McKinley National Parks. A small number of monuments are intermediate in size; an example is the Dinosaur National Monument in Colorado and Utah, an area rich in fossil animals, that aggregates 312 square miles. Yet the extensive areas are the exception, and the majority of the national monuments are relatively small, many being less than 1,000 acres in size.

The most significant difference between a national park and a national monument is found in the comparative value and quality of the natural resources to be preserved, each park being supreme in its special scenic or scientific field. Fortunately no conflict exists; a national monument that is found to possess the outstanding qualities required can, with the approval of Congress, be transferred to the status of a national park.

The national monuments, now eighty-five in number, include cliff dwellings, historic sites, petrified trees, natural bridges, rare geological formations, hot springs, wilderness areas, and other places of unusual interest. The majority of the monuments reserved for prehistoric or scientific features are in the West and in Alaska. Examples of national monuments, in addition to those already mentioned, are the Devil's Tower in Wyoming (Fig. 167), the Muir Woods in California, the Craters of the Moon in Idaho, the Cedar Breaks in Utah, the Petrified Forest in Arizona, the Great Sand Dunes in Colorado, and the Aztec Ruins in New Mexico.

The greater number of the national reservations of historic interest are in the East. These reservations were set aside to preserve landmarks of the colonial period, the Revolutionary War, the early days of the Republic, the War between the States, and the more recent era. Included are national battlefield sites, national cemeteries, national historical parks, national memorials, national military parks, and other spots whose significance is bound up with the country's past. Examples of these areas are the George Washington Birthplace; the Colonial National Historical Park, including parts of Jamestown Island, Williamsburg, and Yorktown; the battlefield sites at Vicksburg, Chickamauga, and Gettysburg; the Washington Monument; and the Lincoln Memorial.

STATE PARKS

Interest in developing state park systems has been in evidence for many years. In 1865 Yosemite Valley and the famous Mariposa grove of big trees, then a part of the public domain, were withdrawn by the national government and given to California for a state park, although later this became a national park. Fifty years ago other state parks were created, among which were those at Niagara Falls in New York, Mackinac Island in Michigan, and Itasca Lake in Minnesota.

State parks serve a very useful place in conservation. They supplement the national park system and make possible the preservation of each state's finest areas of natural scenery and scientific or historic interest. State parks are set aside and developed primarily for recreational use. In these areas, which are easily reached over good roads, the

Figure 167. Devil's Tower National Monument. The Devil's Tower in the Black Hills region of Wyoming is a mass of igneous rock, 600 feet in height and 1,700 feet in diameter at the base. It is visible in some directions for almost a hundred miles. (U.S. Department of the Interior.)

citizens of almost every state have near at hand centers for camping, fishing, water sports, mountain climbing, or other forms of recreation. Hunting is permitted in many of the state parks.

Land devoted to state parks totals almost 3,000,000 acres. Almost four-fifths of this land is found in New York, because the great Adirondack and Catskill forest preserves, over 2,000,000 acres in area, are administered as state parks. At present, the states leading in this development are New York, California, Indiana, Ohio, Michigan, Iowa, Illinois, Pennsylvania, and Connecticut. In the great forest parks of New York many thousands of people from the heavily populated centers annually camp, hunt, fish, and otherwise find their main sources of recreation. New York has also a widespread system of smaller parks that are visited annually by great numbers of people.

Especially noteworthy in the state park system is the reservation of some 40,000 acres of the magnificent Pacific Coast redwoods. These trees, which are closely related to the big trees of the Sierra Nevada forests, were at one time in danger of being cut for lumber. Now, through the efforts of the Save-the-Redwoods League, large areas of virgin redwoods have been placed in the California state park system and preserved for all time. This is a notable step in conservation. Nowhere in the world are these forests equaled for grandeur and impressiveness. Had they been cut, it would have been impossible to replace them.

It is probable that state park development will continue far beyond the status in which it exists today. It is almost the only way in which the local recreational needs of the public as a whole can be met. At the same time, the development will preserve in every state the areas of outstanding scenery and of unusual scientific value.

CHAPTER X

The Western Grazing Lands

THE GRAZING LANDS of the West comprise one of the basic natural resources of the United States. As a problem in conservation the range lands are in many ways similar to the forests. The principal product of the forest is wood; that of the range, grass and other forage for the feeding of cattle, sheep, horses, and other domestic livestock. Like the forest the range is of vital importance in the protection of watersheds, the prevention of soil erosion, and the maintenance of wildlife. The range is closely associated with the agricultural prosperity of the West. The original ranges, which appeared to be inexhaustible, have been severely abused and depleted. The range lands have always been a major problem in the handling of the public domain. Like the forest, the range is a renewable resource. The grazing lands and the forests have much in common both in their history of use and in their present condition. Yet the importance of the range in the general field of natural resource conservation has until recent years been seriously underestimated. In the past neither the general public nor many western stockmen have had a true appreciation of the value of this resource as a whole, the extent of its neglect and abuse, or the way in which its management has affected and will continue to affect human welfare.

HISTORY

The original range. The great western ranges of grass and other forage are estimated to have covered originally 850,000,000 acres, extending from the Mississippi River west to the Pacific Coast and from the Canadian border to Mexico. There were many types of vegetation, including the lush grasslands of the prairies and great plains and, farther west, the lands with bunch, semidesert, and sage brush grasses, the open forests, the piñon-juniper and shrub lands, and the open deserts. West of the Rockies were vast expanses of grazing lands lying between the mountain ranges and other upland areas. Reference has previously been made to the grazing resources in the western forests. In these forests are extensive areas of forest meadows (Fig. 168); in addition, great stretches of forest, in which western yellow pine is predominant, are so open that heavy stands of grass, useful for grazing, have become established. Tall grasses on the prairies and short grasses

Figure 168. A forest range in southern Idaho. Large numbers of sheep are grazed in the open pasture lands that are found in many of the national forests in the West. If grazing is properly controlled, the ranges will provide food for these animals indefinitely. (U.S. Forest Service.)

on the great plains originally covered 320,000,000 acres of land. Another 400,000,000 acres were covered with diverse forms of open-grown and semidesert grasses, shrubs, chaparral, piñon, and juniper. Open forests and forest meadows covered another 130,000,000 acres. The great empire of western range land is said to have produced through the pasturing of livestock five times the wealth of all the gold mined in this country. Bison, elk, and many other animals ranged over this land unmolested. It was a land of varied topography and climate. Rolling plains, with heavy stands of grass to the east, gave way farther west to rugged mountains, intermountain areas, deserts, and plateaus with thinner stands of forage. Numerous great rivers and smaller streams everywhere traversed this vast region.

Use and abuse. Originally consisting of 850,000,000 acres, or 44 per cent of the total area of the continental United States, the range has been reduced to an approximate present area of 750,000,000 acres, or 40 per cent of the country's land surface. This vast domain is larger than the country's total forest area, 624,000,000 acres. Extending originally from the Mississippi River to the Pacific Ocean, the range covered parts of the lands over two-thirds of the western United States. However, most of the prairies, or tall grass lands extending west to the 98th meridian or 30-inch rainfall line, were turned into farms. In addition, a relatively narrow strip of the eastern part of the Great Plains, or short grasslands, was also broken by the plow, this area extending approximately to the 100th meridian or 20-inch rainfall line. This line is approximately the present eastern boundary of the western grazing lands. The transfer of the prairie grasslands to more intensive forms of agriculture, wheat, corn, and cotton, was a natural development. However, the eastern areas of the Great Plains, which were also put largely to agricultural use, have often had disappointing crop yields because of low and uncertain rainfall.

The livestock industry was started on a small scale by Mexicans prior to 1600. The growth was slow and gradual until the late 1870's, when cattle raising had become an industry of major proportions. The range was free, and financial profit seemed certain and immediate. The development of the industry was encouraged by the railroads, and both American and European capital was invested in large amounts. In those years there was little knowledge of the feeding needs of cattle or their effect on the range. Seldom if ever was thought given to possible depletion or exhaustion. Rapid overdevelopment, land speculation, bitter controversies between cattle and sheep owners, and intense competition for the open range were major problems. By the turn of the century serious economic dislocations were taking place, and it was evident, even fifty years ago, that the range lands were being overgrazed and handled without thought for the future. The range industry has always been plagued with a series of booms and depressions. But in spite of this cattle and sheep raising has continuously expanded over all sections of the West.

The grazing lands in general have been utilized with the primary thought of immediate return rather than of long-time use. Too many animals grazing too long on the same areas of land have been the primary cause of the deterioration of much of the forage resources. Extensive grass fires have also played their part, as have other methods of destruction. The continued misuse of these lands has resulted, first, in a cover of grass and forage plants that has progressively deteriorated in amount (Fig. 169); second, in a replacement of desirable grasses and plants by inferior species; and third, after the cover of vegetation was gone or greatly reduced, in severe erosion and loss of surface soil (Fig. 170). There has been all too little appreciation of the correct number of grazing animals that a range could carry and still be con-

Figure 169. An overgrazed range. Overgrazing results first in a thin cover of grass and replacement of valuable plants with those of inferior quality. The next step will be erosion and loss of surface soil. (U.S. Forest Service.)

tinuously productive. Consequently depletion took place steadily over great areas of land.

The Taylor Grazing Act. The unappropriated public domain, over the greater part of its area, has always been used extensively for the grazing of cattle and sheep. Prior to 1934 the public lands were relatively free to the stockmen. For years overstocking and overgrazing were common practices with the resultant steady deterioration of the range resources. Recognizing that much of this vast public land area was almost ruined and the remainder steadily growing worse as a grassland resource, efforts were made to put an end to the misuse and gradually to rebuild the range lands so that they would support indefinitely reasonable numbers of grazing animals. These efforts resulted in the enactment in 1934 of a federal law commonly referred to as the Taylor Grazing Act.

This important law was enacted to stop injury to the public grazing lands by preventing overgrazing and soil deterioration, to provide for their orderly use, improvement, and development, and to stabilize the livestock industry dependent on the public range. The law authorized

Figure 170. Erosion on a forest range. Overgrazing exposes the bare soil, which gullies and washes badly during heavy rains. This picture shows a bad gully that could have been prevented if grazing had been regulated properly. (U.S. Forest Service.)

the establishment of grazing districts of 80,000,000 acres, which included 61,000,000 acres of western range, and 19,000,000 acres of forests, alpine country, and deserts. Pending the classification of lands to be placed in the grazing districts, all public lands were withdrawn from entry. Although provisions under the public land laws for the transfer of federal lands to private ownership still exist, the Taylor Act to all intents and purposes brought about the end of free land disposal on a wide scale from the public domain. The Secretary of the

Interior was granted broad powers to establish districts and regulate grazing practices in them.

There were, in addition to the 80,000,000 acres to be incorporated in districts, more than 60,000,000 acres additional in the unreserved public domain for which no provision was then made for grazing control or management. This was one fundamental weakness of the law as enacted in 1934. Later these areas were all brought under the provisions of the Taylor Grazing Act, and at present 140,000,000 acres in sixty districts are being administered under this law. Though the law had certain faults in relation to various types of administrative procedures, it represented a highly important step in the future plans and policies for handling public lands. Prior to this act the public ranges were, from the national standpoint, a wasting resource of little national concern. With this law the United States recognized its obligations of public land stewardship and adopted the policy of initiating progressive steps of restoring and managing the ranges.

Present ownership and administration. The western range lands are held in three main classes of ownership: federal, state and county, and private. Lands in federal ownership are administered by the Department of the Interior and the Department of Agriculture. The Department of the Interior administers 230,000,000 acres, of which 140,000,000 are in grazing districts, 35,000,000 acres in the remaining vacant, unreserved, and unappropriated public domain, 14,000,000 acres in various reservations and withdrawals, and 41,000,000 acres in the Indian lands. The Department of Agriculture administers 81,000,000 acres in the national forests and, in addition, 7,000,000 acres of purchased submarginal farm lands.

In all, federal grazing lands now aggregate 318,000,000 acres. State and county lands total more than 60,000,000 acres. Privately owned lands amount to approximately 375,000,000 acres.

The ownership problem is far more complex than a mere statement of the acreages owned by private interests and the federal, state, and other public agencies would indicate. The ownership pattern is formed by an intricate system of small farms, railroad lands, state holdings, state and county tax-delinquent lands, ranches of every size, and federal lands, all intermingled. Many of the private lands are in absentee ownership, with the inevitable lack of responsibility or interest in their maintenance. With such a complex ownership pattern, the problems of administration are exceedingly difficult—a fact that has undoubtedly contributed to range-land deterioration.

VALUE AND IMPORTANCE

Economic importance. Along with the forests the western grazing lands rank as one of the most important vegetative areas in the United States. From these ranges come a large part of the nation's meat, wool, and leather supply, which in value runs into hundreds of millions of dollars annually. Also closely co-ordinated with the range is the general agriculture of the West. In fact, the western range is an integral but highly specialized part of western agriculture, and the economic relationships of the two phases are closely interwoven. The direct value of crops in the range states is between $1,500,000,000 and $2,000,000,000 annually. The agriculture of the West involves the standard of living of some two million farm families plus the contribution to all business enterprise that serves agriculture and stock raising. In all, fifteen million people of the range country depend, in large measure, upon the successful handling of the western agricultural and range lands for their welfare and prosperity.

The range and western agriculture. A close interrelation exists between the western farms of a general type and the ranches that are devoted primarily to raising livestock, as the result of a large-scale interchange of the products. The variations in types of crop farming and range livestock operations are innumerable. At one extreme is the wheat and cotton farmer, whose farming may be but indirectly related to range use. At the other is the year-long livestock operation, to which little or no cropland is attached. In between these extremes are many combinations of farming and range livestock operations. Here cultivated crops furnish the main cash income, with sometimes the livestock grower as the only available market. There livestock raising is the major business, with farming carried on merely to produce the necessary supplemental feed. Elsewhere the harvested croplands furnish forage. And again a hay producer depends on the stock owned by his neighbors to furnish a market for his product.

Within the types described there is wide variation in the size of the establishments. At one extreme there may be as few as five to ten head of stock. At the other are great ranches where there may be as many as 60,000 to 80,000 grazing animals. The acreage of land controlled may vary from as little as ten acres of farm land to 500,000 acres or more of range land with some farm land included.

Protective influences. In no part of the United States is the relation of vegetative cover to the conservation of water more important than in the western range country. An adequate grass mantle protects soil from erosion, aids in streamflow regulation, prevents silting of streams and reservoirs, and reduces flood stages. Of the total acreage of the principal watersheds of the West, 64 per cent is covered by grasslands. Most of the villages and cities of the West depend upon an adequate supply of water produced in large part from the range-land watersheds. Likewise irrigation and power enterprises, with investments of billions of dollars, obtain their water from the streams of the range lands. To provide these services to the people of the West every factor that can contribute to a sustained supply of water is essential. The most important of these factors is a protective grassland cover.

Wildlife and recreation. Originally the grasslands harbored the greatest concentration of large animals in North America, including elk, antelope, buffalo, bear, and deer. Many forms of small game including upland game birds and migratory water fowl were present in vast numbers. The streams were rich with fish life. For a number of reasons the wildlife populations have declined to extremely low levels.

Wildlife is of direct economic value. Not only does game produce food, but where abundant it also brings to communities, from hunters and fishermen, annual incomes that amount to millions of dollars. Large sums are spent at present even though the game resources are far more limited than they were in the past. The adoption of effective game-management policies will provide far more wildlife than now exists, and at the same time increase greatly the sums of money spent by hunters and fishermen.

Wildlife exerts a beneficial effect on range lands. The enrichment of the soil by burrowing mammals, the distribution of seed by birds, the influence on stream flow by beavers, when properly controlled, in checking rapid runoff, and the control of insects by birds are all factors of economic importance. Because of the vast areas, scenery, climate, and wildlife, the western grasslands have enormous potentialities for recreational use. Hunting, fishing, camping, and touring provide recreation for millions of persons annually. Tourists and recreationists will continue to come in increasing numbers to the various sections of the range lands, and spend huge sums for the benefit of the states, cities, and communities, provided the wildlife and other attractions are developed and maintained.

USE AND DEPLETION PRIOR TO 1935

The Western Range, Senate Document no. 199. Complying with a request by the United States Senate for a report on the original and present conditions of the western range, the Secretary of Agriculture transmitted a detailed statement to the Senate in April, 1936. This report entitled *The Western Range* was prepared by the Forest Service.[1]

The studies on which the report was based were made in the early thirties and in all probability reflect conditions at their worst. The western country had suffered from several years of severe drought, the unappropriated and unreserved public domain had been open for many years to unrestricted use, and the Taylor Act had just been passed without any opportunity as yet for the initiation of grazing management practices. Yet the results set forth in this comprehensive report are important since they show how serious conditions were when the surveys were made.

It should, however, be emphasized that the facts set forth in the following summary pertain to range conditions prior to 1936 and not to those of today. Though range conditions are still far from satisfactory, a gradual improvement has started for several reasons. Rainfall has been greater in amount, 140,000,000 acres have been withdrawn from unrestricted use and placed in the grazing districts for constructive administration, and soil conservation measures on a broad scale have been initiated. In addition, an increasing number of western stockmen have been trained in range management techniques in the agricultural colleges. These men understand the problems of range management and are definitely interested in improving and sustaining the forage resources that are essential to the development and perpetuation of improved types of range animals, which many of them are now raising.

Some of the more important conditions and the reasons therefor as set forth in the 1936 report follow.

Overstocking. The overstocking of the range has been the primary

---

[1] *The Western Range* (Senate Document 199, 74th Congress, 2d Session; Washington, 1936).

and direct cause of the depletion of much of its area. Not only does the range suffer in the loss of much of its forage cover, but, in addition, the number of animals that a range can carry steadily declines. Further, when conditions become too bad, emaciation, starvation, and an unduly high mortality of the stock take place. On depleted lands calf and lamb crops are low.

In all, the western ranges were carrying more than 17,000,000 head of stock, whereas the estimated capacity was less than 11,000,000. In other words, these figures indicate that the ranges were overstocked by some 60 per cent. The grazing lands in the national forests presented the best picture with only 7 per cent overstocking; the Indian lands were next with 36 per cent. State and county lands were carrying twice the stock of which they were capable. Other classes of ownership were overstocked to the extent of 60 per cent or more.[2]

The causes of overstocking are many and they are not easy to correct. Much of the land was without adequate control, and since everyone naturally wanted to obtain maximum personal benefit, the competition for use was severe. The belief that sustained profits depended on maximum numbers continuously grazed has been general. Stockmen have been in the grip of economic forces that they could not control; they have had their livings to make, regardless of what took place on the ranges as a whole. Not infrequently the range has had to supply feed when supplementary feeding would have been wise. The degree of stocking has often been based on the conditions of better years. Also there has been, on the part of many, little knowledge of the techniques of correct range management, including carrying capacities, proper distribution of stock, and the correct seasonal use of the range.

The problem of correcting overstocking is far from simple. The point of view of the stock raiser must be fully considered. His problems are the result of practices that have developed over many years. Yet a gradual change to restore the grazing lands is imperative and necessitates full co-operation between all parties involved, including both public and private interests.

Types of damage. The types of damage that take place because of overgrazing are, in their major aspects, relatively simple to present. The first and immediate result is the steady exhaustion of the better grasses and the more useful forage plants. The cover becomes progressively thinner, and the desirable grasses and other vegetation are

---

[2] *Ibid.,* p. 164.

gradually replaced with weeds and plants of inferior quality for live-stock feed. Once the cover is reduced to the state where it can no longer protect the soil, erosion begins and continues until sheet and gully erosion commonly render large areas useless for further grazing purposes (Fig. 171).

Range lands cover approximately two-thirds of the principal water-shed areas in the West. Of these lands prior to 1930, 80 per cent were eroding seriously; 50 per cent of these areas were contributing appre-ciable quantities of silt to the major streams and reservoirs of the West.

Figure 171. A result of overgrazing. Overgrazing results in loss of grasses, inadequate food for cattle, and severe erosion. (U.S. Forest Serv-ice.)

In the mountains of all western states accelerated sheet and gully ero-sion was stripping away the valuable surface soil and, in addition, cut-ting into slopes and channeling rich meadows. Floods were increasing in frequency and severity because of the rapid runoff from depleted ranges, causing damage that amounted to millions of dollars. Wind erosion, sometimes resulting in dust storms, not infrequently reduced great areas to wasteland.

Once destroyed the range lands can be restored slowly and only at great expense. Further, when the pasture is reduced or lost, the owners must graze smaller numbers of animals, their incomes are reduced, and yet they must pay as much in property taxes as before. This means that lands are often given up through tax delinquency, and the general prosperity of a region declines. A cycle is started similar to that which takes place when the forests throughout a region are destroyed.

Wildlife has suffered also. It was natural that, as the grasslands were taken over for domestic livestock, the wildlife population would decrease greatly in amount; but the manner in which wildlife of almost every type has been drastically reduced, in some cases almost exterminated, constitutes a gloomy chapter in the story of the wildlife resources of the country.

Overgrazing, fires, loss of soil, silting of streams, and swamp drainage have so changed the environment for desirable animal life that only scattered remnants of the once great numbers now remain. Starvation and disease have taken heavy tolls. Hunting and trapping, often reaching the stage of wanton slaughter, have been common practice. Buffalo, formerly counted in the millions, now number but a few thousands and these are cared for in public parks and reservations. The pronghorn antelope was almost exterminated, but through protection and management, these animals are now increasing in numbers.

Mountain sheep, moose, and grizzly bears have almost vanished from the grasslands, and the few that remain are barely holding their own. Elk and mule deer are crowded on restricted winter ranges. Upland game birds and fur bearers are only small remnants of the former population and are continuing to decline. Many of the streams are depleted of their fish. The great decrease in waterfowl has aroused national concern.

Depletion. On the basis of the studies made by the Forest Service a range once capable of carrying 22,500,000 animal units [3] was in 1935 estimated to be able to support only 10,800,000. On 55 per cent of the entire range area forage values had been reduced by more than half of their original potentialities. The partial or total disappearance of the valuable and nutritious forage plants; their replacement by weeds, by less nutritious grasses, and by undesirable shrubs; and, over large areas, the loss of much of the surface soil were the physical and evident facts of range depletion. As serious as the actual depletion status was, the majority of the grasslands were still further declining in quality

---

[3] An animal unit is considered to be one head of cattle, one horse, one mule, five sheep, five swine, or five goats.

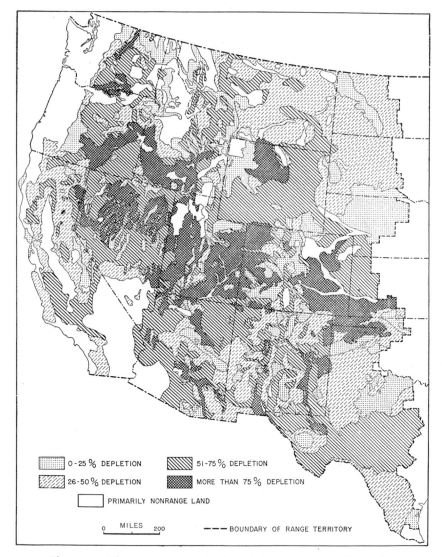

0-25 % DEPLETION   51-75 % DEPLETION
26-50 % DEPLETION   MORE THAN 75 % DEPLETION
PRIMARILY NONRANGE LAND

0   MILES   200   --- BOUNDARY OF RANGE TERRITORY

Figure 172. The western range lands and their present condition. From this map can be seen the geographic location of the western ranges and the extent to which they are depleted. (U.S. Forest Service.)

and quantity of forage. The depletion status of the western grazing lands had reached a critical stage.

These relationships are shown graphically in Figure 172 and statistically in Tables 18 and 19. In the figure are shown the geographic location of the western grazing lands and also the various areas clas-sified by degree and extent of depletion. A study of this map reveals clearly the vast areas in stages of severe depletion (51 to 75 per cent) and extreme depletion (76 to 100 per cent). The areas in stages of only moderate depletion (0 to 25 per cent) are relatively insignificant.

Whatever may have been the over-all situation that brought about forage depletion, the primary cause has been lack of management, a condition closely associated with ownership. The unreserved public domain was practically free, open to unrestricted numbers of stock and grazed without regulation. The ranges in the national forests, aggre-gating 12 per cent of the total grazing area of the West, were in poor condition when grazing regulation started. Though grazed continu-ously, ranges have been managed by the Forest Service so as to per-petuate the forage resources, with the result that less than 14 per cent of the area is in the severely and extremely depleted classes. Thus two agencies in the federal government dealing with the major areas of publicly owned lands administered the forage resources with almost opposite policies and results. Other owners, because of lack of regula-tion, have let the greater parts of their lands reach the stages of severe or extreme depletion. These relationships are shown in Table 18. In this table are presented the areas classified into four depletion classes for each of the major forms of ownership.

For all types of ownership, 13 per cent of the grazing lands were moderately depleted, 34 per cent materially, 37 per cent severely, and 16 per cent extremely; that is, over one-half of all grazing lands were in a condition of severe or extreme depletion. The statistics indicate serious depletion conditions on ranges of all types except those in the national forests, and even there the status was far from satisfac-tory.

Reference to Table 19 will show the depletion trends for each of the several classes of ownership. The largest area, 52 per cent, was in pri-vate ownership, the smallest area, 9 per cent, in state and county ownership, and the rest, 39 per cent, in the possession of the federal government. For the period 1905 to 1935, 76 per cent of this great area steadily declined in condition, 8 per cent remained unchanged, and only 16 per cent improved. This 16 per cent represented 118,408,-000 acres and, of these, 67,880,000 acres were grazing lands in the na-tional forests.

TABLE 18. DEPLETION OF VIRGIN-RANGE FORAGE BY OWNERSHIP AND DEPLETION CLASSES*

Ownership or control	Moderate depletion (0–25 per cent)		Material depletion (26–50 per cent)		Severe depletion (51–75 per cent)		Extreme depletion (76–100 per cent)		All depletion classes	
	1,000 acres	per cent	1,000 acres	per cent	1,000 acres	per cent	1,000 acres	per cent	1,000 acres	per cent
Federal:										
National forests	40,897	46.5	35,172	40.0	10,553	12.0	1,332	1.5	87,954	100
Indian lands	3,171	6.6	17,328	35.8	26,128	54.0	1,764	3.6	48,391	100
Public-domain grazing districts	1,868	1.5	18,320	14.3	61,168	47.9	46,436	36.3	127,792	100
Other federal	463	2.0	4,871	21.2	11,527	50.1	6,136	26.7	22,997	100
All federal	46,399	16.1	75,691	26.4	109,376	38.1	55,669	19.4	287,134	100
State and county	4,676	7.1	30,909	47.2	24,209	37.0	5,722	8.7	65,516	100
Private	43,750	11.7	138,397	36.9	136,885	36.4	56,514	15.0	375,546	100
All ownerships	94,825	13.0	244,997	33.7	270,470	37.1	117,904	16.2	728,196	100

* From *The Western Range* (Senate Document 199, 74th Congress, 2d Session; Washington, 1936), p. 114, Table 22.

TABLE 19. OWNERSHIP OF RANGE LANDS AND TRENDS IN DEPLETION,
1905–1935

Ownership	Areas		Trends in depletion		
			Improv-ing	Declin-ing	Static
	million acres	per cent	per cent	per cent	per cent
Federal					
National forests	88	12	77	5	18
Indian lands	48	7	10	75	15
Public domain grazing districts	128	17	2	93	5
Other federal	23	3	7	81	12
State and county	66	9	7	88	5
Private	375	52	10	85	5
Total	728	100	16	76	8

Again it should be pointed out that these figures were compiled
before the public domain grazing land began to be administered under
the Taylor Grazing Act. Under that act the Grazing Service, in the
United States Department of the Interior, was charged with organiz-
ing the grazing districts and instituting constructive regulations to
stop depletion and restore these lands to productive condition.[4]

RESTORATION AND MANAGEMENT

Conservation needs. A conservation policy is essential for the continued prosperity of the livestock industry. More than 500,000,000
acres of western grazing lands are involved in the broad program of
range restoration and management. Within this great area it will be
necessary first to stop and reverse range depletion; second, to check
erosion and rebuild the soil; third, to restore to productive condition
the overgrazed and depleted lands; and fourth, to place under management the areas which are not at present under control. Such a
program will involve the solution of many problems of a difficult na-

[4] On July 16, 1946, the Grazing Service and the General Land Office, both in the U.S.
Department of the Interior, were consolidated to become the Bureau of Land Management in the Department of the Interior.

ture. Some of the steps to be taken to solve this acute conservation problem follow.

Checking depletion. Previous mention has been made of the fact that on the basis of 1936 figures only 16 per cent of the western ranges were improving, that 8 per cent were static, and that 76 per cent were declining in value. Though these figures would now be changed for the better because of the constructive efforts in administering the Taylor districts, other federal lands, and additional areas in other forms of ownership, the over-all situation is still serious.

Since depletion has been caused by overgrazing, the primary solution is to regulate the number of animals that an area can carry adequately and still be gradually improved. In many locations depletion can be checked only by a definite reduction in the number of animals grazed until the lands start to improve. The extent of reduction can be determined only by experts in the field of grazing management in full co-operation with those who use the range. Where reductions are made, the results will be a more moderate use of the grasslands and the gradual easing of the drain on many forage areas.

Checking soil erosion. Loss of soil through erosion represents the final stages of depletion. On some 100,000,000 acres much of the fertile surface soil has been washed away. The process of rebuilding is slow and will require the establishment of several generations of weeds, grasses, and other plants. In general, the return of a good cover of vegetation will solve most of the soil-erosion problems. On some areas complete closure may be required in order that vegetative cover may be re-established and the various techniques of soil-erosion prevention brought to these lands. Without soil it is impossible to develop a satisfactory forage cover.

Range restoration. Much of the 1936 estimated range area of 728,000,-000 acres can be restored to highly productive condition through proper management. Studies indicated that 250,000,000 acres were in relatively good shape and were in need only of continued management; that 340,000,000 acres still retained their topsoil, but had suffered serious loss of fertility. These lands need reasonable rest for brief periods of years so that the vegetation can renew itself and make for the restoration of productivity. As mentioned in the foregoing section, on 100,000,000 acres much of the surface soil is gone. On these areas there is no solution other than the slow process of soil rebuilding. Finally, on 38,000,000 acres artificial seeding will be required. The restoration of these lands will be slow and expensive. Over much of this land, which includes many acres plowed for dry farming, from twenty to fifty years may be required for rehabilitation. The problem is extremely difficult and will require the highest order of techniques of range-grass production. Once a cover of grass and other suitable vegetation is restored, the ranges will be able to carry on a sustained basis more stock than is now being grazed.

Range management. Range management is the art of restoring and maintaining the range lands so that they will provide feed continuously for maximum numbers of livestock without impairment of their productivity. The art of range management is highly technical. It involves not only those steps that are necessary to check depletion, rebuild soil productivity, and restore a forage cover, but also the procedures of planning for and regulating the quantities of livestock that may be safely grazed on specific areas. In detail, range management must regulate the numbers of animals that a range can carry; the types of animals to which specific types of ranges are best suited; the proper use of ranges during the various seasons of the year; the distribution of stock with respect to watering places, travel routes, and bedding grounds; the development of water resources; the production and use of supplemental feed; and the prevention of overcrowding on local areas. Further, management must plan for the broad use of the range for wildlife, recreational, and watershed services and, where forests are intermingled with the grasslands, take into account the use of timber resources. Obviously range rehabilitation is the primary step, but as this work proceeds the other details of management must be closely integrated.

That the vegetative cover of the range can be restored at the same time it is being used for grazing has been well demonstrated in the national forests (Fig. 173), on some privately owned land, and by research. On probably 90 per cent or more of the total range area the watershed values, along with soil building, can be conserved while grazing is in progress. The one dominant problem is restoration of plant cover.

Range management plans with their maps and basic data include definite prescriptions to be followed in managing the individual areas. Their preparation requires a thorough knowledge of livestock, the useful forage plants, the useless and harmful vegetation, and the sound judgment to co-ordinate all factors.

In fifty years the productive value of the range had been reduced by approximately 50 per cent. In order to restore fully all ranges to a productive state an equal period of time may be required. In addition to the decades of time involved, the cost in money will be high. This, however, is unavoidable and is simply the price that must be paid for the former wasteful and careless treatment of these grasslands. The situation is in no way different from that applying to waste and destruction of soils, forests, and other renewable resources. What it

Figure 173. Forests and grazing—Payette National Forest, Idaho. The grazing lands in the western national forests provide forage for millions of head of domestic livestock, and contribute in large measure to the prosperity of the western livestock industry. (U.S. Forest Service.)

amounts to is a destruction of a large amount of capital wealth, and this wealth can only be restored by large expenditures of money over many future years. If range restoration and management are not undertaken and carried through to the place where the ranges are placed on a sustained-yield basis, depletion will continue, with the result that the livestock industry in all its important economic and social ramifications will steadily decline. If the range is built up and perpetuated, it means that these great areas in the West will not only sustain the great livestock industry perpetually, but they will solve most of the problems that soil erosion and floods create and, in addition, provide a highly favorable environment for many forms of wildlife. Unless the ranges are restored and saved from depletion, much of the land will ultimately become a wasteland.

Activities of federal agencies. In the national forests more than 80,-000,000 acres are available for grazing. On four-fifths of this area range management plans are now in effect. The success of the efforts of the Forest Service in rehabilitating its grasslands and in maintaining them in productive condition attests the good results that come from plans logically worked out and put into practice.

The Department of the Interior is actively engaged in the conservation, improvement, and development of the vast areas of grazing land that it administers. In the grazing districts of 140,000,000 acres, their policies involve the maximum production and orderly use of forage for livestock and wildlife, the stabilization of the livestock industry, and the equitable distribution of privileges to those who use the range. On the Indian lands of 41,000,000 acres, the range lands are being administered in a manner that involves both the conservative handling of the grazing resources and, at the same time, the protection of the interests of the Indians for whom the lands are administered. In the national parks and monuments some 1,000,000 acres are being grazed under strict regulatory procedures. On the park lands increased grazing use was permitted as a war measure, but it is the permanent policy to reduce and eventually eliminate grazing in these areas. On other federal lands administered by the Department of the Interior, including the remaining public domain, wildlife refuges, and areas in miscellaneous classes, the problem of livestock grazing versus other uses is fully recognized. The adjustment of conflicting interests and the regulated use for grazing, consistent with controlling legislation, are definite present policies. To the extent possible, policies of control are similar to those governing the administration of the grazing districts.

Recent attacks on the public grazing lands. As a result of the withdrawal of public lands for national forests, Taylor grazing districts, and other reservations, the activities of former users of these properties have been restricted. Such restrictions have never been fully accepted by some, with the result that legislation is, from time to time, introduced into Congress in order to change in one way or another the provisions of existing laws dealing with these public lands. In general, bills seeking to impair the public land resources seldom have been enacted into laws.

Especially serious are recent legislative proposals dealing with the grazing lands. In 1945 two such bills were introduced in Congress. One of them proposed that 10,000,000 acres of public land in the grazing districts be turned over to the state of New Mexico for the use and benefit of state institutions. The passage of such a bill would mean not only a grant of this huge area to an individual state by the federal government, but it would set a precedent that might well wreck much of the constructive work done to date in handling the federal public lands. The other bill would have given the users of any grazing district the right to dissolve the district upon an affirmative vote of 60 per cent of the users. If dissolved, these lands would again be open to unrestricted grazing, which the Taylor Act was specifically designed to stop.

In 1947 additional bills of far-reaching importance dealing with the grazing lands in both Taylor districts and in national forests were presented to the 80th Congress. These bills, backed by powerful livestock associations, continue the request that the Taylor grazing districts be dissolved if 60 per cent of the present permittees vote for such action. The bills further provide that great areas of grazing lands be turned over to the states with provision for later sale or lease. Pending such transfer no reduction in term permits in the regulated grazing areas would be permitted, and the permits would be frozen at present levels for fifteen years. During this fifteen-year period present permittees would be given exclusive right to purchase the lands that they are now using. In addition, the western states would be given the authority to decide how the funds received from grazing use would be expended. The bills give little consideration to the highly important services that grasslands provide in protecting watersheds or in furnishing a healthy environment for wildlife.

Bills of this type have strong backing, and it is to be expected that they will continue to be introduced in Congress. The lands in the grazing districts are definitely improving under the management practices initiated by the Grazing Service, but, because of the vast areas involved and the exhausted condition of the lands when taken over, many years will be required for adequate restoration. If bills of these types become laws, the grasslands in the grazing districts will soon be back in the condition that existed prior to 1934. Actually the Taylor

Act will be crippled to an extent that it will be useless. Should the laws extend to grasslands in the national forests, they will have a profound and adverse effect on the constructive land policies that started with the federal Law of 1891. Such bills definitely represent backward trends in the conservation policies and practices regarding the country's public lands.

CHAPTER XI

Fish and Fisheries

W ORLD WAR II made the American family fish-conscious. The scarcity of meat demanded substitutes. Fish products, in a measure, relieved this shortage. Without fanfare or advertising, many families throughout the country became accustomed to a fish dinner several times a week. They learned to appreciate this food and have continued to utilize this great natural resource even after the return of an abundant meat supply.

The fishing industry in the United States is a huge one. The total annual catch amounts to more than 4,000,000,000 pounds, valued at $80,121,000. About 140,000 fishermen are employed in making this catch. To conserve this vast resource is of great importance. Without a continuing supply, many thousands of people would be without work, and industries built on the fisheries would collapse. Even more important, we should sorely miss this source of food.

By far the greater share of the fish we eat are taken from the sea. The sea covers about three-fourths of the surface of the world. With this vast area to draw upon, many naturally believe that the supply of sea food is inexhaustible, but this is far from true. Those fish that live offshore on the relatively shallow banks are not difficult to catch, and their numbers in some cases have been greatly reduced. The Atlantic halibut was at one time an important food fish, but the catch has declined to almost negligible quantities, and the haddock has declined about 44 per cent since the peak year of 1929. Moreover, many fish, for example, salmon and shad, spend the greater part of their lives in the ocean but ascend fresh-water tributaries from the sea in great numbers when they spawn. During these migrations the fish have been taken in great numbers and, as a consequence of such overfishing, some species are no longer of commercial importance.

VALUE OF FISHERIES

Food value of fish. Although the people of the United States do not consume so much fish as do the people of other countries, we are beginning to realize the value of fish as food. This natural resource is usually inexpensive and rich in elements that contribute to a strong and healthy body. Every school child knows the importance of vita-

Figure 174. A herring fish plant at Deep Cove, Alaska. The annual output of canned fishery products in the United States and Alaska would provide every individual in the country with seven pounds of fish or shellfish a year. (U.S. Fish and Wildlife Service.)

mins in the maintenance of health. If these are absent in our food, rickets, pellagra, and other nutritional diseases may affect us. Fish oils and fish-liver oils are today the only dependable source of two of the most important vitamins, A and D. Our domestic animals need these vitamins as well as we. In fact, more cod-liver oil is fed to chicks than to human babies.

If we consider fish as a meat, we find it ranks third in quantity consumed. Only pork and beef exceed it. Since canned fish such as salmon and herring (sardines) are less expensive than meat, they are becoming increasingly important to those who cannot afford more expensive meats (Fig. 174) . In 1943 the total production of fishery products in the United States and Alaska was estimated at 4,202,000,000 pounds valued at about $204,000,000 to the fishermen. The New England area alone produced about 600,000,000 pounds of fish in this one year.

Fishery products enter the market either fresh, preserved, or as by-products. According to the Fish and Wildlife Service, in 1943 the output of canned fishery products and by-products in the United States and Alaska amounted to more than 645,000,000 pounds, valued at $200,325,058; the output of by-products was valued at $35,000,000; and the production of frozen fishery products amounted to 110,000,-000 pounds, valued at $10,000,000. Based on the most recent surveys, the supply of cured fishery products amounted to 121,000,000 pounds, valued at $16,000,000, and the output of fresh and frozen packaged fish and shellfish, such as oysters, clams, crabs, and shrimp, totaled 206,000,000 pounds, valued at $27,000,000.

It has been further estimated that about 675,000,000 pounds of fresh fishery products, exclusive of packaged fish (such as fresh fillets and steaks) and shellfish, valued at $56,000,000, were marketed annually during recent years. The total market value to domestic primary handlers of all fishery products is about $240,000,000 annually.

We need only cite the importance of salmon to Alaska to appreciate how vital the sea and rivers are to the lives of those who live by them. Salmon and other fisheries are the real gold of Alaska. Unlike precious metals, the supply is not exhausted by use. More than 28,000 people are employed in the Alaska salmon fishery, and the value of this healthful food taken in 1943 was over $60,000,000. This is more than four times the annual production of gold in the Territory.

More than 125,000 people engage in the marine fisheries. In the fishery plants some 80,000 people find employment. Many more thousands are engaged in selling the products of the sea. Entire communities along the Atlantic Coast, the Gulf Coast, the Pacific Coast, and the coast of Alaska are dependent on this vast industry. We must also include the many thousands who build boats, nets, fishing gear, barrels, cans, and the like, which are so necessary in the fishing industry. These figures have been greatly swollen by the expanded markets of the war years, as the shortage in meat developed.

It is difficult to estimate the value of fresh-water fish caught each year. We do know that these fish furnish great sport to many millions.

Figure 175. The Boston fish pier. From here northeasterners receive much of their marine food. Packaged and frozen fish are shipped all over the country from Boston. (U.S. Fish and Wildlife Service.)

If they had no use as food, their recreational value would be very important. There are far more fishermen than hunters in the United States. This is true partly because little expense need be involved in buying equipment. Guns and ammunition are expensive, but a dollar bill will often provide one with suitable tackle. Even though few fish are caught, the joy of spending a day on a beautiful lake or stream is not soon forgotten.

States with a mild winter climate attract tourists, who spend a great deal of time fishing. These tourists spend much money, and this directly benefits the residents of the state. Thus the excellent coastal fishing in California and Florida brings those states economic advantages. The same may be said of summer fishing. The numerous lakes of New York, Michigan, Wisconsin, and Minnesota attract scores of anglers, who pay handsomely for the privilege of fishing in these waters.

Fishery values other than food. Fish produce many by-products other than the flesh we eat. Formerly many of these were wasted, but recent studies by the fact-finding Fish and Wildlife Service have shown that such supposedly waste products are of great value. More and more are we conserving and utilizing this material, which we formerly considered of little value.

In 1943 the domestic production of fish-liver oil amounted to 851,-854 gallons, valued at $14,970,884. In the same year whole fish and waste produced 22,264,362 gallons of oil, valued at $14,841,970, and 139,735 tons of fish meal was worth $10,242,831. In brief, the total value of by-products of the fishery industry in 1943 was placed at $59,-136,266. The commercial fisherman finds a ready market for material he formerly considered worthless. Fishermen on the West Coast now receive fifty cents per pound for halibut livers, which they formerly threw away.

In the great salmon canneries of Alaska, approximately one-third of each fish is discarded. This represents about 200,000,000 pounds of complete loss if it cannot be commercially salvaged. The head of the salmon is one of the principal sources of vitamin-bearing oils. It is possible that this waste can be utilized in the future, and a great loss to the industry thus prevented.

In terms of pounds landed, the leading United States fisheries in 1946 were those of menhaden, pilchard, salmon, tuna, Alaska herring, and rosefish, in the order named. Together these yielded more than half of the catch of all species by volume. From a little-used and almost unknown species a decade before, rosefish, yielding 180,000,000 pounds in 1946, became one of the leading fishery products of the United States.

Oyster shells are widely used as a poultry food. Such shells have also been used in road building. Fish meal is a valuable food for many domestic animals. Some of this meal is produced from the waste products

Figure 176. A scene on the opening day of the trout season in New York State. (W. J. Hamilton, Jr.)

of commercial fish. Millions of pounds of fish, not edible for humans, are utilized for their oils, and the residue furnishes a high-grade fertilizer. In fact, the by-products of some fish may actually exceed the food value of the fish. The menhaden, a herringlike fish, is a striking case in point.

The menhaden, or mossbunker as fishermen call it, is not edible, or at least is not eaten to any extent. These fish occur in great numbers along the Atlantic Coast. They seldom weigh more than a pound and are twelve to fifteen inches long. These fish swim in immense schools with their heads close to the surface, side by side, and often tier above tier, as close-packed as sardines in a box. The schools of fish are surrounded, caught in huge nets, transported to the factory, and there pressed to remove the oil.

For several generations the manufacture of meal and oil has overshadowed all other uses for menhaden. One-third of all the fish meals and a quarter of the marine animal oils produced in the United States are products of the menhaden industry. The meals are fed to hogs and poultry to provide the indispensable animal protein in their diet; the oils are used in preparing fortified vitamin feeding oils for poultry. The industrial uses of menhaden oil are many. It is a constituent of

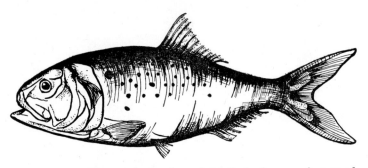

Figure 177. The menhaden is used chiefly in the manufacture of meat and oil, few being eaten. Yet it is one of our most important species, in recent years averaging 600,000,000 pounds. Purse seines are used for the capture of large fish schools.

many paints, varnishes, insect sprays, printing inks, and soap. The oil is used also as a lubricant of machinery, in aluminum casting, and in leather tanning.

Keep in mind that we do not eat this fish. Yet in 1946 the menhaden factories in operation on the Atlantic seaboard utilized nearly 900,-000,000 pounds of fish, thereby making it the principal product of the United States fisheries. Reedville, Virginia, received 147,000,000 pounds of menhaden, its sole fishery product, in 1946.

HABITS OF FISH

It will be well here to point out some requirements and habits of our fish. In this way the reader will be able to see why many fish have declined in numbers, and how they may be conserved in the future.

In general, fish require clean water, suitable food, and a place to breed. The habits of different species vary greatly. Some, like the brook trout, prefer the cold water of a mountain stream. The carp could not survive in such surroundings. It must have the still water of a pond, where it noses in the mud for food. The sunfish and black bass may lay only a thousand eggs, but guard them closely until they hatch. On the other hand, the savage pike may broadcast 100,000 eggs or more but gives them no care, while a large cod may produce three or four million eggs. The eel goes far out into the ocean depths to lay its eggs. The salmon migrates from the sea to the headwaters of fresh-water streams to spawn.

Life history of the salmon. There are five kinds of commercial salmon, all of which have somewhat similar and equally remarkable lives. The sockeye, or red salmon, and the humpback, or pink salmon, are the most familiar to the householder. For convenience' sake, we may consider them all as one, the Pacific salmon. This fish ranges from central California to Alaska.

All salmon spend most of their lives in the sea and enter fresh water only at the spawning time to lay their eggs. After having spawned once, all Pacific salmon die. The eggs are deposited in shallow nests in the gravel, usually in the fall of the year, and often at the headwaters of fresh-water streams. Before the eggs have hatched the following spring, all the fish that produced them have died. After the eggs hatch, some young go down to the sea when still small, while others may remain in fresh water at least a year. They grow very rapidly in the sea, and, upon maturing after from two to six years, they return to fresh water and spawn. One remarkable circumstance in the life of the salmon is that it leads a nomadic existence for much of its life but at maturity, with the unerring instinct of a homing pigeon, it returns to the streams and lakes of its origin to spawn and die. The king salmon of the Yukon River may swim 2,000 miles upstream before it spawns. When starting the spawning run, the fish are very fat, and the commercial catch is made at this time.

The humpback, or pink salmon, reaches a weight of three to six pounds, and the great king salmon may reach enormous size. Specimens weighing one hundred pounds have been taken in Alaska.

Life history of the mackerel. The breeding habits of the common mackerel, a marine species, are quite different from those of the salmon. A common mackerel, weighing scarcely more than a pound, has been known to contain half a million eggs. These eggs are laid in the open sea near the surface, and float about with the currents. Of course, it is quite impossible for the female to guard these eggs, and a very high proportion are destroyed.

Thus we have two fish with entirely different habits. No two species behave alike. The problems of marine and fresh-water fishery conservation are very different. This difference arises in part from the fact that in nature marine fishes produce large numbers of eggs, running often into the millions, and that a tremendous toll of eggs and young is taken by natural enemies. A supply of many billions of mackerel in the Atlantic Ocean could scarcely be affected by the planting of a few million fry, an insignificant percentage of which could be expected to develop to commercial size. On the other hand, the restocking of a stream with a few thousand trout is effectively undertaken by a single fish hatchery.

We must study the life of each kind of fish if we are to know how best to conserve it. Only thus may we maintain suitable numbers of fish, which will continue to furnish food and sport for future generations.

DECLINE OF CERTAIN FISHERIES

To most of us, the supply of ocean fish seems limitless. The habits of many fish are such that they are in no danger from fishermen. They live in the deep sea, where fishing gear and nets cannot reach them. Other species of fish are not so fortunate. Those that must leave the sea and enter rivers to spawn, as salmon and shad do, are in some instances becoming less abundant. Moreover, improvement in fishing gear and boats has made it possible to catch fish that were formerly considered safe from man.

Shad. Shad are among the most prized of food fish. Not so long ago they were one of the three most abundant species of food fish along the Atlantic Coast, furnishing a catch of some 48,000,000 pounds and providing a partial livelihood to 25,000 people. Along the entire coast, fishermen and consumers alike anticipated the spring days when shad would commence to leave the sea and pass up the rivers to spawn. Men came from far and near to watch the countless hordes beat the shallows into foam in their haste to reach the spawning beds. Fish were killed in incredible numbers, some for immediate consumption, some to be salted for winter use.

Now the great shad runs are but history. The practice of overfishing, the building of dams which act as barriers to shad in their breeding

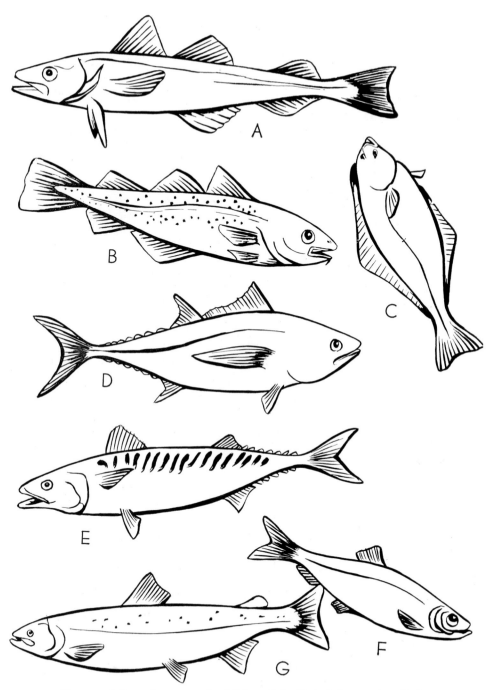

Figure 178. Some important food fishes of the United States: *A,* pollock;
B, cod; *C,* halibut; *D,* tuna; *E,* mackerel; *F,* herring; *G,* salmon.

journey, and the pollution of waters with industrial wastes have nearly exterminated these former hordes. Shad fishing is said to have declined 80 per cent in the past forty years. Such a decline means great loss to fishermen and has deprived the consumer of a sufficient supply of an excellent fish.

In the Chesapeake present catches are about 4,000,000 pounds annually, compared with some 16,000,000 pounds half a century ago. Fortunately, a sound program of restoration is under way. The shad

Figure 179. Transporting shad from nets to the loading boats. The shad fishery has increased in recent years because of better conservation measures and regulation of fishing methods. (Maryland Conservation Department.)

industry has benefited in the Hudson River where the runs have recovered from their low yield of 40,000 pounds in 1916 to 5,000,000 in 1944.

Sturgeon. In earlier days the huge sturgeon, which was little prized for food and had no other economic value, was considered a nuisance by fishermen. Since these great fish, sometimes weighing 200 pounds, would destroy nets, the fishermen usually killed any that they caught. Sturgeon meat, however, grew rapidly in favor. The flesh was cured by smoking or boiled in vinegar; from the eggs caviar began to be produced. With an appreciation of its food value, there began a campaign of slaughter which soon threatened the sturgeon with extinction. Its importance grew until 1890, when it was said that this fish was worth $6,000,000 in a single year to the fisherman. Today it is so scarce that fishing for it is no longer profitable. The catch in 1943 was worth only $36,000 to fishermen. Unfortunately, no means have been found to propagate it artificially.

Haddock. For hundreds of years the shallow seas of New England have furnished us with a great abundance of fish. These banks are rela-

Figure 180. Sturgeon.

tively shallow areas dotting the continental shelf and are thousands of square miles in extent and usually from one hundred to six hundred feet deep. In early days the catch from these banks was small, but the fishery grew steadily. In 1924 New England fishing boats alone caught 190,000,000 pounds of marketable fish. One of the fish represented in this catch was the haddock, formerly considered of little value. About

Figure 181. The haddock is one of the most important food fishes of the Atlantic Coast. Most of the haddock is sold as fresh or frozen fillets. Inland markets sell more of these than they do of any other species.

1924, however, when the packaging of frozen haddock was developed, an immediate and tremendous demand for this fish arose (Fig. 181). In fact, haddock rose from an insignificant product to be the most important food fish on the New England coast. In the five years between 1924 and 1929 the haddock catch of New England jumped from 93,500,000 pounds to nearly 256,000,000.

It is difficult to realize what an enormous amount of fish 256,000,000 pounds really is. It is enough to provide every man, woman, and child in New England with a haddock dinner every Friday in the year. And New England has a population of more than 8,000,000 people. This great demand could have only one effect: overfishing led to an inevitable decline in the catch. Haddock landings at three New England ports decreased more than 25 per cent in the five years from 1929 to 1934.

Figure 182. Landing haddock on the Georgia banks, shallow seas off the New England Coast. To prevent wholesale destruction of young fish, nets with a large mesh should be used. (U.S. Fish and Wildlife Service.)

The Fish and Wildlife Service has carefully investigated this decline. It has recommended that nets with a larger mesh be used. This will permit many small haddock, of little or no commercial value, to escape. It has further recommended that only fish weighing at least one and a half pounds be accepted by the markets. This will, it is hoped, prevent the wholesale destruction of young fish, thus permitting them to reach marketable size. Fishermen must act on these suggestions if they are to profit from future haddock fishing.

In 1943 the catch of haddock off New England totaled 117,216,000 pounds, with $9,199,000 going to the fishermen.

Salmon. In some localities the salmon fisheries have been much reduced. A glance at Figure 183 will show the decline of the salmon catch in the Sacramento River in recent years. By the construction of impassable barriers such as dams, the breeding grounds in this one river have been reduced 80 per cent. Since fishways play an essential part in the conservation of salmon in the Pacific Northwest they have been installed in many dams. Adequate fishery protection can and should be afforded wherever needed.

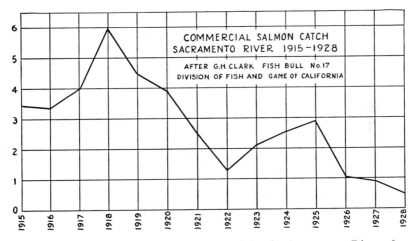

Figure 183. Decline of the salmon catch in the Sacramento River of California. Dams prevent the salmon from reaching their spawning grounds, and where fishways or fish ladders have not been installed, a decline in the fishery is soon noted.

Halibut. The Pacific halibut is a food fish ranking about fourteenth in poundage. This fish first became of commercial significance in 1888, soon after railway communications were established between the East and West Coasts of the United States. The fishery extends for 1,800 miles along the Pacific Coast. The 1943 catch was 54,510,000 pounds, and fishermen received $8,257,000.

At one time as many fish were taken in a 600-mile stretch as are now caught from the entire 1,800 miles. The old grounds produced 21,-000,000 pounds of fish in 1926, where in 1910 more than 50,000,000 were taken. In 1906 the catch per unit of fishing gear, according to the United States Bureau of Fisheries, was nearly 300 pounds. In 1926 it had fallen to below fifty pounds. In other words, in 1926 it took six units of gear to catch as many halibut as one unit caught in 1906. The present high level is maintained only by extending fishing operations to new areas and by increased fishing intensity.

Fortunately the International Fisheries Commission, which represents the United States and Canada, has come to the aid of the halibut fishery. This commission presents an encouraging example of the restoration of a seriously depleted marine fishery by a scientific group with authority to regulate the catch of fish. Restocking the sea is not possible. Investigation by competent biologists indicates that the halibut grows very slowly: at 12 years a female will spawn 200,000 to 500,-000 eggs, but at 20 years she may lay 3,500,000. Furthermore it has been demonstrated that when one bank, or area, is fished out, the area is ruined. It is not repopulated from outside, for halibut maintain themselves in widely separated communities. A good bank can be quite depleted in two years by the power fleets. Under the regulations proposed by the commission an increase in the number of spawning adults and young has been noted, and the yield of halibut per unit of gear has been substantially increased. The present system is to use less gear, because we know that less gear will, over the years, take as much as more did formerly. The boats are now getting their limits in much less fishing time.

The ability of the boats to get their catches in a few days rather than weeks as formerly results in a social problem. If the boats take only a few months to reach their limits instead of a year, the fisherman has an employment problem. The answer seems to be intermittent trips.

Fresh-water fisheries. The Great Lakes have always been famous for their fresh-water fisheries. For the past fifty years the annual production has averaged over 100,000,000 pounds. More than 12,000 persons are directly engaged in this fishery. But will this great number continue to find such employment? Whitefish was formerly the most important fishery product of the Great Lakes, but in 1934 it ranked only sixth. Even that place was closely contested by the bony sucker, which some people would not consider worth eating. In order of decreasing importance on a weight basis the catch is blue and yellow pike, lake herring, lake trout, and perch.

There is no need to consider more of these tragic occurrences. Those who have studied our fisheries agree that many important species have declined. It now becomes desirable to see in detail why such food fishes have been so reduced. It will then be proper to consider how this decline may be avoided, so that future generations may be assured of fresh fish from oceans, lakes, and rivers.

REASON FOR DECLINE

No one cause has been responsible for the decrease in our fishery products. Many reasons for this decline are apparent. Some are not man's fault. But man has been the chief agent in the decline of many of our most valuable species. His selfish greed has resulted in the taking of far more fish than could wisely be utilized.

Excessive fishing. Primitive man took only sufficient fish to meet his needs. In America, for example, the Indian caught such a supply by simple means—hand lines, spears, and small nets. With the settlement of the country, more food was necessary for a growing population, and the demand for fish grew. In narrow-mouthed bays and the mouths of rivers the great maze of nets and traps came to obstruct the passage of fish upstream. These obstructions may effectively prevent shad, salmon, and other fish from reaching their spawning beds. Moreover, new methods of capture have been devised. Legal restrictions have proved difficult to enforce, especially those on the products of marine fisheries. Simultaneously, improved methods of refrigeration have created a wider market, which, in turn, has encouraged fishermen to redouble their efforts.

Overfishing has been especially severe in fresh-water lakes and streams. Great strings of fish are often taken by one or two anglers who cannot possibly utilize all the fish caught. The writer knows of instances where ice fishermen have made such inroads on pike, pickerel, and perch that the summer visitor finds his efforts without reward.

Effect of pollution. Fish must have clean water, with an abundant supply of food. Manufacturing, which has increased tremendously in the last seventy-five years, and the consequent concentration of people in large cities have tended to pollute our streams. Sewage and the waste from factories and mills, creameries and milk plants, contribute undesirable elements to rivers and streams (Fig. 184). Some wastes may rob the water of so much oxygen that the fish will suffocate. Others containing definite poisons destroy countless numbers of fish that should be available for food and sport. Drainage from coal mines, for example, has a particularly devastating effect on the life of a stream.

Even if the wastes are in such minute quantities that adult fish may survive their direct effects, they may kill newly hatched fish and the small animals on which fish feed. Then surviving fish must starve or move to regions that are unpolluted. And it must be remembered that polluted water may have far-reaching effects on the life of a stream. The Illinois River is said to be polluted for 120 miles below Chicago. This fouling of the water has greatly reduced the fish life.

Figure 184. A pulp mill discharging its waste products into a stream. Sewage and the waste from factories and mills often pollute streams and rivers so badly that fish life cannot survive. (U.S. Fish and Wildlife Service.)

It is unfortunate that the wastes that pollute our streams are not in themselves utilized. They are by-products of manufactured gas, petroleum, leather, wood textiles, sugar, and munitions. They might provide us with ammonia, benzene, naphthalene, asphalt, dyes, drugs, material for roads, alcohol, aluminum, fertilizer, and various useful chemicals. When we realize that two such diverse articles as artificial silk and alcohol may be made, in part, from sawdust, we see the possibilities in the utilization of these wastes. When they are not utilized but rather dumped into rivers, they kill fish, contaminate water, produce bad odors, encourage mosquitoes, and spread disease.

Pollution need not be countenanced whether the polluting agency be an individual, a corporation, or a municipality. We have had pollution in the past because we did not have adequate antipollution laws that could be enforced. Those responsible for the pollution of our fresh waters have frequently utilized a lake or river for disposal rather than spend a modest sum for a disposal plant. Too often the ire of the public is aroused after the damage is done. Unfortunately, fines do not remotely approximate the amount of damage. The loss of fish, the effect on public health, and the lesser known damage resulting from stream pollution are beyond measure. A few states have introduced legislation tending to minimize the harmful results of pollution. Occasionally these become law, but such laws are often stripped of their "teeth." Penalties may be eliminated by the changing of the word *shall* to *may*. The 1948 Congress passed a bill that will give us relatively clean water (see Chap. III, p. 100). This empowers the Surgeon General to take action on all matters of pollution brought to his attention.

Barriers. We have seen that many fish, when ready to breed, leave the sea and ascend the fresh-water rivers. Formerly no obstruction prevented the salmon and shad from reaching their spawning beds. When dams are constructed, however, they frequently prove an impassable barrier. Even though the salmon is possessed of great leaping powers, it can seldom jump these man-made barriers.

The striking effect of these dams on salmon abundance is shown in the Penobscot. This great river of Maine formerly supplied immense numbers of salmon, which were used in barter for other goods. The first dam was built in 1830. Other dams soon began to appear, and the run of salmon has declined to the present day.

The Columbia River has long been famous for its salmon fisheries. Now it is being harnessed for power, and the fisheries may be menaced. Fortunately, in the case of the major power dams on the Columbia, the menace to migratory fish has been recognized and provision made for their protection. At Rock Island Dam salmon have been ascending the three fish ladders without difficulty. At Bonneville Dam, where the elaborate system of fishways received its first test, salmon runs have found and ascended the ways without delay. Therefore it by no means follows that we cannot have salmon and power in the same river.

These fishways vary in design according to the height of the dam, the size of the stream, the structure of the dam foundation, and other factors. Fish ladders are similar to cascades. They usually consist of a succession of rectangular pools, varying from 5 to 40 feet across, with a difference in elevation between pools of 1 to 2 feet (Fig. 189, p. 359). Occasionally such artificial means as navigational locks, bracket hoists, or tank trucks are employed to transport the fish over the dam. However well some of these fishways function, the problem of getting the young fish below the dam on their journey to the sea is a serious one. The fingerlings are often killed in the spillway and turbines or swim into the deeply submerged outlets of storage reservoirs. Grand Coulee and Shasta Dams are too immense for fish ladders, and a costly program of artificial propagation must be conducted below these structures.

The salmon in such a river as the Columbia can be conserved only by a well-rounded program that takes into account all unfavorable factors—pollution, obstacles to migration, and irrigation ditches—and provides for reasonable regulation of the fishery.

The menace of irrigation ditches. As young salmon return to the sea, many enter irrigation ditches. Millions of young fish accidentally enter mill races and canals. A survey was made in Washington a number of years ago, in which it was found that about 4,000 young salmon had been stranded in the irrigation ditches of a 200-acre tract. This occurrence could be multiplied many times in a single season, so the loss must be very great. It has been estimated that 90 per cent of the young salmon migrating seaward in some rivers are lost in irrigation ditches.

Various states have laws requiring screening to prevent the entrance of fish into these irrigation ditches, canals, and mill races. This screening results in saving the lives of many fish and is a wise conservation measure.

Other causes for decline. Many minor reasons are also factors in the disappearance of fish from waters once well stocked. The unlawful use of gill nets takes many pike, lake trout, and other game fish in lakes that are not too abundantly supplied with these fish. These nets are made of fine strings, with meshes large enough to permit the head of the fish to pass through. The gills become caught in the net and the fish soon drowns. The use of dynamite to stun fish and make them easier to catch is another destructive practice. Ice fishing, when done to excess, will often seriously depopulate small bodies of water. Drought may cause heavy mortality among young fish.

Another factor in the destruction of salmon streams is gold dredging. Barren hills of raw gravel attest to the industry of man in his greed for gold. Where the dredges worked, the streams were left unfit for salmon or other aquatic life of economic importance. We may wonder if the value of the gold taken by such measures could equal the value of the lost salmon runs, now but a memory in these dredged-out rivers.

An important article on the training of engineers in biological matters has noted the almost complete failure of engineering schools to offer courses in which future dam and highway makers will learn the importance of the conservation of wildlife.[1] Engineers now play a most important part in the daily activities, and thus the general pattern, of American life. Industrial waste and urban sewage render useless a great amount of stream life. Highway construction involves drainage, often to the extent of interfering with the maintenance of ground-water level. Sound engineering design will minimize the often disastrous effects of impounded waters, which frequently defeat the very purpose for which dams were constructed. As an example, a dam built in 1935 at a cost of $20,000,000 was completed without regard to biological factors. Within a few years after completion the dam had intensified flood damage, and the reservoir behind it was silting rapidly, which in turn led to a frantic demand for improved land use upstream. Engineers must reckon with such hazards in future construction.

HOW FISH ARE CAUGHT

The days of the dory trotters are almost a memory. In early days fleets of schooners left the New England ports. On arrival at the banks, shallow seas that support billions of fish, the schooner would drop a dory astern and later pick up the two men who hauled in cod, halibut, and other species by hand or trawl lines. Now steel trawlers, powered by Diesel engines, haul in with electric winches an hour's dragging, which may net four to ten tons of fish, which are dumped into boxed-off pens on the deck. These are rushed to shore, where quick freezing and modern transportation bring the catch to midwesterners. Kansas

---

[1] Paul B. Sears, "Importance of Ecology in the Training of Engineers," *Science*, 106: 1–3 (July 4, 1947).

roadstands serve fillet sandwiches; the fish were caught a few days earlier far offshore in the Atlantic.

Since most of the fish for human consumption live in the sea, various methods have been devised to capture them. Marine fish may be divided into two categories, those that live on or near the bottom and those occurring near the surface. Bottom feeders, such as the cod, haddock, and the various flatfish, are usually taken in trawl nets, less frequently on set lines (Fig. 185F). The otter trawl (Fig. 185A) is a bag-shaped net the mouth of which is kept open by the pressure of water on the trawl boards. Purse seines (Fig. 185B) are used in the capture of a great share of the marine forms. These are large seines with a bag in the center. The fish are gradually encircled, swim or are forced into the bag, and a drawstring holds them until they are landed. Other bottom fish are taken on long trawl or set lines containing a thousand or more hooks. The ends are buoyed and the line is left unattended until time to haul. Cod and halibut are taken in this manner.

Pelagic fish, such as herring and mackerel, which swim near the surface, are taken in drift gill nets (Fig. 185C). One end may be attached to a drifting ship or buoyed. These nets are often nearly 200 feet long and 40 feet deep, a number being joined together so that the seine may extend two or three miles. In an attempt to pass through the seine, the fish is caught by the gills and drowns. The seines are made of light but strong cotton and can intercept and hold sizable fish.

Pound nets are ingenious devices of netting so arranged that the fish, on approaching a long, sunken seine, is guided into an intricate enclosure and finally funneled into a small enclosure. The herring weirs of coastal rivers are similar in design. A good share of the Pacific tuna is taken by hand line, two men on the fishing boats holding separate rods, the short lines of which are joined to a single one with a feathered hook. In a school of large tuna the action can be exciting, and the perfect co-ordination of both men is taxed to land a large tuna (Fig. 185E). When the schools of tuna are sighted by the fishers, dippers of live sardines from tanks on the tuna boats are thrown overboard. Only live fish will attract tuna since the latter are not scavengers.

In an average prewar year, 13,000 fishermen, using purse seines, took 2,100,000,000 pounds of fish; 11,000 fishermen using otter trawls caught 700,000,000 pounds; 24,000 fishermen took 500,000,000 pounds with lines; gill-netters totaling 17,000 caught 200,000,000

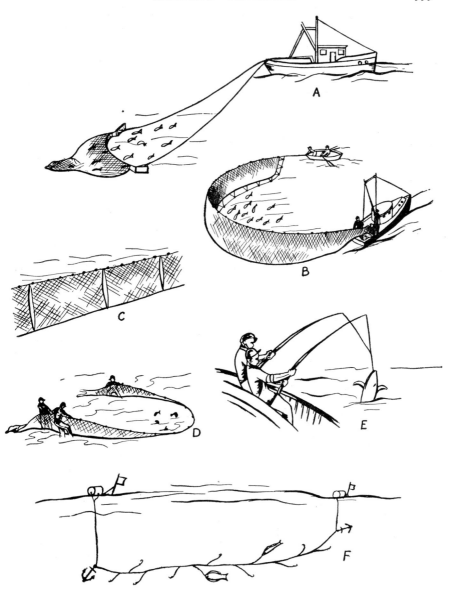

Figure 185. Various commercial fishing methods are employed to make the catch: *A,* otter trawl; *B,* purse seine; *C,* drift gill net; *D,* haul seine; *E,* tuna pole fishing; *F,* trawl or set line for halibut. (Adapted from U.S. Fish and Wildlife Service.)

pounds; and 6,000 pound-net fishermen caught 400,000,000 pounds.

How were these fish processed? The majority were canned (1,500,-000,000 pounds) or made into fish meal, oil, and other by-products (1,600,000,000 pounds), 340,000,000 pounds were fillet-packaged, 150,-000,000 pounds were cured, 130,000,000 pounds were frozen whole, and 680,000,000 pounds were sold fresh. Thus, of all the fish taken irrespective of their use, only 15 per cent currently reach us as fresh fish.

CONSERVATION OF FISHERIES

It is apparent that our fisheries constitute an enormous wealth, but we have seen that some are declining while others are not being fully utilized. To prevent further decline and increase the supply of fish is the duty of conservationists. To safeguard properly this vast resource and to provide wise laws, we must know the habits of the different fish. Closely related fish may differ very much in habits. In the East, the brook trout spawns in the fall, whereas its cousin, the rainbow trout, spawns in the spring. Often they both inhabit the same stream. If we are to permit trout fishing, we must protect the rainbow trout from the fisherman until it has spawned in late March. We must close the trout season by late summer, before the brook trout commences to lay its eggs.

Much research is necessary before we can provide proper laws to protect our fisheries. A very active research group is the United States Fish and Wildlife Service. The Service carries on scientific investigations to determine whether commercially important fishes are declining in abundance and to devise means of conserving them, to improve methods of hatching and planting fishes in fresh waters, and to improve methods of shellfish culture. The Service also makes yearly statistical surveys of the fisheries. Its hatcheries produce about 8,000,000,000 eggs and young fish of game and commercial species. The Service has jurisdiction over the Alaskan salmon fisheries and the fur-seal herd of the Pribilof Islands, studies the effect of pollution on river and stream life, and may study fish-canning problems or investigate the diseases of fish. It is a fact-finding organization of immense importance to the future of America's fisheries.

The state's interest in fish. Each state has a conservation department or commission. This group is interested in the conservation of all natural resources within the state. It enforces the laws that govern the take of fish and game. These departments establish fish hatcheries and provide fish for stocking streams and ponds. They provide a corps of protectors who enforce such laws as are made.

We have previously seen how the shad fishery was greatly reduced. The Hudson River, which empties into New York Harbor, once had great runs of shad every spring. The catch so declined that it was no longer of much importance. The State Conservation Department determined to restore this great industry. The Hudson River is by no means free from pollution, but in spite of this the fish continued to ascend the river to spawn. The state limited fishing to four nights out of each week and established minimum distances between nets. This permitted some fish to escape the nets and reach the spawning grounds. The state likewise releases more than 2,000,000 shad fry on these spawning grounds each year. As a consequence of these protective measures the catch has increased in the Hudson River from a low of 24,000 pounds in 1915 to between 1,000,000 and 2,000,000 pounds annually.

Artificial propagation of fish. It has long been felt by many that unless our waters are replenished with fish life, the natural rate of increase will not meet the needs of the fisherman. For this reason, federal and state fish hatcheries provide many millions of young fish each year to restock our wild waters. At the various fish hatcheries throughout the country, the fall is a busy time. Men press eggs from the fat bodies of trout into pans, then squeeze the sperm or milt from the male trout into the same pans (Fig. 186). Next the eggs and milt are stirred with the finger tips to ensure fertilization. The eggs are then placed in wire trays in troughs of running water. After a period of thirty-five to fifty days, depending on the temperature, they hatch into tiny fish, with a big yolk ball of stored food attached. This is finally absorbed, and the small fish must be fed several times daily in the fish hatchery. When an inch or two long, they are placed in outdoor ponds. Some hatcheries liberate these tiny trout into their streams. Others retain them in rearing ponds until they mature before releasing them in wild streams.

Eggs of marine fish must be placed in jars containing salt water. Mackerel eggs hatch in five days, while cod may take three weeks. The Great Lakes whitefish and herring eggs are incubated in glass jars each having a capacity of four quarts. These jars are about twenty inches high. The water enters the top of the jar through a tube, passes down through the egg mass and then ascends. It may take five months for such eggs to hatch under these conditions.

Excepting the trout, the small fish when hatched are released on their spawning grounds (Fig. 187). They are much too small when hatched to be fed successfully, for the yolk sac with which they are equipped at the time of hatching disappears in four or five days.

Figure 186. Stripping trout, a common hatchery practice. At the proper season the eggs and sperm are pressed from the bodies of trout into pans, a small amount of water is added, and the mixture is gently stirred with the fingers. A high percentage of eggs are fertilized in this manner. Note the stream of eggs being expelled from this brook trout into the pan. (W. J. Hamilton, Jr.)

Bass eggs usually are not obtained as the eggs of other fish are. The bass spawn on artificial nests in outdoor ponds of the hatchery. The parent, usually the male, guards the young until they are large enough to care for themselves, then deserts them. In the late summer or early fall, when the young are several inches long, they are transported in milk cans to a suitable lake or river, where they are released.

Fish culture is indeed a big business. In 1936 the output from the fish hatcheries of the United States Fish and Wildlife Service amounted to 2,750,000,000 young fish. In the same year, thirty-seven states had an output of 3,700,000,000 fry and fingerling fish. Thus over 6,000,000,000 young fish were supplied to the marine shores and inland lakes and streams of our country in a single year, and the demand still far exceeds the supply.

During periods of drought or flood, countless fish become landlocked. If left in temporary pools they would all die. Millions of these fish are returned to larger bodies of water by wardens employed by the state. This work has been particularly important in the Mississippi Valley within recent years.

Improving natural conditions. We have read in previous chapters how the destruction of forests has resulted in erosion, and how the loss of trees and other vegetation will also hasten runoff of water. This runoff results in swollen streams in the spring and dry stream beds in the summer. Fish life cannot continue under such conditions.

Trout do not thrive in streams and rivers that have no pools or

Figure 187. Planting hatchery-raised fish in a stream. The man with the dipper is equalizing the temperature of water in the containers. Thus the fish will not be shocked by a sudden change in water temperature when released into the stream. (U.S. Fish and Wildlife Service.)

suitable shelter. Because of land erosion many fine trout streams have been partly spoiled by stream silting. If conditions more favorable for fish production are created, streams will support a larger population of fish.

It has been demonstrated that small dams, deflectors, and covers under which trout may hide can be installed cheaply and soundly. By the construction of these, life conditions for trout can be much improved. Trout quickly take advantage of these bettered conditions. Long stretches of stream that were formerly without trout can be quickly made to yield good catches of these fine game fish. Unless such stream improvement activities are under the direction of a competent fishery biologist, however, more harm than good may result.

Fish ladders. To conserve the water supply or furnish power, it fre-

Figure 188. Improving stream conditions for trout has received much attention in recent years. These man-made boulder dams improve fishing conditions by providing pools and other suitable retreats for fish. (U.S. Fish and Wildlife Service.)

quently becomes necessary to dam rivers even if these waters may be used by salmon for spawning. If large, the dam may act as a barrier to the spawning fish. This hazard may be overcome by a ladder. A fish ladder is so designed that the salmon or trout, by a series of short leaps, may pass over the dam and continue to the spawning beds (Fig. 189). Some ladders have proved too difficult for the fish. Others have proved very efficient. One is always thrilled to see a large trout or salmon throw its shining body into the ladder and, by a series of lunges, reach and pass over the barrier.

Introduction of new species. Many fish have been introduced into new lands and have thrived there. Carp were introduced into our country from Europe. They now rank with our most important food fishes, although the sportsman may detest them. The fine rainbow trout has been brought from the West and forms a valuable addition to our eastern streams. The shad, greatly reduced along the Atlantic Coast,

Figure 189. A simple fish ladder. It permits trout to pass beyond this otherwise impassable barrier to their breeding grounds. In the great western salmon rivers elaborate fishways have been provided and have resulted in the saving of many commercially important fisheries. (W. J. Hamilton, Jr.)

was carried to California. There it did so well that it is now shipped 3,000 miles to the eastern markets. The striped bass, prized by Atlantic coastal fishermen, has been introduced on the Pacific Coast. California fishermen are delighted with its ever-increasing numbers.

Farm fish ponds. The production of food fish in farm ponds has been developed in the South, and northern ponds of small acreage provide good sport and an additional source of food.[2] Ponds of this nature are

---

[2] H. S. Swingle and E. V. Smith, *Management of Farm Fish Ponds* (Alabama Agricultural Experiment Station, Bull. 254; Auburn, Ala., 1942).

fertilized just as the adjoining land is, and they provide a great quantity of algae for small animal life. These little crustaceans and aquatic insects furnish food for panfish (sunfish and bluegills), which in turn are eaten by bass. If the pond is properly balanced, i.e., the chain of food organisms is provided continuously, the pond will be productive for many years. A well-balanced pond will provide 250 pounds of panfish per surface acre a year. Most of the larger fish, such as bass, must be harvested annually. If not materially reduced, they would eat the smaller food fish to a point where fishing would prove unprofitable. In addition to being a supplemental source of food, the farm fish pond provides recreation.

SHELLFISH

Besides finny fish, we have another important group of marine animals, the shellfish. These include oysters, lobsters, clams, shrimp, and similar sea forms. Shellfish constitute a very important share of the fisheries. Indeed, they even surpass the true fish in value in many parts of the country. From the lobster fishermen of rock-bound Maine south to the shrimp netter of the Gulf, many communities share in the important industry of harvesting these shellfish. We all benefit from this industry since food stores even in small inland cities sell oysters, clams, fresh shrimps, and lobsters. The demand for these foods is increasing.

The oyster. Oysters rank second in value among fishery products. Improved methods of refrigeration and transportation have opened a new field for this industry. Fresh oysters may be had in inland cities today at reasonable prices. A few years ago they were a luxury in the central states. In a recent year 36,570 tons of oysters were taken, their value exceeding $15,000,000 to the oyster fishermen.

Life history of the oyster. In order to understand the need for wise conservation of this important fishery, we must first acquaint ourselves with the habits of the oyster. Oysters breed in the warmer months of the year, when water temperatures reach about 69° F., which may be March or April on the Gulf Coast, June on the middle Atlantic, and July in New England. The oyster exudes a milky substance, composed of millions of eggs. One female may produce 100,000,000 to 500,000,000 eggs in a single season. The eggs are cast out into the water, where they are fertilized. The egg develops in two or three hours into a swimming larva which has small, vibrating hairs, known as cilia. These cilia enable it to be suspended while it drifts about with the current. Before long a tiny pair of shells appear. As these shells grow heavier, the little oyster, now called a spat, drops to the bottom to attach itself to some hard object (Fig. 190). It is no longer able to move about, and where it once settles it must remain until moved by some outside force. The young oyster can attach itself only to clean surfaces. While still young, the spats are easily smothered by mud or silt that may settle upon them. The oyster is equipped with little beating cilia, which carry microscopic food plants to it. We thus see that when the young spat is ready to end its wanderings and make a permanent home, it should be able to find some hard, clean object to which it may attach itself, comparatively free from mud and silt. Otherwise it soon dies.

Conservation of oysters. In general, the oyster catch has declined over much of the area where this valuable mollusk is found. This decline may be attributed to several factors. Pollution of our waters by commercial and sewage wastes in the vicinity of tidewater cities is an important one. The waste from oil wells in Louisiana is believed to have contributed to the decline of oysters in that area.

Oysters have many natural enemies. Starfish are very destructive to oysters (Fig. 191). They wrap their arms about the shell and exert a slow and steady pull by means of small and numerous suction discs. The shells are gradually forced apart and the contents devoured. The starfish is reputed to destroy half a million dollars' worth of oysters annually in Long Island Sound. The most recent control method is the use of quicklime, which can be spread over the oyster beds at a cost of from $2 to $7 per acre. The lime retains its effectiveness for some time, and, so far as is known, is not injurious to shellfish and other commercial species. Another enemy is the drill, a small snail living among oyster beds. It bores through the hard shell of the oyster and destroys great numbers in this fashion.

The oyster's worst enemy is man. Through overfishing he has exhausted once valuable beds of this sea animal. Man has learned how to farm oysters, however, and now many of these shellfish come from planted beds. We have previously seen that the young oyster, or spat, must have a hard, clean surface to which it may attach itself. By planting discarded oyster shells on depleted natural oyster rocks, fine results are obtained. It is the practice of some states to require that a certain percentage of empty shells taken by the fishermen be returned to the beds. The effect of shell planting in parts of the Chesapeake Bay re-

Figure 190. An old boot lying on the bottom of the bay provides a home for these young oysters. The oyster spat must have a clean, hard surface to attach to, otherwise it will be smothered by mud or silt. (Maryland Conservation Department.)

gion has been astounding. Oystermen, who could not catch three bushels a day several years ago in this vicinity, are now able to catch ten bushels.

Frequently oysters may be so thick on the beds as to prevent proper development. Oystermen and conservationists then transplant these

Figure 191. A dredge load of starfish taken from lower Chesapeake Bay, Maryland. When numerous, starfish may be very destructive to oysters. The shells are forced open by a steady pull of the arms of the starfish, which are provided with numerous suction discs, and the contents of the shell are then devoured. (U.S. Fish and Wildlife Service.)

seed oysters to other bars, where, after maturing, they furnish an abundant supply for the fishermen.

Some states limit the size of the oysters that may be taken. By custom oysters are usually not eaten during the warmer months. There is no reason why they should not be except that they contain large amounts of sex products before spawning and are thin and watery after spawning.

Oysters may be caught in several ways. In shallow bays the fishermen take oysters from the beds with tongs. These are metal baskets or rakes, fitted on the end of long handles that work like scissors. The opened baskets or rakes are scraped over the oyster beds and closed by bringing the handles together, and the oysters then are drawn into the boat. In deep water, where shellfish live on a smooth bottom, a metal drag is used.

The shrimp industry. Shrimps are of great importance in the fishery industry of the United States. In 1935 the shrimp fishery was seventh in importance with respect to volume and sixth in value among the food-fishery products. In 1946 this fishery gave employment to more than 20,000 persons.

The Gulf Coast is the chief source of the most popular crustacean in the United States. The American people eat ten times as much shrimp as lobster and half again as much as they consume of crab. And of the 150,000,000 pounds of shrimp taken from the sea for cocktails, salads, and appetizing cooked dishes, 85 per cent comes from the Gulf Coast and 66 per cent from the state of Louisiana alone. About two-thirds of the entire United States catch of shrimp is taken in Louisiana. Texas follows with 10 per cent, while Mississippi, Florida, and Georgia each contribute 5 or 6 per cent, North Carolina and Alabama each 3 per cent, and South Carolina only 1 per cent. Inasmuch as this fishery furnishes a livelihood to entire communities in our southern states, it is essential that the supply be properly conserved.

The common shrimp spawns through the spring and summer in the open sea or gulfs. The eggs are broadcast at random. Soon after the young shrimps have hatched, they move to the warm shallows, where they are fed upon by many fish. By midsummer they begin to appear in the commercial catch. At the peak of the shrimp season in October, great numbers of these young shrimps are taken in the nets. As cold weather approaches, the young shrimps move into the deeper and warmer waters away from shore. The following spring the shrimps, now full grown, reproduce and presumably die, for no trace of them can be found. Because the life of the shrimp is short, it is necessary that a careful watch be kept on the supply from year to year.

Improved methods of capturing shrimps have resulted in much larger catches and the consequent growing importance of this industry. Formerly shrimps were taken in great seines, but now most are captured by means of the shrimp trawl. These trawls consist of a mesh bag, a wing at each end for directing the shrimps into the bag, and a board at each end for holding the wings apart. Tow lines attached to these boards are then secured to the vessel. Such trawls are made of

1½- to 2-inch mesh and vary from 22 feet to nearly 100 feet in width. For two hours the net is carried through the water at about the speed of a walking man. Most shrimp fishing is conducted from mid-August until early December.

Shrimps, like other fishery products, are highly perishable. Handling must be kept to a minimum and the shrimps packed in ice very soon after capture. In the large fishing grounds, where canning factories are from 20 to 100 miles from the fishing boats, larger vessels provided with an abundant supply of ice collect the shrimps from the smaller boats (Fig. 192).

Shrimps are prepared for market chiefly in Louisiana, Mississippi, and Florida. About half the shrimps are canned, a third are sold fresh, and a good share of the remainder are dried and shipped to China. Shrimps possess the same nutritive values as do other sea foods. They are rich in digestible proteins and are a good source of vitamins. Shrimps are rich also in iodine. In the fall of 1948 fresh shrimps were selling for 59 cents a pound in some eastern markets.

Figure 192. Shrimp, a highly perishable product. Larger vessels provided with an abundant supply of ice visit the small shrimp boats and collect their catch at frequent intervals. The shrimp are taken to the canning factories where they are prepared and shipped over the world.

Conservation of shrimp. There is no indication that the shrimps are being seriously depleted. But any animal with such a short life might be considered in a precarious condition as far as overfishing is concerned. If the shrimps should ever be badly depleted one year, it would be extremely difficult, if not impossible, for them to regain their former abundance.

The United States Fish and Wildlife Service has suggested four possible ways of conserving the supply of shrimps. They suggest restrictions on the size of the shrimps taken, closure during certain seasons and in certain areas, and the regulation of fishing gear. Several of the southern states have adopted measures to protect the young, rapidly growing shrimps in their inshore nursery areas during the summer and fall. If the fishermen wait until the shrimps have obtained more of their growth, fewer individuals are required to make up the normal 150,000,000-pound annual catch.

Lobsters. The lobster has long been an important fishery product. Lobsters occur in greatest numbers along the New England Coast, and to a much lesser extent, in the coastal waters of the Middle Atlantic states. In 1940, 11,770,000 pounds of lobsters were taken.

The lobster lives in shallow water in rocky places and is usually captured in traps known as lobster pots. These are made of wickerwork or of hoops covered with netting and having funnel-shaped openings permitting entrance but preventing escape. The traps are baited with pieces of fish and are sunk to the bottom in places frequented by lobsters, the place of each pot being marked by a buoy. The lobsters are often sold alive in the market, although a good share are now canned.

The lobster fishery has declined in recent years. These animals were once caught weighing ten or twelve pounds, but it is unusual to obtain large lobsters in any numbers at present. As the female lobster carries her eggs attached to her body for nearly a year, great mortality to the prospective young occurs when heavy fishing is conducted. Most states fix a minimum size below which it is illegal to sell lobsters, but the law is difficult to enforce. The United States Fish and Wildlife Service considers a maximum as well as a minimum size limit to be perhaps the most important conservation measure for the lobster. This is true because the large lobsters are by far the greatest egg producers and consequently should be protected.

Crabs. Next to the lobster, the blue crab is the most important crustacean of our eastern coast. Crabs swarm in the bays from Cape Cod to Texas. They are pugnacious and feed on almost any small animal. They will even eat their own kind. Soft-shell crabs (those that have recently shed their hard outer shell and have obtained a new soft one) are more desirable than the hard-coated individuals.

Crabs are caught during the warmer months of the year in a number of ways. Trotlines are set, with baited hooks at frequent intervals, for these crabs. They are also caught in small wire traps, or lifted from water with hand nets. Crabs live for a long time out of water and may be purchased alive in the fish markets along our coast.

The polluted waters of New York Harbor support large numbers of these important sea animals, yet their numbers do appear to have declined. For example, during the five years from 1915 to 1920, the Chesapeake Bay crab catch declined from 50,000,000 pounds to about 22,000,000 pounds. The annual catch of blue crabs is about 80,000,000 pounds, the total yielding close to 14,000,000 pounds of crab meat worth between $3,000,000 and $5,000,000. It is most important, from a conservation standpoint, to protect the sponge crab, or egg-bearing female, and to halt the practice of impounding hard-shell crabs for the purpose of holding them in floats until they shed and become soft-shell crabs. A very small percentage of the crabs impounded in the hard-shell condition survive.

Other shellfish. Other important shellfish include clams, which are canned in greater amounts than oysters. Scallops are taken in great numbers along the coast. Many people share in the annual take of 6,000,000 pounds of fresh-water mussels, which are used to manufacture buttons.

OTHER USEFUL PRODUCTS OF THE SEA

The vast ocean provides man with many products other than fish. Whales furnish oil and blubber, seals provide fur, sponges are widely used, and many other lesser creatures add to our wealth.

The whaling industry. Few of us appreciate the importance of whalebone, whale oil, sperm oil, and other commodities of past generations. Whaling was once one of the most important industries of the world, but it is now relatively insignificant because its products have been replaced by those of various other industries. Whale oil, however, is still widely used in the manufacture of soap. During 1919 and 1920, whale fisheries operating along the Pacific Coast of North America supplied one-tenth of the total world output of whale oil. From 1919 to 1929, 15,985 whales were taken on the Pacific Coast. These yielded 530,120 barrels of oil. It was reported that in 1930 the fleet of whaling vessels returning from the South Seas brought the largest cargo of sperm oil and by-products ever loaded. These were obtained from whales that were located and reported by wireless-equipped airplanes and killed by electric harpoons.

Whales are a resource of the world. At one time it was the most important marine resource of our nation. About 1843, the whaling industry engaged some 735 boats and 40,000 people, had an investment of $40,000,000, and took annually whales worth $8,000,000. Just a century later, this country had three boats and 59 people engaged in whaling; the investment was less than a million dollars; and the year's catch was worth $44,000. Why the death of a once great industry? Mismanagement of the industry; the rise of the petroleum industry, which reduced the domestic market for whale oil; and our country's failure to develop new products from whales. Norway has led in the total utilization of the whale catch. In 1937, a treaty was signed by nine governments, including Great Britain, Norway, Germany and the United States. This treaty not only regulates the catch and determines the size and number of different species that may be taken in the whaling season, but likewise prohibits the use of factory ships in many extensive areas of the ocean. During the war the dearth of whaling boats and whalers to man them gave these animals a much-needed respite. At the present time, owing to the scarcity of fats and oils throughout much of the world, soap manufacturers have asked for a two- or three-year suspension of the international agreement limiting the take of whales. Fortunately signers of the treaty are against such a suspension.

The Japanese whaling fleet, under American supervision, is again hunting whales in Antarctic waters. The meat is being used for human consumption.

The fur seal. Look at a map of Alaska, and you will see a chain of islands, the Aleutians, stretching far into Bering Sea. One hundred miles north of this chain are several tiny islands, scarcely shown on our maps. These small, fog-hidden rocks are called the Pribilof Islands. Each spring thousands of fur seals, migrating through storm-swept areas, make their way with unerring accuracy to these rock-bound shores. The huge males, weighing a quarter of a ton, reach the breeding grounds first, early in May. Each male, or bull, selects an area that he jealously guards and where he gathers as many females as he can muster (Fig. 193). Such a harem may number from twelve to fifty females, each weighing about one-sixth as much as the old bulls. Shortly after the females reach the islands, the young are born. When the young grow strong, they take to the water and soon become as accomplished swimmers as their parents.

The young males, those less than six years old, are called bachelor seals. They form huge colonies of many thousands, well removed from the great bulls and their harems. So fearless are these seals that a man can walk among them without arousing the slightest concern.

Figure 193. A herd of fur seals on the Pribilof Islands, Alaska. More than a million dollars' worth of seal pelts were marketed in 1936. (U.S. Fish and Wildlife Service.)

Fur seals once existed in incredible numbers on these islands. It is estimated that, before the purchase of Alaska by the United States in 1867, several million fur seals inhabited these islands in a single season. Their skins were of much value, for the fur seal has a dense, soft fur. The seals were so lacking in suspicion that they could be easily killed, and a tremendous and wasteful slaughter occurred. Many seals were killed at sea. The animals were much reduced and actually threatened with extinction.

In 1911 an agreement was entered into by the United States, Great Britain, Japan, and Russia, whereby the taking of fur seals in the

North Pacific was prohibited except under certain limited conditions. With proper management of these great seal herds by government biologists, the seals have increased from approximately 125,000 animals in 1911 to more than 1,800,000 in 1937 (Fig. 194).

Seals are still taken for the fur trade. More than 50,000 seals are killed each year under government supervision. These are selected from the young nonbreeding males. In spite of this large annual take, the herd is said to continue to increase at the rate of 8 per cent annually. In 1920, 14,852 fur-seal skins were sold by the government,

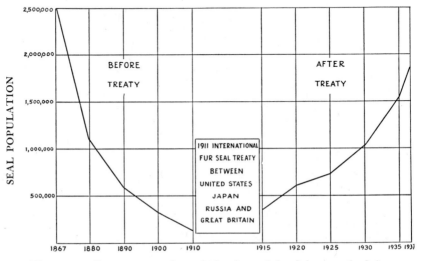

Figure 194. Proper protection of the fur-seal herd has resulted in a marked increase in their numbers during the past quarter-century.

which received $1,707,000 for the hides. In 1936 more than a million dollars' worth of pelts were marketed.

In 1943 the size of the herd permitted the killing of 117,164 young male seals. Of these, 38,655 were sold at public auction for $1,738,000. A by-product of some consequence is seal oil, blubber, and meal from the seal carcasses. In 1943 total sales of these products netted the government $73,234.

The fur-seal herd is now on a stable producing basis. We should feel justly proud of having saved this once-threatened national resource.

The sponge industry. The sponge is a marine animal living in shallow tropical seas. Only on the west coast of Florida does it occur in commercial quantities. It is there so important that its value outranks that of any Florida fish. In 1927 the sponge sales brought $865,510 to the fishermen.

Most of the sponge fleet is centered at Tarpon Springs, Florida. For a modest fee the tourist can go on one of the boats and see the entire operation of the sponge fishery in a few hours.

Most of the sponge fishermen are Greek colonists or their descendants. They obtain sponges in two ways. Deep-sea equipment may be

Figure 195. Buyers examining a lot of marketable sponges. Practically the entire commercial take of sponges in the United States comes from the west coast of Florida. (U.S. Fish and Wildlife Service.)

used, in which case the diver descends and tears the sponges from their resting place. Formerly the diver, with his great leaden shoes, destroyed many valuable sponges by treading on them. A law has been passed that prohibits these divers from operating within several miles of shore, and this measure has undoubtedly proved effective in conserving the supply. The diver usually remains down about two hours, in water sixty feet or less in depth, gathering the sponges by hand and placing them in a net basket to be hauled to the surface.

The other method that is sometimes employed in harvesting the sponge crop is for two men to go out in a small boat and remove the sponges from the bottom with a three-tined hook attached to a pole. Some wastage may occur by this method as the sponges are likely to be badly torn by the hooks.

When we purchase a sponge, we really buy its skeleton. When the sponge is removed from the water, all the hollow places are filled with living tissue. To remove this, the sponges are placed in the shade, and after a short time decomposition sets in. After the tissue has thoroughly decomposed, the sponge is beaten with a board to loosen this now useless matter, strung on a stout cord, and thrown in salt water to soak. A final cleaning makes it ready for market (Fig. 195).

Inasmuch as sponges are of primary importance in the marine fishery of Florida, that state has wisely adopted two laws to conserve the sponge supply. One law makes it illegal to remove for sale sponges less than five inches in diameter. The other regulates the size of the hook that may be used in taking sponges.

CHAPTER XII

Game and Fur Resources

I F WE could turn back the pages of history, we should find that wild animals had a profound influence on civilization. Early man used the hides of the larger beasts for clothing and shelter, and their flesh for food. With the development of civilization wild animals were domesticated. Today we see everywhere the beneficial results of such domestication; what is not so evident is the role wild animals play in contemporary civilization.

Wildlife is a product of the land, just as timber and minerals are. It exists everywhere—in dense forests, in marshes, in streams and lakes, and even on cultivated land. Much of it has an important bearing on human welfare. Wild creatures still provide us with food and fur. They furnish sport to the hunter and delight the traveler in our national parks. They bring joy to millions of nature lovers in every corner of the land.

Value of wild animals as food. Americans are the greatest meat eaters in the world. A relatively small part of this meat comes from the wild supply, largely from deer, rabbits, pheasants, and ducks. Hunters in Pennsylvania legally killed 35,000 deer in 1946, while during the same season more than 100,000 were bagged by Michigan nimrods. The annual average kill of deer in the United States probably exceeds half a million animals. The cottontail rabbit is a favorite with hunters. At least 100,000,000 rabbits are shot annually. The amount of actual meat taken each year probably exceeds 125,000 tons, sufficient to provide at least three game dinners for every adult each year.

Value to business. The food value of wild game killed annually totals many millions of dollars every year, but this sum is insignificant in comparison with the money spent for licenses, arms and ammunition, hunting clothes, travel, and lodging. It has been estimated that four times as many people went hunting and fishing in 1930 as in 1920. Shorter hours and fewer working days are constantly adding to the number of men and women who seek such recreation. The various states issue a total of 18,000,000 hunting and fishing licenses annually. Allowing for duplication in the form of a separate license for each state in which one hunts, it is safe to place the number of individuals who purchase licenses at no less than 13,000,000. This is more than 16 per cent of our adult population. These people are said to spend $650,000,000 annually on hunting and related sports. Both merchants and manufacturers profit from these purchases by hunters. They even capitalize on the harmless pastime of target shooting in which sportsmen indulge. Resort owners, railroad companies, and guides benefit from their activities. Hunting is a big business with an enormous monetary turnover every year.

Figure 196. Trophies of the hunt. Deer are important game animals and provide much sport each fall to thousands of hunters. In the East deer have become more numerous within recent years. (W. J. Hamilton, Jr.)

Esthetic value. Many people care nothing for hunting, but they do have a genuine interest in wildlife. There are just as many people who enjoy seeing, and perhaps photographing, a wild duck and her brood or a deer in the woods as there are people whose chief desire is to kill these animals in the name of sport. This genuine and increasing interest is becoming more evident. Tourists visit the national parks as much to see the wildlife as to observe the great natural wonders. Such visitors are as much attracted to a beaver dam as to a great waterfall. The great bears, the elk herds, or the tiny striped chipmunks add to the beauty of western scenery. The flashing white tail of a startled Adirondack deer lends charm to the summer vacation of the city dweller. Those unfortunate city dwellers who cannot visit the country crowd the city parks to view the captive deer, elks, bears, and monkeys. More than 25,000,000 visitors thronged the national parks in 1947. The wild animals delight these visitors just as much as the majestic cascades, gorges, and great forests.

This awakening interest in our wildlife is a healthy one. A single specific example will show what store some people place on the esthetic value of wildlife. In 1936, of the 30,000 deer killed in Wisconsin, more

Figure 197. A New York trapper with a few weeks' catch of red fox, raccoon, and mink. Fur-bearing animals provide many people with a partial livelihood, and it is thus imperative that their numbers be maintained.

than 10 per cent were killed in Vilas County. Despite the fact that Wisconsin authorized an open season on deer in 1937, there was no hunting in Vilas County. The residents of this county think that the deer are worth more to them alive than dead. The deer are recognized as an important attraction for tourists, who spend more in the aggregate than do the hunters. The Board of Supervisors posted 30,000 acres that the county had acquired through tax delinquency. Sentiment for maintaining the deer was so great that many private owners also posted their land.

The unusual aspect of this case is the recognition by a rural community of the value of its wildlife, and the effort to enlist popular support for a movement that goes beyond the state's conservation policy. **Value of fur animals.** The fur industry is one of the oldest in America. Early exploration and discovery of the West owe much to the fur trade. Adventurous trappers and traders pushing into uncharted regions in their search for new beaver lands opened up much new territory for the United States.

Although the pelts of wild animals are no longer an absolute necessity for human welfare, we must remember that many millions of dollars are invested in the fur industry and that it furnishes employment for thousands of men and women. In New York City more than 14,000 workers are employed in the fur trade. Today the annual fur catch in the United States is estimated to be worth from $100,000,000 to $125,-000,000 to the trappers. More than 300,000 trappers share this wealth. Most trappers in rural districts make but a few dollars each season, but the more experienced trapper will earn from $1,000 to $3,000, depending on the demand for fur (Fig. 197).

The value of the fur catch in the United States far exceeds that of Canada and Soviet Russia combined. Not all furs come from the North. Louisiana trappers take more pelts than do the trappers of Canada and Alaska combined. Within the environs of such great cities as New York and Chicago numbers of muskrats are still trapped by schoolboys.

In 1867 the United States purchased Alaska from Russia for $7,200,-000. Since then the Territory has exported $80,000,000 worth of furs. In 1929 furs valued at $4,513,000 were exported. Fur animals alone have paid for Alaska many times over.

PAST ABUNDANCE OF WILDLIFE

Early American historians have left us a record of the abundance of wildlife a century ago. Superlatives were used to describe the vast herds of big game, the countless flocks of wild fowl, and the teeming wildlife of forest and prairie alike.

Before the coming of the white man, the buffalo herds extended from New York to Georgia and far southwestward into Mexico and north into Canada. Their numbers at that time have been placed at 60,000,000 (Fig. 198). The years following the Civil War witnessed a great emigration of adventurous settlers into the West. A million buffaloes were estimated to have been killed each year for a long period. Prong-horned antelopes, graceful animals that are found in the western plains of North America, once rivaled the buffalo hordes in numbers. A century ago the lordly elks roamed in great herds through territory from Quebec to Georgia and westward to the Rockies. Giant moose abounded in eastern forests, while deer were everywhere abundant.

Figure 198. The great herds of buffalo which roamed the western prairies are but memories. At one time their numbers were placed at 60,000,000. Now a few thousand live a semidomesticated life in national refuges. (New York Zoological Society.)

Game birds and waterfowl were no less plentiful. The history of the passenger pigeon is familiar to many. Flocks of these beautiful birds, living torrents that obscured the light of the sun for hours, have been estimated at more than a billion in a single flight. Wisconsin woods for more than a hundred miles sheltered the breeding birds. In Kentucky a nesting site several miles in width extended for forty miles. In such a place more than one hundred nests were counted in a single tree. Sturdy oaks crashed to the ground from the unaccustomed weight of roosting birds, piled one upon another. Herds of hogs were driven into these roosts to fatten on the eggs and the squabs that had been precipitated from the broken limbs above. As late as 1878 a nesting colony of passenger pigeons in Michigan covered a forested area 100,000 acres in extent. The birds were sold for from twelve to fifty cents a dozen, and many millions were packed in barrels and shipped to the large eastern cities each year.

At one time North America probably contained more wildfowl than any other country in the world. Even in the recollection of men now living, the birds came down from the northland during the autumn in numbers that were beyond description, promising an abundant supply for the gunner forever. Great masses of ducks and geese rose at one time from the water in so dense a cloud as to darken the sky. In early days one might see redhead ducks rafted in bodies miles in extent, probably not fewer than 50,000 ducks in a mass. The redhead is now so reduced in numbers that it requires special protection.

Prairie and forest game was no less abundant. The heath hen ranged along the Atlantic seaboard in countless thousands. Prairie chickens were amazingly abundant, and wild turkeys roamed the northern forests, fattening on the acorns of giant oaks.

The fur animals were so numerous that they beckoned the trapper and trader into the uncharted wilderness. The beaver has rightly been termed a builder of empire. This one animal was largely responsible for the exploration of the North and Far West. Its primitive population ran into millions. The pelts of the marten or sable, fisher, lynx, and beaver were eagerly sought by hardy pioneers, who pushed far ahead of adventurous settlers in their quest for new trapping grounds. Many eastern towns, rivers, lakes, and county landmarks have taken their names from the beaver. This is good evidence of the former abundance of this large fur bearer in areas now thickly populated by man.

DECLINE OF WILDLIFE

Reckless slaughter by man with no thought of the morrow has brought doom to many of America's finest animals. The great herds of buffalo no longer blacken the plains. The former millions are now reduced to a few thousand semidomesticated animals herded on government and private reservations. The antelope millions have been greatly reduced until they number thousands rather than millions. Elks have long disappeared from the East, and are largely restricted to the western mountains. Moose are so rare in the East that their occurrence brings newspaper comment.

Our fur bearers have been greatly reduced. Marten, fisher, and otter are now scarce. The wolverine is almost gone from our forests. Such common fur animals as muskrat, mink, raccoon, and skunk, have declined.

The wonderful and impressive spectacle of immense flocks of passenger pigeons is but a memory. The last pigeon, a captive in the Cincinnati Zoo, died in 1914. The great armies of wildfowl are seen no more, but only the survivors of their broken ranks. The very last of the once abundant heath hen died in 1931. The whooping crane and trumpeter swan seem destined to go.

Reasons for the decline of wildlife. We can lay the blame for the decline of wildlife on no one single cause. Many factors, working singly or together, have wrought destruction upon our wild birds and animals. Much of this destruction was unavoidable.

Settlement of the country. Until a century ago the extermination of wildlife proceeded slowly. The Indian killed only for his wants. When hunting grounds showed signs of exhaustion, the Indian moved to new areas. The former site was soon restocked with game and fish. According to an Iroquois legend, the Indian could never kill for sport. It was a difficult task, with his primitive weapons, to provide meat for himself and his family. The early white settler could find little sale for wild game and shot only enough to supply his needs.

Within the past one hundred years an enormous decline in wildlife has occurred. Advancing civilization with an ever-increasing population encouraged large-scale agricultural operations. These in turn brought on the inevitable destruction of great forests. The western plains could not support millions of cattle and sheep and also the buffaloes. Civilization and indiscriminate slaughter have driven the woodland caribou from our country. In 1927 there were probably not more than thirty in the United States, and these were all banded together in a northern Minnesota swamp. Today they number not more than a dozen and are probably fewer. It appears probable that no measure, however heroic, can now save this pitiful remnant.

Market hunting. The buffalo herds, as we have seen, had been the chief dependence of the Plains Indians. The great animals provided the Indians with meat for food and hides for clothing and shelter. When the white man invaded the West, he needed food. The railroad workers subsisted largely on wild game. The coming of the railroad made available the eastern markets. Then the wanton slaughter really began. Formerly the hides could not be transported easily, nor the meat made available to the easterners. It was a matter of but a few years before the vast herds ceased to exist. It has been said that 50,000 buffalo were killed for their tongues alone, the carcasses being left to rot. Less than one per cent of the meat was shipped, and much of this spoiled in transit. Skins sold for as little as fifty cents each.

The wild sheep of the western mountains are very scarce, yet they are being persistently shot by hunters. The desert bighorn sheep, a great animal of the western mountains, is now seriously threatened. Amateur prospectors wantonly shoot the animals at watering places, often making no use whatever of the carcass. Elks have been illegally killed by the thousands for just two teeth. These trophies dangle on the watch chains of men.

Not so many years ago it was possible to buy game birds in the markets of the country. Immense numbers of waterfowl were killed to satisfy this demand. In southern California during the winter of 1902 two hunters armed with automatic shotguns killed 218 geese in one hour, and their bag for the day was 450 geese (Fig. 199).

Before the coming of the railroad, game had been plentiful in the western markets. Wild turkeys could be had for twenty-five cents, ducks were three for a quarter and wild geese ten cents each. When the railroads reached St. Louis, the great game country was made available to easterners. Price for game gradually rose, while the game rapidly decreased. Hunters and sportsmen came from every land. Market hunters and big-game hunters crowded into this new country. In the early 1890's the platforms of the railroad stations in North Dakota were lined with ducks. In warm weather it was not unusual to see two or three wagonloads of spoiled birds hauled away and dumped. One marvels that any game is left.

Destruction of habitat. Some animals prefer swamps, some prairies, while others may choose the forest in which to live. The conditions under which an animal or bird chooses to live we call its habitat. Many animals are adaptable. They can modify their needs or change their mode of life if their normal habitat is destroyed. Many others cannot thrive with such a change. The ruffed grouse prefers the forests, while the bobwhite quail makes its residence in cleared fields about the farm. We should not, therefore, expect to find a quail in the deep woods nor a grouse in the hedgerow.

The habitats of many wild animals and birds have been destroyed.

Figure 199. This 100-pound illegal gun was confiscated in Dorchester County, Maryland, by federal and state deputy game wardens. Such a gun is capable of killing and crippling many ducks in a single discharge. (Maryland Conservation Department.)

Much of this destruction was unavoidable. We could not retain all of our forests and still have pasture lands for our cows. Man has greatly modified the country to suit his needs. This change in habitat has made for a profound change in animal life.

Figure 200. A typical marsh area of the Malheur Migratory Bird Refuge in Oregon. Such marshes provide breeding grounds for vast numbers of wildfowl, fur-bearing animals, and other wildlife. Ill-advised drainage projects have destroyed many acres of these valuable marshes, to the detriment of wildlife generally. (U.S. Fish and Wildlife Service.)

Drainage. One of the worst features of this change by man has resulted from the great drainage projects. Many animals and birds require swamps and shallow lakes to breed in and rest upon during their migrations (Fig. 200). Numerous striking examples of the loss to wildlife wrought by drainage could be given. One will be sufficient.

On the boundary of southern Oregon and northern California there once existed the great Lower Klamath Lake. The naturalist William Finley gave a vivid picture of this huge, shallow lake in 1905. Many varieties of ducks—mallards, redheads, pintails, teal, and others—swam and bred in its marshes. More than 1,500 old and young geese were counted in a small, open area among the rushes. Gulls, herons, cormorants, grebes, terns, and pelicans were here in thousands. The nesting multitudes whitened the marsh. These shallow lakes and wide, bordering marsh lands maintained the waterfowl nurseries of the Pacific Coast. Such areas were a haven to the great migrating flocks of geese, swan, and other wildfowl on their long flight to the south. Malheur Lake, in southeastern Oregon, was at one time the largest and most important breeding area within the United States for Canada geese.

Klamath Lake and Malheur were partly drained. Klamath Lake and surrounding marsh lands, 85,000 acres of teeming wildlife, became a desert waste of dry peat and alkali. The alkali has caused duck sickness, which has destroyed thousands of wildfowl. If this drainage had been of benefit to man, it might have been excusable. The homesteaders who settled on these marginal lands learned that they had been fooled by promotional schemes and, when possible, they anxiously sold out and returned to a land where they could make a living. The United States Fish and Wildlife Service is reclaiming these areas and trying to transform them once again into havens for wildfowl.

Much useless drainage of this nature has destroyed wildlife habitats. Muskrat marshes, which are valuable in themselves, are disappearing. Wildfowl areas are being depleted. We have seen in an earlier chapter (p. 94) that these countless marshes serve to keep a uniform water table and are a necessity to us in many other ways.

Mosquito control and wildlife. In recent years there has been urgent necessity for the control of disease-carrying and pestiferous mosquitoes near centers of large populations and resorts. Mosquitoes breed in enormous numbers in salt marshes, ponds, and swampy areas. Unfortunately, these places are also the principal breeding, feeding, and resting places for waterfowl and fur-bearing animals. Such areas also support small food plants and lesser wildlife, which is none the less attractive even though it has no commercial value.

Federal, state, and local agencies have taken extensive steps to free communities from the annoyance of mosquitoes. To eliminate such pests, the authorities have ditched many mosquito breeding grounds. This is one of the most practical methods of destroying these pests. However, such operations have, in many instances, seriously disturbed the favorite natural habitats of wildlife and have proved disastrous to it. Much of this ditching has been done in areas where mosquitoes have never caused concern to man.

Destruction by oil pollution. Essentially, all agencies that engage in the production, transportation, or use of oil are a potential menace to wildlife. This is particularly true along our coasts. When a duck or gull lights on oil-covered water, its feathers quickly become so saturated that it cannot again take flight. The fine down which insulates its body becomes water-soaked, and the bird soon dies from exposure. Thousands of ducks have been destroyed in this manner in both the Atlantic and Pacific coastal waters.

The disaster to the steamer *Robert E. Lee* near Plymouth, Massachusetts, in the spring of 1928 was a veritable calamity to waterfowl, caught as they were in full migration to their nesting grounds. Fuel oil was released in large quantities, and it was not long until the beach on the north side of Cape Cod was literally covered with dead and dying ducks. One report stated that thousands of dead ducks were found along the East Sandwich Beach.[1]

The California Fish and Game Commission has made an effort to stop oil contamination of coastal and interior waters, and fines of several hundred dollars have been imposed upon ships' engineers and oil companies. But such laws are difficult to enforce, and the evil persists.

On the coastal regions of Louisiana and Texas the destruction of wildfowl by oil is particularly severe. Here we find a heavy winter concentration of ducks and geese near the extensive oil fields, which at times have been responsible for the contamination of large areas.

Overtrapping. There has been a steady decline in our valuable fur animals. This is largely due to an increased demand for furs of all kinds. The people of America are truly fur-conscious. Shortly after World War I the value of pelts increased tremendously. Trappers were paid four dollars for a muskrat skin, and skunk pelts brought six dollars. These were formerly worth from a few cents to a dollar each. This decided increase in value spurred trappers to greater efforts.

As a result, many species became scarce. Records show that more than

---

[1] F. E. Lincoln in *Proceedings of the North American Wildlife Conference* (Washington, 1936), p. 556.

100,000,000 skins of twenty-three kinds of fur-bearing animals passed through the principal fur markets in 1921. This was only a part of the number killed for their pelts, many being unreported.

Lack of food. Man, intentionally or otherwise, sometimes upsets the so-called "balance of nature." His activities frequently destroy food plants suitable for wildlife. He may, and often does, kill the natural enemies of game animals. The animals may then become so numerous that they eat up the available food supply and perish from starvation. A number of such instances have occurred (Fig. 201).

Figure 201. Starved deer collected by game wardens in the Pennsylvania forests. It is not often that wildlife is threatened with food shortage. The deer in Pennsylvania have increased so rapidly that food shortage has resulted. Hunters have been permitted to shoot female deer so that the numbers may be reduced. (Pennsylvania Game Commission.)

During severe winters, the ice of Lake Superior connects Isle Royale with the Canadian shore line, thirteen miles distant. Moose crossed this ice span and populated the island, supposedly in 1912. With no wolves or other natural enemies to molest them, the animals increased yearly until their numbers were estimated to have reached 2,000 in 1933. The food supply proved inadequate to meet this increase, and many of these fine animals died of starvation. By 1937 their numbers were reduced to a few hundred. We might call this an instance of too much wildlife.

Other agencies of destruction. Hunting for the market, destruction of habitat, advancing civilization, intensive trapping of fur animals, and ill-advised extermination of vermin are a few of the factors that have caused a decline in our wildlife. Many other agencies have been responsible for a decline of game and fur animals within recent years. Poaching and illegal killing of game have contributed in no small way to the decline. In recent years the high price of meat has encouraged unlawful practices. New Yorkers were fined $84,000 in 1946 for taking game illegally. Currently we are experiencing the most lawless era in outdoor history, an aftermath of the war.

The great floods of the last few decades have taken their toll of many valuable animals. High water has flooded the great fur country of the

Figure 202. A deer killed by a forest fire in the Santa Barbara National Forest, California. Such fires are responsible for terrific mortality of wildlife annually. (U.S. Forest Service.)

Mississippi Valley, destroying unnumbered fur bearers and game animals.

Forest fires can outrace or trap even the deer (Fig. 202). Every year these disastrous fires, by destroying habitat suitable for wildlife or by the actual destruction of wild animals and birds, cause a very appreciable loss in the United States. Following the month-long drought in October, 1947, forest fires flared repeatedly through the northeastern forests, destroying incalculable numbers of animals.

The automobile takes a very great toll of wildlife. Deer, rabbits, birds of many kinds, fur animals, especially the skunk, and many smaller creatures are killed. This highway mortality is increasing, and the time may come when action to prevent it is warranted. More deer were killed by cars in one agricultural county of New York in a recent year than were taken by hunters in another favored deer county. In 1946, 2,714 deer were killed by automobiles in Pennsylvania. Much of such destruction is wanton and could be avoided.

Dogs which run wild kill much game. They are particularly destructive to deer. Cats destroy some forms of wildlife. However useful they may be about the home, their benefits are far overshadowed by their destructive habits when they go into the fields at night. Small game animals and song birds are the chief sufferers.

PRESENT STATUS OF WILDLIFE

We have painted a rather dreary picture of wildlife conditions in the United States. Many wild creatures are gone, and others are faced with early extinction. But Americans are not by nature wanton murderers. Much of the destruction of our useful wildlife has been due to ignorance and thoughtlessness.

A new day is at hand for our wildlife resources. Public-spirited citizens, legislators, hunters, trappers, game officials, and nature lovers alike see the need of immediate conservation efforts if our birds and animals are to survive. Is it too late to save most of them? The answer is decidedly No.

Wildfowl have decreased immeasurably, but drastic efforts to conserve them in recent years have been effective. Protection furnished fur-bearing animals has resulted in a very decided increase in one or more species. The otter is now common in Massachusetts, whereas a dozen years ago it was considered rare.

The sea otter possesses the most valuable fur of all animals. A single pelt has sold for $2,000. It once existed in incredible numbers, but shameless persecution brought it to the point of extinction. With proper protection it has now increased. Lately a census by federal biologists on the coast of Alaska placed its numbers at 2,000.

Some wildlife increasing. Not all animals and birds have been reduced in numbers. The clearing of the forest, while destroying the homes of moose, bears, and other large animals, has made existence possible for many smaller creatures. The cottontail rabbit is probably far more abundant now than formerly. The prairie chicken, as its name would indicate, was a bird of the open prairies, but in recent years it has moved northward 300 miles or more; it is now found in Canada. The opossum, in past years a typical animal of the South, has noticeably increased its range in the past half-century. It is now found over almost all northern states and is still advancing. It is an animal which is important to the trapper for its fur and also provides many southerners with a savory meal.

As the North was settled, forest and prairies disappeared; pastures and fields of wheat and corn took their place. The bobwhite quail responded to this change, and, where winters are not too severe, it is a year-round resident.

Beaver have increased greatly within the past two decades. Their numbers have now approached a point where damage is frequent. Highways are flooded, the forest is often inundated, drowning large tracts of timber, and apple orchards have been seriously damaged by these big rodents. Practically extinct in New York State in 1900, more than 4,000 beavers were taken during the 1948 trapping season.

At the turn of the century, deer were at the crossroads. Their extinction was threatened in many areas. Now the reverse obtains in many eastern states, where an excessive deer population in the rural areas and farm lands threatens the truck crops and orchards.

Abandoned farm lands, clothed in second growth hardwoods, provide excellent food for these animals.

Wildlife, while generally not so abundant as in the past, is still fairly plentiful. It can be increased. Everyone interested in the out-of-doors must help in this task. All can lend a hand in restoring our wildlife resources.

CONSERVATION OF WILDLIFE

Wild game birds and mammals, if given a measure of protection, quickly respond. Many become quite tame. We can see evidence of this on every hand. The wild duck flies at the approach of a gunner but will take bread from the hand of the same individual in a sanctuary or city park. Bears are notoriously shy creatures but become unbelievably tame in the national parks. Even the wary antelope has been known to enter the streets of a Montana city when given proper protection.

When we look back a century, we wonder that all the larger game birds and mammals were not destroyed. There were few champions of wildlife. Very few laws safeguarded our birds, and none enforced the laws even when they existed. Market hunters plied their trade in ruthless fashion. If a voice was lifted in protest, it was soon stilled. Now the wildlife of our country has entered a new era. It has many defenders, while the government agencies and the various states are interesting themselves in this natural wealth as never before.

Federal laws. Many laws have been provided to protect birds and animals. One of the most useful of these has been the Migratory Bird Treaty Act. Previous to 1918 hunters were permitted to shoot wild fowl and other migratory game birds in the spring. Had this practice continued, it is very likely that ducks would long since have ceased to be an important source of game. Formerly many birds were killed while returning to their northern breeding grounds. Swamps suitable for nesting were left deserted, while geese and ducks winged into Canada rather than attempt to breed in this land of guns. Now all this is changed. By treaty with Canada, the federal government has been given control of migratory birds. Spring shooting of waterfowl is now prohibited both in this country and in Canada.

Prior to 1900 great numbers of game birds and animals were shot illegally and shipped to markets outside the state in which they were killed. Thousands of grouse were snared and carted to the city markets. Ducks and quail were illegally killed and shipped to the great urban restaurants. The Lacey Act put an end to this outrageous practice. This act prohibits the interstate shipment of the dead bodies of illegally killed wildlife. Under its provision the importation of wildlife from foreign countries is prohibited, unless approved by the United States Department of Agriculture. Thus we are unlikely to have further introductions of undesirable species such as the English sparrow and starling.

Pittman-Robertson Act. In 1937 this important act was passed. It is officially an aid to wildlife restoration, providing for a 10-per-cent excise tax on sporting arms and ammunition. Congress authorized appropriations, the proceeds going to the states for assistance in purchasing lands for wildlife, developing lands for game and other species, and conducting wildlife surveys and research. Every state that qualifies for such support matches the federal funds on a 25- to 75-per-cent basis. Thirty-eight states reported on the progress of eighty-four different research projects in the summer of 1947. These ranged from state-wide game censuses to life-history studies of individual species.

State regulation of hunting. Wildlife is considered the property of the various states. It is, therefore, the duty of the states to provide suitable protection for those species that are not migratory. Such protection has been provided in the majority of states. Restricted open seasons allow for a short open season in the fall, when the hunter may kill a limited number of certain game species. Formerly the hunter was permitted to destroy all the game he could shoot. The bag limit has been reduced. No longer can the gunner use large-bore weapons. Duck hunters are restricted to the use of three shells in their shotguns. Some states prohibit the use of live decoys (tame ducks tethered in the water) to lure their unsuspecting wild cousins.

Night hunting was formerly the cause of great killings. A boat could be poled into the midst of flocks of sleeping ducks and dozens killed with a single discharge. Many more were hopelessly crippled, and died where they could not be recovered by the market hunter. Today waterfowl can be hunted only after sunrise and before sunset.

Many of our rarer game species have been afforded even greater protection. The quail, recognized as a great destroyer of insects and weed seeds, has been removed from the game list in some states. Realizing their importance as mouse destroyers, some states have given a measure of protection to certain of our hawks and owls. The rarer fur animals, such as the marten and fisher, have been given a long closed season.

It is well to remember that protection from aggressive persecution by man is not sufficient to save our vanishing species. Without proper conditions for feeding and breeding, an animal cannot survive. We shall now see what other methods have been adopted for conserving our wildlife.

National refuges. The map (Fig. 203) indicates the extent of bird refuges and game preserves maintained by government. More are being added continually. Within these areas wildlife is protected from the gunner and trapper. Unmolested by man, great flocks of wildfowl find resting and breeding spots. Most of these areas are too small, however, and do not allow proper protection to animals that require much space in their daily movements. Some people have suggested that a considerably larger area surrounding existing preserves be closed to hunting and trapping. This would add in no small measure to the safety of such predatory animals as the mountain lion, wolf, and bobcat, and also the migratory elk.

State preserves. Most states maintain areas where no hunting or trapping is permitted. Here animals increase rapidly and stock surrounding country with the overflow from this increase. The preserves serve as a refuge for harassed game during the hunting season.

Restocking. Many states, finding their wildlife much reduced or actually exhausted, have purchased birds and animals from neighboring states that were better supplied. With a nucleus for breeding stock, and no hunting permitted, these introduced species have often shown an amazing increase.

It has been said that deer in Vermont had been practically exterminated by 1870. In 1875 thirty were introduced. These were protected until 1897. From that time until the present a short open sea-

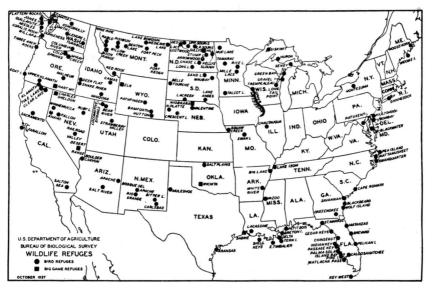

Figure 203. Federal and state refuges are of immense benefit to wildlife. Note the numerous refuges in North Dakota and Montana, where extensive marshes attract immense numbers of breeding wildfowl and other interesting birds. (U.S. Fish and Wildlife Service.)

son permitted hunting. In 1901, only 211 were killed, but the number taken by hunters in succeeding years rapidly increased. During the fall of 1937 Vermont hunters killed 2,449 deer with an estimated value of $54,788.

One of the most successful reintroductions occurred in Pennsylvania. This state has much ideal beaver country, and the animals were once very abundant. By 1895, because of excessive trapping, no beavers were left. From 1919 to 1924 the Pennsylvania Game Commission secured 92 beavers from Canada and released them in suitable parts of the state. One might expect that in the course of ten or fifteen years these beavers would increase to 500 or even 1,000. Everyone was amazed when a careful census revealed 15,000 beavers in the state.

As they increased, some of these beavers became a nuisance. They cut down desirable trees, entered reservoirs, and in general made themselves objectionable. The state authorities trapped the most undesirable ones alive and removed them to wilderness areas. This proved too expensive, so the state, in 1934, decided to permit the animals to be trapped for their fur. There was an immediate outcry from many nature lovers. Some protested that the beavers would again be exterminated in the state. In spite of this, an open season of six weeks was declared. Let us see what happened.

Some 6,408 beavers were trapped in the state. Beavers were caught in fifty of Pennsylvania's sixty-seven counties, showing how well they had spread about the state. The trappers received $64,000 for the pelts. While the state received none of this money, it did get the beaver situation controlled at no cost. That the beaver was not seriously threatened by this open season is evident. Two years later trappers took 2,231 beavers, and the animals still are not reduced to a point where they no longer cause damage. It now looks as though beaver trapping will become an annual event with no further protests.

A number of eastern states have for many years bought cottontail rabbits from dealers in Kansas and other prairie states. These were liberated in suitable surroundings in order that eastern hunters might be provided with greater sport. Now many western states have prohibited the sale of such live game. Pennsylvania, New York, and other states must find new means of replenishing their supply.

Introduction of exotics. An animal introduced into a country where it has never been a native is called an exotic. Almost every country has several to many exotic plants and animals. Some are very useful, while others may be a menace to the welfare of native animal life. The pheasant and Hungarian partridge have been widely introduced into the United States. The former has adapted itself well and is now a most important game bird in the northern part of the country. It is hardy and resourceful and is able to survive where other species fail.

Some introductions have not proved successful. The English sparrow and starling are not held in much esteem by Americans as they are considered to be more harmful than useful. Although both species devour many destructive insects, they also drive away more desirable native birds.

The mongoose, an animal somewhat smaller than our cat, was introduced into Jamaica to combat the rats, which had proved a great enemy of poultry. These mongooses destroyed large numbers of rats, but themselves became destructive to the poultry. They are today probably a greater menace than the rats.

The muskrat is a valuable fur animal in the United States. In Europe and Great Britain, where it has been introduced, it is a pest. Its burrows have undermined banks and dikes so that much valuable

Figure 204. This farmer combines mink ranching with other agricultural pursuits. More than 200 adult mink are kept in this area of less than two acres. Mink are the most important fur bearers raised in captivity. (W. J. Hamilton, Jr.)

land has been flooded. A strenuous campaign involving large sums of money has been launched to control it. So far, these campaigns have been only partly successful.

FUR FARMING

Fur farming is the practice of raising commercially important fur animals in captivity. The surplus stock is killed when the pelts are prime in the early winter. Sixty years ago silver-fox skins brought the trappers the fabulous sum of $1,000 each. It was the custom to dig fox pups from the den in the spring. These were held in suitable cages until their fur became prime in the winter. Early efforts to breed silver foxes in captivity were cloaked in secrecy. From 1890 to 1900 breeding stock sold as high as $34,000 a pair, and individual pelts brought $2,700. Just before World War I the bubble broke and many fur ranchers lost fortunes. With present-day knowledge of nutritional requirements and disease, fur ranching is now an established industry and many people make a living from the sale of pelts raised in captivity.

Kinds of fur animals raised in captivity. From 1915 to 1935 silver fox was the mainstay of fur ranching. Nearly 200,000 ranch-raised silver foxes were marketed in 1937 and about the same number in 1938. The number of silver foxes caught wild is negligible. The price of a good

Figure 205. Muskrat houses on a Maryland marsh. Trappers catch about one million muskrats every year in Maryland. The pelts have averaged two dollars apiece the past few years. (Vernon Bailey.)

silver-fox pelt has declined from $250 in 1928 to an average of $50 in recent years.

Mink breeding has become increasingly popular within the past decade. More mink are raised for their fur than all other wild species combined. More than 300,000 pelts of ranch-raised mink were marketed in 1947. The pelt of a natural brown mink raised in captivity in 1947 averaged less than $15. The new mutation mink, of blue and pastel shades, is in greater demand and commands prices of $60 or more. Since mink are only slightly larger than a gray squirrel, they take much less room than a silver fox, and are easier to handle. A few mink farms are located in city back yards.

The most important wild fur-bearing animal in the United States is the little muskrat. Muskrat farming consists chiefly of maintaining suitable living conditions on natural swamp and marsh lands. These marshes may be fenced, but more often they are merely posted to keep off trespassers. Good swamp land will produce a harvest of 4 to 6 or more muskrats an acre (Fig. 205). Owners of extensive marshes employ men to trap these areas. Important muskrat marshes are located on the east shore of Maryland. About 1,000,000 animals are trapped here each winter. The muskrat is valuable for its flesh as well as its fur. It is dressed and sold for food in the markets of Washington, Baltimore, and other cities, where it is called *marsh rabbit*. The carcasses sell for fifteen or twenty cents each.

The future of fur farming. Although practically the entire production of silver-fox skins comes from ranch-raised animals and although many of the mink pelts marketed annually are raised in captivity, it is doubtful that fur farming will ever provide a sufficient supply of furs to satisfy the world demand. However, the ranching of fur animals will in a measure relieve pressure on the trapping of wild animals. By so doing it will perform a useful service to conservation.

GAME MANAGEMENT

Because of the ever-increasing interest in game birds and mammals, it has become desirable to manage these wild creatures so that we may always have not only an adequate stock but a surplus for hunting and trapping. The improvement or modification of farm and waste lands to ensure that game species will find suitable food and shelter is called *game management*. Such management makes it possible for the landowner to increase the game on his property. This adds another crop to those already produced. The farmer may profit by this additional crop in several ways. Not the least of these is the opportunity to sell hunting privileges, as has long been done in Great Britain.

Game management can be practiced by the individual farmer or property owner. Far better results may be accomplished by the co-operation of a large group on adjacent properties. Game management is, fortunately, not a complicated practice. The landowner can, with little effort, provide suitable areas where game species will find a suitable haven. Sometimes this area may have a foundation of game; again it may be totally barren of game birds and animals. Trained men who will advise on the kind of game best suited to the farm may be found in the state colleges and conservation departments.

Game management practices. Wildlife is one of the easiest crops to grow. It is a natural product of the land, and as such will produce abundantly if given half a chance. All one needs to do, in some instances, is to let the waste lands grow to natural vegetation. Weeds, fruit-bearing shrubs, tangles of grape and brier, and dense vegetation along hedgerows and roadsides will materially aid wildlife. We can recommend a few practices which have been beneficial to the increase of wild game.

Game cover. Wild animals, whether they be prairie chickens or cottontail rabbits, cannot exist without suitable shelter. Such a retreat provides protection against enemies and against storms and other climatic disturbances, and furnishes a safe place for breeding. It is desirable to provide such cover in close relationship to available food. For instance, a dense cover of shrubs or a thicket adjoining a field of buckwheat, clover, lespedeza, or corn is helpful. After the harvest a few shocks of corn or several bundles of buckwheat may provide food for a covey of quail or pheasants.

Planting for wildlife. We have seen that one of the methods of controlling erosion consists of establishing a vegetative cover [2] on the soil. Many of the plants recommended to check soil erosion are highly beneficial to wildlife in that they furnish fruit or browse for wild creatures.

Commenting on Cecil clay loam, a soil of the Piedmont section of North Carolina that is often seriously eroded, two government investigators have said that abandoned fields first grow up in broom sedge and brambles, followed the second year by sassafras and sumach bushes and yellow pine, and that in a few years, except on badly eroded areas, there is a good stand of pine. Forested areas support a fair or good growth of white, red, black, post, scarlet, and chestnut oaks, shortleaf or yellow pine, spruce, pitch and white pine, hickory, black gum, yellow poplar, dogwood, and a few persimmon, locust, sourwood, black walnut, white elm, sweet gum, red cedar, and hemlock trees.[3]

Of these plants, broom sedge affords good cover, and brambles (that is, dewberries, blackberries, and the like) provide both cover and food for small forms of wildlife, including cottontail rabbits, quail, and other game species. Sassafras and sumach fruits are eaten by many birds and mammals. Yellow pine, according to its height, furnishes cover for both ground and above-ground fauna and, when mature,

---

[2] Frank C. Edminster, *Wildlife Management Through Soil Conservation on Farms in the Northeast* (U.S. Department of Agriculture, Farmers' Bull. 1868; Washington, 1941).

[3] W. D. Lee and S. R. Bacon, *Soil Survey of Burke County, North Carolina* (U.S. Department of Agriculture, Bureau of Chemistry and Soils, Section 1926, no. 22, 1930).

produces in seed years a food supply that is relished by many species. In the forests the various oaks, through their acorn crops, contribute heavily to the upkeep of wildlife; the hickory and walnut are valuable to squirrels and a few other species; the black gum, dogwood, persimmon, and red cedar yield fruits that are sought by a variety of wildlife; the yellow poplar, locust, white elm, and hemlock bear seeds that are eaten in small quantity; and the red cedar, in addition to its fruit-bearing role, affords first-class cover.[4]

Thus practically every plant deserving of mention as a pioneer on eroded clay loam is of some value to wildlife.

Winter feeding. In the South wild game finds an abundance of food throughout the winter. Wild birds and animals of the North, on the contrary, are severely affected by prolonged storms and by deep snows that effectively cover the available food. It has long been realized that wildlife in many northern states is dependent on man's help in winter. In severe weather, when an ice crust covers the snow for several days or a week at a time, great numbers of birds perish. Natural foods available to wildlife are inadequate on many farms. Even the very important ragweed so abundant in fields and pastures does not provide enough food for many birds, and the seeds may be covered with snow. Under such conditions winter feeding is necessary.

An abundant supply of food may be provided in several ways. Shocked corn is the most useful. These shocks should be on the borders of cultivated fields, adjoining hedgerows, swales, or marshes. Brush heaps will provide cover where such is lacking. Buckwheat is of much value, and it is utilized more fully than corn. Wheat, rye, barley, sorghum, sunflowers, soybeans, and many other plants provide natural food during the winter. The daily spreading on snowy fields of manure that contains undigested grain attracts many game birds in the winter.

If feeding is commenced in the fall, it should be carried on throughout the winter. Ducks attracted to feeding stations may elect to remain well into the winter (Fig. 206). If feeding is then discontinued, the birds will be pressed to find suitable food and many will eventually perish.

Winter feeding of wildlife, whether it be song birds or game species, can be conducted by almost anyone. It provides healthy outdoor exer-

---

4 W. L. McAtee, *Groups of Plants Valuable for Wildlife Utilization and Erosion Control* (U.S. Department of Agriculture, Circ. 412; Washington, 1936).

cise and lasting satisfaction. There is probably no better way in which to arouse interest in the conservation of wildlife than through this very worth-while practice.

Feeding stations. Birds seem never to forget places where food is abundant. They will return to these places time after time if the supply is dependable. For this reason it is desirable to establish permanent feeding stations where suitable food is available throughout the winter.

Figure 206. Wildfowl become quite fearless if fed during the winter months. These Canada geese are attracted by the abundance of corn that has been provided by city officials. Note the ice in the water. (W. J. Hamilton, Jr.)

Such shelters may be very simple. They may consist of a pile of brush or hay thrown over a support of poles lodged against a fence. Or they may be rather elaborate, containing substantial food hoppers, as shown in Figure 207. In these hoppers are placed cracked or whole corn, buckwheat, or other grains. Chaff from the barn floor may be thrown under such shelters. Sheaves of grain may be set upright and will provide the birds with many feasts. Corn on the cob is sometimes impaled on nails driven into boards and placed in the shelters.

Feeding big game in winter. Normally big game animals can take care of themselves in winter. There are, however, conditions that may so reduce the normal food supply that deer, elk, and other large game animals may starve if they are not provided with food. These conditions may arise from a number of factors. Grazing of livestock in the West may reduce the available food supply. Western farmers may cut the hay in the valleys where elk are accustomed to feed. Lumbering removes browse trees that are normally utilized by deer and moose. As a consequence it becomes necessary at times to supplement the natural supply of feed (Fig. 208).

Figure 207. A well-constructed feeding station. The hopper containing food is protected by a substantial shelter. Even after heavy snowfalls food is available to pheasants, prairie chickens, squirrels, and other game. Food should be available from early winter until all danger of a heavy snowfall has passed. (Wisconsin Conservation Department.)

Most of our western big game concentrate in the valleys during the winter. The herds have become so large that sufficient food is lacking. Thus it becomes the duty of custodians of the national parks or state officials to feed such animals.

PROPAGATION OF GAME

Many birds and animals can be successfully raised under semi-domestic conditions. In some instances birds are propagated on state-owned game farms and liberated when they have attained sufficient size to care for themselves. In general, this has proved an expensive procedure. Some states find it more profitable to improve conditions for wildlife and thus create better breeding conditions for such birds and animals as may be considered game.

Game farming. The practice of game farming is essentially similar to poultry husbandry. The eggs of pheasants, quails, or other game birds are placed under hens or put in an incubator. They are cared for at hatching in a manner similar to that employed in rearing young chickens. The conservation departments of the various states may provide farm lads with a setting of eggs and instructions in their care,

Figure 208. The elk herd on their winter feeding ground in Jackson Hole, Wyoming. Food has become so scarce in the valley that winter feeding of hay has become necessary. (U.S. Fish and Wildlife Service.)

upon the understanding that when the young birds become several weeks old, they are to be released in a suitable habitat.

Attempts have been made to raise cottontail rabbits under artificial conditions. Such experiments have met with little success. Nor has a similar experiment in the propagation of fur-bearing animals such as the raccoon and muskrat, with a view to liberating them in areas where they are now scarce, proved any more successful. Future efforts, however, may bring about better results.

The economic weakness of game farms is evident when one considers the cost of raising the birds. Public shooting on a nation-wide scale demands that pen-raised pheasants or other game species must be raised at a cost that will parallel, in a measure, the price of the hunting license. If a state charges $2 for a hunting license and permits three birds to be taken, the practice is unsound. This is evident when we realize that a pheasant raised on a game farm costs the state $1.50 to $2 or more before liberation.

Obviously it is better to manipulate the land, encourage growth of suitable food plants and cover, clean sluggish streams to provide marsh land, or take other steps than to raise the various game species in captivity. A landowner of eastern New York has averaged a dozen muskrats from a half-acre tract for several successive years merely by giving heed to proper marsh-management practices and providing a measure of protection to the animals during the closed season for pelts. It is the writer's belief that, in the future, less attention will be directed to the propagation of game species under artificial conditions and more emphasis will be placed on improving the habitat to encourage natural reproduction.

THE FARMER AND THE GAME SUPPLY

If we are to replenish and maintain the supply of game in the country, we must rely upon the support and co-operation of the farmer. Furthermore, if the farmer is to become interested in game as a crop, he must first be assured of a share of the profits that such a crop provides. Even though existing laws pronounce game a property of the state, the farmer owns the land that produces much of this game. He provides the food and cover on which game depends. By posting a trespass sign on his property he may prevent the hunter from killing game on his land.

Within recent years many groups of farmers and sportsmen have co-operated to their mutual advantage. One group of twenty-eight midwestern farmers, on an area of 11,000 acres under central management, has charged $2.50 for hunting permits for the area. In one season 200 such permits were issued, returning a revenue of $500, or an average of $18 for each co-operator. The farmer will be interested in wild game if he can harvest it as a crop by permitting hunters, for a fee, to shoot on his premises.

ORGANIZATIONS CONCERNED WITH THE PROTECTION OF WILDLIFE

Great interest has been aroused in the conservation of our natural resources. Much of this attention has been directed toward a restoration of our wildlife. Below are listed a few of the nation-wide organizations, federal or otherwise, that have given prominent attention to the conservation of wildlife. The list is far from complete but it gives an indication of the widespread interest now being accorded the nation's wildlife.

Federal agencies.

United States Fish and Wildlife Service. For half a century the Fish and Wildlife Service has dealt with wildlife problems. This organization has a well-trained staff of scientists who investigate many kinds of wildlife problems. It is the most important single organization that has for its objective the investigation of the habits of wild animals.

There are, of course, many problems that the Fish and Wildlife Service must study. The status of wildlife in the various states is investigated, and maintenance methods are studied. The food habits of many birds and animals are recorded. In this way it can be determined just what food plants are desirable for wildlife. The economic value of the bird or animal may be studied. If such studies indicate that the bird is harmful to man's interests, methods of reducing the numbers of such birds are sought. If, on the other hand, the food of the bird proves that it is useful, this knowledge is made public and the bird is given full protection.

Fur-animal conservation is carried on by the Service. Extensive studies of disease, nutritional requirements, and general care of silver foxes and mink are undertaken. The Service has a large rabbit experiment station at Fontana, California. Here feeding tests are made to obtain knowledge of the quality of fur and meat in different breeds of rabbits, and of the diseases that afflict them.

Bird banding is one of the most interesting phases of the Service's work. Metal bands supplied by the Service to co-operating individuals and state agencies are placed on the legs of various captured birds, and the birds are then released (Fig. 209). If, later, the bird is shot, the band is forwarded to the Service's office in Washington. Each band is numbered, and a record kept of when and where it was first placed on the bird and when removed. Many recoveries have enabled the federal biologists to determine the migration routes of birds, and have provided much useful information on their habits. The main duck highways during migration have been plotted. It is thus possible to determine where refuges will do the most good.

The Fish and Wildlife Service, with funds supplied by Congress, investigates and purchases large tracts of land suitable for wildlife refuges and provides men to patrol and study these areas. Suitable control measures for rats, mice, and other destructive animals are studied by the Service. It conducts many rat-control campaigns.

Many foreign birds and animals have been introduced into the United States with dire results. The Service determines what foreign animals may be introduced into our country and what species must be excluded. Recently a customs guard at New York seized a smuggler

Figure 209. A banding trap at Malheur Migratory Bird Refuge in Oregon. The practice of banding the legs of birds with numbered bands has provided much useful information on the habits, migration routes, and distribution of many species. (U.S. Fish and Wildlife Service.)

who had attempted to bring four finches into the country. The would-be smuggler had tied the birds around his ankles inside his socks.

These are but a few of the many duties of the Fish and Wildlife Service. This bureau of the United States Department of the Interior is becoming yearly more important.

Soil Conservation Service. This Service has a section devoted to wildlife management. Its duties are varied and include many activities that are of immense benefit to wildlife. It directs erosion-control planting made for the benefit of wildlife. It develops other soil-conservation practices so as to enhance their value to wildlife. It attempts to develop an appreciation on the part of the farmer, other conservation agencies, and the general public of the direct relationship between wildlife welfare and soil conservation. Many notable achievements have been accomplished since the wildlife section was established. Conservation nurseries have been planted in many parts of the country. Demonstration areas have been set up in strategic localities throughout the country so that the landowner may have first-hand information on the desirable plants that will check soil erosion and at the same time furnish suitable food and cover for wildlife.

Bureau of Animal Industry. For more than forty years the Bureau of Animal Industry has been accumulating information on the variety and control of parasites of many species of wild game, although its major work is with domesticated animals.

Bureau of Entomology and Plant Quarantine. A large number of bobwhite quail chicks are destroyed in the South every year by fire ants. This bureau is seeking to reduce the death rate of quail from this source by developing practical means of controlling the fire ant. The Bureau is also seeking means of controlling mosquitoes that will not be deleterious to wildlife. Control measures for insects have been devised that will be least harmful to useful wildlife.

National Park Service. The Wildlife Division of the Service conducts research on wildlife similar to that of the Fish and Wildlife Service. The staff of the Wildlife Division investigates the economic relationships of predatory animals to other animal life. They have made extensive studies on the lives of threatened species such as the trumpeter swan and bighorn sheep. Another investigation now under way is upon the effects of artificial lakes on wildlife.

Forest Service. The Forest Service administers the national forests and is responsible for the management of national forest resources, of which wildlife is one. It co-operates with federal and state officials in the enforcement of game laws in the national forests and in the development and maintenance of wildlife resources in these forests.

National organizations.

National Audubon Society. The Audubon Society is a well-organized national group, which has done much to arouse interest in conservation. Its aims are varied. The society attempts to arouse public appreciation of the beauty and economic value of wildlife and to stimulate action to protect and preserve it. It establishes sanctuaries and seeks regulation of hunting and the commercial use of wildlife. The Audubon Society also conducts vigorous educational programs. The training of teachers and other youth leaders to develop genuine, lasting interest in wildlife is one of its primary purposes. The society is very active in preparing and distributing conservation material and natural science facts among children. For many years it has waged a vigorous defense of the much-persecuted hawks and owls. Audubon wardens patrol the great swamps of southern Florida and protect the few remaining birds of many large subtropical species, which are so attractive to the tourist and nature lover. The Audubon Society has been instrumental in having a law passed that prohibits all traffic in wild bird plumage in the United States.

Wildlife Management Institute. Formed in 1946, with headquarters in Washington, D.C., the Wildlife Management Institute is dedicated to wildlife restoration. Its immediate objective is a sustained effort to promote more widespread use of present knowledge, the practical application of which often lags far behind the research. Its over-all aim is to restore wildlife to the greatest possible abundance in a country devoted to agriculture and industry.

State agencies. Every state has one or more commissions, departments, sportsmen's organizations, garden clubs, and allied groups interested in furthering the conservation of wildlife. Some of these are nationally known for their efforts. On the other hand, many clubs are composed of a few individuals who seek relaxation from the cares and worries of everyday life by conducting conservation programs. These may be of a varied nature, such as winter feeding, the preparation of a birdhouse, or the dissemination of knowledge of wildlife by arranging for public lectures.

State conservation departments. Every state has a department or commission that has partial jurisdiction over its wildlife. These departments establish or suggest to the state legislature laws designed to protect the wildlife of the state. Investigation is carried on in many phases of wildlife. The departments operate game farms, raise game birds, and release these in suitable parts of the state. They also maintain fish hatcheries, where trout, bass, and other game fish are propagated, to be released in favorable waters when they attain sufficient size.

State conservation departments have a number of handicaps. Many of their employees are politically selected. Lack of basic knowledge of the needs of animals, birds, and fish renders these departments liable to costly mistakes in administration. Frequently little attention is given to animals and birds other than those having significance to the hunter. And even though the suggestions of trained biologists for the management of wildlife are placed before the residents of a state, hunters are often loath to have them adopted for fear their sport may be curtailed for a time.

All in all, however, the conservation departments of the various states are performing a splendid task in restoring our game and fish life. It would be desirable for them to place more stress on nongame species, for these are yearly becoming of more interest to the layman.

CHAPTER XIII

Conservation of Other Useful Wildlife

WHEN we use the word *wildlife,* most of us think in terms of game animals. In reality, the term should connote all forms of living creatures that bring pleasure to us in one form or another. The hunter thinks of a deer as a living target to be shot and proudly displayed before his friends. The camera enthusiast also thinks of the deer as a living target, but even more difficult to "shoot" with his lens. Both enjoy and profit from the chase, but in entirely different ways.

The marmot in his rockslide is as much an integral part of the wildlife of our western parks as are the bears. The pelicans, ibises, herons, and spoonbills all delight the tourist in Florida. The majestic condor, with a wingspread of nearly ten feet, is one of California's natural assets (Fig. 210). The great herons, the eagles, and the loons of our northern lakes are welcome residents. The ocean voyager long remembers the glimpse of a huge whale or a school of porpoises. And who has not thrilled on first hearing the roar of a bull alligator in a southern swamp or glimpsing a prairie-dog village on the western plains? Even the sweet trill of a toad and the voice of the peeper are a welcome chorus, for they proclaim to the initiated that spring is at hand.

Before we study the relationships of this wildlife to the larger and more spectacular animals, we shall discuss briefly the intricate and often complex interrelationships between animals and the plants upon which many of the former are dependent. With knowledge of this phase of wildlife one can better understand the necessity of protecting many of the lesser creatures of field, wood, and waterways.

THE WEB OF LIFE

Although most people think of nature as being nicely poised and balanced, in reality it is not. Even in situations where man has not in-

Figure 210. The California condor. This grand bird of the wild mountain valleys of California is quite rare. It breeds slowly, having but one young every other year. While it is given much-needed protection, irresponsible people still shoot these noble birds. (New York Zoological Society.)

terfered, there is no "balance of nature." The many species of animals and plants vary in their numbers from one year to the next, never approaching a so-called mean or normal population. These changes may not be readily apparent, centuries being required to indicate the succession of events. Man, with his drastic alterations of natural environments, has modified these changes so that they may be apparent in a few years' time. Drainage, grazing, and fires all contribute to radical upheavals in the plant world and, as a consequence, modify the habitat of the animals dependent upon them.

Over a relatively short space of time an observant individual can note the interdependence of animals and plants. Birds and other animals kill insects, and at the same time the lesser parasites of the insects also contribute to their control. Where such checks are destroyed or removed, insects increase rapidly and may often prove a menace to man. It is not difficult to point out examples that are familiar to many of us.

The gypsy moth was accidentally released in Massachusetts in 1869. It is not a particularly destructive pest in its native Europe, where parasites keep its numbers in check. Without these parasites, it rapidly became a scourge in the eastern United States, where extensive damage to forests has resulted. Millions of dollars have been spent on its control, which has proved only partly successful.

No common animal can be destroyed or greatly reduced in numbers without affecting others. When lemming mice and rabbits of the Arctic become scarce, as periodically happens, snowy owls migrate southward into the United States to feed on our small animals. Formerly wolves and coyotes preyed upon antelope, buffalo calves, and small animals. As these wild creatures made way for the cattle and sheep of the western ranchman, the wolves found it easier to obtain young cattle and sheep. Hence in the early days of the range they were a real pest to the stockmen.

Interrelationships. We have seen that no animal can live unto itself alone. Each species is intricately associated with its neighbors, and dependent, directly or indirectly, upon them for its survival.

Chipmunks occasionally roll the eggs of grouse from the nest, which is then deserted by the bird. Foxes like to feed on grouse, but they also like chipmunks, which they find easier to capture. In brief, the fox is a predator of both chipmunks and grouse. Since chipmunks are far more numerous than grouse, and are a menace to them, the fox seems to be entitled to a few grouse because in the long run it may be an actual asset to the bird by destroying an enemy potentially far more dangerous.[1]

---

[1] W. J. Hamilton, Jr., "The Value of Predatory Mammals," *New York Zoological Society Bull.*, 40^2: 42 (1937).

An animal may be a decided asset to man at one place or time; a few miles removed it may be a pest of the first order. Deer in the orchard are a menace to young fruit trees. Their increasing numbers in the agricultural lands of the eastern United States present a real problem for the wildlife manager. Yet in forested areas they provide good sport and good food for the hunter and good fun for the camera fan. In the western states coyotes kill many destructive rodents, but all too frequently they also destroy lambs and poultry. Rabbits are an important game species, but they often cause extensive damage to young orchards and gardens.

VALUE TO MAN

By keeping in check the insects that are ever ready to injure crops and by performing numerous other helpful acts our small wildlife is of direct benefit to man. The esthetic value of these lesser creatures is even greater than that of our larger wildlife, for they are available to a greater number of people.

Value of birds. Few people fully appreciate the role of birds in controlling insects. The great diversity of their food habits, their willingness to consume the food most available, and their ability to move from place to place with great ease give birds a most important position in nature.

One of the best-known events illustrating their value to mankind occurred many years ago in Utah. When the Mormons first settled in Utah, they were visited by plagues of black crickets that totally destroyed one crop and were again rapidly devastating the fields, threatening the pioneers with starvation. But gulls appeared by the thousands, cleared the fields of insects, and saved the crops. The people of Utah, in grateful remembrance of what they considered an act of Divine Providence in their behalf, erected a beautiful monument to the gulls at Salt Lake City, at an expense of $40,000.[2]

Birds do not completely destroy any insect pest, but they tend to lessen the insect tribe and thus reduce damage.

The amount of food consumed by birds is truly prodigious. Many young birds eat more than twice their own weight of food daily. A young robin which weighed 3 ounces consumed, in one day, 165 cutworms that weighed 5½ ounces. The stomach of a yellow-billed cuckoo contained 250 tent caterpillars, and an owl stomach yielded 17

---

2 J. Henderson, *The Practical Value of Birds* (New York, 1927), p. 127.

mice. Meadowlarks consume quantities of grasshoppers, weevils, cater-pillars, and weed seeds (Fig. 211). It has been estimated that in Virginia and North Carolina the bobwhite quail eats 1,341 tons of weed seeds between September 1 and April 30. Tree sparrows in Iowa destroy over 875 tons of weed seeds annually. The tiny chickadee, no larger than one's thumb and weighing only a quarter of an ounce, will eat from 200 to 300 destructive cankerworms at one meal. Birds sometimes become destructive to crops, but their good services in rid-

Figure 211. A meadowlark returning to her hungry nestlings. These birds consume great quantities of injurious insects. Their sweet, clear call is a welcome note of spring. Note how well the bird blends in with its surroundings. (W. J. Hamilton, Jr.)

ding the fields and woods of destructive weeds, rodents, and insect pests far overshadow any damage they may do.

Value of mammals. We have spoken previously of the importance of mammals as game and fur producers. Those which are not of value in this respect may provide benefits to man in less spectacular but equally essential fashion.

We sometimes think of field mice and moles as providing furrows or small ditches that may start erosion. But they also make the soil more friable and porous. The pocket gophers in Yosemite Park alone raise 8,000 tons of earth an average height of 8 inches every year.[3] The

---

[3] Joseph Grinnell, "The Burrowing Rodents of California as Agents in Soil Formation," *Journal of Mammalogy,* 4: 137–149 (1923).

burrowing helps to aerate the soil, and the soil brought to the surface is subjected to more rapid weathering, thus releasing minerals needed by the plants. The exposed soil buries surface vegetation, which decomposes and enriches the soil, while the loosened soil absorbs moisture more readily.

When we speak of mice, we customarily think of the pantry mouse that pilfers our food and eludes our traps. There are more than a hundred kinds of wild mice living in the United States. Some destroy quantities of insects, of which they are very fond. Indeed, one little rodent is called the grasshopper mouse, for it has a particular fondness for these pests. Wild mice in Michigan had opened and destroyed the contents of 60 per cent of the larch sawfly cocoons examined. Shrews, little mouselike animals related to the moles, consume quantities of insects. Moles also perform a useful service in this respect.

These small creatures furnish food for many birds of prey and other predatory animals. Were they not so abundant, these predators might feed on more desirable species.

Bats are almost entirely insectivorous and perform a very useful service in their war against insect pests. The droppings of bats, rich in nitrogen, accumulate in caves where these little animals roost. When the Carlsbad Caverns in New Mexico were discovered, the droppings (called *guano*) filled some of the largest chambers to a depth of 100 feet. More than 100,000 tons of it have been removed and marketed for fertilizer at from $20 to $75 per ton, or a total of much more than $2,000,000.

Skunks are useful in destroying grubs, while foxes and weasels keep in check the mice and rabbits. We could enumerate many more instances, unfamiliar to the average individual, that would show the value of this lesser wildlife. The point to be kept in mind is that probably no mammal, excepting the house rat and house mouse, can be classed as entirely injurious to man's interests. It is equally true that the most desirable mammals may, upon occasion, become destructive.

Other useful wildlife. In their eternal quest for food, toads and snakes all help to keep within bounds a great number of small, harmful animals, many of which are destructive to man.

When large, white grubs became abundant in Puerto Rico, it resulted in a race by man to harvest the sugar cane before the grubs destroyed the roots and killed the plant. Other control measures failing, the giant toad was introduced into the island and soon became abundant. It shortly reduced the number of grubs so that the planters no longer had to contend with this major pest of the sugar cane. Our common toad destroys great numbers of caterpillars, grubs, and other injurious insects, and for this reason is a welcome addition to our gardens (Fig. 212). The writer once examined a toad that had been killed by a boy. Its stomach contained twenty-one cutworms, destructive pests of our lawns and gardens.

Lizards feed largely on insects, and it has been demonstrated that they are of great importance in reducing these pests. A study in Utah

Figure 212. Toads are found in every state, and their usefulness as insect destroyers is recognized. (W. J. Hamilton, Jr.)

has clearly indicated that lizards are a great asset to livestock by reducing the number of insects that compete for the food of cattle. Large numbers of live and mounted young alligators are disposed of each year to the tourist trade in Florida. Many alligator skins are marketed for the manufacture of leather goods. Snakes are very useful because they control rats and mice and rarely do any appreciable harm to birds. **Esthetic value.** The lesser creatures of field and wood provide many people with enjoyment. Each year adds to the growing legion of nature lovers, whose chief interest may be in birds but who find the study of mammals, frogs, fish, snakes, and salamanders also fascinating. The fisherman may object to the kingfisher's and watersnake's sharing his favorite trout stream, but this wildlife adds much enjoyment to the interested lover of nature. The enjoyment of nature by the American public is becoming yearly more evident. We are at last realizing that wildlife is not the property of hunters and fishermen alone, but that it contributes materially to the pleasure of all Americans.

DESTRUCTION OF WILDLIFE

Many animals of no value either for food or sport have been so persecuted that their numbers have been greatly reduced until not a few are threatened with extinction. Many of these, notably our hawks and owls, have been killed under the mistaken assumption that they are entirely harmful. Economically these persecuted species often are of direct benefit to man, and therefore deserving of adequate protection.

Destruction of birds. A few instances of bird destruction will suffice to show the reader that many useful birds are killed, often under the guise of conservation.

Brown pelican. The pelican (Fig. 213), the state bird of Louisiana, is a large fish-eating bird that lives along coastal waters of the South. Pelicans are still found in Louisiana and Florida, where they furnish a valuable attraction to tourists. In Texas, however, large numbers of pelicans have been killed by fishermen and hunters who had the mistaken belief that pelicans destroy many edible fish. Careful observations indicate that the fish eaten by pelicans are largely of a worthless character. There were seventeen colonies of pelicans on the Texas coast in 1918, but now a single colony remains. The former population numbered 5,000 birds, but it has been reduced to 500.

Bald Eagle. Nothing in its habits justified the killing of our national bird, the bald eagle. Unfortunately its numbers are being greatly reduced by the desire for killing that far too many hunters possess. It is a pity this lust cannot be restrained when opportunity is had to kill such a magnificent bird.

The bald eagle of Alaska has been accused of killing wild sheep and goats, deer, and salmon, but no unbiased study of its habits has been conducted in the Territory. Alaskans receive a dollar bounty for a dead eagle; in ten years 67,798 eagles were killed in Alaska for this bounty.

Hawks and owls. Both hawks and owls destroy some useful animals, but many studies have shown that field mice, insects, and other destructive pests are their chief food (Fig. 214). Indeed, their perpetual warfare against such pests should bring them praise rather than censure. That an occasional hawk will visit a poultry yard with evil designs and perhaps kill a few chickens is small reason for condemning all hawks. If a horned owl should visit the turkey roost and make off

Figure 213. Sportsmen often crusade against fish-eating birds. The brown pelican shown above feeds largely on fish that have no value to man and is valued by nature lovers for its grotesque appearance and queer habits. Campaigns to destroy these interesting birds have met with some success, and their numbers have been reduced. (S. A. Grimes.)

with a bird or two, we would not be justified in killing its cousin, the little long-eared owl. The fierce goshawk may visit our wood lot in winter and prey upon the grouse, but surely we are not justified for this reason in shooting the sparrow hawk, no larger than a robin, which feeds chiefly upon mice and grasshoppers.

Unfortunately, most farmers and sportsmen alike remember only the lapses from good behavior of these birds and shoot them at every opportunity. If their true status were fully understood, then these use-

Figure 214. The barn owl, a highly beneficial bird. All owls feed largely upon small mammals, chief among which are destructive rats and mice. The indigestible remains of hair and bones are cast up by the owl, and scientists who study the dried wads can tell what species of animal the owl has eaten. The nest of this barn owl, found in an old deserted attic in the Bronx, New York City, is composed of these undigested pellets. (Allan D. Cruickshank, Audubon Society.)

ful birds would be more kindly considered by those individuals who are now ever ready to kill them.

Many states give protection to all but a few hawks and owls. Other states, less informed as to the true economic worth of these birds, give them no protection, or even place a bounty on their heads. Contrast this situation with that in Germany, where, realizing the value of owls, the government has established an owl farm where these birds are raised and distributed to areas from which they have been exterminated.

Destruction of mammals. If we owned a flock of chickens and a skunk or weasel killed several, we should feel justified in killing the culprit if it were possible. But we ought not to condemn all predatory creatures for the faults of a few. Unfortunately, many sportsmen would like to see the end of all hawks and owls, foxes, skunks, and weasels, so that a few more quail and rabbits might be saved for them to shoot.

Federal and state hunters have for some years waged a vigorous campaign against the coyote, an animal that looks somewhat like a police dog. Coyotes do kill some sheep and may be responsible for the death of a few calves and some poultry. But their useful habits probably balance their destructive ones. To reduce the numbers of these wild dogs, poisoned baits have been distributed. But the campaign brought about unlooked-for results. Many useful animals have taken the baits placed about for coyotes. In consequence, many fur-bearing animals such as the desert fox, badger, and skunk, other useful animals, and many birds have been destroyed.

Payment of bounties. Some states offer a bounty for hawks, owls, weasels, wildcats, foxes, and the like. These misdirected efforts have proved of little or no value. The animal upon which a bounty is offered is often worth far more to the farmer alive than dead. Hawks and owls feed chiefly on mice and other pests of the farmer. Weasels and foxes destroy great numbers of rodents. Skunks eat quantities of grasshoppers, white grubs, and cutworms, all of which feed on useful plant matter. Even the coyote serves a useful purpose, for it preys upon ground squirrels. These little squirrels of the West carry disease, destroy game birds, and ruin crops. Were it not for the coyotes, badgers, and foxes, we should have to charge an even greater bill against these abundant pests. Bounties have been paid on the inoffensive harbor seal of Maine, because fishermen said these seals fed largely upon lobster and salmon. Research has proved that their food consists largely of species that have little or no commercial value. Moreover, they are a continual source of enjoyment to summer residents of the Maine coast.

Then too, bounty payments permit much fraud. Foxes and dogs

have been passed off as wolves. The county clerk, who usually pays such bounty claims, is often unfamiliar with animals and cannot tell one species from another. This is particularly true where the entire carcass of the animal need not be presented for the bounty. At one time a middle western state paid a bounty on ground squirrels. The fee was paid upon the presentation of the tail of the squirrel. Boys would catch those squirrels alive, cut off the tail and release the squirrel. The loss of the tail in no way affected the breeding behavior, and thus the squirrel supply was maintained for the bounty hunters.

Poisonous snakes, or, for that matter, other snakes, do not delight the tourist unless they are in a pit next to a roadside gas station. Some counties in Florida have offered bounties on rattlesnakes and the poisonous coral snake. Just why a bounty on poisonous snakes is necessary is hard to understand. Those who have little fear of a poisonous reptile never miss the opportunity to kill one, bounty or no bounty. Others who fear these snakes could not be induced to approach one irrespective of a fat bounty.

Rodent control. Many species of rodents often become destructive and must be controlled by man. Field mice, woodchucks, gophers, and ground squirrels consume quantities of vegetation, girdle trees, and prove a menace to agriculture in many other ways. Local control of these animals, where they have become a pest, is justified, for their inroads on crops must be minimized. These measures should be for control only and not for extermination of the species.

The prairie dog, a picturesque rodent of the early West, was once so abundant that it was a major cause of concern to the farmer. Poisoning and the use of gas have materially reduced these little animals, so that they can no longer be considered of major importance over extensive areas. Nevertheless, measures to reduce their numbers, even where they are of no economic significance, continue unabated. In Arizona, one colony of prairie dogs numbering about twenty, was marked for destruction by a state agent. They were in no way a problem to the agriculturist, nor were they likely to become so, for the colony was in a small, grassy depression in the midst of alkali flats which in themselves would not favor the extension of the colony. Where prairie dogs colonize within sight of the highway, they are a source of interest to the tourist. Recently a convention of biologists met in Denver. One of the highlights of this meeting, certainly to the eastern representatives, was viewing a sizable prairie-dog "town" on waste lots within the city limits.

Destruction of "vermin." Animals that are supposedly injurious to game species, or which prevent their natural increase, are called *vermin* by hunters. In this group fall the skunks, weasels, foxes, snakes, kingfishers, hawks, owls, cats, and many other creatures. It is generally thought by sportsmen that the elimination or reduction in numbers of these animals will be beneficial to game and will permit an increase in their numbers. For this reason campaigns called *vermin hunts* are often sponsored by the members of fish and game clubs in the mistaken belief that they will benefit more desirable wildlife.

While it is true that such animals may occasionally destroy a pheasant or quail, which man would rather shoot, the good services of skunks, foxes, weasels, snakes, and others far overshadow the harm they do. Weasels in a poultry yard may become a pest, but in the orchard they feed largely on rodents. Skunks destroy great numbers of cutworms, grasshoppers, and white grubs, which are a major problem to the garden owner. Foxes eat many rabbits and mice, and are also fond of ground squirrels and woodchucks. Furthermore, by culling the weak and diseased game these so-called vermin may actually benefit the hunter.

In general, those animals which are looked upon as vermin perform many useful services to man. Moreover, there is a great army of bird and animal lovers who delight to see and study such species, and their rights should be considered as well as those of the hunter.

Destruction of other useful wildlife. Most of us, uneducated to the value of our native wildlife, see it as a living target to be stoned or shot as opportunity affords. Small sport is it to kill a hapless frog or run down a plodding turtle as it crosses the highway, but many consider such wanton destruction to be fun.

Most people kill snakes whenever opportunity permits. The sight of a grown man clubbing to death a small reptile scarcely thicker than a pencil would be amusing were it not so tragic. Such a sight, all too common, merely illustrates how little the American public appreciates the value of these creatures. Until the economic value of these animals is stressed and made apparent to all, we can expect such destruction to continue unabated.

It is said that the "glass snake," a peculiar legless lizard, is becoming scarce in parts of Florida because of its habit of resorting to the highway. On the smooth surface its progress is impeded, and large numbers are killed by traffic.

When the South was first colonized, alligators were numerous, and specimens fourteen feet or more long were often shot. Today it is rare to secure a ten-foot specimen, and one which measures twelve feet is considered a monster. Many of the alligators that were shot were partly utilized, but as many more were left to rot in some subtropic marsh (Fig. 215).

Figure 215. Part of a single night's kill of alligators by Louisiana hide hunters. The increased use of alligator hides has been responsible for an alarming decrease in the numbers of these reptiles. (Stanley C. Arthur.)

The widespread use of DDT in the control of insect pests, through the use of extensive plane dusting, has not yet been demonstrated to cause any measurables loss of birds and mammals. It is conceivable that the breaking up of food chains through the suppression of insects and cold-blooded vertebrates may in time have serious indirect consequences. Since little is yet known of the accumulative effects traceable to DDT, intensive research by trained biologists is urgently needed to determine any ill effects to useful wildlife that this important chemical may have.

REASON FOR DESTRUCTION

Much of the destruction of useful wildlife has been due to ignorance of its value to man. Another reason has been our amazing lack of knowledge of the habits of our most abundant and common species. Without this knowledge we are powerless to restore any threatened species.

Illegal shooting and plume hunting have been disastrous to many of our birds. As many species of birds become scarce, collectors are seized with a frenzied desire to possess the few remaining ones. The ivory-billed woodpecker, a handsome bird of the southern cypress swamps, has been threatened with extinction because its rarity attracts the professional bird collector to secure specimens before the birds become totally extinct.

A Florida bird warden counted sixteen parties with rifles along six miles of highway, all in quest of living targets. These targets may be the harmless cormorant or pelican or the hapless ibis. The great white heron, the roseate spoonbill, and the glossy ibis are all on the brink of extinction.

The commercial traffic in eggs of wild birds was, until recently, a regular business on the Kissimmee Prairie in

Figure 216. One of the few remaining trumpeter swans that now find sanctuary on the Red Rock Migratory Waterfowl Refuge in Montana. The buglelike call of these beautiful birds used to be heard in many parts of the western United States before hunting and the development of the country almost wiped them out. Recently, however, the swans at the Red Rock Refuge have begun to show an increase in numbers. (U.S. Fish and Wildlife Service.)

Florida.[4] The illicit traffic in these eggs has threatened the very existence in that state of such magnificent species as the Florida crane, the caracara, the burrowing owl, the limpkin, and several others. In certain places spikes have been found driven into practically every cabbage palm tree on the prairie where the caracaras nested, a mute reminder of past havoc wrought by professional egg collectors. Wild swans were once very numerous in the United States, but destruction

---

[4] R. P. A., "A True Story of Commercial Egg Traffic," *Bird Lore,* 40: 145 (1938).

by man has greatly reduced their numbers (Fig. 216). The commercial collector is, of course, in the business for gain alone. The rarer the bird, the higher price the eggs will command; and inasmuch as these collectors have no ethics, one can readily see how rare species may become increasingly scarce. Fortunately the Audubon Society wardens have been instrumental in lessening the activity of the egg collector. The past few years have witnessed remarkable increases on the part of some of the birds which were subjected to this commercialization.

Destruction of sea lions. A new menace to wildlife is the business of canning cat and dog foods. A company engaged in this activity is operating a canning factory off the west coast of Lower California. Two boats supply this factory with sea lions. One hundred eighty of these animals have been reported killed daily. The sea lion is a large, inoffensive seal, which affords much pleasure and amusement to visitors of our California coast. If these operations continue, the sea lion will soon be exterminated.

There are further dangers. The ships that collect these sea lions are equipped for handling whales. It is feared that the gray whale may next be slaughtered for dog food, or the rookery of elephant seals destroyed on Guadalupe Island. There is some hope that the Mexican government, keenly interested in its wildlife resources, will prevent continuance of this wanton slaughter.

We merely point out this instance to show that no animal is safe from man's exploitation if a market for the species can be found.

CONSERVATION MEASURES

Laws give a measure of safety to much of our valuable wildlife, but all too many people disregard these laws and destroy useful animals whenever the occasion permits. To conserve better our wildlife most of us need to be informed as to the true value of our native species. When we fully appreciate the services of snakes, we shall no longer make pointed efforts to run over them with our cars, or to club them to death on every occasion. Nor shall we continue to shoot harmless birds because they furnish a living target for our guns. Much of this useless persecution is carried on by uninformed or irresponsible people who have no appreciation of nature.

Educational measures. To offset this apathy toward the destruction of wildlife and to provoke an interest in our wild animals, federal, state, and private agencies have campaigned for better protection. Through the offices of these organizations, news releases, lantern slides, motion pictures, and other publicity services are available. Lectures on wildlife also can be obtained from them. The National Audubon Society has pioneered in this field with amazing success. The United States Fish and Wildlife Service has fostered an active program of conservation, while women's clubs, schools, and many other agencies have actively aided in conserving our lesser wildlife.

The greatest boon to our wild neighbors is the increasing interest shown by the younger generation. With a better understanding of and sympathy with our natural resources than their parents possessed, young people of today want to enlist in the fight for wildlife. They can best help by becoming better acquainted with the birds and other useful animals all about them. Such a study will awaken a lively interest and is perhaps the best way to make one conservation-minded.

Conservation by the individual. There are many ways of practicing conservation, but none pays greater dividends than attracting wildlife about one's home. This may be accomplished in many ways. The simplest and most interesting way is to set out plants useful to birds both for food and for nesting shelters. During the spring of 1941 the writer found nine nests of yellow warblers, robins, catbirds, chipping sparrows, and song sparrows on his home grounds of scarcely more than an acre. The birds nest in the bushes of honeysuckle, forsythia, spiraea, and barberry, or in the elms and arborvitae. They add to the value of property by their sweet songs and quaint ways, to say nothing of their destruction of countless cutworms, cankerworms, and other insect pests. Providing bird houses and feeding the birds in winter are both practical measures. Information on the construction of these houses, the methods of preparing food and placing it for the birds, and a list of desirable food plants attractive for the home grounds may be had from several sources. The Fish and Wildlife Service in Washington, the Audubon Society in New York, or the various state colleges will supply those interested.

Local wildlife refuges. Local refuges provide much pleasure to nearby residents. Many bird clubs have established wildlife areas where birds and other creatures may find secluded sites in which to live and breed unmolested. These havens may vary greatly in size from a single acre of shrubs to large areas of many hundreds of acres.

At the head of Cayuga Lake at Ithaca, New York, there is a small bird sanctuary (Fig. 217). It is scarcely more than an acre in extent, but contains much water with several shrub-covered islands. A caretaker feeds the multitude of ducks and geese that pass the winter on this little refuge. Here the wild birds become unbelievably tame. They take bread from the hands of children and delight the visitor with their queer antics. Many remain to rear their young. Tree swallows, marsh wrens, and swamp birds of many kinds may be seen here

Figure 217. A small sanctuary often attracts many species of wildlife and provides much pleasure to people interested in birds and other animals. At this sanctuary in central New York wildfowl are fed and remain throughout the winter. (W. J. Hamilton, Jr.)

in the spring. Painted turtles bask on floating logs and lay their eggs in the sandy bank, providing an added attraction to the visitor.

Golf courses, if not too destitute of shrubs and trees, become a sanctuary for birds. The writer has often seen coveys of bobwhite quail on golf courses within the limits of New York City. The dense grass that clothes the "rough" of such courses provides nesting sites for meadowlarks. Bluebirds and flickers nest in the maples bordering such areas. Not only do these feathered songsters add to the enjoyment of the golfer, but they serve a very useful service in ridding the grounds of countless cutworms, ants, and other injurious insects. Wrens, bluebirds, martins, and other species may be attracted if suitable bird houses are erected.

Cemeteries, if not barren of trees and shrubs, often provide a haven for wildlife in the midst of large cities. If shrubs are planted that provide berries and fruits during winter and early spring when food is difficult to secure, many birds will take advantage of such a favorable refuge.

CHAPTER XIV

Economics of Mineral Resources

UNDER the term *mineral resources* we include all those minerals of which deposits are found on our planet, the earth, and which in crude or manufactured form are of value to man in almost every phase of his daily life.

To be more specific, the mineral resources include the various metals used for making machinery; structural materials for buildings, bridges, railroads, airplanes, automobiles, and various kinds of apparatus; mineral fuels such as coal, oil, and natural gas; building materials such as stone, clay, and cement; fertilizers such as potash and phosphate; and a host of mineral products of use in the chemical and other industries. Even food products may contain mineral preservatives and cannot be made without machinery manufactured from metals. Moreover, the power to drive the machinery or the heat needed in the manufacture of a food may be supplied by mineral fuels.

It can be understood, then, that the mineral treasures of a nation are to be regarded as one of its most valuable and indispensable possessions. They represent, furthermore, resources that enable a nation to attain industrial importance and even to maintain commercial supremacy if it possesses supplies of mineral raw materials that other countries need, and either lack completely or are deficient in, because these other countries must look to the more fortunate ones for a supply.

A country, therefore, which has a sufficiency of commercially valuable minerals of all kinds should be the envy of all other nations. Comparatively few of them occupy such a position, and this fact was brought out some years ago by the chart in Figure 218, which at that time showed the interdependence of the important countries of the world in respect to minerals. While conditions have been changed by

World War II, and the relationships are somewhat altered, the chart is still instructive and not entirely unreliable.

This chart makes clear several interesting facts. It indicates that, of 28 minerals which are of industrial importance, the United States possesses 11 in sufficient quantity for its own needs and 3 in a large enough supply to export. In the case of 11 others, the United States is depend-

METALS AND THEIR ORES	UNITED STATES A B C D	GERMANY A B C D	FRANCE A B C D	U. KINGDOM A B C D
ALUMINUM	_B_		_A B_	_D_
ANTIMONY	_B_		_B_	_D_
CHROMITE	_C_		_B_	_D_
COPPER	_B_		_B_	_D_
IRON	_A_	_B C_	_B_	_C_
LEAD	_B_	_B_	_B_	_D_
MANGANESE	_B_		_B_	_D_
MERCURY	_B_		_B_	_D_
NICKEL	_C_		_B_	_D_
TIN	_D_		_B_	_C_
TUNGSTEN	_B_		_B_	_D_
ZINC	_B_	_B_	_B_	_D_
NON METALS				
ASBESTOS	_C_		_B_	_C_
BARITE	_B A_		_B_	_D_
CHINA CLAY	_A_	_B_	_B_	_B C_
COAL	_A_	_B_	_B_	_B_
FLUORSPAR	_A_	_B_	_C_	_B_
GRAPHITE	_B_		_B_	_D_
GYPSUM	_A_	_B_	_B_	_B_
MAGNESITE	_B_	_B_	_B_	_D_
MICA	_B_		_B_	_D_
NITRATES	_B_	_B_	_B_	_D_
PETROLEUM	_A_	_C_	_B_	_D_
PHOSPHATES	_A_	_C_	_B_	_D_
POTASH	_A_	_B_	_B_	_D_
PYRITES	_B_	_B_	_B_	_D_
SULPHUR	_A_	_C_	_C_	_D_
TALC AND SOAPSTONE	_A_	_B C_	_B_	_D_

JAPAN A B C D	BELGIUM A B C D	ITALY A B C D	SPAIN A B C D	METALS AND THEIR ORES
_C_		_A B_	_D_	ALUMINUM
_C_		_B_	_C_	ANTIMONY
_A_		_B_	_C_	CHROMITE
_A_		_B_	_C C_	COPPER
_B_		_B_	_C_	IRON
_B_		_B_	_B C_	LEAD
_B_		_B C_	_B_	MANGANESE
_C_		_A B_		MERCURY
_C_		_B_	_C_	NICKEL
_C_		_B_	_C_	TIN
_C_		_B_	_C C_	TUNGSTEN
_A_	_A_	_B_	_C_	ZINC
NON METALS				
_A_	_B_	_B_	_D_	ASBESTOS
_A_	_B B_		_C_	BARITE
_A_		_B_	_C_	CHINA CLAY
_B_	_B_	_C_	_C_	COAL
_A_		_B B_	_C_	FLUORSPAR
_A_		_B C_	_C_	GRAPHITE
_A_		_B B_	_C_	GYPSUM
_B_		_B_	_C_	MAGNESITE
_B_		_B_	_C_	MICA
_B_		_B_	_C_	NITRATES
_B_		_B_	_C_	PETROLEUM
_B_		_B_	_C_	PHOSPHATES
_B_		_B_	_D_	POTASH
_A_		_B B_	_C_	PYRITES
_A_		_B B_	_D_	SULPHUR
_A_		_B B_	_C_	TALC AND SOAPSTONE

Figure 218. A chart showing the interdependence of the important countries of the world in respect to minerals. *A,* minerals available in large quantities for export. *B,* minerals adequate to meet domestic demands without appreciable excess or deficiency. *C,* minerals inadequate to meet domestic demands and supply partially dependent on foreign sources. *D,* minerals for which the country depends almost entirely on foreign sources. This table is based on geographic boundaries in existence before World War II. (Modified from *Mineral Raw Materials,* U.S. Bureau of Commerce.)

ent on other countries in part, and wholly dependent for 6, of which we have practically no commercially valuable deposits. The different nations are more dependent on each other than they used to be, but the chart shows that the United States is compelled to import a smaller percentage, on the average, than any of the others.

A more recent estimate, prepared by government bureaus, is given in Table 20. This shows the mineral position, actual, impending, and potential, of the United States. It is based on known commercial reserves, which are those that can be exploited under present economic and technologic conditions, and on submarginal or potential reserves, which are those that cannot be worked with profit except under more favorable economic and technologic conditions.

TABLE 20. RELATIVE SELF-SUFFICIENCY IN MINERALS OF THE UNITED STATES *
Actual and Impending Position

(Based on present technologic and economic conditions and on known commercial reserves)

A. Virtual Self-Sufficiency Assured for a Long Time:

Bituminous coal and lignite	Magnesium	Fluorspar (metallurgical)
	Molybdenum	Helium
Anthracite		Magnesite
Natural gas		Nitrates
		Phosphate rock
		Potash
		Salt
		Sulfur

B. Complete or Virtual Dependence on Foreign Sources:

1. Small or remote expectation of improving position through discovery:

Chromite	Industrial diamonds
Ferro-grade manganese	Quartz crystal
Nickel †	Asbestos (spinning quality)
Platinum metals	
Tin	

2. Good expectation of improving position through discovery:

Cobalt †	Graphite (flake)

C. Partial Dependence on Foreign Sources:

1. Little hope of improving position through discovery:

Antimony †	High-grade bauxite
Vanadium	Strategic mica

2. Good expectation of improving position through discovery:

Petroleum	Arsenic †	Fluorspar (acid grade)
	Bismuth †	
	Cadmium †	
	Copper	
	Iron ore	
	Lead	

Mercury
Tantalum †
Tungsten
Zinc

Potential Position
(If technologic and economic changes permit use of known submarginal resources)

A. Virtual Self-Sufficiency:

Bituminous coal and lignite	Aluminum ores	Fluorspar (all grades)
	Copper	Graphite (flake)
Anthracite	Iron ore	Helium
Natural gas	Magnesium	Magnesite
Petroleum	Manganese	Nitrates
	Molybdenum	Phosphate rock
	Titanium	Potash
	Vanadium	Salt
		Sulfur

B. Complete or Virtual Dependence on Foreign Sources:

Platinum metal   Industrial diamonds
Tin   Quartz crystal
     Asbestos (spinning quality)

C. Partial Dependence on Foreign Sources:

Antimony   Strategic mica
Arsenic
Bismuth
Cadmium
Cobalt
Chromite
Lead
Mercury
Nickel
Tantalum
Tungsten
Zinc

In World War II the United States called for thirty minerals that were used little or not at all in World War I.

---

* From U.S. Bureau of Mines and Geological Survey, *Mineral Resources of the United States* (Washington: Public Affairs Press, 1948).
† Domestic production chiefly a by-product.

POLITICAL AND COMMERCIAL CONTROL

The data just given show us that, comparatively speaking, the United States occupies a position of superiority, primarily because it can supply many of its own needs. If a nation has within its own boundaries practically all of the supply of a certain mineral that other nations must have for use in their manufacturing industries, that nation is in a particularly strong commercial position. The United States can truthfully be said to be the greatest producer and consumer of minerals among the nations of the world.

The British Empire is regarded by some as being the foremost example of self-sufficiency in mineral wealth, but this is offset by the fact that the several parts of the Empire are widely separated. Great Britain alone has large supplies of only iron and coal.

American enterprise and capital have shared with the British in the development of fully three-quarters of the world's minerals. Two examples of our dependence on Great Britain, however, will illustrate how valuable are the resources she controls.

Tin is a most important metal, vast quantities being used in the United States in the manufacture of tin cans (which, by the way, have only a thin coating of tin), and yet we are almost completely dependent on foreign countries for our supply, the amount imported being many times that produced in the United States. The supply is largely controlled, directly or indirectly, by Great Britain.

Again, we might ask what we would do without asbestos, used in such enormous quantities for brake linings in automobiles. The United States has not enough of this even to make a beginning in supplying its own needs, and most of what we use comes from Canada. In contrast to this situation, the United States has a sufficient supply of coal and several other minerals (see Table 20).

In spite of the fact that the United States has been the most self-sufficient country in the world regarding minerals, it has always had to import some of its supplies, and it may have to import more in the future, because it is continually drawing on its own resources.

STRATEGIC MINERALS

Certain minerals are needed in the production of war materials such as armament, naval vessels, airplanes, etc., or in the manufacture of instruments necessary for war work. If these much-needed raw mineral products are lacking or occur only in small amounts we call them *strategic minerals*. Under the Strategic Minerals Act of 1939, the metals antimony, chromium, manganese, mercury, nickel, tin, and tungsten were so called, but by 1942 the list included about fifty-three mineral products. The government has endeavored to build up stock piles of strategic minerals which are essential to our needs in time of war, but these stores should be built up of foreign minerals if possible. It is easy to accumulate such stock piles in time of peace, but not during war, because in such periods stock piling may be interfered with by: (1) scarcity of ships; (2) embargoes on exports; (3) blockades; and (4) competitive demand by other countries.

It will of course be understood that the list of strategic minerals will be different for different countries.

THE DOMINANT DEMANDS OF ONE INDUSTRY

One branch of the manufacturing industry may use a large portion of the country's supply of different mineral products. A good example of this is the automobile industry. It has been stated that this industry uses the following percentages of our total annual supply of each of the materials named: steel, 18.1; copper, 13.7; lead, 34.2; zinc, 12.1; aluminum, 9.7; tin, 11.4; nickel, 23.0; gasoline, 90.0; lubricating oils, 52.0.[1]

THE SEARCH FOR MINERALS

In the past much of the search for new deposits of minerals has been for those of high market value. The one which naturally comes to our mind is gold. It is said to have been the hope of finding supplies of this noble metal that brought the early conquerors from Europe to South America and Mexico. For many years during the past century the search was carried on by prospectors, men who had little scientific knowledge but who recognized the yellow metal when they saw it in outcrops, that is, in surface exposures.

Prospecting for gold has carried men into many uninhabited regions, and its discovery has led to subsequent development of these areas. But while it is true that the mining industry may have been responsible for the development of a country or subdivision of it, mining was probably followed by agricultural pursuits and manufactur-

---

[1] Automobile Manufacturers Association, *Automobile Facts and Figures* (Washington, 1937 and 1940).

ing industries, which accounted for the continued importance of the country.

DISTRIBUTION OF MINERALS

Although minerals of commercial value are widely distributed geographically, from the Arctic to the Antarctic, their distribution is very uneven, and while certain ones are common to a large number of countries, some, including a few that are important to industry, are very irregularly distributed. There is a perfectly good reason for this, because certain minerals are associated with certain kinds of rocks, and not with others. Had the nations of the world known this before their present boundaries were established, they might have tried to locate them elsewhere. Occasionally some mineral which turns out to be of great strategic importance is obtained only in one country. Thus our supply of quartz crystals—of importance in radar and radio work —comes entirely from Brazil.

HOW MINERALS OCCUR

The mineral deposits of the world are found mostly in the rocks below the surface, some being so near that they can be worked like a stone quarry. Others, although appearing at the surface, may extend below it to great depths. As a result, such products as coal and many metals can usually be extracted from the earth only by underground mining.

The various deposits, having been formed by different natural processes, will, of course, vary in their shape. Some of them, like clays, limestones, sandstones, phosphates, salt, and some iron ores, occur as beds of material which has accumulated as a sediment on the ocean bottom, just as mud or sand settles in a pond. These beds were later covered by many feet of other sediments, the weight of which packed them down. Hardening followed, and then nature's forces which are at work on the earth's crust lifted these beds up to form dry land.

Coal occurs in similar beds but has been formed in a somewhat different manner, as will be explained later (p. 468).

Many minerals, especially the metallic ones like those carrying gold, copper, lead, and zinc, have been deposited by hot waters, which have ascended from deep in the earth, carrying the minerals in solution and depositing them along fractures to form veins, or in irregular masses of variable size where these solutions worked into the smallest pores of the rocks through which they traveled.

The formation of any one deposit may have required thousands of years, and in some cases millions. This enables us to appreciate that once a deposit is worked out or exhausted, there is no chance of its being renewed. Forests, after being cut off, can be regrown, and soils which have lost their supply of plant food can be refertilized or rejuvenated, but not so with mineral deposits. When exhausted, they are gone forever. Even soils, when washed away, take hundreds of years to reform, because they were derived originally by the decay of rocks, which is an exceedingly slow process.

Of course, we have larger supplies of some kinds of minerals than others. Our coal resources will last for a long time. Some, like the common nonmetallic mineral products such as building stone, brick clay, and cement materials, are practically inexhaustible. The same cannot be said of our supplies of metals. Some deposits are already worked out, and others are on the way to exhaustion. A pathetic example of this is the gold district of Cripple Creek, Colorado. In 1900 this area was producing about $18,000,000 worth of gold a year, and Cripple Creek in its prime was a town of over 20,000 inhabitants, but in 1926, owing to the exhaustion of many deposits, the town had dwindled to 2,500, and its production in 1941 was only about $133,000.

By-product sources. In the treatment of many low-grade deposits, the extraction of the material sought may be made profitable by saving certain minor ingredients. Thus in the roasting and smelting of some lean metalliferous sulfide ores many thousands of tons of sulfur are recovered annually. Salt, borax, magnesium compounds, and gypsum may be saved as by-products in the extraction of potash from lake brines. Vanadium, an important metal in steel alloys, is found in small amounts (about 0.3 per cent) in the extensive phosphate and phosphatic shale deposits of Idaho and Wyoming. In recent years some of this has been recovered as a by-product.[2]

CONSERVATION OF OUR MINERAL RESOURCES

While it is true, as has been pointed out, that our supplies of certain mineral products may last for a long time, there are others which may

---

[2] U.S. Bureau of Mines and Geological Survey, *Mineral Resources of the United States* (Washington, 1948), p. 204.

be exhausted, not in a year but perhaps in twenty years or even less, and this should awaken us to the need of conserving these resources to make them last as long as possible. This might be accomplished in several ways:

(1) In nearly every kind of mining there is a certain amount of waste, but by more careful mining methods this may be reduced. It might appear that another waste incidental to mining—the loss of agricultural land—caused by open-pit workings and accompanying waste heaps of many deposits such as iron, coal, clay, building stone, phosphate, and gold gravels, would be extremely serious; but this is an exaggerated idea because the land is often of low agricultural value; the mineral products thus obtained are far more valuable than the crops would ever be; and the total acreage thus destroyed is relatively small.

(2) Many minerals as mined are mixed with useless minerals from which they have to be separated, but this separation is sometimes not completely accomplished, and so there is loss of valuable minerals. Methods are devised from time to time to reduce this loss further, and thus to help conserve our supplies.

(3) A more economical use of the finished product will serve to prolong our supply.

(4) Some mineral products, like coal or oil, are lost when used, and cannot be replaced. Others, like iron or copper, can be made into manufactured goods, and these when worn out can be resmelted and the metal used over again. Right here, as we shall see later, is a fine chance for conserving our supply of certain metals.

(5) The initiation of conservational measures by both federal and state governments as well as by certain industries may promote considerable saving of our mineral resources. Those recommended thus far have applied particularly to coal, oil, and gas.

It is admitted that there is not the same need for conserving all kinds of raw mineral products. Thus, our supplies of stone, clay, and sand, all materials used in the building industry, are so abundant that we have little need to fear for their exhaustion, although locally they may be scarce, as, for example, supplies of building stone in the Great Plains area. Our unmined beds of coal contain an enormous tonnage, but the better varieties are not so abundant and are more or less localized in the eastern half of the country. Supplies of some of the metals such as lead, zinc, gold, and silver are exhaustible, and in some districts already have been exhausted.

Taking the world as a whole, however, the mineral supplies are so large that we need not fear the early exhaustion of any particular mineral. Some have suggested, however, that if we can obtain a given mineral from some foreign country at a cheap price, it is better to do so than draw on our own supplies. Tariffs sponsored by domestic mining industries may discourage this.

DISCOVERY OF NEW DEPOSITS

We may naturally ask whether the exhaustion of our stores of mineral wealth cannot be made up for by the discovery of new deposits. Those nations which are greatly favored with mineral resources are doing all they can to increase their natural advantages, which also includes getting control of foreign sources of supply, while the less-favored nations are at the same time exerting their best efforts to improve their position.

The important countries of the world probably already have a fairly good knowledge of their mineral wealth, and yet even at the present day unexpected discoveries are sometimes made, as in the case of copper (p. 455) and zinc (p. 460) deposits in the United States, as well as in some foreign countries (p. 456 and 460). Potential reserves of oil and gas may also be discovered, as, for example, in the shallow water areas off the coast of the United States and Alaska (p. 485) and also in western Canada.

There may, however, be discoveries in those parts of the world where exploration is made difficult, either because a region may be inhabited by hostile peoples, or because of jungle growth or general inaccessibility. Such conditions exist in certain parts of Asia, Africa, and South America. There are also parts of northern Canada and of Russia which have not been thoroughly explored.

Turning to the United States, it is interesting to note that of the thirty-five leading metal-producing districts that have been developed, only five have been discovered since 1900, and none since 1910. With oil, however, the case is different, for of the fifty largest pools, twenty were discovered between 1920 and 1930; but their potential supply is not sufficient to equal the rate at which petroleum is being consumed.

DEMAND FOR NEW MINERALS AND
MINERAL PRODUCTS

Since 1850 there has been an ever-increasing demand for the more common and better-known minerals and their products, and, in addition, rarer and less well-known ones have come into use. It was found, for example, that iron could be alloyed [3] with such relatively rare elements as chromium, nickel, cobalt, tungsten, molybdenum, titanium, vanadium, and others. These steel alloys had desirable properties that permitted their being more widely used, and for purposes not previously considered. In addition to this, minerals enter into many artificial products where their presence may not be suspected. When we look at an automobile tire, we think only of the rubber in it, little realizing that its durability is due to various mineral ingredients mixed with the rubber.

ARTIFICIAL PRODUCTS

One might hope that if a mineral product which is found only in limited quantities could be replaced by an artificial one, it might help conserve our supply, but this does not hold in all cases.

Artificial graphite is made from coal or coke, both of which can be obtained in greater quantities in this country than natural graphite. Unfortunately most of the graphite deposits in the United States have not been found profitable to operate except in wartime. Since, in this case, the artificial product can be used to replace the natural one for many purposes, it serves to some extent to decrease imports.

Our supplies of natural emery and corundum are not abundant, and artificial products are made to replace them, but they are manufactured from an aluminum-bearing mineral known as bauxite, which is not found in this country in unlimited amounts, although more abundant than the original mineral which it replaces. Carborundum made from coal and silica replaces emery and corundum to some extent.

MINERAL WEALTH OF THE UNITED STATES

The United States has for some time been, and is still, the leading producer of many minerals of value to industry, the value of the out-

---

[3] An alloy is a mixture of two or more metals formed by melting them together.

put having reached almost staggering figures. The following table shows the approximate average for several decades:

Years	Average
1890–1899	$ 660,673,000
1900–1909	1,557,962,000
1910–1919	3,175,449,300
1920–1929	5,575,346,000
1930–1939	3,913,070,000
1940–1946	7,650,857,142

It is also interesting to compare the total annual value of production of the metals, nonmetals, and coal, oil, and gas. The figures for 1946 are:

	Total values
Metals	1,823,000,000
Nonmetals, other than fuels	1,311,000,000
Coal, oil, and natural gas	5,725,000,000

The United States is, in addition to being the greatest producer, also the greatest consumer of mineral products. This country has within its boundaries a larger variety of useful minerals than any other country of the world. In spite of this, however, it lacks a sufficient supply of about twenty minerals which are of industrial importance. Prominent among these are tin, nickel, manganese, chromium, and antimony.

It may be of interest to mention here the six leading states in the production of minerals, and the mineral products which are responsible for the rank of each.

			Value in 1946
(1)	Texas	Petroleum, natural gas, sulfur, natural gasoline	$1,518,111,000
(2)	Pennsylvania	Coal, petroleum, natural gas, cement ..	1,090,784,000
(3)	California	Petroleum, natural gas, gold, natural gasoline	696,997,000
(4)	West Virginia	Coal, natural gas, petroleum, stone	632,654,000
(5)	Illinois	Petroleum, coal, stone, cement	355,578,000
(6)	Louisiana	Petroleum, natural gas, natural gasoline, sulfur	342,944,000

CHAPTER XV

The Metals

ANYONE interested in what goes on about him cannot fail to notice the extent to which metals are used in many branches of industry, and how their use has increased our comfort and happiness in this world; in other words, how they have contributed to civilization.

It takes but a few moments to think of a number of metals which are being used. Iron (or steel) for automobiles, machinery, rails, fireproof buildings; copper for electrical goods and wire; aluminum for cooking utensils and airplanes; gold for coins and jewelry; silver for coins and tableware; tin for containers; zinc for coating iron (galvanizing) to preserve it against rust; mercury in thermometers and scientific apparatus. These are all uses which cannot escape our notice, and to stress their importance let us imagine what we should do if we had to get along without even half of them.

Aside from these metals, there are others widely used, not by themselves, but alloyed with commoner ones such as iron or steel (p. 451) to improve the properties of the product. We are not likely to realize how valuable they are. An example well known to everyone is stainless steel, made by coating steel with chromium.

Metal deposits not inexhaustible. Realizing then that the metals are of such value to man and that the deposits of them are not inexhaustible, we can appreciate the need for conserving our supplies. The need of this is well brought out by a few comparisons. The gold production of the United States reached its peak about 1915 and decreased to 1929, rose again to 1940 and then dropped again. The supply may give out in a few decades. The Lake Superior district, which supplies about four-fifths of our iron ore, is said to have reserves, of the commercial grade and in the quantity being mined at present, sufficient to last about fifteen years. When these are exhausted, we shall have to turn to poorer iron ores. Our copper reserves may last no longer than our high-grade iron ores. The reserves of lead and zinc are stated to be only half as great, or about twenty years' supply.[1]

The richness of ore. Few metallic elements except gold and platinum are commonly found in ore as the metal (p. 465), but are usually combined chemically with other elements. Thus zinc, lead, and copper are commonly combined with sulfur to form sulfides. Iron is usually combined with oxygen to form oxides.

Ore bodies are very rarely composed solidly either of gold or of any copper, iron, zinc, or lead minerals, but contain also minerals of a nonmetallic nature. Unless the ore contains a certain percentage of the metal sought, it is not only unprofitable to mine it but also difficult or impossible to smelt it and extract the metal by itself. This brings us up directly against a conservation problem. There may be a certain minimum richness below which it does not pay to work the ore. In general, we can say that the higher the market value of metal in the ore per unit of weight, the lower the grade of material which can be worked.

As an example we may compare iron with gold. Because of the much lower market value of the former, an iron deposit to be workable must be considerably higher in its metal content than a gold ore.

If the market value of a metal rises, it permits us, other things equal, to work a lower-grade ore. This is illustrated by the fact that in 1934, when the price of gold rose from $20 an ounce to $35, many idle gold mines were reopened. Thus the possibility of working deposits not hitherto regarded as profitable tends to increase what we may regard as reserves of gold ore.

In general the percentage of metal in the ores mined at the present day averages much less than formerly.

Concentration of ores. Since few ores of the metals, except sometimes those of iron, are rich enough to smelt as they are mined because of the admixture of nonmetallic minerals, it becomes necessary to crush the ore and separate the metallic minerals from the nonmetallic impurities. This gives us a product called the *concentrate,* which is rich enough in its metallic content to smelt.

As time has gone on, methods of concentration have been gradually improved so that in many cases it is possible to work a much lower-grade ore than was handled formerly. Indeed, in some cases material

---

[1] K. Leith and D. M. Liddell, *The Mineral Reserves of the United States and Its Capacity for Production* (Washington, 1936).

which had formerly been regarded as waste rock and thrown on the dump heap at the mine was at a later date put through an improved concentration process and the metallic contents were saved. In addition to this, the percentage of metal recovered in the concentration process is greater than formerly, and thus less is allowed to go to waste.

One of the most important developments in the mining industry, which has been a strong ally in the conservation of our metal resources, was the discovery and introduction of the process of flotation about 1900. This consists of making a pulp of finely ground ore and water and mixing it with small quantities of one or more chemical reagents. This mixture is made into a froth. The mineral particles desired stick to the air bubbles and float, while the waste particles settle. We can thus make a separation of minerals which could not formerly be accomplished by other means. This process permits the treatment of low-grade ores not formerly workable and thus increases our reserves.[2]

No more striking example of the use of low-grade ore is to be found than that of the Bingham copper deposits of Utah, where in 1945 224,284 short tons of copper were produced from ore averaging 0.87 per cent copper. Such ore cannot be utilized, however, unless the deposit is of great size, so that it can be worked on a large scale.

Mixed ores, that is, those containing two or more metals, represent another conservation problem. In former years it was difficult to separate the minerals containing certain metals such as lead and zinc, but improved methods of treatment have now made this possible, thus adding to our available supply.

Use of scrap metals. Many metal products become worn out with use or broken. The quantity of this discarded material during the course of a year in the United States alone represents millions of tons.

Much of this material is sold as scrap (Fig. 219) which can be remelted and used over again. It thus becomes, in some instances, a competitor with new metal obtained from the mines, but it is of direct benefit in one way in that it may reduce the amount of metal mined and help conserve our supplies. Great quantities are also exported. The demand for this scrap metal will vary somewhat depending on the market; when the price rises, the sale of new metal increases.

Scrap iron is a most important element in the iron and steel industry (Fig. 219). In the United States in 1945, of the total amount of

---

2 Flotation is now also applied to some nonmetallic products.

steel produced, 51.4 per cent was scrap and 48.6 per cent pig iron.[3]

Copper is another easily recoverable metal. It is stated that in 1934, for every pound of primary copper produced in the United States, 1.62 pounds were obtained from scrap material.[4] In 1945 the secondary copper produced amounted to about 130 per cent of the domestic mine output.[5]

Figure 219. A pile of scrap iron. This will be remelted and cast into new articles. Thousands of tons of scrap are reused annually. (F. Steinach.)

Not all of the metal used in industry can, however, be saved. Zinc and lead are used in vast quantities for paints and are not recoverable. If we could find an equally satisfactory substitute for them, it would be a step in the conservation of these metals. Another loss of zinc occurs in its use for galvanizing sheet iron and wire fencing. The same is true of titanium, much of which is now employed for a similar purpose. The tin used in making tin plate is not all recovered. Aluminum-coated steel might be used as a substitute, but this would mean a drain on the supplies of another metal. Conservation would be best served if

3 U.S. Bureau of Mines, *Minerals Year Book*, 1945 (Washington, 1947), p. 528.
4 Leith and Liddell, *op. cit.*, p. 65.
5 *Minerals Year Book*, 1945, p. 122.

we could find a common nonmetallic mineral which could be used as a covering substitute.

THE MAJOR METALS

Gold. Gold is a metal most eagerly sought, and the world production of it has shown a tremendous increase since 1900, chiefly because of the increasing output from mines in the Transvaal, South Africa.

The total value of gold produced in the world in 1940 was about

Figure 220. Washing gold gravels. The powerful stream of water directed against the bank washes the gravel into sluices where the gold settles, and the gravel is carried off. (W. W. Bradley.)

$1,518,000,000, representing about 42,325,000 ounces. From 1940 to 1945, because of the war, there was a great decrease in the world production of gold, which in 1946 was estimated by the United States Bureau of Mines as 27,777,000 ounces. In 1940 the Union of South Africa produced about 54 per cent; Soviet Russia, 12.6 per cent; Canada, 14 per cent; and the United States, 12.5 per cent.

Up to about 1902, the United States was the leading country of the world in the production of gold. Around 1940 Canada and the United States were practically tied for second place. Since 1940 the Union of South Africa has been the only large producer which has maintained its production. Both Canada and the United States have dropped off in production; the great drop in the latter is due to the closing of gold mines by government order because of the need for miners in essential metal-mining industries. In 1946, however, the United States gold production increased about 60 per cent over that of the preceding year.

In 1940 about 55 per cent of the United States' gold was obtained from ores which contained gold alone, and about 31 per cent from

Figure 221. Gold dredge, Helena, Montana. The gravels underlying the flat valley carry small amounts of gold. The buckets on the traveling belt scoop this up and discharge it on the dredge where the gold grains are separated from the gravel, after which the latter is discharged at rear end of dredge. The pile of gravel in the background is refuse. (H. Ries.)

gravel deposits (Figs. 220, 221), the remainder coming from those ores in which the gold is associated with the less valuable metals, copper, lead, and zinc. In these the percentage of gold may be very small, amounting often to a value of only a few cents per ton of ore mined. Yet this small amount may be important because the money received for the gold helps toward the cost of mining and treatment of an ore which might not otherwise be profitable; and incidentally, it opens up larger supplies of the commoner metals.

From 1940 to 1945 the percentage of gold extracted from straight gold ores and placers in the United States showed a great decrease, but on the other hand the amount extracted from copper ores was more than twice as great, owing, of course, to the demand for copper. When normal peacetime conditions return, the relative amounts of gold obtained from different sources may become again what they were before the war. Figure 222 shows the domestic production from 1840 to 1945.

One outstanding feature of the United States gold-mining industry is the shift that has taken place in the areas of production. Gold was mined in North and South Carolina as early as 1800, and the eastern states were important until the discovery of gold in California in 1848. This started the famous gold rush which attracted thousands to that

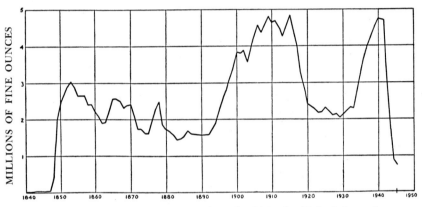

Figure 222. Graph showing production of gold in the United States from 1840 to 1945. (U.S. Bureau of Mines.)

state. The gold produced from river gravels of California caused a tremendous jump in this country's production. Later other deposits of gold were found in the western states (Fig. 223), but in most of them the gold was obtained from bedrock deposits which had to be mined, as contrasted with the gravels from which the gold nuggets or grains were washed. Still later came the great gold discoveries in Alaska between the years 1896 and 1909.

The gold content of most ores worked for this metal alone is relatively low, and every effort is made to save as much of the gold as possible and thus conserve the supply. Some 20 or 30 years ago gold ores carrying one-eighth ounce per ton of ore were considered low grade, but now ores with one-half that amount are worked. Gravels carrying as little as 8 to 15 cents' worth of gold per cubic yard are worked. According to the *Minerals Year Book* the average for all Oregon placers in 1946 was $0.105 and for Washington ones $0.141. As already stated, the revaluation of gold upward by the United States government from $20 an ounce to $35 an ounce has encouraged the development of many low-grade deposits.

After the ore has been smelted, all gold is cast in the form of bars (bullion), which are held in treasuries as a monetary gold reserve or are used in industry. Very few gold coins are now in circulation anywhere and none at all in the United States.

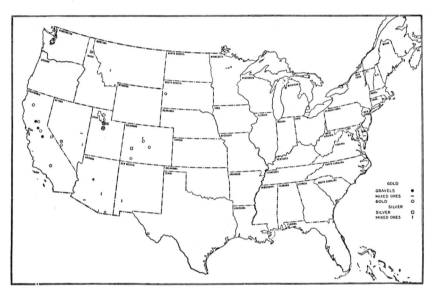

Figure 223. Map showing the more important gold- and silver-producing areas of the United States.

A new and interesting use for gold reported in 1946 is in connection with spectrography. The transmutation of gold to mercury gives a type of the latter that presents much sharper lines.

A considerable amount of gold is used in jewelry and dental work, in chemical plants and laboratory ware, in thermocouples, watches, radio and electrical equipment, and other items. Much of that so used can be saved, when discarded, and reused. There are some substitutes for gold such as platinum metals, mercury, and palladium alloys in dentistry and sometimes other metal alloys. Since our gold reserves are small, every effort should be made to conserve them.

The reserves of the United States and Alaska of recoverable gold as of January, 1944, were: estimated, 35,130,000 troy ounces; inferred, 33,855,000 troy ounces.[6] Of this, about 21,000,000 is in placers, 37,000,000 in dry and siliceous ores, and 11,000,000 in base metal ores, chiefly copper. At the 1940 rate of production of 4,800,000 ounces, this would give a life of at least fourteen years. New discoveries may add to this.

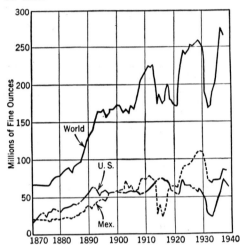

Figure 224. Graph showing production of silver in the United States, Mexico, and the world from 1870 to 1938.

Silver. Up to the year 1860 the United States' production of silver was small, amounting to but a few thousand ounces annually, but in 1859 there was discovered in Nevada a famous deposit, the Comstock Lode, which contained both gold and silver in enormous quantities. This was followed by other discoveries in the Far West, so that the United States was the world s leading producer of silver until 1896, when Mexico became the leader. The latter country has held the position of leadership most of the time since then.

Silver, even more than gold, is found with other metals, and has to be mined in connection with them; indeed not over 25 per cent of our silver is obtained from straight silver ores. Copper ores supplied 24.4 per cent in 1946, lead ore 7.5 per cent, zinc ore 2.3 per cent, and mixed zinc, lead, and copper ores, 41.1 per cent. We get almost no silver from gravel deposits, which have been a great source of gold.

Silver has a wide variety of uses. Much of it was used for war equipment: of primary importance were the uses in solders and brazing alloys; next came uses in photography, electrical appliances, engine bearings, etc. All of these uses, especially photography, are important in time of peace. In addition, large quantities of the metal are used for silverware and jewelry.

Silver is widely used for coinage in certain countries such as China, Indo-China, and Mexico, and some of this may be lost by wear.

---

[6] *Mineral Resources of the U.S.*, p. 106.

The amount of secondary silver recovered in the United States in 1946 is said to have been about 36,000,000 ounces and came chiefly from silverware and photographic wastes. The mine production of silver in the United States dropped from about 67,000,000 fine ounces in 1941 to 23,000,000 fine ounces in 1946. We are partly dependent on foreign sources of supply.

The estimated silver reserves of the United States and Alaska as of January, 1944, amounted to approximately 763,000,000 ounces of silver that could be recovered under present economic and technologic conditions.[7] This is said to be about seventeen years' supply, but since at least three-fourths of the silver is obtained as a by-product of base metal mining, its output would depend on the production of these metals. The reserves may be extended by improvements in the methods of mining and treating these low-grade ores.

Iron. Iron is the most useful of all the metals. It is so cheap and has so many advantages for use that the demand for it is greater than for any other metal. It can be cast into various shapes, hammered, rolled, drawn into wires, and welded. Moreover, its hardness can be varied by proper treatment, so that we may obtain products ranging from the soft, easily bent horseshoe nail to a hard razor blade.

In a country like the United States the demand for iron ore is enormous, and on the average it has been rising in recent years, having reached a total of 106,312,399 gross tons in 1945. This is in excess of the domestic production, which in the same year was about 88,000,000 long tons. In 1946 it had dropped to 70,000,000. About four-fifths of our domestic production has been coming from the Lake Superior region. Because of the great demand every effort should be made to conserve our stores of this metal.

Iron ores vary in their richness of iron content, and they cannot be mined profitably unless they contain a certain amount of the metal. Much of the ore mined in the United States has contained around 50 per cent iron. If the ore is not rich enough, it can in many cases be beneficiated (concentrated) by washing or magnetic concentration (p. 450).

There are some ores, like those in the southern states, which do not carry more than 30 per cent iron, but which can be worked partly because they are so located as to be outside the zone of competition with the Lake Superior ores, and partly because the impurities consist of

---

[7] *Ibid.*, p. 181.

calcium carbonate (practically the same as limestone) which would have to be added separately in the blast furnace if it did not exist in the ore.

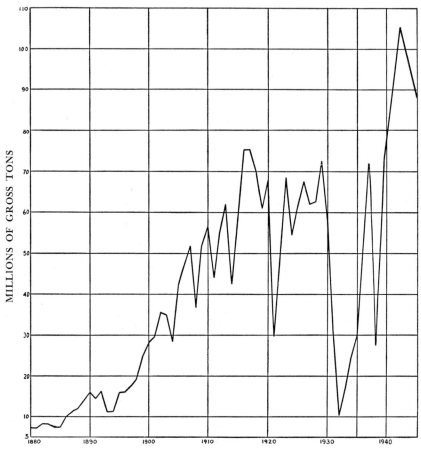

Figure 225. Graph showing production of iron ore in the United States from 1880 to 1945. (*Minerals Year Book,* 1940, 1945.)

Estimates of the reserves of iron ore in the United States have varied. The figures given in *Mineral Resources of the United States* as of January, 1944, are as follows:

	Long tons
Measured and indicated	3,726,000,000
Inferred	1,750,000,000
Potential	62,915,000,000

The sum of the first two is said to be the equivalent of forty years' supply even at the expanded rate of production during wartime.

The reserves of the Lake Superior district, one of the richest iron regions in the world, are estimated at 1,806,000,000 long tons of measured, indicated, and inferred ores, and 61,000,000,000 long tons of potential ores. It is believed that the district contains large reserves of low-grade ores that can be used if suitable methods for their concen-

Figure 226. Iron ore pit near Hibbing, Minnesota. The ore is extracted with steam shovels; some of these pits have yielded over 1,000,000 tons of ore a year. (Aubin Studio.)

tration are developed. Both governmental and industrial interests are engaged in trying to develop economic methods for concentrating this low-grade ore (taconite). However, when such methods are found, it will take years to build the plants. If a process for successfully treating taconite is developed, it will make available a reserve of many billions of tons.[8]

Labrador is also thought to contain large reserves.

Mikami [9] estimated the world's reserves of actual iron ore at 35,200,-

[8] W. O. Hotchkiss, *Economic Geology*, 42: 205 (1947).
[9] *Economic Geology*, 39: 1 (1944).

000,000 tons, and 164,800,000,000 tons of potential ore, the latter including those deposits which cannot compete with actual ores because of their low iron content but which may become usable at some future date with improved methods of concentration.

In 1945 we imported 1,193,534 gross tons of iron ore, nearly three-quarters of which came from Canada; but in the same year we exported about 2,000,000 gross tons, most of which went to Canada.

In Europe large quantities of iron ore running much lower in iron content than our Lake Superior ore are used because of lack of better material. When our supplies of good-grade ore give out, we too shall have to turn to lower-grade material, of which there is a large amount.

The fact that in 1945 twenty-eight of our mines each produced over 1,000,000 tons of ore and thirty-seven produced over 500,000 tons may well cause us to wonder how long our supplies will last.

There are several ways in which conservation may be accomplished, and some of these are already being followed. Low-grade ore, which owes its low iron content to the presence of mineral impurities, can sometimes be purified. A striking and interesting example of this is that type of iron ore in which the iron-bearing mineral is attracted by a magnet, while the other minerals in the ore are not. If this ore is crushed so as to separate the mineral grains, it is possible by using a machine called a *magnetic separator* to remove the iron-mineral grains from the others. The result is that an ore which did not contain more than about 20 per cent of iron might yield a concentrate running 50 or 60 per cent. Other kinds of iron ore may sometimes be concentrated in other ways.

A second method of keeping up our supply is to import foreign ores, and this has been done for some years; the imports in 1945 were about 1,000,000 long tons—which is not as large as those in 1940. Most of our imports came from Chile, Canada, and Algeria.

A third and a most important method of conservation already touched upon (p. 440) consists in the reuse of scrap iron. In case of necessity an additional quantity of scrap iron could be obtained by shutting off exports. In 1939 the United States exported 3,500,000 long tons, of which nearly 57 per cent went to Japan, but in 1945 the exports were about 95,000 short tons, most of which went to Canada and Mexico.

Iron is a metal which rusts easily, and to conserve our supply every effort should be made to protect it and prolong its life. Everyone has noticed workmen painting the cables and girders of a bridge. This is done to prevent rusting. Galvanizing iron with zinc or coating sheet-iron cans with tin has the same effect. Rustless steel, which is coated with the metal chromium, is another example of this type of conservation, but to follow this plan with all steel would be too expensive.

Another way of conserving iron has resulted from the development

Figure 227. A group of blast furnaces in which iron ore is reduced to molten pig iron. The molten pig iron is tapped about every five hours from the bottom into the car seen on right. Each of these furnaces can turn out as much as 600 tons of pig iron every 24 hours. (Bethlehem Steel Company.)

of high-strength steels. These are made by adding some other metal to the steel when it is molten, thus forming an alloy. The result is greatly increased strength, so that one ton now does the work that formerly required two.

Copper. Copper is an indispensable metal for certain purposes. It is widely used in the electrical industry, which consumes more than one-third of the production. The automobile industry takes perhaps 10 to 15 per cent. Enormous quantities are called for in time of war for the making of shells and bombs.

Some idea of the importance of copper is gained from the fact that in 1946, the United States alone produced 62,232,342 short tons (one short ton equals 2,000 pounds) of ore, which yielded 608,737 short tons of copper.[10] The United States is the world's leading producer of copper, but the average content of copper in the ore mined in this country is very low; in 1946 it was only 0.91 per cent. That the United States is not independent of other sources of supply is shown by the fact that in 1945 we imported 853,196 short tons of copper in the unmanufactured form, and 393,275 short tons in 1946.

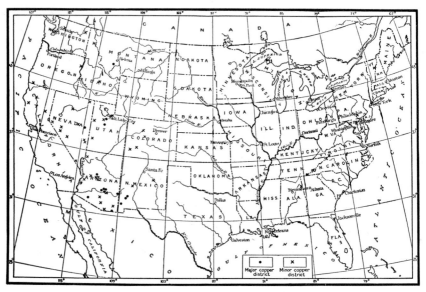

Figure 228. Map showing distribution of copper deposits in the United States. (*Copper Resources of World.*)

It is interesting to note how the site of the copper-mining industry has shifted, and that had it not been for new discoveries in the Far West, our present supplies of this metal would be very meager (Fig. 228). The early production of copper was in the eastern states, which are now of no importance in this respect except for an area in southeastern Tennessee. Then, about 1845, came the development of the famous deposits of native copper in northern Michigan, which by 1880 were producing from 70 to 90 per cent of all the copper mined

---

[10] In 1943 it was 1,027,000 short tons of copper, owing to the demands of war industries. Imports for the same reason established new records.

in this country. Some of these mines have reached a depth of 6,000 feet, but they find competition with rival mines difficult because the ores do not have the gold and silver content which many others have, and which helps toward paying for the cost of mining and treatment. Now the great centers of production are in Arizona, Utah, Montana (Fig. 230), New Mexico, and Nevada, with Michigan a poor sixth.

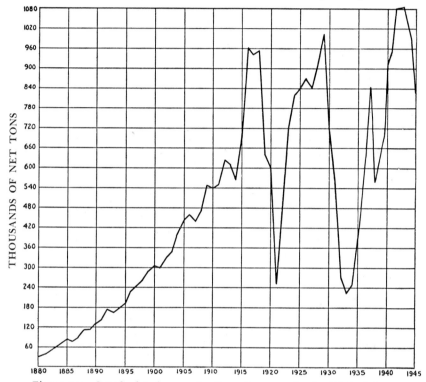

Figure 229. Graph showing production of copper in the United States from 1880 to 1945. (*Minerals Year Book,* 1940, 1945.)

Since 1942 most of the producing districts in this country have shown a decrease.

Most of the copper ores now obtained from the great ore bodies of the West are low grade, and the ore has to be concentrated. As a matter of conservation, therefore, it is desirable to save as large a percentage of the copper mineral as possible. Formerly not more than half of the copper was saved, but, with improved concentration methods, it is now possible to save from 80 to 90 per cent from an ore that carries but 1 per cent of copper, and even 95 per cent with richer ores.

It is perhaps hard to imagine such a low-grade ore as 1 per cent, which means that every ton of rock mined carries only 20 pounds of copper, of which 18 pounds are saved. This is truly a case of conservation.

Figure 231 will give some idea of the vast scale of some of the western copper mining operations. Here we see what practically amounts to a mountain of rock which is being blasted down, crushed, and concentrated to obtain the small percentage of copper that it contains.

But this is not all. In some cases great masses of rock containing a very small percentage of copper, too little to obtain by mining, have

Figure 230. View of a hill at Butte, Montana, in which copper mines are located. Note the head frames surmounting the shafts, up which ore is hoisted from depths of as much as 3,000 feet. The ores taken from these mines have supplied to date more than 12,000,000,000 pounds of copper, and over 3,000,000,000 pounds of zinc, as well as much manganese, gold, and silver. (Al's Photo Shop.)

their copper contents dissolved out by letting water trickle down through the mass. At the bottom this water is diverted into tanks containing scrap iron on which the copper is precipitated. Many tons of copper which would otherwise have been lost have been saved in this manner. Not only this, but the waters flowing from a copper mine may have their small amount of copper saved in the same way. About 23,-000 short tons were recovered in 1939 by these methods.

When we consider the enormous tonnage of copper mined, we can appreciate what large and expensive plants have to be built at many localities to concentrate and smelt the ore (Fig. 232).

Conserving our supply. Copper is one of the easiest of metals to reuse, and so we find that a considerable amount is reclaimed. In 1945 the amount obtained from scrap copper was 1,006,506 short tons valued at about $237,537,776. When we consider that the production of copper in the United States in the same year was a little over 772,000 short tons, it is easy to see that scrap copper is a strong competitor of the copper-mining industry. So, although the saving of this scrap copper works for saving our supply of this metal, it does have a depressing effect on the mining industry.

It is of interest to note that within recent years several important discoveries of additional copper-ore reserves have been announced.

Figure 231. Mine of Utah Copper Company, Bingham, Utah. A mountain of low-grade ore is being removed by blasting and steam shovels. Height from top to bottom of the excavation is 1,600 feet. (Utah Copper Company.)

Thus near San Manuel, Arizona, a newly prospected deposit has shown the presence of 120,000,000 tons of ore running 0.81 per cent copper with small amounts of molybdenite,[11] and another tract adjoining the preceding one of perhaps 100,000,000 tons with 1 per cent copper. At Ajo, not far away, they have been increased to 150,000,000 tons, while at Yerington, Nevada, 50,000,000 tons of 1.02 per cent copper ore have been proved.[12]

An estimate of the country's reserves made by the Bureau of Mines and Geological Survey in 1944 amounted to about 20,000,000 short

[11] C. W. Pehrson, *Mining and Metallurgy*, 28: 52 (Feb., 1947).
[12] C. D. Hulin, *Mining and Metallurgy*, 28: 57 (Feb., 1947).

tons of copper ore, measured, indicated, and inferred, with an average copper content of 1.1 per cent. The reserves of the world as of 1934 have been estimated at 104,830,200 short tons.[13]

Should our domestic reserves be worked out, there are large supplies in South America and Rhodesia. The United States is at present supplying about one-third of the world's production, but it controls about 56 per cent of the known world reserves. Also, silver can be used

Figure 232. View of Anaconda Reduction Works, Anaconda, Montana. The concentration mill and smelting plant can handle 25,000,000 pounds of copper per month. The stack is 585 feet high. (Anaconda Copper Mining Company.)

as a substitute for copper. During the war the United States Treasury expressed a willingness to loan some of its tremendous stored supply.

In this connection it is interesting to note that two enormous deposits, one of which is said to contain 250,000,000 tons of 2½ per cent copper, have been recently reported from Peru.[14]

---

[13] *Mineral Resources of the U.S.*, p. 96; G. H. Barbour, *Engineering and Mining Journal*, 135: 448 (1934).
[14] Hulin, *op. cit.*, p. 57.

A point to be borne in mind is that copper ores are not always what might be termed pure. That is, other metals in small but recoverable amounts are associated with them; if therefore the output of copper slows down, it affects the production of these other metals. Some idea of the small but commercially valuable quantity present may be gained from the fact that according to the U.S. Bureau of Mines the average yield of gold in domestic copper ores in 1946 was 0.004 ounces

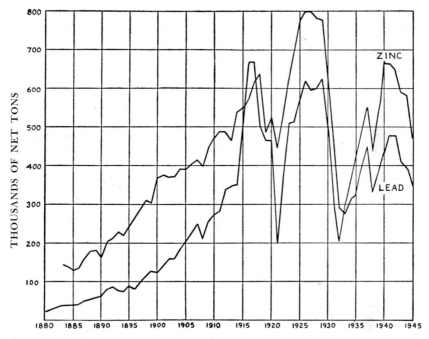

Figure 233. Graph showing production of lead and zinc in the United States from 1880 to 1945. (*Minerals Year Book*, 1940, 1945.)

per ton, and of silver 0.098 ounces, but it paid to save it. The Canadian copper ores contain appreciable nickel, but when the copper output is curtailed, as it was in the past year, it affects the nickel production also.

Labor difficulties may have a deterrent effect on production as was the case recently in the United States, Chile, and Rhodesia.

C. D. Hulin states that our commercial copper reserves are sufficient to last for 34 years.[15]

---

15 *Ibid.*

Unfortunately, with the tremendous copper reserves there has at times been an overproduction of the metal, with a consequent reduction of the market price. International agreements have sometimes been entered into to restrain production, but they have not always been effective.

Lead. Lead in nature is often found closely associated with zinc as well as silver, but in southeastern Missouri, which is our leading producer,

Figure 234. View at Picher, Oklahoma. The chert rock mined contains about 4 per cent zinc, and 1½ per cent lead. The great white conical piles represent the waste chert after separation of the metallic minerals. Some of these piles are being reworked to save the small amount of zinc that was left in them. (Tri-States Zinc and Lead Producers Association.)

both these metals are absent. Aside from this, most of our supply comes from the western states. In 1929 this amounted to about 670,000 short tons (Fig. 233), but, owing to the depression, it has dropped off considerably since, and in 1946 was only about 293,306 short tons. An additional 44,888 tons came from imported materials.

Since much of the lead used in industry is not recoverable, conservation should be followed in every way possible. This has been done in part in recent years by the introduction of flotation (p. 440), which permits us to use lower-grade ores and separate the lead from the zinc minerals.

The chief uses of refined lead for 1946 are listed in Table 21. None of the lead, except that used in storage batteries is recoverable. Lead used in paints is not recoverable, but this loss is somewhat offset by the fact that white paints are now made from other minerals, such as titanium ore and barite.

TABLE 21. USES OF REFINED LEAD, 1946 *

	Short tons	Per cent
Red lead, white lead, and litharge	133,920	24
Cable covering	72,540	13
Tetraethyl lead for ethyl gasoline	50,220	9
Storage batteries	1,380	11
White lead	4,640	8
Solder	3,480	6
Ammunition	16,740	3
Sheet lead	27,900	5
Pipe, traps and bends	27,900	5
Miscellaneous	89,280	16

* From U.S. Bureau of Mines.

It is curious that as fast as lead has been replaced by some other mineral product in one industry, new uses have been found for it elsewhere. Thus while iron pipe has largely replaced lead pipe for many uses, in recent years an extensive use has been found for lead in making ethyl gasoline. Another unfamiliar use is for making mats of sheet lead and asbestos, which are placed under tall buildings to prevent vibration. Much lead is used in glass manufacture and for pottery glazes, from which it is not recovered.

Where lead is used in its metallic form or in alloys, much can be recovered. In 1946 that saved from what we call scrap amounted to 392,787 short tons, or an amount equal to about 116 per cent of the total production of refined lead from domestic and foreign sources in the United States.

One authority states that the estimated lead ore reserves have about 3,300,000 short tons of lead, which would be about seven years' supply at the present rate of production, which is below normal. The Bureau of Mines estimates that the lead recoverable from measured and indicated ore by present methods is equivalent to the domestic needs of the country for four years if there is a minimum peacetime production of 500,000 tons of primary metal per year. The additional inferred reserves should add another nine years. A wartime demand of 750,000 tons would be equivalent to a nine-year supply. Two-thirds of our lead supply comes from ores which produce also zinc, copper, silver, and some gold, so the demand for these will to some extent govern our lead output.

Since our own supplies of lead ore are limited we are naturally interested in foreign sources of supply. What may be the biggest deposit found anywhere in twenty years has been discovered in Tanganyika.[16] There appears to be a sufficient supply in Mexico to meet our needs to a large extent.

Zinc. The mine production of recoverable zinc, which includes that recovered as zinc pigments and salts directly from the ore, in the United States in 1946 was 574,833 short tons, which is an appreciable drop from the preceding four years. Of the 1946 production about 459,000 short tons was primarily slab zinc. In addition, about 269,000 short tons were made from foreign ores, which indicates the extent to which we depend on foreign sources of supply. Idaho, Oklahoma, and New Jersey are the three leading states in production, in the order named, the balance coming chiefly from states west of the Mississippi River.

Unfortunately, much of the zinc used is not recoverable, particularly that employed for galvanizing and paints. That which goes into the manufacture of brass can be recovered.

It is these losses which may account for the greater amount of zinc than lead produced. Could we find a substitute for zinc, it would be desirable, as our domestic supplies are by no means inexhaustible. However, about 360,000 short tons of zinc were recovered from zinc articles and alloys in 1945.

The production of zinc in the United States is given in Figure 233 (p. 457). According to C. D. Hulin the zinc reserves of the United States are calculated at nineteen years, over half of them being inferred.[17] A reported find is in the Central Mining District of New Mexico, which it is thought may yield 1,500,000 tons of ore. New lead-zinc deposits also are being developed around Pioche, Nevada.

---

16 Hulin, *op. cit.,* p. 56.
17 *Ibid.*

THE MINOR METALS

A number of metals are spoken of as minor because their production is small compared with that of metals described on the preceding pages. They may be of great importance to industry, either for the reason that some of them alone have special uses, or because when alloyed with iron in making steel they greatly improve certain of its qualities.

During World War II all of these assumed great importance, and the domestic supply was insufficient to fill the greatly increased demand. We shall refer briefly to aluminum, chromium, magnesium, manganese, mercury, molybdenum, nickel, tin, titanium, tungsten, and vanadium.

Aluminum. This metal is of particular value because of its very light weight, it being lighter than any of those commonly employed except magnesium.

Important uses are for making cables, in airplane and other transportation industries; for instruments, cooking utensils, incendiary bombs; and for many other metal products where lightness is desired. Aluminum can also be alloyed with other metals.

New uses for aluminum are also being found, as in the manufacture of railroad passenger cars, sheet roofing, and clothespins.

Aluminum is widespread in the earth's crust, but it does not occur in the metallic or elementary form; it is combined with other elements to form minerals. All clays contain it and so do granites, and if we had any commercially practicable process of extracting the aluminum from these two, it would be possible to get it from many localities in all parts of the world. Since this is not the case, we have to obtain our entire supply from deposits of a mineral known as *bauxite,* from which the aluminum can be extracted without much difficulty. So far as the United States is concerned these deposits are restricted, the main source of supply being Arkansas, with much smaller amounts in Alabama, Georgia, Tennessee, Mississippi, and Virginia. Extensive deposits occur in Dutch Guiana or Surinam, which supplies three-quarters of our imports; British Guiana; and France. More recently others of importance have been developed in Yugoslavia and Hungary. European sources of supply, however, were shut off during the war.

According to G. H. Branner, in an estimate made in 1941, our reserves of first- and second-grade bauxite amount to 20,000,000 tons, which according to the 1937–1939 rate of consumption should last about 28 years. If, however, it were all to be used in making aluminum and the annual production were to be increased fourfold during the last war, the supply would last only about six and a half years.[18] Harold L. Ickes, former Secretary of the Interior, stated in 1945 that we have only a 35-year commercial supply of bauxite.

The United States' production of bauxite in 1945 was about 1,155,-808 long tons, while the imports were 739,581 long tons; in other words, we import over half of what we need. This country consumed 796,081 short tons of aluminum in 1945, about 62 per cent of which was produced here. The great demand for aluminum which came with World War II led to an intensive search not only for further sources of bauxite, but also for high-alumina clays for which some practical method of treatment may be found.

The aluminum industry consumed over 80 per cent of the domestic bauxite production in 1945, the balance being used chiefly by the chemical industry and by the abrasive industry in the making of artificial emery wheels. The latter two uses do not permit recovery. An example is the manufacture of large quantities of aluminum paint. The amount of this can be appreciated when we find that one large bridge, connecting San Francisco with Oakland in California, required 50,000 gallons for its final coat.[19]

The United States in 1946 produced about 409,000 short tons of aluminum and imported about 339,000 short tons. The only possibility of conserving our supply of aluminum occurs when it is used in the metallic form or in alloys. The quantity saved in 1946 from these two sources amounted to 278,073 short tons, valued at about $80,000,000. This was about 60 per cent of the aluminum consumed in the United States in the same year.

In discussing conservation we naturally think of possible substitutes. So far as lightness is concerned, a possible substitute is magnesium, but this is more expensive. Neither is it likely that aluminum will be extensively substituted at present for some of the cheaper metals because of its market price.

Chromium. This metal is added to steel during the process of manufacture. Stainless steel is a well-known product. The mineral chromite is also used for refractories and in chemical work.

---

18 *Mining and Metallurgy*, 22: 351 (1941).
19 This is the equivalent of five average tank cars.

Very little chromium ore is produced in the United States because the deposits are small and often not of a sufficiently rich grade to work. We therefore have to import nearly our entire supply. About two-thirds of it comes from Rhodesia, South Africa, and Cuba. The imports in 1945 amounted to 914,765 long tons, or 65 times the domestic production. This large increase was due to war needs.

In the United States, efforts to treat the many known low-grade deposits of chromic iron ore are now under way, and these may prove to be successful.

Magnesium. The airplane industry calls for a large amount of light-weight metals. Aluminum, as already stated, is widely used, but in addition magnesium has recently become of great importance. It is used by itself or in alloys, and is especially desirable because of its great lightness and strength.

Magnesium can be made from magnesite or brucite, of which there are deposits in Nevada, from sea water, or from the brine obtained from salt wells. Dolomite has also been used.

There was a large demand for it during the recent war, but since then the demand has fallen off, and salt water is now the sole source of supply. One plant erected at Freeport, Texas, is capable of yielding an unlimited supply. The falling off in production is well illustrated by the fact that in 1943 the United States produced 183,584 short tons, ingot equivalent; in 1945 43,496 short tons; and in 1946 only 8,916 short tons.

Manganese. This is an exceedingly important metal in steel manufacture, the production of every ton of steel requiring about 15 pounds of manganese. Manganese makes the steel very hard, and also brings about certain desirable changes in its chemical composition during smelting. Not all the manganese remains in the steel; some goes off in the slag.

Since manganese is so essential in steel making, which is one of our leading industries, there is a considerable demand for it. But to be of value for steel the ore must contain 45 per cent manganese, and here is where the trouble comes in, because this country lacks a sufficient supply of high-grade material. As a result of domestic deficiency we have to import large amounts from Cuba, Russia, Brazil, India, and the Gold Coast, in the order named, the amount in 1947 being 1,297,992 short tons of manganese ore and 81,307 short tons of ferromanganese. This is truly not a pleasant situation to contemplate in case our imports were shut off by war, although in that event small deposits might be worked which cannot compete with the imported product at other times. The United States has abundant supplies of ore running low in manganese.

Mercury. This metal is liquid at ordinary temperatures. It is widely used in industry in the manufacture of electric appliances, drugs, paints, explosives, etc. Its largest use is for electrical apparatus, with pharmaceutical uses second.

Mercury is found in ore deposits, sometimes in the elemental form (quicksilver) and sometimes combined chemically with sulfur (cinnabar). The domestic ores are low grade, averaging less than 1 per cent mercury.

Since we supply less than one-half of our domestic requirements in peacetime, it would be an advantage if our supply could be conserved. The military uses of mercury for making fulminate to detonate high explosives, as well as the civilian uses, make it indispensable. The quantity used for recovering gold from the crushed ore has decreased, as another chemical compound can be used. Mercury is also being replaced by silver nitrate for silvering mirrors. On the other hand, new uses for the metal are being developed which will counteract the saving. Hulin estimates our reserves at 3 years.[20]

Spain, Italy, and the United States were the most important producing countries in 1945.

The changes in production and prices of mercury show how war may affect domestic industry and prices. When the war shut off imports there were two hundred mines in production in the United States, whereas at the end of 1946, when imports were resumed, there were only six mines in operation. The price per flask (72 pounds), which had reached $200 during the war, had dropped to $88 at the end of 1946 when imports from Europe were resumed.[21] Our domestic production was about 52,000 flasks in 1945 but dropped to 28,000 at the end of 1946.

Molybdenum. This is a metal valuable for making extra hard, high-speed tool steels. Molybdenum steels are also much used in the construction of airplanes and automobiles, as well as in the radio industry. It has replaced tungsten and nickel to some extent; but while this conserves two metals, it does not save the other.

---

[20] *Op. cit.,* p. 56.
[21] Pehrson, *Mining and Metallurgy* 28: 50 (Feb., 1947).

The United States produces about 90 per cent of the world's supply of molybdenum. The production in ore and concentrates in 1947 was 27,047,000 pounds, which was less than half of the 1942 output. Colorado supplies over half the output. In some states molybdenum is associated with copper or tungsten. We have abundant reserves.

Nickel. This metal is widely used for making alloy steels which have great hardness, strength, toughness, elasticity, and resistance to corrosion. Some other metals like chromium and molybdenum are sometimes added to such alloys.

Nickel was an important metal in World War II, and the United States was almost entirely dependent on foreign sources of supply. Fortunately most of our supply comes from Canada, the world's leading producer.

Some nickel is recovered for reuse. However, it is but a small fraction of that imported annually. Secondary nickel in 1946 amounted to 8,248 short tons, and the imports in 1945 were 122,528 short tons.

There is no complete substitute for nickel.

Platinum. The term *platinum* is sometimes used in a general sense to refer to a group of metals called the platinum metals. These are platinum, palladium, osmium, rhodium, and iridium. When we find them in stream gravels as grains and nuggets, we cannot tell whether only one or more than one of these metals is present. They are also found sometimes in ore veins mixed with metals other than those of the platinum group, and they have to be separated from these during the process of smelting and refining.

Russia and Colombia get their supply from gravels. Canada obtains a large amount from the nickel-copper ores of Ontario. These three countries are the leading producers.

Much platinum is used in jewelry and dental work. This metal also plays an important though small part in X-ray apparatus, telephone transmission, and the electrical apparatus in airplanes. Our fountain pen points resist wear because they are tipped with an alloy of two platinum metals. The chemical industry is the second largest user. There are many other uses in spite of platinum's high price per ounce.

The United States is a small producer and the largest consumer of platinum metals. In 1946 it produced 22,949 ounces of platinum metals. Of this 22,882 ounces came from placers mostly in Alaska, and the balance from gold and copper ores. It imported 76,012 troy ounces of unrefined platinum metals, and 331,198 ounces of refined metals. We see then that we are quite dependent on foreign sources of supply. Fortunately for us, the largest producer is again our friendly neighbor Canada. In 1946 we exported 26,555 ounces of platinum metals in manufactured and unmanufactured form.

The total reserves of platinum metals as estimated by the Bureau of Mines amounts to 600,000 troy ounces. This would mean a two and a half years' supply at the rate of consumption, but since the output of platinum metals is limited by the rate of exploitation of the ores with which they occur, the supply will last longer.[22]

During World War II the use of platinum and platinum alloys in new jewelry was prohibited.

Tin. The two great consumers of tin are the automobile and the food industry. The latter uses the so-called tin cans, which are really thin sheet steel, coated with tin. This is why a tin can, if exposed to dampness, will eventually rust. We can see how little tin there is in cans when we find that only one pound of tin is required to cover 220 square feet of tin plate. Tin is also required in the manufacture of roofing, gas tanks for automobiles, and many other products.

The United States is the largest consumer of tin, but its production of this most useful metal is very low. Before World War II tin metal was obtained mostly from British Malaya, with smaller amounts from China, the Netherlands Indies, and the United Kingdom. In 1941 we imported 140,873 long tons of metal, which was over half the world's production, but owing to the war this dropped to 8,440 long tons in 1945, most of it coming from the Belgian Congo. In addition, in 1945 we imported 33,527 long tons of tin concentrates, mostly from Bolivia. These were treated at a government-financed smelter in Texas, which in 1946 produced 43,488 long tons of pig tin. In 1946 the imports of tin metal had risen to 15,520 long tons, but the Netherlands Indies and the United Kingdom were the largest sources of supply. Bolivia, however, was the largest producer of tin in concentrates, with 25,984 tons.

Much of our tin can be used over again; the amount of this in 1946 was equal to 26,316 long tons.

There is not much use in talking about conservation so far as this country is concerned, because we have practically no workable deposits except in Alaska, from which, as we can see from the above figures, the supply is not large. There are two ways of conserving this metal: (1) by reusing as much tin as possible, and (2) by using aluminum as a

---

[22] *Mineral Resources of the U.S.,* p. 170.

substitute for coating steel. If the latter works, it may seriously affect the demand for tin which we have to import. In automobile manufacture, the use of tin is said to be diminishing because of substitutes, one of which is the metal cadmium, producible in some quantity in the United States.

Titanium. There is little use at present for this metal in the metallic form, but it is interesting to know that a black mineral (ilmenite, FeO, TiO_2) carrying titanium can be used for making white paint, which is its chief use. Smaller amounts of ilmenite are used for titanium alloys and for carbide. The ore has to be concentrated after mining, the domestic production of concentrates in 1946 being in excess of 282,000 short tons, making the United States the world's leading producer. India and Norway were next in order of production.

Rutile (TiO_2), another titanium mineral, is used chiefly for welding rod coatings. About half the demand is supplied by the United States, the remainder coming almost exclusively from Australia. Sands on the east coast of Florida carry ilmenite, rutile, and zircon.

We have abundant reserves of ilmenite and rutile.

Tungsten. This is another metal employed for making hard tool steels and lamp filaments; it was an important war mineral. The United States production has been dropping off so that we have to import it from foreign countries, notably Bolivia, Brazil, and Argentina. China has large resources, but exports dropped off in 1945. In the United States Idaho and Nevada produced about equal amounts, with California supplying a quarter of their total.

Vanadium. This is an important metal in the steel industry. It gives toughness, strength, and hardness to alloy steels. Most of it is used in the form of ferrovanadium. It is also employed to a limited extent in the chemical industries.

The chief world sources of vanadium have been sulfide minerals in Peru, vanadium-bearing sandstones in the United States, and deposits in Northern Rhodesia and South Africa. The western sandstone deposits yielded about 25 per cent of the world's production, but due to war requirements this rose to 60 per cent. We have an appreciable supply of this important metal.

CHAPTER XVI

Coal

COAL represents one of the most valuable mineral resources that we possess, because of its wide and well-known uses in providing heat and steam power. In addition, certain valuable substances can be extracted from it. It is an important source of the compounds now so widely used in the manufacture of the various substances known as plastics.

PRODUCTION

Some coal was mined near Richmond, Virginia, as early as 1767; but the first production in any amount was in 1814. However, it was not until the use of steam for power that coal began to be of importance, and at first it had to compete with wood. From that time the production of coal rose steadily up to 1918; since then it has varied (Fig. 235). In recent years the total production has dropped off somewhat, partly because of competition with other fuels.

HOW COAL OCCURS

In order to understand what follows, it is necessary to consider how coal is found and also how it is formed.

All coal is found in beds which lie between beds of sandstone or shale. Individual coal beds can sometimes be traced over a large area many square miles in extent.

In many coal beds and in the rocks associated with them we find plant impressions, and carbon, which is an important element of plant tissue, makes up a large part of the composition of coal. Putting these facts together, we suspect then that coal must have some connection with plants and may have been formed from them.

When dead plants collect in a swamp, the decaying plant tissue forms peat, with which many persons are familiar. Put a sample of this under tremendous pressure, and it begins to look like coal.

Millions of years ago there existed thousands of square miles of peat swamps. When these deposits sank below sea level, they became covered by many feet of sediments washed in from the land. This had the effect of putting them under great pressure, and the material was also heated by the interior temperature of the earth. As a result of this the peat gradually changed to coal.

Longer time and greater pressure changed the coal more and more. This gives us a series of coal types ranging from those in which the

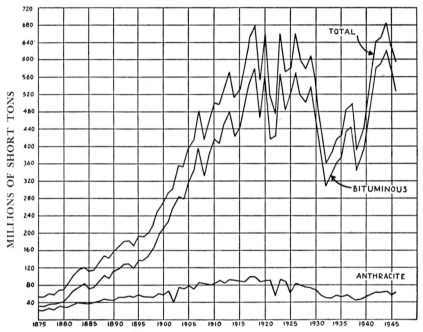

Figure 235. Graph showing the production of coal in the United States from 1875 to 1946. (*Minerals Year Book.*)

vegetable matter has undergone relatively little change to those which represent an extensive change. The greater this change, the higher the carbon content. We speak of a coal's position in this series as its *rank*. So, depending on the amount of change which the vegetable matter has undergone, we get varieties known as lignite, subbituminous coal, bituminous coal, semibituminous coal, and anthracite, the last being hard coal, or coal of the highest rank. Heating value varies in these different ranks, there being a gradual increase as we pass from lignite, the lowest, to anthracite, the highest rank.

Reference to the map (Fig. 236) shows how extensive are the areas underlaid by coal in the United States. In many cases there may be a number of beds of coal separated by beds of other rock.

A further study of the map will show that the several ranks of coal are not evenly distributed throughout the United States. Thus anthracite, our highest rank of coal, is found almost nowhere except in northeastern Pennsylvania and a small area in Colorado. The bituminous coals, which are the next highest rank, are most abundant east

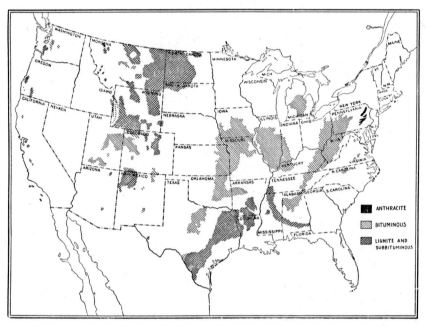

Figure 236. Map of coal areas of the United States, showing that the better ranks of coal are of more importance in the eastern half of the country. (U.S. Geological Survey.)

of the Great Plains; the lignites occur in the greatest quantity in the Far West, the northern Great Plains, and the Gulf Coast States.

In many areas the coal beds, as now found, lie level; in others they are tilted and sometimes bent into folds, a condition characteristic of the anthracite region.

MINING OF COAL

The mere fact that a bed of coal is present in the rocks is no guarantee that it is worth working, for to produce coal at a profit depends on several things: (1) the thickness of the bed, which should be not less than 15 inches for high rank coals like anthracite and 3 feet for lignite; (2) the depth of mining; about 3,000 feet is set as the extreme depth for any kind; (3) the purity of the coal; an impure coal may need cleaning before shipment to market, and to balance the cost of this, that of mining should be reduced as much as possible; and (4) the amount of waste in mining.

COAL RESERVES

The wide distribution of coal beds in the United States naturally leads us to think that the supply must be enormous. Calculations made by experts indicate that the coal deposits of the United States contained originally something over 3,000,000,000,000 short tons. This included all coal lying within 3,000 feet of the surface, and having a minimum thickness of 14 inches for bituminous coal, 2 feet for sub-bituminous, and 3 feet for lignite.

At the beginning of 1944, what was left was calculated as follows: [1]

Net tons

Bituminous	1,329,984,000,000
Subbituminous	817,996,000,000
Lignite	936,460,000,000
Anthracite	15,727,000,000

Of the first three there is probably enough to last nearly 3,400 years, at a yearly production of 600,000,000 tons. The reserves of anthracite are calculated to last 100 years at a current rate of 60,000,000 tons.

These figures do not, however, tell the whole story, because, in the first place, the total amount of coal mined annually in the last few years has not shown a tendency to increase greatly, partly at least because of competition with oil and natural gas. This might, therefore, defer the date of exhaustion of our supplies.

Against this is the fact that we cannot get 100 per cent of a coal deposit out of the ground, for there is an appreciable loss in mining. Some years ago a commission which made a special study of this question found that in our eastern states the average loss in mining was about 35 per cent, of which 15 per cent might be avoided. This loss resulted from leaving coal in the ground because of careless mining, or leaving pillars of coal to prevent the mine workings from caving in. In some cases it became necessary to leave considerable coal in the ground

[1] *Mineral Resources of the U.S.,* p. 84.

to prevent settling of the surface and thus endangering buildings. There has been much trouble from settling in some of the Pennsylvania anthracite fields.

COMPETITION IN THE COAL INDUSTRY

The coal industry has sometimes been considered an ailing one. We can easily understand that in times of prosperity, when manufacturing and allied industries are active, there will also be a great demand for coal, and many mines will be started to meet the demand. But when business drops off, and the demand for coal falls with it, there are more mines than are needed, and they naturally have a hard time making money. Add to this the increasing competition of oil and gas with coal, and it is not difficult to understand why the coal mining industry is unhappy. Coal mining recently has been seriously interfered with by strikes.

There is still another difficulty. The coal producer will work only his best beds of coal, taking out all he can of them. This may mean a caving of the ground, breaking up other overlying, less pure although workable, beds of coal, which are practically ruined for future working. This amounts to the same thing as destroying some of our reserves.

CONSERVATION OF OUR COAL SUPPLIES

The mere statement that our reserves of coal are sufficient to last several thousand years should not mislead us.

As already mentioned, not all of the coal in the ground can be saved, and much of that included in the estimated reserves is of quality that is not marketable at present. Furthermore, a large portion of our reserves consists of coals of a lower rank, like lignite and subbituminous coals. In addition to this, that coal will be mined in the greatest quantities which is nearest to the markets, because this means a shorter freight haul to the points where it is used.

In other words, we find that the greatest consuming markets for coal are east of the Mississippi and Missouri Rivers, because that is the region which is thickly settled and has many centers of industry. Studies of statistics show us that the coal fields of this region supply over 90 per cent of the country's present output of coal but contain only about 34 per cent of its reserves. We can therefore assume that with such conditions, the long years of life mentioned on page 471 do not hold true.

As the coal beds of the eastern part of the country become worked out, we must turn to the West for more of this mineral fuel. That, however, means using inferior fuel and paying increased freight rates, as a result of which coal might cost us twice as much as now.

We are at present mining the cream of our supplies. The exhaustion of certain varieties may come at no very distant date in the future.

It should be clear that large as our coal reserves are, they are not inexhaustible, and every legitimate effort should be made to make our supply last as long as possible. There are several ways in which this may be accomplished:

(1) *By less waste in mining.* As already stated, when prices are good and the demand is great, more waste is likely to occur. This is difficult to stop by law, but it is possible if the coal underlies government-owned (public) lands. Then, if mining privileges are leased by the government, it can control mining methods. According to the United States Geological Survey records of September 1, 1947, the area in the public-land states that has been formally classified as coal land aggregates 34,924,529 acres, and there is an additional 24,008,480 acres in such states under federal withdrawal awaiting examination and classification for coal. It is estimated that the United States owns between 55 and 60 per cent of the coal reserve here involved, with title to the remainder vested in various land-grant railroads, states, Indian tribes or allottees, and agricultural entrymen, and in numerous individual and corporate purchasers who acquired title prior to February 25, 1920.

According to the June 1, 1946, statistics, the segregated coal lands of the Choctaw and Chickasaw Indians in Oklahoma aggregated 377,-443 acres, of which 31,482 acres were currently under lease or mining permits for coal development.

(2) *By cleaning the coal after it is mined and before it is shipped to market.* In anthracite beds, for example, there may be thin layers of shale (called slate); many lumps coming from the mine are mixtures of coal and slate which could not be used as mined. With the use of modern methods (Fig. 237), these lumps are crushed, and the coal is separated from the slate, thus increasing the amount of marketable product. Bituminous coal may also be cleaned. Such concentration also saves paying freight on impurities in the coal.

In the past, much coal of small size was washed into the streams in the preparation of anthracite. Now the greater part is caught in the coal preparation plant. From 1909 to 1940, inclusive, about 17,-500,000 net tons of this were recovered by dredging, and in 1945 over 1,000,000 short tons were recovered. Here is an interesting example of conservation.[2]

(3) *By coking.* Many coals, on being heated out of contact with the air, lose certain compounds, and there is left behind a hard, porous mass called coke, which can still be used as fuel. In former years all

Figure 237. Anthracite coal breaker. In this the coal is crushed to different sizes and freed from the associated "slate." This breaker can treat 10,000 tons of coal in seven hours. (Philadelphia and Reading Coal Company.)

of the volatile matter driven off by the heat was allowed to escape into the air. In recent years coke ovens (called *by-product ovens*) have been constructed which save these by-products for the market. These products include tar products, oil, illuminating gas, ammonia gas, and other gaseous compounds.

Some idea of the size of the coking industry is gained from the fact that in 1946 the United States produced 58,497,848 short tons of coke, valued at about $486,729,382. Of this, 92.2 per cent was made in by-product ovens, and the total value of the by-products saved was about $173,000,000.

[2] U.S. Bureau of Mines, *Information Circular,* 7213 (1942).

Unfortunately the by-product coke industry has met with some obstacles. Formerly, much of our gas for lighting and heating purposes was made from coal, but in recent years coal has been unable to compete with natural gas, which, as mentioned on page 490 may be piped many miles to the market. Competition also comes from natural oil, and, finally, there must be a market for the coke.

(4) *By greater saving in the use of coal.* Much coal is used for power by the companies generating electricity. The less coal that must be used to generate a given quantity of electricity, the more saving will be accomplished. Thus, a few years ago it took something over 5 pounds of coal to generate 1 kilowatt hour of electricity, whereas later this was reduced to 1.7 pounds or even less, through increased efficiency of boiler plants.

(5) *By proper combustion.* Everyone is familiar with the fact that in some communities where soft or bituminous coal is used, the chimneys pour out great volumes of smoke which settles as a blanket over the town. This smoke means that unburned coal is lost. How much saving of fuel could be made if this were all burned is not difficult to imagine. If more attempts were made to burn the coal properly, there would be a tremendous saving of fuel. It is said that in some large heating plants where automatic stokers are used the fuel loss has been reduced from 50 to 70 per cent. Some communities have also passed laws to stop this smoke nuisance.

(6) *Prevention of fires.* Fires are sometimes started in mines from one cause or another, and some coal beds are fired by lightning. Such fires have occurred in different parts of the country and attract attention by their spectacular character, but the total amount of coal lost is relatively unimportant.

(7) *By legislation.* One step in this direction was the passage by Congress of the Guffey Coal Act, which created a Federal Coal Commission. This has the power to stabilize production, prices, and labor conditions. The object of the bill is partly conservational.

THE FUTURE OF COAL

Much of what is to happen will depend on the use of oil, natural gas, and water, which compete with coal as sources of power. The figures of production show that in the period from about 1880 to 1935, there was a great rise in the use of all of these, but that, since 1913, the use of coal has not increased so rapidly as that of oil and gas. There seems little hope for increased use of coal until our supplies of oil and gas begin to give out; but, according to one authority, the fact that coal is our cheapest fuel will always help it to keep its place in industry.

A hope for the future lies in the fact that by putting coal through a process called hydrogenation, liquid fuels like oil can be extracted from it. This is now done in some countries which lack oil, but it is not practical to do so in the United States at present. If the time comes when this is necessary, we shall find an abundant reserve of coal to supply our needs for this purpose.

CHAPTER XVII

Petroleum
and Natural Gas

PETROLEUM and natural gas are two mineral products of the greatest importance in our daily life. Natural gas is widely employed for heating purposes in stationary heating plants. Oil, whose chief use is as a fuel, is employed in factories, ships, locomotives, automobiles, and airplanes, and the oil burner is now widely used for domestic heating. Petroleum is also employed for lubrication and to a considerable extent for lighting. In addition, petroleum and its products are used in vast quantities for destroying insects that attack plants. It is mixed with rubber to make automobile tires, increasing their mileage, and it has many other uses. At present it is particularly important in the manufacture of synthetic rubber. It is indeed alarming to contemplate what we should do without petroleum, and, because it is so important, every effort should be made to conserve our supplies.

DISCOVERY, ORIGIN, AND DISTRIBUTION

Oil—*crude oil,* it is called—coming from the well is of little use except for oiling roads. Crude petroleum is made up of a number of different compounds of hydrogen and carbon. Some of these are very volatile at ordinary temperatures, and, although dissolved in the petroleum below ground, evaporate from it readily on exposure to air. If the petroleum is heated to successively higher temperatures, other compounds are driven off, until finally there is left behind a solid residue, which is asphalt, paraffin, or in some cases, a form of coke. The major products obtained in the refining process are petroleum coke, fuel oil, lubricating oil, kerosene, and gasoline.

The separation of these products is accomplished in the refinery. In the refineries at present operating in the United States more than

4,000,000 barrels a day can be treated. By the modern refining process some of the petroleum compounds can be broken down or *cracked,* and new ones made. By this means, for example, a larger quantity of gasoline may be obtained from a given oil than it contains naturally. Egloff says that "the cracking process is the greatest force for conservation that has developed in the oil industry."

A number of different grades of oil are obtained from the crude petroleum by refining. These different grades are used for different purposes. The gasoline that we use in our automobile is a very light oil. Kerosene, still used in considerable quantities for oil lamps in spite of the widespread use of gas and electricity, is also a light oil, but slightly heavier than gasoline. Still heavier is the oil with which we lubricate machinery and that which we burn in an oil burner.

The oils obtained from different areas are not all the same, some being of high specific gravity and others of low specific gravity, but in no case is the oil heavier than water. The crude petroleum obtained from wells in Pennsylvania and other eastern states contains a high percentage of the lighter oils. Much of that from Texas and Louisiana, on the other hand, contains a smaller proportion of the lighter oils, but a larger percentage of the heavier ones.

Discovery of petroleum. In 1859 when Colonel Drake drilled a well in western Pennsylvania and, at a depth of 69 feet, struck oil-bearing rock which yielded 20 barrels a day to the well, he little suspected that this discovery represented the beginning of one of our greatest industries.

Up to the time of the discovery of oil, illumination was obtained largely from candles and whale-oil lamps. What kerosene was available was made by the distillation of coal. All these fuels were largely replaced by kerosene from oil.

In refining the oil to make kerosene, the refiners obtained a byproduct called gasoline, which if not separated from kerosene, was likely to cause explosions in kerosene lamps. At first this gasoline was allowed to go to waste. About 1886, however, an engine was invented that could use gasoline as fuel, a use that has revolutionized the transportation industry.

Origin of petroleum and natural gas. When they think of oil and gas, most persons think of them as lying imprisoned in the rocks in what are often called pools, ready to rise to the surface when tapped by wells.

Few pause to consider what complicated natural processes have been at work to produce these two valuable mineral products. Millions of years ago low forms of plants like seaweed became buried in the mud of ancient seas. As this buried plant material decayed, it was converted into compounds like those found in petroleum and natural gas. The muds in which this change took place are called the source beds, and it is from these that the oil and gas have moved into the porous rocks (reservoirs or pools), particularly sandstone, where they are now found by the drill. This, however, does not tell the whole story. It is necessary that the oil- and gas-bearing rocks have certain structures which form a trap to catch and hold these two materials. Such a structure may often be an archlike fold, near whose crest the oil and gas accumulate, but other varieties of structure may serve the same purpose. Should the rocks be cracked all the way to the surface, the oil and gas may escape upward, thus disclosing their presence, but in most cases this condition does not exist.

In some oil districts of California, the oil is found oozing out at the surface; these oil springs are called seeps. At one place within the city limits of Los Angeles the thick seepage oil collected in depressions years ago, and in these tar bogs many animals of kinds no longer living were caught. Their bones have been preserved in the thick tarry oil.

The fact that oil and gas are found only in certain kinds of rock should save much money in useless search for them. Since, however, these reservoir beds may lie deep below the surface, it becomes impossible at times to determine the existence of the characteristic structures from surface observations, and delicate instruments are used to detect the arrangement or position of the rocks at considerable depths. In some cases the underground structure can be inferred by the use of electrical methods, in which the passage of artificially produced electric currents through the rocks indicated their nature because different kinds react differently to these currents. In other cases a charge of dynamite is set off at some selected point. This causes vibrations to travel through the rocks below the surface. Some vibrations are reflected by certain kinds of rock and return to the surface, where they are detected and recorded by means of suitable instruments. Even the difference in gravity pull exerted by rock masses of varying size can be used to determine their position.

These *geophysical methods,* as they are called, are important. Many thousands of dollars are spent annually by the oil companies sounding out the formations underground in this way, and many a new oil or gas area has been found through this kind of exploration.

These methods are used not only on land but also beneath the water. Off the Gulf Coast there is a continental shelf, which extends 70 to 140 miles seaward and covers about 132,000 square miles and which may be underlain by oil-bearing structures. Estimates are that within a 31.4-mile offshore limit there may be reserves of 4 to 5 billion barrels of oil.[1] More than thirty possible structures have been indicated off the Louisiana coast in water not over thirty feet deep.[2]

Drilling wells in the water is a costly process, but a number of operations are about to be started. One well eleven miles offshore is already producing. It has not yet been definitely decided whether these offshore operations will be under state or federal control.

Below the surface of the Coastal Plain which borders the Gulf of Mexico in Texas, Louisiana, and Mississippi, there occur huge dome-shaped masses of rock salt. They occur at varying depths below the surface, from perhaps one hundred to several thousand feet. The beds of soft rock are often bent up around them, and in these beds much oil has been found. The important fact is that, although the presence of these great salt masses may not be suspected from surface conditions, they have been detected by geophysical methods.

We hear much in popular literature about the use of divining rods and similar devices, referred to collectively as *doodle bugs,* to find oil and gas, or even other mineral deposits, but they are regarded by scientists as worthless. Scientific prospecting for oil, however, is of untold value, because unless new areas were discovered from time to time, our reserves would soon be exhausted. Even with scientific methods it is not possible to tell beforehand whether oil or gas is actually present, even though the rock structure may be favorable. Only the drilling of a well will determine this fact.

Distribution of petroleum and gas. A glance at the map, Figure 238, will show how widely petroleum and natural gas are distributed in the United States. However, these localities are grouped together in regions with nonproductive areas between. Within each region there are a number of separate districts. These districts may be still further subdivided into what are called pools.

---

[1] R. Spann, *Wall Street Journal,* May 24, 1948, p. 8.
[2] H. F. Beardmore, *Mining and Metallurgy,* 28: 96 (Feb., 1947).

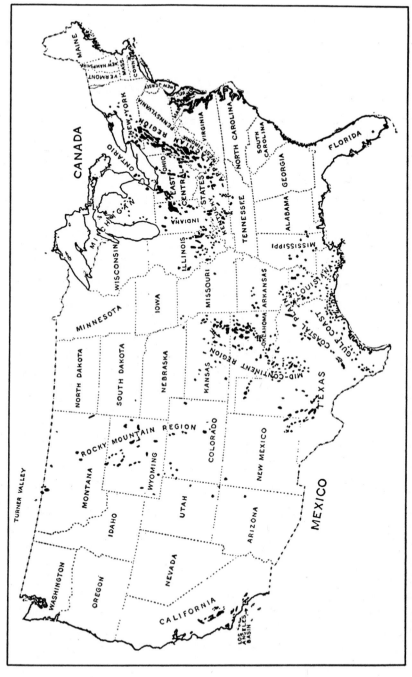

Figure 238. Map showing oil and gas fields of the United States. (Ries and Watson, *Elements of Engineering Geology*, 1947).

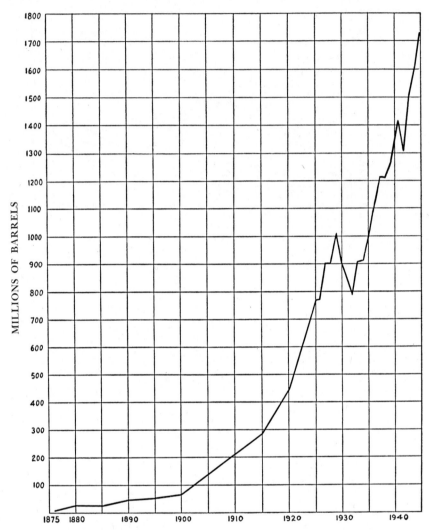

Figure 239. Graph showing production of petroleum in the United States from 1875 to 1946. (*Minerals Year Book.*)

The earliest developed of these regions was the Appalachian of the eastern states, which has consistently yielded oils of the lighter type as well as gas. It is, however, of much less importance as an oil producer than formerly. Of the twenty-nine states producing oil in 1945, California, Oklahoma, and Texas supplied over 70 per cent of that pro-

duced between 1859 and 1939, and these same three states now supply
about 71 per cent of the yearly output.

Natural gas occurs in most of the areas where oil is found, with

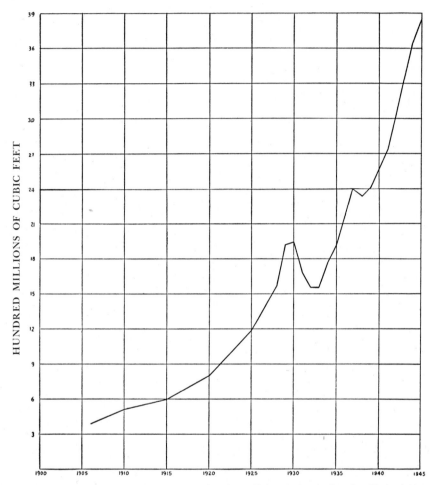

Figure 240. Graph showing production of natural gas in the United
States from 1906 to 1945. (*Minerals Year Book,* 1940, 1945.)

Texas, California, Louisiana, and Oklahoma yielding about 79 per
cent of the supply in 1945. Some wells yield only oil, others only gas,
but many oil wells yield gas in quantity in addition to the oil.

PRODUCTION AND RESERVES

Production of petroleum and natural gas. In the first year of oil production, it is said that 2,000 barrels were produced, but the quantity obtained annually has increased rapidly as is shown in Figure 239 and the following figures:

Years	Barrels
1859–1875	74,072,000
1876	9,133,000
1880	26,285,000
1890	45,824,000
1900	63,621,000
1910	209,557,000
1920	442,929,000
1930	898,011,000
1940	1,353,214,000
1945	1,713,655,000
1946	1,733,424,000

This country's production of crude petroleum in 1945 represented 65 per cent of the world's production. The United States in the same year imported 74,085,000 barrels of petroleum. Our imports of crude petroleum, residual fuel oil, and distillate fuel oil in 1945 came chiefly from Venezuela (85 per cent) and to a lesser extent from Colombia (11 per cent) and Mexico (3 per cent). Our consumption of oil in 1946 amounted to an average of 5,280,000 barrels per day, of which 4,745,-000 barrels were domestic, and the rest was from natural gasoline and crude oil imports.[3]

In 1944 there were in the United States 412,220 producing oil wells and an additional 14,297 were completed in 1945. The average yield per day in 1944 was 11.2 barrels, with a range of 0.4 to 106.3 barrels. The number of producing gas wells in 1944 was 52,780 with 3,227 completed in 1945. The number of dry holes drilled for either oil or gas in 1945 was 7,471.[4]

The production of natural gas in 1946 was 4,095,000,000,000 cubic feet.

Depth of petroleum or gas. The original Drake well in Pennsylvania was only 69 feet deep, but many producing wells are now several thou-

---

[3] Beardmore, *Mining and Metallurgy*, 28: 96 (Feb., 1947).
[4] *Minerals Yearbook,* 1945.

sand feet down. One in California, drilled as the result of geophysical exploration, is 11,302 feet (over two miles) deep, and has produced 1,400 barrels of oil per day. A newer one in California, 15,000 feet down, produced over 3,000 barrels daily from a depth of 13,000 feet.

Up to the beginning of 1947 the deepest producing well was one on Week's Island, Louisiana, which yielded oil at 13,778 feet. The deepest drilled hole in the world at that time, a dry one, was in Kern County, California, which was bottomed at 16,668 feet.[5]

Reserves of petroleum. With the yearly production of oil now running in the neighborhood of 1,000,000,000 barrels, the question of how long our supplies will last naturally arises.

Oil and gas reserves are more difficult to estimate than those of coal, which lies in well-defined beds. It is particularly difficult to make a calculation of reserves of gas, because much of it is associated with the oil and dissolved in it.

The American Petroleum Institute Committee on Petroleum Reserves in a special report estimated that the proved crude oil reserves on December 31, 1947, amounted to 21,487,685,000 barrels. The natural gas liquids totaled 3,253,475,000 barrels. This made a grand total of 24,741,610,000 barrels of liquid hydrocarbons. According to the committee, additions to the reserves since December 31, 1946, amounted to 705,000,000 barrels.

At the present rate of production this does not mean a long period of production unless new reserves are found.

The increase in reserves may be brought about in several ways: (1) by oil discoveries under improved portions of partly developed fields; (2) by oil discoveries under untested areas, of which there may be a number; (3) by the recovery of oil by means of secondary recovery methods in fields where such methods have not yet been employed; (4) by the recovery of oil through the processing of natural gas; (5) by obtaining oil from oil shale, coal, or other substitute sources; (6) by the discovery of potential areas, such as the continental shelf off the coast of the United States or the Arctic slope of Alaska. Already investigations are being made in this last direction (p. 480).

In California it was said that, for the first time in ten years, the 1937 discoveries of new oil reserves were greater than the annual production from that state. In southern Louisiana in the same year fifteen

---

[5] F. H. Lahee, *Bulletin of the American Association of Petroleum Geologists,* 31: 941 (1947).

new oil pools were discovered, and much oil is coming from depths of about 10,000 feet below the surface. It makes one wonder how much deeper man may drill for oil. This will probably be decided by the cost of such deep drilling and the engineering skill required to operate drills at such tremendous depths.

Quantity of petroleum recovered. Not all of the oil in the reservoir rock is extracted. One estimate regarding Pennsylvania is that probably 40 per cent of the oil is recovered.[6] The percentage of recovery varies in different parts of the country, and while it may be as low as 10 per cent in some cases, it is much higher in others. In one Texas field it is expected that it may reach 70 per cent. One thing is certain—with natural water drive and improved practice higher recoveries may be expected.

There are several ways in which recovery can be increased. One of these consists of forcing water or air into the exhausted sands. These drive the oil before them, and an additional quantity can be obtained. This was discovered accidentally some forty years ago in a Pennsylvania field, when surplus water flowed down an abandoned well and caused an increase in the production of the surrounding ones. The practice of flooding wells is allowed by special permission in the states of Pennsylvania, Texas, Kansas, and Oklahoma. In the Bradford field of Pennsylvania, the use of the watering process is said to have made available a reserve of some 600,000,000 barrels from an area that was about to be abandoned.

When oil-bearing rock is struck by the drill, the oil often rises to the surface and even overflows from the well. In some cases it rises with such force as to spurt high into the air. Such wells are called *gushers* (Fig. 241), and they may sometimes flow uncontrolled for several days, resulting in the loss of an enormous quantity of gas and often considerable quantities of oil.

One well drilled at Oklahoma City, Oklahoma, suddenly began to flow uncontrolled. It first blew gas, then oil spouted out until it reached an outflow of 1,000 barrels a day, while the volume of gas accompanying the oil was estimated at 100,000,000 cubic feet of gas a day. This wild well was not brought under control for eleven days.

The cause of this pressure is the gas which is imprisoned with the oil, and which tends to expand and force the oil out. The oil from different wells contains different amounts of imprisoned gas. The

---

[6] *Pennsylvania Mineral Industries Experiment Station, Bull. 45,* November, 1946.

greater the amount of gas, the greater the pressure, other things being equal. If too much of this gas is allowed to escape with the oil, it means a needless reduction of the pressure in the reservoir. Many oil companies attempt to prevent the escape of this gas. There is a law in California which limits the amount of gas that may be produced with each barrel of oil.

In some pools the gas is caught and forced back into the rocks to keep up the pressure. In other cases compressed air is forced down into the oil sand to force the oil out just as gas does. A third method consists of properly spacing the wells.

Since our oil reserves are limited, every effort should be made to save as much of the oil as possible.

Gas reserves. As was said before, it is very difficult to estimate our reserves of natural gas. Some of it is obtained from porous rock in which the gas occurs by itself, but according to the United States Bureau of Mines, about 55 per cent of the gas comes to the surface with oil. According to the Committee on Natural Gas Resources of the

Figure 241. A "gusher" oil well, Goose Creek Oil Field, Texas. The pressure of the gas in it caused the oil to rush to the surface when the drill penetrated the oil sand. This pressure is sometimes sufficient to throw out the heavy drilling tools. (Humble Oil Co.)

American Gas Association, the proved natural gas reserves as of December 31, 1947, amounted to 165,930,000,000,000 cubic feet. The total reserves of natural gas liquids, which include condensate from natural gasoline and liquefied petroleum gases, amounted, as stated on p. 485, to 3,253,475,000 barrels.

METHODS OF CONSERVATION

There are two ways of conserving our supplies of these two mineral products. One consists in making a greater recovery from the oil and gas fields, and the other depends on preventing loss of these materials between the well and oil refinery.

Spacing of wells. When a new oil pool is discovered, there is sometimes a tendency to put down an excessive number of wells placed close to each other, let us say less than 100 feet apart. In some pools

Figure 242. Huntington Beach Oil Field, California. Many of the derricks have now been replaced by pumps. (H. Ries.)

they have been drilled so close together that the bases of the framework towers called derricks, used to lift and lower the drilling tools, almost touch each other (Fig. 242).

The bad effects of this are twofold. First, the oil supply becomes exhausted in a much shorter time, and second, the excess production from a new pool being put on the market lowers the price per barrel and has a bad influence on the petroleum market, a thing that has happened several times in the United States.

Proper spacing of wells in order to give maximum production of oil and gas and lengthen the life of a pool, is a matter of the highest importance, and has already been made the subject of state laws by California, Texas, and Michigan.

Control of production. Not all of the oil or gas land in a given area may be owned by one company or one individual, and so unless there is some form of general agreement regarding spacing of wells, over-production and rapid depletion of the reserves may follow. If this were not done, intensive drilling on adjoining properties would soon exhaust the supply.

The term *unit production* is sometimes mentioned; the meaning is that if several companies own adjoining tracts of oil land, they agree to space the wells on their combined properties so as to give the best results and thus conserve the supply. This is usually done voluntarily, although it would be very desirable if it could be required by law. When unit production is agreed upon, the value of the oil or gas produced and sold is divided between the owners or lessees according to the acreage which they control.

Proration is another term used to indicate control of production. It means keeping down the production to a point where it will satisfy the needs of the consumer. If proration is country-wide, then each state, property, or pool is assigned an allowable amount of production, proportional to its share of the country's output.

There is no law governing proration, but it has been practiced voluntarily for about fifteen years in some states, as Texas, Oklahoma, Kansas, Michigan, Louisiana, and California. While there is a difference of opinion regarding its value, it certainly tends to prevent overproduction and thus controls the price of oil per barrel. In a sense it amounts to storing the oil underground until needed. An interesting case of what happens where proration is not practiced is that of Illinois. In 1937 this state ranked tenth in the list of producers, but in 1939 it was fourth, because of new production from new fields or deeper sands whose product could be marketed unrestrictedly. In 1945 it was sixth.

Abandonment of wells. In times of overproduction, many wells of small daily production may be abandoned; the piping lining the drill hole is pulled out, and thus the oil in the reservoir rocks is lost. This oil could have been saved by using improved equipment, although the cost of the equipment would have eaten up some of the profit from it. Also, a well shut down for a period is often a loss, because for various reasons it cannot be started up again.

Waste of gas. There is no doubt that there has been an enormous waste of natural gas in the United States. For many years little was done about it, but now those states in which it is produced have passed laws to prevent waste.

Much of this waste has come from oil wells because the companies seeking the oil have simply allowed the gas which issued with it to escape into the air. As a result of conservation laws in California, the waste of natural gas was reduced from 40 per cent in 1930 to 6 per cent in 1935. The gas issuing from the well with the oil, instead of being allowed to escape into the air, is caught by a special device called a *trap*.

One of the most glaring cases of gas waste, as pointed out by J. L. Rich in radio talks, occurred in the Texas Panhandle field. This is probably the largest gas field thus far discovered in the world. The gas is conducted through pipe lines to the cities of St. Paul, Minneapolis, Indianapolis, and Chicago, and these lines represent an investment of $200,000,000. At first much of the gas from this field was freed of its small gasoline content, and the gas allowed to go to waste. The original reserves of gas were estimated at 16,000,000,000,000 cubic feet, which would have been enough to supply the pipe lines mentioned above for fifty years, but it is maintained that, after five years, there is only sufficient gas left for a ten-year supply. Fortunately, the state of Texas now has passed laws to prevent such waste.

An interesting method of conservation, mentioned above, is the growing practice of returning natural gas to oil sands for the purpose of keeping up the pressure of the oil in the wells. Gas can also be stored in depleted natural reservoirs for future use.

Loss after leaving well. Evaporation and leakage of either oil or gas may take place at many points. It may begin at the well and continue in storage tanks, pipe lines, refineries, and even service stations. When we consider that there are over 360,000 miles of pipe lines in the United States [7] that are used to transport oil and its products as well as natural gas, we can see what a chance for loss there may be through leaky joints. Because of improved construction of these lines, however, losses have been greatly reduced. Refined gasoline can now be carried hundreds of miles through pipe lines with little loss; in fact, during

---

[7] American Petroleum Institute, *Petroleum Facts and Figures* (New York, 1947). It is practically impossible to show all the pipe lines on a small map. The reader is referred to a large map showing the principal crude oil, natural gas, and refined product pipe lines in the United States published as a supplement to the *Oil Weekly* of June 24, 1946.

recent years, gas pipe-line leakage has been reduced as much as 65 per cent.[8]

Ways to conserve our supplies of oil and gas, therefore, consist of increased recovery at the wells, and decrease of waste, which in the case of gas, especially, has been inexcusable. Efforts have been made by the states and the federal government to bring about agreements looking toward the conservation of our oil and gas resources. The plan of saving our supplies by unit production and proration, both previously referred to (p. 489), is an important conservation measure.

Purchase and lease of petroleum and gas lands. Companies producing oil and gas rarely purchase outright the land in a productive area, although a great many acres are actually owned by oil companies in California. Such purchases might be costly if drilling later proved that the territory yielded neither of the two substances sought. The commonest method is to lease the mineral rights from the property owner and pay him a royalty. This means that he is usually paid a definite percentage of the gross production from the wells.

Certain states like Oklahoma, Texas, and Louisiana own land which may be oil- or gas-bearing. These may be leased to oil or gas producers under certain conditions.

Large acreages of possible oil- and gas-bearing lands are also owned by the United States government. Prospecting permits may be issued for these, which require drilling within a certain time. If oil or gas is found, the lands can then be leased on a royalty basis. It is required that a certain number of wells be drilled to a specified depth within a given time. The Secretary of the Interior has the power, in the interest of conservation, to order stoppage of operations and production of oil and gas at any time that he thinks it desirable to do so.

There are 2,970,918 acres of oil and gas land under federal development leases, and about 135,474 acres under federal oil and gas permits, but it is not definitely known whether all of the latter contain oil and gas. Within Indian reservations, under government supervision, there are at present 2,076,445 acres under lease for gas and oil.

Competition. Oil and gas compete not only with each other, but with coal, manufactured gas, and water power. If we could shift to that material of which we have the greatest reserves, it would mean a saving.

---

[8] E. L. Rawlins and L. D. Work, U.S. Bureau of Mines, *Technical Papers,* 565 (Washington, 1935).

Natural gas is an excellent fuel, but oil can be used as a substitute in all stationary plants. Oil is not used as a fuel in its natural state; the lighter oils must first be extracted.

Conservation of oil may be accomplished by using coal as a substitute. Unfortunately perhaps, the greater convenience of using oil as fuel has caused many to turn to it from coal. However, the use of mechanical stokers in furnaces, and the fact that soft (bituminous) coal is practically smokeless if properly burned may restore coal to greater favor in the future.

FUTURE PROSPECTS

It is well to consider what will happen when our present supplies of oil and gas give out.

Several possibilities appear: discovery of new pools; mining of oil; imports of oil from foreign countries; oil from oil shale; oil from coal; oil from natural gas.

No predictions can be made regarding new discoveries, and as already said, the new pools found do not compensate for the withdrawals. The improved and scientific methods of prospecting, and the fact that in many areas new supplies are being found at greater depths than those hitherto reached, lead us to hope that our supply will last longer than estimated.

It has been suggested that when an oil well gives out, it might be possible to sink a shaft to the oil sand, run out tunnels from it, and let the oil remaining in the rocks drain into these.

Some have also advocated the possibility of drilling holes into bituminous coal beds and extracting the gas which they contain, and which sometimes is the cause of explosions in mines.

It may seem strange, but oil can be made from natural gas. A plant is being built near Brownsville, Texas, which can process 7,000,000 cubic feet of natural gas a day and produce about 5,000 barrels of gasoline plus 2,000 barrels of other liquid petroleum products.[9]

HELIUM

For many years balloons and airships have been filled with hydrogen, the lightest of all gases. This gas, however, is highly inflammable, and a great stride forward was made when helium, a gas which has

---

[9] W. Miller, *Mining and Metallurgy*, 28: 102 (Feb., 1947).

about 92 per cent of the lifting power of hydrogen, was found in small quantities in the natural gas of some western states.

Helium occurs in the atmosphere but in exceedingly small amounts. It is also found in natural gas at a number of localities, but in very small quantities. The only known sources of low-cost helium are a few gas fields in Texas, Kansas, and Colorado. The first of these has been under control of the United States government, and the other two are said to have been acquired by it recently. In order for helium to be commercially extractable, the natural gas should contain not less than 0.5 per cent of it. It is said to range from 0.9 to 2 per cent in the more important fields.

It is said that before World War I, not more than 10 to 15 cubic feet of helium had been extracted, but that up to 1921, the government plant at Fort Worth, Texas, had produced 2,300,000 cubic feet. Now five plants in Texas, New Mexico, and Kansas produce large amounts. The United States has produced 434,190,000 cubic feet of helium in the last six fiscal years. More than half of the 63,000,000 cubic feet of helium produced in 1946 was returned to underground storage at Amarillo, Texas.[10]

When we consider that a great dirigible like the *Macon* required 6,500,000 cubic feet of helium, and a smaller one, the *Shenandoah,* 2,000,000 cubic feet, we can understand what a large amount is needed, and that our supplies should be carefully guarded.

Helium changes to a liquid at the remarkably low temperature of minus 450 degrees Fahrenheit. Atmospheric air becomes a liquid at minus 312 degrees Fahrenheit. The treatment, therefore, consists of cooling the natural gas under great pressure to a tremendously low temperature at which everything except the helium is liquefied. It can then be separated, and the natural gas, freed of its helium, can be discharged into pipe lines and conducted to market.

CARBON DIOXIDE

Most gas wells produce natural gas, which burns readily, but occasionally a well is drilled which yields a noninflammable gas composed mostly of carbon dioxide. Several wells of this kind have been drilled in some of our western states.

Carbon dioxide is best known for its use in charging beverages like

---

[10] *Annual Report, Secretary of the Interior,* 1946 (Washington, 1946), p. 173.

ginger ale and pop. Dry ice is a product made by cooling carbon dioxide to a low enough temperature to make it freeze.

Ordinarily carbon dioxide is produced artificially, since most of the wells yielding it are rather far from the markets where the product can be sold. Some of the natural product, however, is utilized.

OIL SHALE

Oil shale is a shale rock, containing decomposed plant remains, which yields no oil to a well, but from which oil can be obtained by distillation. Such shales are known to exist in large amounts in some of our western states, but there is no attempt at present to develop them commercially as a source of petroleum for the reason that oil from a well can be obtained much more cheaply.

Estimates have been made that the oil shale reserves of the United States would yield approximately 98,000,000,000 barrels of oil.[11]

We have seen that in the old days before Colonel Drake's well was drilled, some oil was distilled from coal. More recently, processes have been developed to obtain gasoline and other oils from coals, but the process is still too costly to compete with oil drawn from wells.

As a final comparison between oil and gas on the one hand, and coal on the other, attention may be called to the fact that, although oil and gas made up 42 per cent of the mineral fuels used in 1935, they constitute less than 1 per cent of the total fuel reserve. This should serve as a warning to use them carefully and avoid waste.

---

[11] H. H. Hill, address before U.S. Chamber of Commerce, April, 1947.

CHAPTER XVIII

The Nonmetallic Minerals

UNDER this heading are included mineral substances of non-metallic character exclusive of coal and oil. Although not always so valuable per pound as the metals, many of these are nevertheless indispensable to industry. The value of those produced in the United States in any one year is considerable (p. 437). The nonmetallic resources include stone, sand, gravel, cement, lime, and clay, used largely as structural products; millstones, emery, garnet, diatomaceous earth, and tripoli, employed for grinding or polishing; borax, gypsum, salt, potash, phosphate, asbestos, graphite, magnesite, mineral pigments, and other commodities.

Some of these nonmetallic resources occur in inexhaustible quantities; but others are found in only limited amounts, and our supplies of them should be carefully conserved. There are still others for our supply of which we are largely dependent on foreign sources.

NONMETALLICS USED CHIEFLY FOR STRUCTURAL PURPOSES

Building stone. The rocks used for building include granite, limestone, sandstone, marble, and slate.

The building-stone industry, except in the case of stone for special uses, such as monumental and decorative stone, has met with much competition in recent years. Thus, ordinary blocks of cut stone, such as are used in walls, have had to compete with concrete.

Granite. This is one of our most valuable building stones, being widely used for monumental, structural, and decorative purposes, as, for example, in polished columns. It is a widely distributed stone, being found in the eastern states as well as in Texas, Missouri, Wisconsin, the Rocky Mountain region, and the Pacific Coast states. Some of these areas are far removed from important markets and hence not so actively worked at the present time.

In the working of granite, there is a variable amount of waste. Some of this can be sold for crushed stone, but the demand for it is not so great as the demand for waste from other stones because, on account of its greater toughness, it is harder to crush. Nevertheless, in 1946 this country produced 10,584,260 short tons of crushed granite.

A competitor of granite is architectural terra cotta made of fired clay.

Limestone. This is one of our most widespread building stones. It is to be found in many states in unlimited amounts. Certain types, like a

Figure 243. A large limestone quarry in eastern Pennsylvania, which supplies rock for the manufacture of Portland cement. (H. Ries.)

limestone quarried near Bedford, Indiana, are shipped all over the United States.

The refuse from limestone quarries can be used for crushed stone and lime; in fact, certain deposits may be worked entirely for this purpose. In a way, therefore, quarrying of limestone may have less loss than that of other kinds of rocks. The crushed-limestone industry used 134,213,340 short tons in 1946. Since much limestone not suitable for buildings may be used for other purposes (Fig. 243), large supplies are available. Much limestone is used in the manufacture of Portland cement.

Sandstone. This rock, like limestone, occurs in inexhaustible quantity, and the refuse from the quarries can also be sold for crushed stone. However the output is less than that of limestone. Many quarries can be opened to serve as local sources of supply, although one area in northern Ohio supplies material for the building industry all over the country. It is in these quarries that we see an interesting case of conservation, for here the stone is cut up into blocks (channeling process)

Figure 244. A sandstone quarry, South Amherst, Ohio. The stone is cut in blocks by channeling machines. Horizontal ledges indicate thickness of blocks. (Cleveland Quarries Company.)

by means of special machines (Fig. 244). This process avoids the waste that might occur if the stone were blasted out with dynamite.

Marble. This is a form of limestone which has been recrystallized by nature's forces. Many marbles take a high polish, and this, together with their color, may make them of value for decorative purposes. The chief domestic supply is obtained from our eastern states, notably Vermont, Tennessee, and Georgia; but most of the highly decorative, brightly colored marbles, so much used for interior decoration, come from foreign countries.

The supply of white and gray marble is large, and probably is in little danger of exhaustion for some time. It is also conserved by the use of the channeling process.

Figure 245. A Vermont marble quarry. The channeling machines in the bottom of the quarry cut out blocks of the marble, which are then removed to the mill for finishing. (Vermont Marble Company.)

Although most marble quarries are open pits (Fig. 245), some are worked as great underground chambers, where pillars of the stone are left to support the overlying formations.

Slate. This is unique among the building stones, because of its peculiar property of splitting into thin sheets. That which splits best can be employed for roofing, a familiar use; but other portions which do not cleave so thin are used for table tops, sinks, switchboards, and stair treads.

A matter of some concern is that, in slate quarrying, there is at least 60 per cent waste material (Fig. 246).

Slate granules and flour in recent years supplied a use for slate not usable for millstock. The granules, of which 513,780 short tons were

Figure 246. Dump heap of a slate quarry. This shows the huge piles of waste rock that accumulate at many slate quarries. No use has been found for much of it. (H. Ries.)

sold in 1946, are used chiefly in surfacing prepared roofing. The flour, recovered chiefly as a by-product in the granule industry, is employed as a filler in road-asphalt surface mixtures, paints, roofing mastic, linoleum, etc. The production of flour in 1946 was 149,740 short tons.[1]

Most of our slate supply comes from Vermont, New York, and Pennsylvania. Trouble in the slate industry is not so much because of a lack of reserves, but because of competition with other roofing materials such as metal sheeting, or tiles of fired clay, of cement, or of asbestos composition.

---

[1] *Minerals Yearbook,* 1946.

Sand and gravel. Those required for ordinary construction work, as in the mixing of concrete or mortar, are to be found in great quantities in many parts of the country, and some single deposits are large. Those sands which are used for making glass must be high in silica and are not so abundant, and those employed for molds (called *molding sands*), in which molten metal is cast, are likewise not to be found everywhere. We do not have to be worried about our supply of most sands.

Clay. This is another structural material widely used for the manufacture of brick, tile, and sewer pipe. There are inexhaustible supplies

Figure 247. A kaolin mine in North Carolina. The white clay is freed of its sand by washing and then shipped to potteries for use in the manufacture of white china. (J. L. Stuckey.)

of it, which are being actively worked. The greatest development is in the eastern half of the country. We need have no concern about our supply's running short.

Almost equally abundant are those clays which resist a high degree of heat and are used for making fire bricks to line furnaces for melting metals, glass, and other products.

Not so abundant, however, are the white clays (Fig. 247) which are used for making white china and white tile, electrical porcelain, and as a paper filler. These are obtained almost exclusively from the southeastern states and occur in limited quantities as compared with the others. Some of them have to be purified for the market. In recent years this refining process has undergone great improvements, which have enabled domestic white clays to compete more successfully with similar clays imported from England. The result is that there has been a marked decrease in the quantity imported.

NONMETALLICS FROM OCEANS AND SALINE LAKES

Few persons realize how much we owe to the oceans past and present for certain supplies of minerals. They think of the ocean as con-

Figure 248. A plan of the underground workings of a salt mine at Retsof, New York. This was printed over an airplane view of New York City to show the extent of the mine workings. There are 119 miles of workings in this mine. (International Salt Co.)

taining merely salt in solution; but it has, in addition, small yet important amounts of gypsum, potash, bromine, magnesium, and other materials. In all the oceans of the world the quantity of dissolved minerals is enormous.

Not all of the substances dissolved in ocean water are equally soluble. In other words, a given volume of ocean water can hold a much larger amount of one substance in solution than it can of another. To illustrate, a large amount of sugar can be dissolved in a glass of water, but only a very small amount of plaster of Paris. If in this glass of water we dissolve as much of each of these two substances as possible, when the water evaporates the one which is least soluble will separate out first and the more soluble last. The same thing happens if a basin of ocean water evaporates. Gypsum, the compound of lime and sulfur, would separate out first, then common salt, and finally the most easily soluble compounds like those of potash. So it is that at different places in the rocks of the earth's crust, we sometimes find deposits of these

Figure 249. Searles Lake, California. The salt which fills this great depression contains common salt, potash salts, and borax. The brine in the deposit is pumped to the works on the farther side of the lake, where the borax and potash are separated from it. (American Potash and Chemical Corporation.)

materials that were formed from the evaporation of ancient seas millions of years ago.

Great Salt Lake in Utah is an inland body of salt water, about eight times as salty as the modern ocean, but it has not yet evaporated enough to cause the common salt which it contains to separate out. Other less soluble materials have been precipitated.

In some parts of the desert region of the West, we find the beds of former salt lakes which have dried up completely and left behind a crust of different substances formerly dissolved in the water (Fig. 249).

In many regions where beds of rock represent layers of sand and mud which settled out on the bottom of ancient oceans existing millions of years ago, there lie, between these, beds of materials which were formerly dissolved in the old ocean waters. They include deposits of rock salt, gypsum, potash, and sometimes phosphate.

Salt. Few, probably, realize the value of salt to industry. It is estimated that about 33,000,000 metric tons were produced in the world in 1944. In 1946 some 15,000,000 short tons came from the United States.

The salt used in chemical industries of the United States in a year amounts to about two-thirds of the annual production. Among the uses may be mentioned the bleaching of cotton and paper, soap making, and glass manufacture. The chlorine obtained from salt is used in the manufacture of lacquer and metal work for automobiles and in making ethyl gas. This does not mean that salt enters into the composition of these products in all cases, but it is, at least, necessary in the process of producing them. Much salt is now used in sand-gravel roads for laying dust and hardening the surface. Table and other household uses took about 680,000 tons in 1945.

With such an enormous demand for salt, there might be some fear that our supply would give out, but it seems inexhaustible. Like oil and natural gas, the salt does not always show on the surface. It is often found as deposits of massive salt—rock salt—in rocks many feet below the surface. These rock salt beds were formed by the evaporation of ancient seas millions of years ago. This salt is often obtained from the deposits by dissolving the salt in water passed down through wells. The brine formed is then pumped to the surface, where it is evaporated to get the salt. In some places (Fig. 250), a shaft is sunk to the salt, and the latter is mined like coal or ore.

Where salt is obtained by evaporating sea water as is done on San Francisco Bay (Fig. 251), that portion of the water which remains after the salt separates out is piped off to factories where bromine and magnesium are separated from it. Formerly this liquid was allowed to run back into the bay, and these materials were lost. The additional products conserved in this manner have an annual value of more than $750,000.

Gypsum. Plaster of Paris is a well-known commercial product, being used for wall plaster and many other purposes. It is obtained by heating gypsum rock to 400 degrees Fahrenheit. This process converts the rock into plaster of Paris, which sets to a hard mass when mixed with water. In 1945 about 2,485,000 short tons of calcined gypsum were produced in the United States.

Gypsum is found in a number of states, but over 50 per cent of the

Figure 250. View in mine of Avery Salt Company, Avery Island, Louisiana. The huge pillars are solid rock salt left to support the overlying rock. (H. A. Costain Studio.)

annual production is contributed by Michigan, New York, Iowa, California, and Texas. In 1946, 5,629,000 short tons of it were produced in the United States. Since many of the deposits are inland, much material from eastern Canada is shipped by boat to our eastern seaports, the quantity in 1945 being 548,697 short tons. The domestic supplies are larger, however.

Potash. As mentioned on page 141, this is an important plant food, and the value of the potash salts sold in the United States in 1945 was not far from $30,000,000. Since it is such a valuable material for agriculture, we can well be concerned regarding our supply.

Potash was originally obtained by dissolving it out of wood ashes. This was done by boiling the ashes in large pots, hence the name pot ashes, or as we call it, potash.

Potash salts are found in sea water with common salt, but they are

Figure 251. Salt ponds on San Francisco Bay, California. In these the sea water from the bay is evaporated by the heat of the sun. The white material is salt, and the conveyor belt in foreground carries it to the stock piles. (H. Ries.)

more soluble. If we can imagine the waters of an ancient sea evaporating, we can understand that both the salt and the potash will be left behind. But since the potash is more soluble than the salt, the latter will be precipitated first, and the former on top of it. Somewhat the same thing might happen if a lake in the desert region evaporated, providing both materials were present in its water.

We have many deposits of rock salt in the United States, but the only places where potash has been found in association with them, and that have been developed are in New Mexico and Texas. Other sources of natural potash at present are Searles Lake in California, and Utah.

In Germany and some other European countries, however, large supplies of potash are associated with rock salt. The German mines have been actively worked for a number of years; much of the product was exported to the United States.

When World War I broke out in 1914, the European supply was shut off, and we had to content ourselves with what could be obtained from different localities, most of which were not important and could not compete with sources of foreign potash after the war was over.

Figure 252. View in a potash mine, New Mexico. The material between roof and floor is potash salts. A mechanical loader is used for filling the mine car shown at the left. (United States Potash Company.)

About this time, the New Mexico deposits were discovered in drilling for oil, and they are now being mined (Fig. 252). This is fortunate because the German, French, Spanish, and Polish producers, after World War I, formed a selling organization to keep up prices. At present, the American deposits are supplying a large part of our needs, and it has been demonstrated that if necessary they can satisfy them completely.

The potash industry of New Mexico is under federal and state control. This means that the present known deposits are mostly on state and federal lands and are operated under leases given by the state or federal government. This is desirable, for it prevents such overdevelopment as has been the case in Germany. The estimates are that the area contains over 100,000,000 tons of potash salts, an amount which is sufficient to last the United States for some years.

One difficulty is that the location of our sources of supply in the Far West means a high freight rate to eastern markets, which can be reached more cheaply by foreign producers.

Bromine. Many persons may not have heard of bromine, but they have heard of ethyl gasoline, of which it is a constituent. The manufacture of ethyl gasoline consumes most of the production of bromine. Bromine is also used for other purposes, particularly in medicine and photography. It is found in small amounts in sea water, and for some years it has been obtained from wells drilled down to ancient sandstone formations which contain salt water in their pores. This represents ancient sea water which was imprisoned between the sand grains when they settled on an old ocean bottom some millions of years ago.

The largest producers now are plants at Wilmington, North Carolina, and Freeport, Texas, where the bromine is extracted from sea water. Other sources of supply are salt wells in Michigan and other states, and the bitterns from the San Francisco Bay salt works.

The bromine and bromine compounds sold or used by producers in the United States amounted to about 43,000,000 pounds in 1946, and to about 78,000,000 pounds in 1947.

Phosphate. Here we have another mineral compound, phosphate of lime, which is of great value to agriculture as a fertilizer. The phosphate rock is not, as a rule, ground up and placed directly on the soil, but by treatment with acid is converted into superphosphate, in which form it is more soluble.

Unlike limestone, with which it is often associated, phosphate rock of commercial value is not found in many states. The earliest deposits worked were near Charleston, South Carolina; then later came the discovery and development of those in Florida (Fig. 253) which are very important. Still later, the deposits of Tennessee were developed, and last of all came the western ones in Idaho, Montana, and Wyoming.

The United States produces annually more phosphate rock than any other country of the world, the quantity in 1946 being 6,860,713 tons. It exported about 8 per cent of the production in 1945.

About 80 per cent of the annual domestic production goes into artificial fertilizers, and about 7 per cent is ground in its raw condition for direct application to the soil. The remainder is used chiefly for making the phosphorus employed in matches, rat poison, tracer bullets,[2] poisonous war gases, fertilizer filler, and stock and poultry feed.

Probably 95 per cent of the phosphate rock consumed in the United States is used east of the Mississippi River.

It is a little difficult to make an accurate estimate of the tonnage of reserves in this country. Mansfield has conservatively estimated that

Figure 253. Landpebble phosphate pit, South Pierce, Florida. The material is washed down by powerful streams of water and pumped to the washing plant where the phosphate pebbles are separated from the impurities. (American Agricultural Chemical Company.)

the phosphate reserves of the United States amount to not less than 13,000,000,000 long tons, of which 5,000,000,000 are credited to Florida. This is sufficient to last us for a long time at the present rate of production.[3] Waggaman,[4] on the other hand, makes an estimate of about 51,000,000 long tons, but includes deposits of a much lower grade.

While there are in the United States reserves (Fig. 254) sufficient to

---

[2] Bullets which are phosphorescent in flight.

[3] American Institute of Mining and Metallurgical Engineers, *Technical Publication,* 1208 (New York, 1939).

[4] *Chemical and Metallurgical Engineering,* 46: 66 (1939).

last us for many years, when the eastern supplies have given out the long freight haul from the West is bound to raise the price of phosphate unless importations begin from North Africa, which also contains extensive phosphate deposits. These latter find a ready market in Europe and have come into serious competition with exports from the United States. From the point of view of conservation this is desirable, as it keeps our most accessible supplies at home.

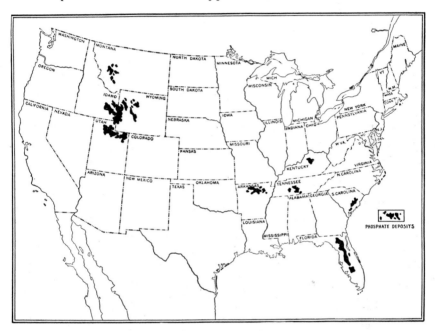

Figure 254. Map showing distribution of phosphate deposits in the United States. Note the extensive areas in the Far West which represent our greatest reserves. (U.S. Geological Survey.)

Borax. This substance is one with which everyone is familiar, for it has been extensively advertised as a cleansing material and preservative. In addition, however, it is used in the manufacture of glass, medicine, and flame-resisting paints; also for treatment of hard water and for fertilizer. Those who have read the advertisements have probably learned that it comes from desert regions, but few realize how it occurs. In many desert regions we have shallow salty lakes, which dry up easily and leave crusts of different salts in the soil. Such deposits formed also in the distant past and are now buried under other rocks.

In the desert region of the West, in California, and to some extent in

Nevada, there are a number of such deposits containing borax minerals. In addition there are underground deposits in California. At present, the United States supplies over 90 per cent of the world's production, about one-third of this being exported to other countries. Since, however, the actual reserves of this material are not known, the supply should be carefully guarded. The United States is the largest producer in the world, the production in 1947 being reported as 501,935 short tons.

MISCELLANEOUS NONMETALLICS

Sulfur. A most important nonmetallic element is sulfur. It is widely used for the manufacture of sulfuric acid, which, in turn, is employed in the manufacture of superphosphates and explosives, in refining crude oil, in sugar refining, and in other ways.

The sulfur itself is used in making matches, in medicine, in insecticides and fungicides, and as a fertilizer for some soils.

The United States' production in 1946 amounted to about 4,000,-000 long tons, with a value of about $16 per ton.

We ordinarily think of sulfur as being a substance given off by volcanoes. While this is a common source, the quantity so obtained at any one place is relatively small.

In the United States, probably 98 per cent of the supply is obtained from deposits found resting on huge buried domes of rock salt which lie beneath the surface in Texas and Louisiana. It is difficult to estimate the Texas-Louisiana reserves. These deposits have made the United States the world's largest producer, Italy being second. It has caused serious competition between the two countries, so that they have divided the world's markets between them.

Graphite. When we use a lead pencil, it probably does not occur to us that all the graphite, or *black lead* as it is sometimes called, has probably come from some foreign country. The United States contains many deposits of graphite, but while mine after mine has started up, hardly a one is now in operation because the American product has not been able to compete with the high-grade foreign product, and it was only during the last war that any of the domestic deposits could be worked. Even so, in 1946 the American deposits produced only 4,844 short tons. Thus, although we possess moderately abundant supplies of a needed material, they are practically useless to us. This is unfortunate, as the United States is one of the largest consumers of graphite. It is employed in pencils, as a lubricant, in paints, in electrical work, and in crucibles for melting steel, to mention only some of its uses.

Natural graphite, however, has to compete with artificial graphite, which is made from anthracite coal or coke in an electric furnace. The production of it has already become important, and where it can be used for the same purposes as the natural product, the manufactured one may serve to reduce the importation of foreign material. The imports of natural and artificial graphite in 1945 were 36,288 short tons. The domestic production is not published because of the small number of producers.

Mica. Mica is a mineral which is of special value in certain industries because of its property of splitting into very thin sheets, which are characterized by their great thinness, transparency, lack of color, flexibility, and nonconductivity of heat and electricity. The great difficulty lies in finding it in sheets of sufficient size and necessary purity.

Two important commercial varieties are known as muscovite and phlogopite. Deposits of value are found only in pegmatite dikes.

Mica is of great importance in the manufacture of electrical insulators, aircraft, autos, and radios. Hence it is most essential in war and is regarded as a strategic mineral.

Ground mica is also used in roofing, wallpaper, rubber, and paint.

Vermiculite (commercially known as zonolite) is used for insulation.

North Carolina and New Hampshire yield about 75 per cent of the domestic sheet mica, but we had to import some $7,000,000 worth in 1946, which is nearly seven times the domestic output. Our chief supply of muscovite comes from British India and of phlogopite from Madagascar.

Spark-plug materials. Everyone knows how important a good sound spark plug is for the successful operation of an automobile engine. A spark plug has the look of unglazed porcelain, but while originally this product was made from the same type of white clay that is employed for making ordinary porcelain, at present the mixture contains a large percentage of one of a group of peculiar minerals sometimes collectively referred to as *sillimanite*. This is not widely distributed in the United States; some is mined in California and Nevada, and the remainder in Virginia, Georgia, and South Carolina.

One spark plug does not require much raw material, but since the number of them made amounts to millions, the quantity of sillimanite required is very large. One company in the ten years from 1922 to 1932 produced 350,000,000 spark plugs.

Unless new deposits of the type mined in the West are discovered, we may eventually be forced to depend entirely on the eastern deposits, the mineral of which, although usable, possesses some features not so desirable.

Much kyanite, a mineral of the sillimanite group, is imported from India.

Asbestos. Asbestos is a most remarkable mineral of great commercial importance because of its long silky fibers. This enables it to be made into cloth, rope, and various textile products particularly valuable for their resistance to fire. For this reason it is used for theater curtains, suits for men exposed to heat, and, last but not least, automobile brake linings. This last use calls for an enormous quantity of asbestos. The shorter fibers are used for asbestos-cement shingles, boiler and pipe packing, and similar insulating purposes.

A large part of the domestic output of the variety known as chrysotile asbestos comes from Vermont, and some from Arizona. Amosite asbestos, a type used extensively for making high-temperature insulation, is obtained only in South Africa. A newly suggested use for this is as a substitute for kapok. Blue asbestos (crocidolite) comes chiefly from South Africa. Tremolite asbestos, used chiefly for filtering chemicals, is obtained from California and Alaska.

The United States in 1946 produced 14,075 short tons and imported 456,688 short tons. Unfortunately, we have not enough to supply more than about 3 per cent of our needs. All the rest, therefore, has to be obtained from foreign countries, particularly eastern Canada and Africa. The value of this imported material has recently amounted to about $16,000,000 each year.

Selections for Supplementary Reading

GENERAL

Chase, Stuart. *Richland, Poorland.* New York: McGraw-Hill Book Co., 1936.

Cheyney, E. G., and T. Schantz-Hansen. *This Is Our Land.* St. Paul: Webb Book Publishing Co., 1940.

Elliot, Charles N. *Conservation of American Resources.* Atlanta: Turner E. Smith and Co., 1940.

Florida, Department of Education. *Florida: Wealth or Waste?* Tallahassee, 1946.

Foundations of Conservation Education, The: Symposium. Washington: National Wildlife Federation, 1941.

Glover, Katherine. *America Begins Again.* New York: McGraw-Hill Book Co., 1939.

Holmes, H. N. *Strategic Materials and National Strength.* New York: Macmillan Co., 1942.

Mitchell, Lucy Sprague, Eleanor Bowman, and Mary Phelps. *My Country 'Tis of Thee.* New York: Macmillan Co., 1940.

National Resources Board Report. Washington: Government Printing Office, 1934.

Osborn, Fairfield. *Our Plundered Planet.* Boston: Little, Brown and Co., 1948.

Parkins, A. E., and J. R. Whitaker, editors. *Our Natural Resources and Their Conservation.* 2d ed. New York: Wiley and Sons, 1939.

Proceedings of a Conference of Governors in the White House. Washington: Government Printing Office, 1909.

Renner, George T. *The Conservation of National Resources.* New York: Wiley and Sons, 1942.

Report of the National Conservation Commission. Senate Document 671, vol. I, 60th Congress, 2d Session. Washington: Government Printing Office, 1909.

Van Hise, Charles Richard. *The Conservation of Natural Resources in the United States.* New York: Macmillan Co., 1910.

Van Hise, Charles Richard, and Louis Havemeyer. *Conservation of Our Natural Resources.* New York: Macmillan Co., 1930.

Vogt, William. *Road to Survival.* New York: Wm. Sloane Associates, 1948.

Wales, H. Basil, and H. O. Lathrop. *The Conservation of Natural Resources.* Chicago: Laurel Book Co., 1944.

Zon, Raphael, and others. *Conservation of Renewable Natural Resources.* Philadelphia: University of Pennsylvania Press, 1941.

CONSERVATION OF SOIL AND WATER RESOURCES

American Society of Agronomy, *Proceedings,* 1907–1912; *Journal,* 1913–.

Ayres, Q. C. *Soil Erosion and Its Control.* New York: McGraw-Hill Book Co., 1936.

Bear, F. E. *Soils and Fertilizers.* New York: Wiley and Sons, 1942.

——. *Theory and Practice in the Use of Fertilizers.* New York: Wiley and Sons, 1938.

Bennett, H. H. *Elements of Soil Conservation.* New York: McGraw-Hill Book Co., 1947.

——. *Soil Conservation.* New York: McGraw-Hill Book Co., 1939.

—— and W. R. Chapline. *Soil Erosion, a National Menace* (U.S. Department of Agriculture, Circular 33). Washington, 1928.

Burgess, Austin E. *Soil Erosion Control.* Atlanta: Turner E. Smith, 1936.

Collings, G. H. *Commercial Fertilizers.* Philadelphia: Blakiston Co., 1941.

Cox, Joseph F., and Lyman E. Jackson. *Crop Management and Soil Conservation.* New York: Wiley and Sons, 1937.

—— and Lyman E. Jackson. *Field Crops and Land Use.* New York: Wiley and Sons, 1942.

Ely, Richard T., and G. S. Wehrwein. *Land Economics.* New York: Macmillan Co., 1940.

Gaines, Stanley H. *Bibliography on Soil Erosion* and *Soil and Water Conservation* (U.S. Department of Agriculture, Miscellaneous Publication 312). Washington, 1938.

Gustafson, A. F. *Conservation of the Soil.* New York: McGraw-Hill Book Co., 1937.

——. *Handbook of Fertilizers.* 4th ed. New York: Orange Judd Publishing Co., 1944.

——. *Soils and Soil Management.* New York: McGraw-Hill Book Co., 1941.

——. *Using and Managing Soils.* New York: McGraw-Hill Book Co., 1948.

Hunger Signs in Crops: A Symposium. Washington: Judd and Detwiler, 1941.

Israelson, O. W. *Irrigation Principles and Practices.* New York: Wiley and Sons, 1932.

Kellogg, Charles E. *The Soils That Support Us*. New York: Macmillan Co., 1941.

Lord, Russell. *To Hold This Soil* (U.S. Department of Agriculture, Miscellaneous Publication 321). Washington, 1938.

Lyon, T. L., and H. O. Buckman. *The Nature and Properties of Soils*. New York: Macmillan Co., 1943.

McDonald, Angus. *Old McDonald Had a Farm*. Boston: Houghton Mifflin Co., 1942.

Millar, C. E. *Soils and Soil Management*. St. Paul: Webb Publishing Co., 1937.

—— and L. M. Turk. *Fundamentals of Soil Science*. New York: Wiley and Sons, 1943.

Peterson, Elmer T. *Forward to the Land*. Norman, Okla.: University of Oklahoma Press, 1942.

Sears, Paul B. *Deserts on the March*. Norman, Okla.: University of Oklahoma Press, 1935.

Soil Conservation, monthly publication of the U.S. Department of Agriculture, Washington, D.C.

Soil Science Society of America. *Proceedings, 1936—*.

Turrentine, J. W. *Potash in North America*. New York: Reinhold Publishing Co., 1943.

Van Dersal, W. R. *The American Land*. New York: Oxford University Press, 1943.

——. *Native Woody Plants of the United States, Their Erosion-Control and Wildlife Values* (U.S. Department of Agriculture, Miscellaneous Publication 303). Washington, 1938.

Wier, W. W. *Productive Soils*. 5th ed. Philadelphia: J. B. Lippincott Co., 1946.

——. *Soil Science*. Philadelphia: J. B. Lippincott Co., 1936.

Worthen, E. L. *Farm Soils*. 4th ed. New York: Wiley and Sons, 1948.

In addition many state experiment stations and extension services and the U.S. Department of Agriculture, especially the Soil Conservation Service, have published bulletins dealing with the management and fertilization of soils and the control of erosion. Many state conservation departments have published material dealing with the conservation of their water resources.

CONSERVATION OF FORESTS, PARKS, AND GRAZING LANDS

Allen, Shirley W. *An Introduction to American Forestry*. New York: McGraw-Hill Book Co., 1938.

American Forests, monthly publication of the American Forestry Association, Washington, D.C.

Boerker, Richard H. D. *Behold Our Green Mansions*. Chapel Hill, N.C.: University of North Carolina Press, 1944.

Butler, Ovid M. *American Conservation in Picture and Story*. Washington: American Forestry Association, 1935.

Cameron, Jenks. *The Development of Governmental Forest Control in the United States*. Baltimore: Johns Hopkins Press, 1928.

Forest Outings: A Symposium. Washington: Government Printing Office, 1940.

Forestry and Forest Products, World Situation 1937–1946. Report of Food and Agriculture Organization of the United Nations. Stockholm, 1946.

Graves, H. S., and others. *Problems and Progress of Forestry in the United States*. Report of Joint Committee on Forestry of the National Council and the Society of the American Foresters. Washington, 1947.

Harlow, William M., and Ellwood S. Harrar. *Text-Book of Dendrology; Covering the Important Forest Trees of the United States and Canada*. New York: McGraw-Hill Book Co., 1937.

Hawley, R. C., and P. W. Stickel. 2d ed. *Forest Protection*. New York: Wiley and Sons, 1948.

Illick, Joseph S. *An Outline of General Forestry*. New York: Barnes and Noble, 1936.

Ise, John. *The United States Forest Policy*. New Haven: Yale University Press, 1920.

James, Harlean. *Romance of the National Parks*. New York: Macmillan Co., 1939.

Lillard, Richard G. *The Great Forest*. New York: Alfred A. Knopf, 1947.

A National Plan for American Forestry (Senate Document no. 12, 73d Congress, 1st Session). Washington: Government Printing Office, 1933.

National Resources Board Report. "Forest Land Resources, Requirements, Problems, and Policy." Part VIII, Supplementary Report of Land Planning Committee. Washington: Government Printing Office, 1935.

Natural Resource Problems. Annual Report of the Secretary of the Interior. Washington: Government Printing Office, 1946.

Nature Magazine, monthly publication of the American Nature Association, Washington, D.C.

Proceedings of the American Forest Congress. Washington: American Forestry Association, 1947.

Pinchot, Gifford. *Breaking New Ground*. New York: Harcourt, Brace and Co., 1947.

A Reappraisal of the Forest Situation: Report 1, *Gaging the Timber Resource of the United States;* Report 2, *Potential Requirements for Timber Products in the United States;* Report 3, *The Land Management Status of Forest Lands in the United States;* Report 4, *Wood Waste in the United States;* Report 5, *Protection Against Forest Insects and Diseases in the United States;* Report 6, *Forest Cooperatives in the United States.* Washington: Government Printing Office, 1946–1947.

Robbins, Roy M. *Our Landed Heritage, the Public Domain.* Princeton: Princeton University Press, 1942.

Timber Shortage or Timber Abundance. Annual Report of the Chief of the Forest Service. Washington: Government Printing Office, 1946.

The Western Range (Senate Document 199, 74th Congress, 2d Session). Washington: Government Printing Office, 1936.

Yard, Robert S. *The Book of the National Parks.* New York: Charles Scribner's Sons, 1928.

—— *Our Federal Lands.* New York: Charles Scribner's Sons, 1928.

Yeager, Dorr G. *Your Western National Parks.* New York: Dodd, Mead and Co., 1947.

Numerous federal publications on the various aspects of conservation of forests, grazing lands, and parks are available from the Superintendent of Documents, Government Printing Office, Washington, D.C. Lists of titles can be obtained without charge. Many of the individual states, through their departments of conservation, colleges of forestry, and colleges of agriculture, have for distribution material dealing with the use and conservation of their forest resources. These organizations will supply available publications and motion picture films, usually free of charge. The American Forest Products Industries, of Washington, D.C., also makes available to schools maps, pamphlets, films, and other teaching materials on the subject of forest conservation.

CONSERVATION OF WILDLIFE

Allen, Arthur A. *The Book of Bird Life.* New York: D. Van Nostrand Co., 1930.

Anthony, H. E. *Field Book of North American Mammals.* New York: G. P. Putnam's Sons.

Audubon Magazine, bimonthly periodical of the National Audubon Society, New York, New York.

Beard, Daniel E. *Fading Trails.* New York: Macmillan Co., 1942.

Ditmars, Raymond L. *The Reptile Book.* New York: Doubleday, Doran and Co., 1933.

Facts—The Key to Progress (U.S. Department of Commerce, Bureau of Fisheries). Washington: Government Printing Office, 1938.

Fishery Resources of the United States (Senate Document 51, 79th Congress, 1st Session). Washington: Government Printing Office, 1945. (This is an excellent report. All university libraries should obtain a copy.)

Gabrielson, Ira. *Wildlife Conservation.* New York: Macmillan Co., 1942.

Gabrielson, Ira. *Wildlife Refuges.* New York: Macmillan Co., 1943.

Graham, Edward H. *The Land and Wildlife.* New York: Oxford University Press, 1947.

Grange, Wallace. *Winter Feeding of Wildlife on Northern Farms* (U.S. Department of Agriculture, Miscellaneous Publication 159). Washington, 1933.

Grosvenor, Gilbert, and Alexander Wetmore, editors. *The Book of Birds.* Washington: National Geographic Society, 1932. 2 vols.

Hamilton, W. J., Jr. *American Mammals.* New York: McGraw-Hill Book Co., 1939.

——. *The Mammals of Eastern United States.* Ithaca, N.Y.: Comstock Publishing Co., 1943.

Hornaday, William T. *Our Vanishing Wildlife.* New York: Charles Scribner's Sons, 1913.

Jordan, David S., and Barton W. Evermann. *American Food and Game Fishes.* New York: Doubleday, Doran and Co., 1934.

Journal of Mammalogy, quarterly publication of the American Society of Mammalogists, U.S. National Museum, Washington, D.C.

Journal of Wildlife Management, quarterly publication of the Wildlife Society, Columbus, Ohio.

Leopold, Aldo. *Game Management.* New York: Charles Scribner's Sons, 1933.

McAtee, W. L. *Game Management on the Farm* (U.S. Department of Agriculture, Farmer's Bulletin 1759). Washington, 1936.

——. *Groups of Plants Valuable for Wildlife Utilization and Erosion Control* (U.S. Department of Agriculture, Circular 412). Washington: 1936.

——. *Local Bird Refuges* (U.S. Department of Agriculture, Farmer's Bulletin 1644). Washington, 1937.

Nature Magazine, monthly publication of the American Nature Association, Washington, D.C.

Peterson, Roger Tory. *A Field Guide to the Birds.* Boston: Houghton Mifflin Co., 1947.

Pope, Clifford H. *Snakes Alive and How They Live.* New York: Viking Press, 1944.

Pough, Richard H. *Audubon Bird Guide.* New York: Doubleday, Doran and Co., 1946.

Transactions of the North American Wildlife Conference. Investment Building, Washington, D.C.

Walford, Lionel A. *Marine Game Fishes of the Pacific Coast.* Berkeley, Calif: University of California Press, 1937.

Many free publications on wildlife of the United States are available.

Others may be secured at small cost. Write the Superintendent of Documents, Washington, D.C., for a list of these publications.

The conservation department of your state will provide publications on wildlife. Many state colleges and universities also prepare information on wildlife for free distribution.

CONSERVATION OF MINERAL RESOURCES

Ashley, G. H. *A Syllabus of Pennsylvania Geology and Mineral Resources* (Pennsylvania Topographical and Geological Survey, Bulletin G-1). Harrisburg, 1931.

Bean, C. F., and C. K. Leith. *The University and Conservation of Wisconsin Minerals* (Bulletin of the University of Wisconsin 2253). Madison, 1937.

California's Natural Wealth. (Bulletin of the California State Department of Education, vol. 9, no. 4, December, 1940) .

Cawthon, W. S. *Minerals* (Course in Conservation of Natural Resources, Florida High Schools). Tallahassee, 1936.

DeMille, J. *Strategic Minerals.* New York: McGraw-Hill Book Co., 1947.

Egloff, G. *Earth Oil.* Baltimore: Williams and Wilkins Co., 1933.

Fanning, L. M. *Our Oil Resources.* New York: McGraw-Hill Book Co., 1945.

Hendricks, T. A., "Coal Reserves," ch. i, pp. 281–286. *Fuel Reserves of the United States* (House Document 160, 76th Congress, sec. 1, part 2). Washington: Government Printing Office, 1939.

Leighton, M. M. "Illinois Geological Survey Conserves and Develops State's Mineral Heritage," *Illinois Blue Book,* 1935–1936.

Leith, C. K. "Conservation of Minerals," app. 8, pp. 357–372. *Science Advisory Board, Second Report.* Washington, 1935.

——. "Principles of Foreign Mineral Policy of the United States." *Mining and Metallurgy,* 27: 6 (Jan., 1946).

——. *World Minerals and World Politics.* New York: McGraw-Hill Book Co., 1931.

——, J. W. Furness, and C. Lewis. *World Minerals and World Peace.* Washington: The Brookings Institution, 1943.

Leith, D., and D. M. Liddell. *The Mineral Reserves of the United States and Its Capacity for Production.* Washington: National Resources Committee, 1936.

Lovering, T. S. *Minerals in World Affairs.* New York: Prentice-Hall, 1933.

McGill, W. M. *Outline of the Mineral Resources of Virginia* (Virginia Geological Survey, Educational Series, 3, 1936).

Miser, H. D., G. B. Richardson, and C. H. Dane. "Petroleum Reserves," ch.

2, pp. 286–294. *Fuel Reserves of the United States* (House Document 160, 76th Congress, sec. 1, part 2). Washington: Government Printing Office, 1939.

Parsons, A. B., editor. *Seventy-five Years of Progress in the Mineral Industry: 1871–1946.* New York: American Institute of Mining and Metallurgical Engineers, 1947.

Read, T. T. *Our Mineral Civilization.* Baltimore: Williams and Wilkins Co., 1932.

Rice, G. S., A. C. Fieldner, and F. G. Tryon. *Conservation of Coal* (Third World Power Congress, sec. IV, paper 11). Washington: U.S. Department of the Interior, Bureau of Mines, 1936.

Richards, R. W. "Natural Gas Reserves," ch. 3, pp. 294–297. *Fuel Reserves of the United States* (House Document 160, 76th Congress, sec. 1, part 2). Washington: Government Printing Office, 1939.

Roush, G. A. *Strategic Mineral Supplies.* New York: McGraw-Hill Book Co., 1939.

Sampson, E. "Mineral Commerce and International Relations," *Journal of the Franklin Institute,* vol. 221, no. 1 (1936).

Simoneaux, N. E., and C. K. Moresi. *The Conservation Laws in Relation to Minerals.* New Orleans: Louisiana Department of Conservation, 1936. See also Department of Conservation, Louisiana, *13th Biennial Report* (1936–1937).

Stout, W. *Mineral Resources of Ohio* (Geological Survey of Ohio, Fourth Series, Information Circular, 1) Columbus, O., 1938.

Thom, W. H. *Petroleum and Coal, the Keys to the Future.* Princeton: Princeton University Press, 1929.

——. *Conservation of Petroleum and Natural Gas* (Third World Power Congress, sec. IV, paper 12). Washington: U.S. Department of the Interior, Bureau of Mines, 1936.

Tyler, P. M. *From the Ground Up.* New York: McGraw-Hill Book Co., 1948.

U.S. Bureau of Mines and Geological Survey. *Mineral Resources of the United States.* Washington: Public Affairs Press, 1948.

Voskuil, W. H. *Postwar Issues in the Petroleum Industry* (University of Illinois, Business Studies, no. 3) Urbana, Ill., 1946.

Works Progress Administration, National Research Project and Bureau of Mines, Technology and the Mineral Industries, Rept. E-1 (1937).

Index

AUTHORS

SUBJECTS